BUNBURY'S WAR

Charlie Snell, the Bunbury community and the Great War

Former humanities teacher, Margo was born in Bunbury and educated in Busselton and the University of Western Australia. During her career, she furthered her studies in education and languages and pursued interests in music, travel and local history. Recently, she has completed a PhD at Murdoch University. She is now studying French at UWA and, with the UWA Historical Society, is examining the WW2 service of UWA students, graduates and staff.

MARGARET JANE WARBURTON

BUNBURY'S WAR

Charlie Snell, the Bunbury community and the Great War

Australian Scholarly

I dedicate this work to my mother, Nancy Margaret Sherwood, née Snell, 1928 –2024, who knew the sadness.

First published 2021 by
Australian Scholarly Publishing Ltd
7 Lt Lothian St Nth, North Melbourne, Vic 3051
Tel: 03 9329 6963
contact@scholarly.info / www.scholarly.info

ISBN 978-1-922669-13-1

Cover design: Amelia Walker

CONTENTS

PREFACE

Researchers have concluded that, in regional Australia, World War I exacerbated existing social divisions. My study demonstrates that, for the Wellington community of Western Australia, the war intensified the existing sense of community, altered private and public gender beliefs and relations, and yet left the community struggling to adequately manage the needs of veterans. When Charlie Snell of Harvey, Western Australia, wrote of enlisting in the war, his parents kept his letters, creating an archive of his experiences at war, his death in France and his community's grief at his death. Research into the background to the 200 names from Western Australia's Bunbury–Harvey community found in the archive has revealed the private and public lives and community relationships of the population, before, during and after World War I, showing how they were transformed by war. In the Wellington district, social capital developed during the pioneering period provided the community structures and social cohesion needed to fight the war on the home front and the battle front, as existing community organisations became committees of men and women working tirelessly to support their young men at war. In the aftermath of war however, the efforts of local committees, veteran support associations and families were insufficient to adequately cater for the needs of veterans. The repatriation files of returned men and women depict the war's long-term consequences in the private suffering of veterans from a multiplicity of injuries, illnesses and emotional traumas. Limited understanding of trauma and government repatriation policies that effectively diluted social capital, ultimately isolated veterans in their confrontations with the repatriation system. The testing of gendered behaviours, roles and relationships in wartime led to new understandings as men expressed their emotional selves in new ways and women moved from the pre-war domestic sphere to the public sphere where they learnt new skills and rhetoric and interacted as equals with men. While some women retreated into the domestic sphere after the war in response to the needs of their disabled men, many continued to use their newfound skills in their private dealings with Repat, while others continued to make an impact in the public sphere.

ACKNOWLEDGEMENTS

Historical research often has personal roots and this is no different. As a child, my grandfather's shed in the back garden of my grandparents' house in Bunbury held great fascination. It was full of the objects of his interests, 'killing bottles' of preserved insects, beetles and worms, coral and rock specimens collected on his travels through the north of the state as the 'expert' (mechanic) for shearing teams, and the tools and materials for his hobby of manufacturing metal packing cases for shearers. I became aware of Charlie Snell at twelve years of age, when my grandfather opened an old trunk of letters and memorabilia in his shed and began talking about his brother who was killed in 'the war', of which I was vaguely aware. I remember picking up old embroidered cards and sheets of music. My grandfather soon became upset and sent us away, but his distress had a profound effect on me and the memory remained. The letters in the trunk have provided the inspiration for this thesis.

I acknowledge Murdoch University for providing me with a maintenance fund which enabled me to attend a conference at the University of New England, Armidale New South Wales, and to visit the Australian War Memorial and the National Library in Canberra; and a Conference Travel Award which allowed me to present my work at a conference at Kings College, London. The research and writing of this work have been largely self-funded and I am grateful to family and friends who have provided moral support.

My thanks to academic staff at Murdoch University: my supervisors Prof. Michael Sturma and Drs Janice Gothard and Andrew Webster for their patience, timely advice and attention to detail; to my mentors, Drs

Julia Hobson and Liana Christensen, for their belief in my work and help in teasing out the tangled web of material and ideas.

To the staff of the Geoffrey Bolton Library at Murdoch University, the Battye Library, the State Records Office, the National Archives, Perth, the National Archives and the Australian War Memorial in Canberra, the Armidale archives and historical society, the Beardies Museum in Glen Innes and to the Bunbury and Harvey Historical Societies, thanks for their response to my requests. Thanks to the staff of the AH Bracks Library in Melville for technical assistance and a congenial place to work. Thanks to the staff of the National Library of Australia for the marvel that is the *Trove* website of Australia's historical newspapers. Thanks to Jeff Pierce of Bunbury, for his *Anzacheroes* website which documents all the Wellington men who took part in the war and provides such a useful ready reference for my research. And to those who listened, questioned and supported: Nancy, Natalie, Sophie, Wes, David, Louise, Patsy and Luciana. Thanks also to David Maynier, John Thomson, Elizabeth Sherwood, Francesca Meehan and Dr Joan Pope, AM, for their meticulous reading of the final drafts.

Finally, to Prof. Peter Stanley of UNSW, my sincere thanks for his generous comments and criticism which guided the transition from thesis to book.

ILLUSTRATIONS

ABBREVIATIONS

10LH	Tenth Light Horse
ABS	Australian Bureau of Statistics
ADB	Australian Dictionary of Biography
AWM	Australian War Memorial
CCS	Casualty Clearing Station
DC	Deputy Commissioner of Repatriation.
DOTAG	Department of the Attorney General, now Department of Justice, Western Australia
JRAH	Journal of the Royal Australian Historical Society
MLA	Member of the Legislative Assembly
MLC	Member of the Legislative Council
NAA	National Archives of Australia.
NSW	New South Wales
pp	percentage point/s
Repat	Repatriation Department
RGH	Repatriation General Hospital
RTA	Returned to Australia
SD	Statistical District
SRO	State Records Office
VAD	Voluntary Aid Detachment (volunteer nurse)
WA	Western Australia

Snell Family

CS	Charles Snell
AJS	Alfred James Snell (Mr Snell, Snell senior)
CAS	Caroline Amelia Snell (Mrs Snell)

Individuals, especially servicemen and women, once identified, are often referred to by their initials in the notes, for example, AG (Alf Gray) CC (Claude Clifton), CP (Cyril Paisley), IP (Ivy Paisley), JB (Jack Blythe) JS (Janie Sutton), LP (Les Paisley), MBW (Mervyn Bailey Wenn), MEC (Mervyn Ephraim (Dick) Clarke), NH (Norman Holtzman), RC (Ray Clarke), RI (Reg Ibbotson), SP (Selwyn Paisley), TR (Tom Rose), VP (Vera Paisley), WHS (Wisbey Harrington Sinclair).

INTRODUCTION

In order to understand any community … it is essential to know who lived in it.[1]

Charles Snell was born in Kuala Lumpur in 1891, the second son of British parents and died on 22 July 1916, on the Western Front in France, digging jump-off trenches in preparation for the Battle of Pozières. His older brother, Alf, was born in London, while a younger sister, Marjorie, was born in Bunbury, Western Australia. His father, Alfred James Snell, born in Exeter, had begun his working life with the Great Northern Railway (UK) in 1879, was railway superintendent in Kuala Lumpur (Malaya) from 1889–96, making a three-month inspection tour of the Japanese railway system, before working for New Zealand Railways for two years. The railway between Bunbury and Perth opened in 1893, and from 1898 to 1910, Snell senior was superintendent of railways for the Wellington district of Western Australia, based in Bunbury. On his retirement from the railways, he ran an orchard and fruit-packing business at *Devonia*, in Harvey. Snell's mother, Caroline Amelia Graves, born Haworth, Yorkshire, was a servant before her marriage. Snell senior had relatives in London and Devon and Caroline had a sister in Sydney.[2]

Snell's father became a well-known figure through his position as district railway manager. He was a witness in a 1910 trial presided over by Dr Joel and A.R. Foreman, when a 'Welshman' was charged with unruly behaviour on a local train.[3] Soon after, he suffered a 'severe nervous breakdown' and needed medical care as a result of his heavy workload.[4] The illness was the catalyst for the family's move to Harvey, where Bunbury contacts were maintained through visits, letters and newspaper reports.[5] Mrs Snell was also well-known. In early 1911, she was reported to be in 'better health' and enjoying life in Harvey, while her husband was still 'in a very weak state of health'.[6] Later in the year, however, her 'many friends' were advised that she was 'in a very low state of health' and had been taken by ambulance to 'Nurse Bruton's Private Hospital'.[7] While Caroline Snell continued to suffer poor health, by 1913, Mr Snell was busy with his fine crop of passion fruit and advertising orchard and farm produce for sale, including poultry, 'prime navel oranges, onion seedlings and split oranges for marmalade'.[8] Condolence letters to the family after Charlie's death testify to the influence of the press in maintaining the flow of information when Caroline Snell was hospitalised around the time of her son's death. She compiled lists of visitors and condolences so she could reciprocate with notes of thanks.

The Snell's younger son, Charlie, after schooling in Bunbury and several years' apprenticeship in the mixed farming practised in the Bunbury district, worked his sea-passage to Sydney in January 1914, and began work at the Glen Innes Experiment Farm in northern New South Wales later that year. He enlisted as a private in the Australian Imperial Force (AIF) at Armidale in August 1915 and underwent four months' training at Liverpool Camp in Sydney with the 4th Battalion AIF. He embarked for Egypt on the TS *Medic* in January 1916, was transferred to the Western Front in France where he died.[9]

Charlie's family kept his letters, diaries and photographs from the time he first mentioned enlisting. The archive was held by my grandfather, Alf Snell, until his death in 1971, later passing to 'the eldest son of the eldest son', my uncle Charlie, then to his son. It came to my mother, Nancy Sherwood, née Snell, before passing to me in 2000.

The Snell Archive contains around 600 pages of letters and photographs dating from 1905 to 1920, written by Charlie himself from New South Wales, Egypt and France, and by family, friends and colleagues in Western Australia, New South Wales, New Zealand, England, Scotland and Siam (now Thailand).[10] Sensing the significance of the war, Charlie bundled up letters he received and sent them home to his family with the instruction to 'keep these for me'. The archive includes condolences sent to the family after his death and copies of his father's replies. This work is an attempt to understand the sense of community that infuses the letters.

The names of two hundred Bunbury district residents appear in the letters, representing the leadership group in the community. Through these names, we can explore the historical background of the community, its participation in the war and war's impact on the community. Details from census records, post office directories, indexes of births, deaths and marriages, and newspaper reports identify the community. Official sources such as attestation papers and service records also held in the National Archives place Charlie Snell among his military cohort. The repatriation records of Australian servicemen, held in the National Archives of Australia, document the post-war lives of Snell's cohort who survived the war.

The community connections which sustained AIF troops and their families at war are the subject of many studies, including those by Gammage and Young.[11] The memoirs of Australian nurses too, are filled with the names of fellow-nurses and servicemen, friends and relatives encountered in Egypt and later in France.[12] Like Snell, the nurses record the numbers of letters received, newspaper reports and the movements of friends. While Janet Butler's studies of nurses' letters and diaries shed light on the community networks which supported individuals at war, Ruth Rae explores the broader themes of military nursing and the contribution of women generally to the Great War.[13]

The Snell archive shows that the men and women of Snell's parents' generation were eminently capable of interrogating their wartime experiences through their writing. Hassam also explores the concept of liminal space as a threshold between the old and the new, which is also applicable to a community at war, when continuity and tradition became uncertain, accompanied by an expectation that a new reality would finally emerge.[14] For the community at home, the liminal period was filled by patriotic activity and letter-writing as they awaited the outcomes of the war, which for many, could never have been anticipated. The modern reader learns of a new reality that is reconstructed from artefacts of the past which had lain unexplored since the deaths of Charlie's parents. This reconstruction is informed by the perspectives of the researcher, whose life has been strongly influenced by the family's oral culture.[15]

The narrative of Charlie Snell's war service is informed by studies of the part played by the Australians on the Western Front, the effects of battle on the soldiers, and the consequences for the Australian community. Private sources in the Snell Archive are supplemented by official records in the Australian War Memorial and the National Archives of Australia, as well as the Battye Library of Western Australia, the Bunbury Museum and the Harvey and Glen Innes Historical Societies. Belford and Devine's battalion histories, and the personal memoirs of Hartnett and Lynch, elucidate the wartime experience of Australian soldiers.[16] Maze, a Frenchman who worked for General Gough provides a unique view of the Australians.[17] The memoir of a medical officer who served in a casualty clearing station and the diary of Casualty Clearing Station 44 assist in evaluating Snell's medical records.[18] Bennett examines the Battle of Pozières from the Australian perspective, while Bean's official history describes the preparation for the Battle of Pozières.[19] Pedersen's battlefront guidebook enables the location of places mentioned by Snell's diary and official diaries.[20] Van Bergen's study enables a reconstruction of Snell's final hours.[21] Damousi and Luckins explore the social and cultural effects of losses of Australians in World War I.[22] Myer's examination of masculinity and war also informs this study.[23]

Condolence letters to Snell's family introduce us to the community that supported the Snell family in their time of bereavement, provide a 'window into the soul of the author'[24], while Snell's father's replies help us to identify masculine networks. In the absence of letters from Snell's mother, the surviving letters to Charlie from women of his parents' generation epitomise the 'long distance mothering' identified by Roper.[25]

For most of his short life, Snell resided in regional communities. Wellman shows how, traditionally, 'community' meant neighbourhood communities that provided wide-ranging social support and companionship, extending the range of national and international ties evident in Snell's pattern of movement and communications.[26] Letters provide the means for the expression of affect when community members are scattered and in prioritising mail services in the early days of the war, the British authorities recognised this need.[27] Studying a family and community network such as Snell's enables us to reconstruct his world and investigate the local solidarity which was so significant during the Great War.[28]

Among studies of Australia's home front at war, Sir Ernest Scott's official history depicts the frenetic activity of the patriotic and munitions funds on the home front, which was reflected in Bunbury's wartime press.[29] Bill Gammage's pioneering 1974 study of the close links between the soldiers and loved ones at home, and the supportive relationships between family and friends, is reflected in the present study by news reports of the wartime movements of soldiers and by the personal expressions of comfort and loss when Charlie Snell died.[30]

McKernan's study of regional Australia at war, emphasising the New South Wales experience, resonates closely with the present study of the Bunbury community at war.[31] Gammage and McKernan highlight the intimacy of the country experience, where the newspaper editors and journalists were themselves members of the community.[32] McQuilton's descriptions of intense wartime activity in rural communities and the role of newspapers in spreading news of casualties were all strongly reflected in the Bunbury community.[33] Payton's study of a South Australian mining district traces the transition from mining into agriculture, creating the cohesive population which faced the trials of war.[34] This suggests comparisons with Collie, the coal mining district in Bunbury's hinterland. McKernan, McQuilton and Payton all distinguish the regional experience of war from that of the cities, emphasising 'the sense of intimacy between regional Australia and the Great War'.[35]

Anstey and Oliver have examined the impact of the Great War on Western Australia. Anstey compared an agricultural and a mining community, finding that community attitudes to the war were polarised along employment lines.[36] He finds much greater division within the mining community than within the agricultural region; however, the present study finds that the Collie coalmining district was as united as the agricultural districts in its support of the war. Oliver identifies wartime attitudes to recruitment, conscription, aliens, and loyalty to Britain as sources of conflict in Western Australia.[37] Like Oliver, Evans in Queensland and Lake in Tasmania find that the stresses of war exacerbated pre-existing class, ethnic and ideological divisions, presenting a contrasting perspective to the united Bunbury community.[38] Damousi's study of grief and mourning in Australia examines the formation of supportive community networks around soldiers and their families.[39] Alistair Thompson's *Anzac Memories: Living with the Legend* provides a useful outline of the post-war experiences of some Great War veterans.[40] Belford and Gill's studies of the 11th Battalion examine the wartime experiences of many of Charlie's Bunbury friends.[41]

British researchers Jay Winter and Antoine Prost have identified the critical role of the debate over the outcomes of the war for women.[42] Feminism and gender were already before the Australian public in the 1890s and a visit to Bunbury by American feminist Jessie Ackerman ensured that the Wellington district was in the forefront of the debate.[43] Carmel Shute, John McQuilton and Philip Payton have concluded that women's patriotic work entrenched the idea of separate spheres for men and women.[44] However, Marilyn Lake and Joy Damousi, Stephen Garton, Beverley Kingston and Bruce Scates show how women renegotiated traditional roles and were empowered to act in the public sphere on the home front.[45]

Ruth Rae, John McQuilton and others, have examined the ambiguity of the role and position of nurses at war, while S. Williams, Janice Bassett and Kirsty Harris have researched the interactions of nurses with the repatriation system.[46] Alistair Thomson has shown how, in these roles, the women were forced outside their expected domestic roles.[47]

The present work is driven by the names in the Snell letter archive, the 'Snell population'. Appendix 1 shows the archival connection between individuals and the Snell family, sorted by place of residence, whether

Bunbury, Harvey or Perth. Newspaper sources identify some former Bunbury or Harvey residents who had relocated to Perth. Others, such as W.J. George, had professional ties or owned properties in the Wellington district. Other connections, such as Alfred Goss and the Dunlop family predated the Snells' move to Western Australia. Agricultural shows, social gatherings and rifle clubs drew residents from far afield, especially after the arrival of the railway in 1893.[48]

Contemporary newspapers are an invaluable source but are complicated by the use of titles such as Mr, Mrs and Miss without their forenames, for example, 'Mrs George Reading', or 'Miss Foreman' for the eldest daughter of a family.[49] Department of Justice records of births, deaths and marriages are useful in identifying married women born in Western Australia.[50] However, the records are incomplete. Individuals born outside Western Australia are difficult to identify, but if they became well-known, obituaries often identify place of birth and death. Birth dates, when unknown, have been estimated according to known ages of family members.

Names such as 'Smith', 'Robinson', 'Moore' and 'Johnson', or common forenames such as 'William' have eluded identification.[51] There were several families of Smiths, as well as Robinsons and Moores, which came with the earliest British arrivals in the district, but were joined by other unrelated individuals of the same name in later migrations.[52] The *ANZAC Heroes* website, a compilation of names of enlistees connected to the Bunbury district, is useful in distinguishing between the old families and the new.[53]

This work is a response to Stanley's call for community-based studies of the experience and impact of the war and its aftermath.[54] Already the subject of local histories by Staples, Sanders and others, the work places Bunbury in the context of World War I with its diverse, profound and enduring impact.[55]

The Bunbury district's wartime experience has been partially examined through a compilation of the names of the men and women associated with the Wellington district who served in the war.[56] This study shows how the community framed the lived experience of the individual, shaping him or her into an active participant in the war on the battle front and on the home front. It explores the ties of kinship and friendship that motivated the population to participate in World War I and endure its aftermath.

The theme of gender and war completes the study. Women figure prominently in the Snell archive, including Snell's mother, Caroline Amelia Snell, his sister, Marjorie, female friends and the wives of male correspondents. The changing roles of women on the home front and caring for ailing veterans, and the renegotiation of gender roles in the war and its aftermath, show that for the Bunbury district, the war did produce change in the lives of women. Throughout the study, individual narratives illustrate the community's response to the war and its aftermath.

Snell's correspondence community stretched across Australia and as far as Britain, however this study focusses on the Wellington Statistical Division,[57] encompassing the towns of Bunbury and Harvey and associated villages to the south of Perth in Western Australia. Situated between the Mandurah–Pinjarra (Murray) region to the north and Augusta–Busselton (Sussex) region to the south, the area was defined by administrative boundaries, newspaper distribution patterns and the rail network centred on the Bunbury port.

The study extends from the early days of European settlement of the Bunbury district, to the death of the last of the veterans and their wives in the 1980s, more than six decades after Charlie lost his life in the trenches of France. Charlie's parents died in the 1930s, his brother Alf in 1971 and his sister Marjorie in 2001, none having fully recovered from the death of their son and brother. The work is set in the Bunbury middle class, with its public citizens and their wives, who were largely invisible prior to the war but came into public view through their wartime activities.

Charlie Snell did not fight at Gallipoli but served and died with the Australian Imperial Force (AIF) on the Western Front. He was a hero to his community, but never exhibited the larrikin[58] behaviour associated with the ANZAC legend. He was known as 'Charlie' to his family and friends, 'Mr Snell' in Glen Innes, and 'Snell' in the military. His father and brother were both named 'Alfred'. His father will be referred to as 'Snell senior' and the brother as 'Alf'. The women were usually addressed as 'Mrs' and 'Miss', but Christian names are used when known. The Commonwealth Department of Repatriation will be referred to as 'Repat', its colloquial name. In the repatriation files, the individual will be referred to by his or her first name. Around 70% of the individuals named in the letters regularly appeared in press reports of district activities. Therefore, the 'Snell' population will be simply referred to as 'the community' or the 'Bunbury' or 'Harvey' communities, depending on the context.

Overview

Chapter 1 describes Charlie Snell's enlistment, training in Sydney, war service, death and the condolences which introduce us to his community. Chapter 2 examines the community in which Charles Snell was raised, and examines its historical background and community structures. Chapter 3 examines the Bunbury community during the war years, including its civilian patriotic activity on the home front, as well as the military contribution of the district. Later chapters explore public and private transformations in the aftermath of war through personal narratives. Chapters 4, 5 and 6 examine repatriation, first looking at soldier settlement and the problems arising from wartime injuries and war neurosis; the second at medical outcomes of the war, including lung disease, trench foot and thyroid conditions; and the third examines the interactions of individual women with Repat. The final chapters look at the gendered outcomes of the war for Bunbury people, through the experiences of the men, the wives of war-damaged soldiers and nurses. Narrations of the lives of four Wellington women reveal the subtle adjustments experienced by some women after the war.

During the pioneering period between 1840 and around 1900, the Bunbury community grew by the addition of waves of mostly British migrants. Isolation from the centre of government in Perth forced the community to manage almost all aspects of its development. Churches operated in an ecumenical setting and enabled cultural expression. 'Public men' rose to prominence as the governing class of the community, their wives sharing in public duties.[59] Shared community activity resulted in a high degree of social capital which was available for the war effort. Meanwhile, state government intervention gradually increased as the need for railways, irrigation and harbour extensions outstripped local resources. The war intensified the existing sense of community, altered private and public gender beliefs and relations, and yet left the community struggling to adequately manage the needs of veterans.

When war came, men were sent to war to the sound of patriotic songs and approval from the whole community. Men's organisations transformed themselves into 'munitions' committees to manage recruitment, fund-raising, repatriation and employment, while the women's social circles became patriotic committees dedicated to raising funds and manufacturing 'comforts' for the men at the front. Local newspapers documented and promoted the feverish wartime activity. Although the conscription debates aroused dissention, and despite the community's overwhelming support for conscription, harmony was quickly restored once the votes were counted. Meanwhile, 'communities of mourning' supported grieving families when news of casualties arrived.

In the aftermath of war, the community was unable to adequately cater for the needs of veterans. When wounded and sick men began returning to the district following the Gallipoli campaign, women's committees welcomed them and men's committees arranged local employment. The local repatriation committee expanded to include soldier settlement, while veterans' organisations supported the social needs of returned men and their families.

Limited medical understanding of trauma and repatriation policies implemented from a distance diluted social capital, and in their confrontations with repatriation officials, veterans were alone. Since local committees were dependent on funds from state and federal government, three-way conflict between Repat, the local committee and the individual veteran became the norm. Private sufferings are revealed in the repatriation files of the men and women through tales of the physical and emotional pain of old wounds and developing illnesses such as war neurosis and lung disease, added to financial hardship resulting from run-down farmland, crop failures and growing families. Repat's doctors and other officials greeted veterans' complaints with a mixture of sympathy and scepticism, but were governed by financial constraints as they sought to balance needs against resources.

The testing of gendered roles and relationships in wartime led to new understandings as men discovered their emotional selves. Their correspondence shows a deep humanity and sympathy over wartime losses, alongside growing self-awareness and concern for their women folk. Women moved from the domestic sphere to the public sphere, learning new skills and rhetoric and interacting as equals with men. In the Bunbury district, the wives of the public men emerged as the leaders of women's patriotic activity, adopting masculine rhetoric and taking their place in the community's wartime work. The men, in turn, accepted women in the public sphere and willingly worked alongside them.

Post-war, some women retreated into the domestic sphere in response to the needs of their disabled men, while others remained in the public sphere, using their newfound skills in their private dealings with Repat and in their public activities. Veterans' wives became increasingly assertive in pleading the cause of their men, earning consideration and respect from Repat officials. Women without needy husbands transferred their activities to other community needs or entered new fields.

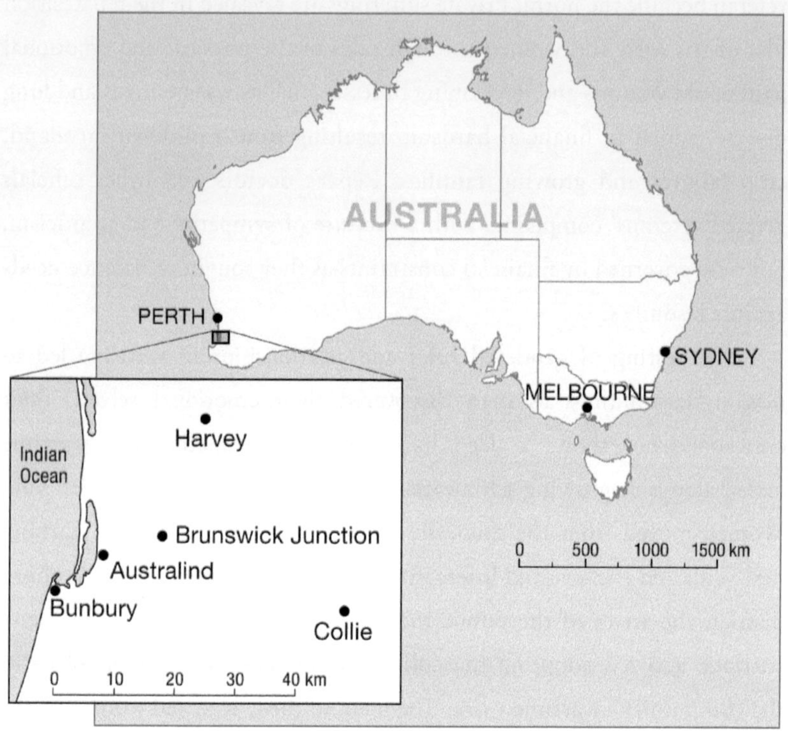

Locating Wellington District in Australia.

I

PRIVATE CHARLES SNELL, SERVICE, DEATH AND COMMEMORATION

> *We should of all things like to know … how Charlie met his death and where … if you could … gather any particulars of the circumstances attending his injuries – and death – I should be exceedingly grateful.*
>
> *Alfred J. Snell, 1916*

Private Charles Snell died at Pozières, France, on 22 July 1916, one of 295,000 Australians who fought, and the 46,000 who died on the Western Front. In 1914, at the age of 22, Charlie worked his passage to Sydney and, after a year there, moved to Glen Innes to work at the Experiment Farm.[1] He was embraced by the local community and became unofficially engaged to Gladys Whatham, who divided her time between Sydney and Glenn Innes. Critical of those who married before going to war, Charlie was determined to have an income of 200 pounds a year and a home before marriage.

After a year in Glen Innes, a sense of duty to Britain, and fear of censure on himself or his family, led Charlie to enlist as a private at the Armidale Recruiting Depot on 12 August 1915 and left Glen Innes amid emotional farewells. Initially in the 6th Battalion, he transferred to the 4th Battalion on arrival in Sydney. He was promoted Acting Corporal, reverting to private on arrival in Egypt. He delighted in sharing his wartime experiences with family and friends, showing an intense interest in everything he saw and heard in Australia, *en route* or in Egypt and France.

Charlie was 'anxious to get into the business part of the war' and would 'rather be here than letting someone else fight my battles'. He was proud to be in the firing party for a funeral and to lead a procession through the crowds in Sydney. He encountered a Bunbury friend who assured him that life at the front 'wasn't too bad'. About his fellow soldiers, he expresses some reservations. Their trench digging was 'poor work, a lot will fall into the trenches with a lump of lead in them', 'this camp is ruining many a good man', and after a tour of duty in Sydney to round up drunken men, he commented that he could write a book on 'a soldier's temptations'. He escaped injury when a train returning from Sydney with 600 men on board was derailed at Liverpool Station after the brake lines were tampered with.[2]

Charlie embarked on TS*Medic* in Sydney on 7 January 1916, arriving in Fremantle nine days later. After meeting his father and brother in Fremantle, and friends in Claremont, his convoy crossed the Indian Ocean, arriving in Alexandria on 17 February. Acting Corporal Snell, 12th Reinforcements, joined the original 4th Battalion, which had taken part in the Anzac's Gallipoli landing.[3]

After six weeks' arduous training in Egypt, a sea journey to Marseille and 60 hours by train, the Australians arrived in the northern sector of the Western Front, where they held a ten-mile section of the line from Fromelles in the south to Armentières and the River Lys in the north, in what was known as the Nursery Sector.[4] Snell gave avid accounts of training, route marches, and trench digging under fire. 'Wonderful things were happening' at the nearby front, and the men quickly learnt to identify whether danger threatened.

Snell, in D Company, 4th Battalion, 1st Brigade, was one of 42,000 troops in the 1st and 2nd Australian Divisions in the north of France, joining the 50 British divisions already there.[5] Although the Australians were initially in a relatively quiet sector, there were periods of sharp fighting, shelling and some heavy raids. Between early April and the end of June over 600 men were killed.[6]

The Australians held an area bounded by the towns of Hazebrouck in the north west, Bailleul, Fleurbaix, Estaires and Morbeque. Snell named many small villages and hamlets within this area which are not shown on the map.

Bare sheds, barns and outhouses that served as billets were often subject to enemy fire. Training in grenade handling, bayonet drill and rapid loading practice, care of ammunition, physical drill and company drill was visible to the Germans on Aubers Ridge and provoked shellfire. Regular route marches of 10 to 12 miles, carrying a full pack, gave the keenly observant Snell the opportunity to survey the local landscape. He described being 'thoroughly knocked out' after a march which was immediately followed by another trek to guard duty. Two days later, headache and pain in the kidneys earned him 'light duties', which consisted of guard duty, followed soon after by another 36-hour stretch. Another march was a 'Human Endurance Test', accompanied by an officer on horseback. He reluctantly acknowledged, however, that he was the fittest he had ever been.

There was more physical work to be done than fighting. The ground in Flanders was marshy and low lying, necessitating sandbag parapets and parados (back walls) for the trenches which were in constant need of repair. Rain added mud and slush. Trench work was usually carried out at night, and a rum issue at 4am ensured a good three hours' sleep. Trench digging was done under the danger of shelling, and deaths of 100 men a month were common.[7] 'Fatigues', or general duties involved moving equipment and ammunition, and the constant loading and unloading of vehicles. Snell's diary noted: 'June 21st went to Fleurbaix, work behind firing line, 22nd, various duties, June 23rd, working in communication trench, June 18th, ammunition taken from Elbow Farm to Chappelle Farm'.

Snell's letters, mindful of the censor's pencil, were often ironic: 'one 'sees things', and, 'generally speaking all going well'. The enemy were 'our friends', their shelling was 'free fireworks', and guns were 'talking'. Heavy bombing created some 'hot corners', and the enemy was sending a 'good supply of shrapnel and high explosive shells over'. Flares looked 'pretty at night'. Near misses by a shell or a bullet were 'close shaves'. So far, he had dodged a sniper's bullets, but 'unfortunately couldn't locate the —'. He had 'put a couple of Germans out of action'. He assured the family that everything was A1 with 'this chicken'. The planes at an aerodrome were a sight worth seeing, with their 8-cylinder engines, 100-horsepower Daimler and Austin motors. Rats ran over sleeping men in the trenches, but they developed ingenious methods for exterminating them. 'Leave the war to us!' he wrote, everything was going well and the war would soon be over.

His only reference to death was 'my friend Smithy shot and killed 8pm' soon after arrival in France. However, when his brother expressed a desire to be with him, he tersely responded: 'take a fool's advice and stay away'. He was sorry the Gibbs boys were not accepted for service, but their mother had already lost one son. 'I didn't think I could stand what we have had, but am fitter now than I ever was in my life, feed me on kerosene and chips and I'll be a fine perpetual motion machine.'

Charlie took the French and the village life to heart and remarked on the women working the railways and the farms. He took a country-man's interest the landscape and noted crops, farming activities and the condition of the stock. He remarked on the lovely avenues of trees, and at the firing line, the contradiction of larks singing. He enjoyed the company of the little French 'kiddies' as each attempted to speak the others' languages, and a French lady friend obligingly posting mail for him. France was 'always interesting and instructive', and he would 'love to see it in peacetime'. The local village offered food and souvenirs, a meal, a couple of bottles of wine, or a visit to the local YMCA. The Empire Theatre in Sailly held concerts, vaudeville, picture shows and boxing tournaments. He enjoyed wandering the country roads, strawberry picking with friends and a game of bridge.

The arrival of the 11th Battalion provided the opportunity to catch up with friends from Bunbury and Harvey, school friends or former rifle club rivals. Among them were bombers and snipers, medal winners, absconders and VD cases. Many were wounded or killed in action. Their stories will be told in a later section. Charlie was encouraged by reports of the first week of the Somme Offensive. He noted Lord Kitchener's death at sea, and news of the Battle of Jutland came first hand from Maud Dunlop in Edinburgh.

News of events at home provided a sense of normality, and in his letters, Charlie reflected on the doings of his siblings, the arrival of the telephone, the development of irrigation in Harvey and his father's venture into potato growing. His Glen Innes employers were keeping a position for him on his return. He followed the romantic affairs of family friends but was 'not building castles too high' in his expectations of Gladys Whatham. 'Comfort' parcels came from Gladys and from Maud Dunlop in Scotland. His mother sent a sandbag, which did 'good service at front'.

The Firing Line

While in the northern sector, Snell spent a two-month period with the Signals Company, in the support trenches and the front line. Signallers' duties included laying, patrolling and repairing communication wires, signalling and telegraph instruction, buzzer and semaphore 'key and station' drills, memorising and delivering messages and escort work, usually under fire.[8] In two months, signallers laid many kilometres of new cable in trenches, crossing ditches, roads and culverts.[9] Snell relished the work and his diary meticulously recorded his training and visits to various headquarters, the Signal Station and the Trench Mortar Battery, and escort duty with a sick patient to Croix Blanche. It involved increased responsibility and included assisting with the handover to the incoming 11th Battalion. He passed examinations for Signaler 'B' class but reverted to his former position when the size of the group had to be reduced.

In the lines, the 'evening hate' involved the exchange of trench mortars and grenades.[10] The men anxiously watched the wind vanes to assess the likelihood of gas attacks. In early May, the 4th Battalion spent their first few days in the firing line and the support trenches, living in billets near Fromelles under occasional heavy shelling which wounded one of Snell's officers. Snell recorded the frequency and duration of the shelling, the repulse of a nearby attack, the cutting of the communication wire under bombardment, the laying of barbed wire over the parapets and the shelling of a signal station. Nightly raids and patrols were sent out to explore no man's land, often provoking intense counter-attack. The area was again relatively quiet until 30 May when Cellar Farm communication trench was destroyed by German shelling, that was reportedly heavier than any experienced at Gallipoli. The Australian First Brigade diary recorded 47 men killed and 71 wounded in May.[11]

On 10 June, the 4th Battalion supported the firing line outside Fleurbaix, and moved to the front-line three weeks later. Over the next two weeks, eleven raids were conducted, incurring significant casualties on both sides.[12] Brigade casualties for the month of June were three officers killed and 21 other ranks, nine officers and 155 other ranks wounded, one missing and 100 men in hospital.[13] When a raid by the 11th Battalion destroyed German trenches, Snell reported the 'finest display of fireworks and death works, terrific noise, hundreds of flashes of bursting shells, bombs and hundreds of flares sent up, green star rockets and red flares sent up as signals, the heaviest bombardment yet'.[14] The following night, the Germans retaliated, killing and wounding more than forty Australians under a heavy bombardment. 'Rifle fire pretty hot, and the Germans were using searchlights which showed the outline of the head and shoulders of their own men.' The 'lads anxiously waited to get a shot', the light being more of an advantage to the Australians than to the Germans.[15]

After eleven days under fire, Snell's battalion left the line to the 46th (Victorian) Battalion, marching through the night to Sailly along duckboards in muddy communication trenches and wet roads. Snell had 'never shot for trophies or spoons as I do here, accounted for a couple of Germans'. He was 'still in the land of the living', but it was difficult to write with the 'lads whistling and singing and in good spirit – old bill will have had enough of us soon'. He expected peace at any time: 'the end is near – I'd give something to know what the next 12 months will hold'.

Orders were received on 11 July for the 60,000 men of the 1st Division to move south to the Somme battlefront.[16] Reveille was called at 4.30 a.m. the next morning and at 8.55 a.m. the troops entrained at Bailleul 'in full marching order and packed like sardines', 40 men each in cattle trucks: 'hommes 40, chevaux 8'.[17]

The seven-hour journey, followed by a ten-mile march, and continuous marching during the next four days, was 'a very interesting trip through lovely country scenery passing trains packed with troops going in the opposite direction'. The men detrained at Feinvillers-Candas, and departing at 3.40 p.m., marched fully-loaded to St-Léger-lès-Domart, (8 p.m.) and St Ouen, a total distance of 9 miles (8.45 p.m.). Local residents treated the men to brandy and rum. The men marched the entire distance from Doullens to the front line, approximately 40 miles (64 km), in a week, with route marches on the days when they were not moving forward. The sight of the retiring British troops, singing and wearing German helmets reassured them that the Somme campaign was successful.[18]

The evening of 12 July was spent at Vignacourt, now 1ANZAC headquarters, and almost deserted by the local inhabitants. Thousands of Australian and British troops, and the 13th Light Horse packed the village.[19] Snell meticulously recorded the march from Vignacourt (12.15 p.m.) through Flesselles (1.35) Bertangles (2.50), past an aerodrome, through avenues of trees, Allonville (3.50) to a billet outside the village in an old farm, with the English Motor Transport and Australian Horse Transports nearby. They were now five miles (8 km) north east of Amiens, and for the first time since arriving in northern France, could not hear the guns at the front.

The Australians had been allocated an east-west swathe of land from St Ouen through Berteaucourt, Herrissart, Warloy and Senlis to Albert for rest and training. Local farmers lived in villages of timber-beamed buildings, with whitewashed walls surrounded by open fields. The area between Amiens and Albert was alive with horses, tents and troops and a constant stream of ambulances and official vehicles crowded the roads.[20] Training and lectures, on 'Infantry in Attack' and 'Artillery Formation Drill', were held on the hillsides overlooking Amiens.[21] The Australians were now 'on the move nearly every day now', and finally 'where there is Somme fighting'.

Snell's diary ends 15 July, with a tally of letters and newspapers received, including 'long and newsy' letters from the Dunlop family in Bangkok and Edinburgh.[22] His last letter, written six days before his death, closes:

> *with all good wishes and fondest love to all, I remain, your loving Charlie.*

The account of his remaining days and his death must now be reconstructed from other sources.

To the Somme Front

Snell spent his last days in the area around la Boiselle under the intense artillery fire of the Somme Offensive which had opened on 1 July. Attacks resulted in hundreds of deaths and thousands of wounded, with many dead unburied.[23] The villages of la Boisselle and Ovillers and nearby woods had been reduced to rubble.[24] The Australian assault on the German stronghold of Pozières over the next few weeks became famous for the intensity of the bombardments, the casualties suffered and the heroic endeavours of the Australians, who lost nearly 7,000 dead and 17,000 wounded, Charlie among them.[25]

Heavy rain prior to the Australians' arrival had turned the ground to mud, leaving trenches and roads almost impassable.[26] Labour battalions were remaking roads amid a constant stream of supply vehicles, and the area was dotted with cages for prisoners of war. The men were in constant view of the Germans on Pozières ridge.[27] At the village of Pozières where the Australians entered the Somme fighting, a double line of tree stumps marked the remains of the main street, and the base of a windmill was visible at the top of the street.

One Anzac Corps marched through Albert, with its Hanging Madonna, to join the Reserve Army under General Gough. The 1st Brigade was well rested and in high spirits. They were guided to positions in Sausage

Valley through a stream of heavy traffic and explosions. Maze noted:

> *'The Australian Corps was coming, moving like long snakes, swaying under heavy haversacks and singing tunes that were heard everywhere they went, battalion after battalion swarmed all over the whole area'.*[28] *With their 'wild escapades', they were 'a glorious set of men, the last word in physique and general bearing'.*

The 1st Brigade was to lead the attack on Pozières, which they delayed in order to build new jump-off trenches. [29] Now within 200 yards of the German lines, the nightly digging occurred under artillery fire.[30] The Australian bombardment of Pozières began at 2 a.m. on 19 July, the day of Snell's last church parade. The same day, unknown to the men on the Somme, the recently arrived 5th Australian Division made its disastrous attack 50 miles to the north at Fromelles (Fleurbaix), the area they had recently vacated.

The Chalkpit, one mile from Pozières, with its ammunition dump, first aid station and cooking area, was the departure point for parties moving to the front line. The German trenches were now approximately 150 yards away, in front of Pozières. The Australians' movements were lit by enemy flares, routes were heavily shelled and casualties occurred as soon as the men began work on the unfinished jump-off trenches. In spite of casualties, several long sections of trench were completed prior to assault.

Snell's tone remained positive to the end, and although errors in his writing suggest wavering confidence, he relied on an inner strength and faith in God for protection. We can only imagine the determination it took him to make his final preparations for the days to come, placing this slip of paper in his pocket:

> *In the event of my being wounded in the movement about to take place will the finder of this note please inform Mrs Snell, 45 Cassland Road, South Hackney, London, England.*
>
> *Pte C. Snell, No 3911, D Coy, 4th Battalion.*[31]

While Snell was engaged in trench-digging, there was a two-way bombardment overhead, with shells big enough to uproot trees or to cause a dozen deaths.

On the night of 21–22 July, Snell was wounded under the bombardment of Pozières. There are conflicting versions of his activities at the time. The sergeant who sent the group out reported: 'Mr Hay told me Snell had died before they left the trench, and had been buried where he fell'.[32] Lt Percy Hay, Snell's commanding officer since training in Sydney, wrote after a period in hospital in England:

> *I was in charge of the party that was making some assembly trenches on the night of 21st July at Pozéries [sic]. Private Snell had just finished his turn of duty and was resting in a dugout with two of his mates. A shell came through the roof, killing both his mates and wounding himself very badly. I was there when he was unearthed and could see at once that he was fatally wounded. He never regained consciousness and died shortly afterwards.*[33]

Private Hamilton of the 4th Battalion, who was not present when Snell was hit, reported:

> *I knew Snell well. He was hit at Pozeries [sic] on the 22nd – he and some others were sent to dig the lines for us, when we were back in the supports. He was killed by a bomb. He was taken back to the dressing station and died there.*[34]

However, official records, verified by the Red Cross, show that Charlie was taken to a Casualty Clearing Station a considerable distance behind the lines.[35] Lt Hay had been repatriated to Britain, where he wrote his condolence letter with his account of Snell's death; and Sgt Collins and Pte Hamilton had returned to Australia where they made their statements, so doubt can be cast on them.

Sniper Dugald Leitch of Harvey claimed that when he lay wounded in no man's land, Charlie, on stretcher duty, applied a tourniquet, and promised to return for him.[36] However, Leitch was wounded on 22 July during the assault on Pozières, so it seems unlikely that Charlie was the stretcher bearer. In the event, Leitch lay injured in no-mans-land for at least another 24 hours and was lucky to survive at all.[37]

Charlie was transported by horse ambulance to the 1st Division Field Ambulance at Bécourt Chateau, then by motor ambulance to Warloy then by train to Casualty Clearing Station 44 at Puchevillers to the north.[38] CCS 44 was allocated to the Australians, and on 22 July, received more than 200 wounded.[39] The casualty report states that Snell died of wounds received in action and that he was buried at Puchevillers British Cemetery.

> *Casualty Report: 12th Reinforcement 4th Battalion.*
> *'Died of wounds received in action at No 44 Casualty Clearing Station, GSW base skull, foot and thigh, GSW face, skull, foot, thigh. Abrasions to face and arm.*
> *Buried at Puchevillers British Cemetery, 7 ½ miles SSE Doullins'.*[40]

Charlie was attended by the Church of England chaplain attached to the clearing station.[41] After his death, the contents of his pockets were placed in a calico bag and reached the family three months later. Among the items was his New Testament presented at Glen Innes, containing a portrait of Gladys Whatham.[42]

Charlie's family received the urgent telegram advising of his death, on Monday 7 August, nearly three weeks after the event.[43]

> *Please inform Mr A.J. Snell of Harvey that his son Private C Snell fourth battalion died of wounds on 22nd July and convey Defence Department's sympathy.*
> *Military Commandent* [sic].

Reacting to the news: community in mourning

Charlie's father had sent his mother to hospital in Bunbury that morning, and was obliged to telegram the doctor with news of their son's death. He inserted a notice in the *Southern Times*:

7 August 1916: Killed in Action: On July 22nd 1916 died of wounds received in action in France, Charles Snell 4th Battalion. Beloved youngest [sic] son of Alfred and C.A. Snell. Inserted by his loving parents, brother and sister. A. Snell, Devonia Orangery Harvey.[44]

Mrs Snell wrote from hospital in Bunbury:

My dears

No words, no writing can express my feelings.

I can't realise my baby boy in heaven I have that one consolation.

Every heart knoweth its own bitterness.

Oh, I've had such a lot of visitors.

The Lord gave and the Lord taketh away. Love to you both.

Fourteen-year-old Marjorie attended to practical matters: 'My dears, I am spending two or three days with Mum in the hospital and will write you tomorrow. Love from us both.'

Alf wrote: 'Dear Mum, no need to tell you how I feel about losing poor old Charlie.'

Mr Snell despatched telegrams to family and friends in New South Wales and the United Kingdom. He then made enquiries through the Red Cross and the YMCA.

To the Red Cross: 'My son was yesterday reported as having died of wounds on July 22nd. On the same date, a cable from our relatives reported him as well. I beg your good offices in trying to find the actual truth for his bereaved family.'[45]

The Red Cross replied:

We regret very much to have to inform you that the information your son died on the 22nd July is only too true. You have the consolation, however, that your son died, as he would have liked to have died, in the defence of the honour of his country.[46]

An enquiry to the YMCA elicited both personal and official responses.[47]

Just a few lines to add my personal sympathies. Although I do always with all soldiers everything possible under such circumstances, any experience I have picked up whilst in charge here is freely and fully yours. Kindest regards to Mrs Snell and Marjorie. John Beecham.[48]

Mr Snell responded:

The loss of our boy has broken us all up badly, but time is softening the wound, and we are hoping to soon see sunshine again. We should of all things like to know if possible how Charlie met his death and where, that he was game right thro', we have no doubt. If he left any little odds and ends they would be valued if they could be sent to us. We deeply appreciate your kind feeling and must congratulate the YMCA in having in yourself one who is exceptionally well fitted in uplifting sorrowing souls'.[49]

Sir Newton Moore's own enquiries to the Red Cross elicited a further fragment of information:

He was buried in the cemetery and his grave is marked with a Wooden Cross bearing his name, so that after the war is over, his friends will be able to find out where he lies. Pte C. Snell was admitted to this (44) Casualty Clearing Station on July 22nd, wounded. He had a compound fracture of the femur, and the base of his skull was fractured, he only lived a few hours and died the same day, being unconscious the whole time. [50]

In September, Charlie's note of 19 July was returned to his aunt in London, enclosed in the letter from Percy Hay, Charlie's commanding officer, which she forwarded to the family in Harvey. An official card from the AIF enclosed a photograph of a grave at Puchevillers Cemetery. Mr Snell's brother in London made his own enquiries to the AIF In London, and received a confirmatory letter on 14 September. Mrs Blanche Martin in Glen Innes also made inquiries, and forwarded the two responses seen above to the Snell family.

We now meet the Snell community as men and women, many of

whom had sons and daughters at war, wrote to express their own grief at Charlie's death. The majority of the letters (60) are from Harvey and Bunbury and surrounding districts; there are fifteen from the Perth region and fifteen from Sydney and Glen Innes relatives, friends and colleagues. Wounds were reopened some months later, when a dozen letters arrived from England. Most letters were addressed to Mrs Snell, but it was Mr Snell who answered them, from lists of correspondents compiled by Mrs Snell. Carbon copies of many of his replies tell of his grief and loss and the hope of a happy reunion 'on the other side'.

Nellie Gibbs was with Mrs Snell in Bunbury soon after the news was broken. She later wrote:

> *My own dear girl, so brave, so dear, I never spent such a sad day as Monday – nothing would ease the pain in my heart for very sorrow for you – and for us. Thank God you have Marjorie, she's such a mother's girl just as Win is to me, and there's Alf, so affectionate and so fond. And I know Mr Snell is just full of sorrow. When I returned, he was in his office. He asked all about you, and he spoke so splendidly of his and your terrible loss. Mrs Mayne was a bit upset at not seeing you, I asked her to let me go alone at first. Ever your loving friend, Nellie Gibbs.*[51]

Mrs Mayne waited her turn, and later wrote:

> *Dear Mrs Snell, get strong, dear, and come back soon as you can. I did not come in again, I thought I would not intrude, but my loving wishes for your recovery and speedy return I leave. Enclosed, dear, a few words of loving memory just for you. Your always affectionate, Mabel Mayne.*[52]

The 'few words' are a poem on the theme of a mother's sacrifice.[53]

> *In Memory of a Beloved Son (abridged)*
> *Hail beloved, splendid son of a beloved mother …*
> *Thy life grandly yielded, great evils to smother*
> *… Triumphantly thy manhood rose in arms …*

There are wrongs to right, Mother,
Yet did the gods demand of thee thy all …
Greater love hath no Man,
Fearlessly with heart and courage high
For love of Mother home, your duty clear
Now faced the foe to do your part and die.
But in your Mother's heart, fragrant and sweet …
In deathless memory, your love lives yet …
Spirit shall Spirit greet …
Sweet natured, gentle, honourable, Beloved of all,
To thee, Pure in Heart, comes clear and sweet The Call. To his dear Mother.

Gladys Whatham, Charlie's fiancée in Sydney, expresses disbelief, but acceptance that he had died doing his duty.[54]

Please accept my deepest sympathy in your very sad loss, I cannot tell you how grieved I am and only wish I could comfort you in some way. It came as a great shock to me as although I knew Charlie was in the firing line I did not once think anything would happen him, and cannot yet realise the awful truth. But, dear Mrs Snell, he died as I am sure he would wish to die doing his duty and fighting for those he loved. I had a letter from him only last week, in which he sent me a little bunch of flowers, I am enclosing half for you. I have had several very nice letters from Glen Innes friends and they are all very sad, he was a favourite everywhere. I only pray that he did not have to suffer long. I hope you are well and being brave for his sake. Give my kindest wishes to Mr Snell, your son, and dear little Marjorie, and love to your dear self. I remain, Yours lovingly, Gladys Whatham.

Charlie's childhood friend, Wedd Tuxford, a munitions worker in Sheffield, England, wrote:

I have a sad task before me, expressing my sympathy to you in the loss of poor old Charlo [sic]… I can't think of anything else but the years and years of happy outings with Charlie and Alf, and can't imagine I'll never see him again. He was the only real mate I had up to the time I met the wife, as you know. Believe me, my regret is that I was not with him at the last. I remain your foster son (as you used to say).

Communities of mourning surrounded the grieving family as people sought to comfort the bereaved family and themselves.[55]

I have a splitting headache, it's awful when it comes near[56]*, my heart has been rudely lacerated.*[57] *It seems so cold to write,* [58] *I have been sitting with a sheet of paper for half an hour,*[59] *if I wrote reams I could not say very much',*[60] *I will write a proper letter when I can collect my thoughts,*[61] *this letter is only a poor poor expression of what I really feel.*[62]

Your old Bunbury friends feel greatly for you.[63] *There was universal grief in Harvey:*[64] *The day the news came it caused quite a gloom around Harvey, and many had a weep over it, wrote Emily Daddow, adding that she had spoken with Charlie before he left for Sydney.*[65] *How many hundres of parents in your position, mourning dear sons, fathers, husbands and relatives … sadness and bereavement for one and all.*[66] *We can sympathise with each other*[67] *– doesn't all the trouble make us look back on their childhood days?*[68]

The Sydney and Glen Innes communities felt a similar sense of loss.

Miss Tonkin, a friend of Charlie's has just come in to condole, and we had a letter from Glen Innes and everyone is so sorry. He was a favourite wherever he went, [69] *we have his photo in a corner among our soldier friends.*[70]

Steve and Polly Snell wrote from London:

our fears for dear Charley [sic] were correct. We missed the dear boy's letters and feared that something had happened.[71] *Mrs Jefferson wrote: my husband had corresponded for the last three years.*[72] *Wedd Tuxford's mother suggested 'a pilgrimage to Charlie's resting place'.*[73]

Some wrote of the close relationship between Charlie and his mother:

> *she was simply wrapped up in him;*[74] *how he adored his mother.*[75] *Any mother might be proud to own him.*[76] *You know every mother will feel for you … he was so much more than many sons.*[77]

Some were more matter of fact:

> *your dearly loved Charlie is dead oh my own poor darling friend, how my heart aches for you. How proud you were of your handsome good boy. Only think of his worth and how all honoured him;*[78] *the whole world of mothers must indeed be suffering, but they are safe from any more pain and horror.*[79]

Cousin Susie wrote:

> *yours is indeed a sacrifice. Words – and heart – fail me. I can only commend you to God, who can and does heal the broken hearted, as one whom his mother comforted, so will I comfort you.*[80]

Friends advised Mrs Snell to resign herself to her situation and count her blessings:

> *he has given you a wonderful gift – your endless pride in him,*[81] *comfort yourselves in remembering that you were the mother of such a brave good son,*[82] *and try and be brave for the sake of the others.*[83] *Siblings were a source of consolation, but elder brother, Alf, must have felt some consternation at the admonition that he must try to fill his shoes … brace up dear old girl.*[84]

Mourners recreated Charlie's identity:[85]

> *He was a model of model sons, honoured by all who had the privilege of knowing him,*[86] *a boy in a million,*[87] *a dear old boy,*[88] *a fine manly boy,*[89] *and a clean souled young man.*[90] *Mrs Jefferson wrote: your dear son was a noble young man, who trusted and hoped in God. I should love to send you his last letter, but my husband will not part with it.*[91]

Employers, teachers and organisations such as the Harvey Citrus Society, Lodge and the Rifle Club, spoke of a promising future cut short. The Bunbury Municipal Council wrote of:

> *your most illustrious son,*[92] *while others expressed sincere regret at the loss of such a bright young promising life.*[93] *Teacher, Ethel Middleton wrote of a beautiful life cut off so early, he stood out from among his school mates, when I saw him again in later years I found the promise of his boyhood fulfilled.*[94] *Thomas Paisley wrote: how well we all remember him, I always looked on him as a good and promising lad.*[95] *Isabel Rhead wrote: As you know I was very fond of your dear boy, and of bright young lives lost to us forever.*[96]

The manager of the Experiment Farm at Glen Innes spoke of Charlie's 'trustworthiness, efficiency and honourable conduct',[97] while his wife described Charlie as 'full of life and bright, good and true: he was a splendid character.'[98] W.J. Allen wrote of a 'most promising junior officer, enthusiastic, energetic and painstaking; he conducted himself well, and would have soon filled one of the best positions in the branch. He was highly thought of by officers, workmen and students alike. We did not like to let him go, but he felt it was his duty. We have lost one of the most promising officers and you the best of sons.[99] Charlie gave everyone the impression he would go far;[100] he was a loyal character and I saw in him a great future if God had spared him.'[101]

The masculinity of war[102] was echoed in the condolences:

> *he did his duty right manfully,*[103] *fighting for his country as any man should:*[104] *a man grown he felt he must do a man's work.*[105] *None displayed a cleaner and truer manhood than your dear lad.*[106] *He wrote such a fine, manly letter, full of hope and cheerfulness.*[107]

Expressions of grief focussed on duty and patriotism, reassuring the bereaved that their son had not died in vain.[108]

> *Your hero son, doing his duty, will wear a crown of glory.*[109] *You*

must try console yourself in the thought that your son gave his life fighting for freedom under a banner of justice and died a glorious death.[110] *That darling boy of yours who passed away doing his duty*[111] *died for his country on the field of honour,*[112] *doing his duty so gloriously.*[113]

Others found solace in the fact that Charlie was fighting for

Australia and the great cause of humanity,[114] *and was preserving our honour and the purity of our womanhood*[115] *and saving our loved ones being trampled on by the vicious hordes.*[116] *From London, pride was evident: the dear lad was a hero. We were so proud of having a nephew from the colonies, fighting for us.*[117]

Faith was a source of comfort:

those whom God loves die young … we are the better for having known and loved him.[118] *He trusted and hoped in God and he will surely get his reward. They laid down their lives for God and Empire, in this awful sacrifice, none possessed a cleaner and truer manhood than your dear lad.*[119] *The minister's wife wrote: the widespread roof of the father's home overshadows your boy … be still my soul … we shall meet at last.*[120]

Privately, Dr Dermer confided to Mr Snell that while Mrs Snell could find strength in her religion – 'personally I cannot take it, but I quite recognise its good as a comfort to a woman'.[121]

Lieutenant Percy Hay, Snell's commanding officer, wrote to Snell's aunt in London.

It is with the deepest regret that I write concerning the death of Pte Snell but as he enlisted in my company in Australia, came over to Egypt with me, I feel in duty bound to write you concerning the end of your nephew. Pte Snell was always formost (sic) in matters of duty, his character was exemplary, his disposition was such as to make him a favourite among his friends and I always looked upon him as one who would receive promotion. He did all a soldier possibly could for King and Country. I regret having to open what must be a most painful wound, still it is respect to your nephew or son that it is done.[122]

English correspondents were unanimous in their dismay at the costs of the war, Australians less so. England was close to the fighting: London was the subject of Zeppelin raids, the Battle of Jutland was heard in Edinburgh, and returning wounded were ever present.[123] English correspondents commented on this awful,124 cruel,[125] wicked, endless war.[126] How very dreadful this war is … the young good lives lost,[127] it is hard to realise the awfulness of this shocking war,[128] the men simply can't speak of it, it is so awful to see their dearest friends falling in the most terrible agony.[129] At last we have them beaten but it will be some time before it is all over.[130]

Mr Snell's male friends wrote:

from one who, like yourself has the cloud of sorrow hovering thro' this awful crime of war. We are brothers and sisters in one common grief,[131] *and William Robinson, a veteran himself, referred to the inferno that is the Western Front.*[132] *Dr Dermer had a son in Mesopotamia.*[133] *Selwyn Paisley was still in the midst of all this fearful fighting, while Cyril had been delighted to meet Charlie in the trenches, and could not have been far away when he died.*[134] *Mrs Bythe has lost another son. They were such strong big men.*[135] *Mrs Whatham wrote: we have not heard from my son for some time and feel very anxious,*[136] *and Ethel Smith commented: my son if alive is fighting in France.*[137] *Nora Snell in London was concerned that 'her' Charlie had gone to Salonika, not very fit after his skull being cracked in two places.*[138] *George Goss wrote of a mutual friend in London who had suffered the loss of two sons, and now a third was going to the front. Goss's own son was in France and his wife and daughter were anxiously awaiting his return.*[139]

Mr Snell's replies reflecting on the pain of loss, the consolation of knowing that Charlie had done his duty, and assurance of a spiritual homecoming.

Your few words of sympathy came at a time when we were tasting the full bitterness of the first death in the family. Letters received show that the loss is not ours alone,[140] *and help to ease our sore hearts. We are greatly cut up:*[141] *we only had one Charlie, the great hope we had for our boy is so suddenly and completely wrecked. Even now we can hardly realise we will never see him again this side. I never credited myself with so much sentiment.*[142]

We could hardly have wished for a more noble life – or death – for he was as much to us as Kitchener was to the nation.[143]

After the knowledge that our boy had lived and died as a man should do, the one thing more than another that gave us the greatest consolation was the amount of fellow feeling shown by so many friends, many of whom had themselves sore hearts from a similar cause.[144]

I am hopeful that the sun will soon be shining again.[145] *The worst now is over and kindly time bringing its influence to bear; I hope we shall all have a fresh lease of life.*[146] *When my own time comes it will be eased by the thought that Charlie is waiting.*[147]

Memorials to the Australian troops are a prominent feature of the former battlefields of northern France. The memorial to 1st Division dead at Pozières Windmill site commemorates *Australian troops who fell more thickly on this ridge than on any other battlefield of the war.*[148] The Commonwealth War Graves Commission maintains the war cemeteries in perpetuity in honour of the Australian sacrifice on French soil and family have visited Charlie's grave. His name is on the Australian War Memorial in Canberra and on memorials in Glen Innes and Bunbury. His mother erected a headstone in the Bunbury Cemetery as a tangible symbol of his death.[149]

Charlie was in France for four months before he died in the Somme offensive, mortally wounded in the preparation for the Australians' first engagement. He enlisted through a sense of duty. More proper than many but amused by his less reverent comrades. He did not endure the extreme hardships suffered during the worst winter in modern memory and the horrific battles in which his fellow Australians later participated. Nor did he endure a long post-war life of suffering as many of his friends did.

His father searched for certainty around his death, reconnecting with male friends in an emotional environment dominated by women. Neither Charlie's parents nor siblings ever recovered from the loss of their son and brother. The sadness endured until his parents' deaths in 1935 and 1936, his brother's, at the age of 82, and his sister's at 99. Their sadness lingered too in the memories of their children. Some of the names mentioned here – Hymus, Gibbs, Paisley – were uttered by Martha, Snell's sister in law, who inherited through marriage many of the community relationships which sustained the Snell family after Charlie's death.[150]

Charlie's father resisted the Australian War Memorial's request for the personal papers of servicemen and women and kept them in the trunk Charlie sent from Sydney prior to his departure to war.[151] He instructed that the papers should go to the eldest son of the eldest son. Eventually, they made their way to his eldest great-granddaughter.

2

THE PRE-WAR WELLINGTON COMMUNITY: 'SOMETHING IN BETWEEN'

When the Snells arrived in Bunbury in 1896, they found a dynamic community which had evolved in the formative decades of the Swan River Colony, welcoming new residents and creating 'fictive kin' relationships which helped to assuage community grief in wartime.[1] Isolation from the centre of government in Perth forced the community to manage most aspects of its development. Contemporary newspaper reports and oral histories document the establishment of housing, food production, hospitals and schools, roads and bridges, timber milling and coal mining. Churches and cultural activities enriched community life. Public men rose to prominence as the governing class of the community while women largely remained in the domestic sphere. Shared activity resulted in a high degree of social capital. State government intervention gradually increased as infrastructure needs, such as railways, irrigation and harbour extensions outstripped local resources.

The Bunbury–Harvey community represented a middle ground between Bean's bushmen and Robson's urban soldiers through community networks that encompassed both the rural and the urban population.[2] The rural community included farmers, their wives and children and residents of timber towns. The townspeople engaged in administrative, service and commercial activities and included medical, legal, business, and government officials, members of the press, sea captains and clergy. The population was surprisingly mobile as a list of visitors to Caroline Snell while in hospital shows. It included Mr Harcourt Ward, 'Glengarriff', Collie; H.M. Beigel, brewer; George Reading, proprietor of the *Southern Times*; Kenneth Eastman, lawyer; and George Stead, who was General Manager of the Midland railway workshops, where Alf Snell did his apprenticeship. Community interactions were fostered by business and farming activity and social, religious and sporting events.

The Bunbury population was therefore, neither wholly bushmen nor urban dwellers, but something in between since they lived when 'but few years had intervened between country and town' and boundaries were fluid.[3] The Bunbury–Harvey community combined the bushman's sense of independence and resourcefulness, with the town dweller's sense of community. The Snell family arrived only 60 years after Europeans first settled the district, when many individuals were directly linked to the district's earliest European settlers. While the majority of the Snell family's Western Australian correspondents resided in the Wellington district, twenty individuals corresponded from elsewhere, indicating some movement away from the district. Most were former Bunbury residents, whether young people or families who had moved to Perth for education or employment, or former business associates of Snell's father. Some former Wellington residents wrote from England where they were residing, either temporarily or permanently.

Until at least 1920, local inhabitants were referred to in the press as 'settlers'. For example, 'the Logue family were amongst the oldest and most respected settlers of the district', and 'Mr Rose was a son of one of Bunbury district's oldest and best-known settlers'.[4] A debating society was formed to bring 'settlers' together, government decisions were communicated to 'the settlers', and social evenings welcomed 'new settlers'.[5] After the war, the term was only applied to soldier settlers.

Residents retained close ties to Britain, although immigrants came from all the countries of Europe, as well as small numbers from other locations. Charlie Snell was unique in the Wellington district in having been born in the Straits Settlement (Kuala Lumpur). Nearly 40 Snell correspondents were British-born, including the Ibbotson brothers, whose mother still lived in London.[6] Northern European names appearing in the correspondence include Dannell, Fabricius, and one 'Rupert', surname illegible, possibly Swiss. Mrs Dannell, whose son's name was 'Sig', used some German spellings and grammatical constructions yet 'Rupert' clearly identified as Australian through his outrage at the reported actions of the 'Hun'.[7] Victoria provided the largest numbers of interstate arrivals, although many were born elsewhere. W.J. George, born in the UK, Fabricius, born in Denmark, Leitch, born in Scotland, and the Holtzman family all migrated from Victoria.[8] South Australia provided the Tuxford, Gibbs and Roy Hayward families, while the Eastmans came from New South Wales.

The Snell Archive identifies around 120 families, of whom a significant number were among the earliest European arrivals in the district.[9] Of these, the year of arrival of around 100 are known, enabling them to be placed in the broader settlement history of the district. For example, Martha MacGregor, the daughter of one of the earliest arrivals in the district, married schoolteacher Thomas Paisley who arrived in a later wave of settlement.[10] The settlement history of the district has been notionally divided into three periods, 'original settlers', who arrived between 1838 and 1860, Bunbury expansion, 1860–1910, and Harvey 1890–1910.

After the earliest European settlement at Bunbury, which included Martha Paisley's father, a second wave of settlers at Australind in 1840–41, brought 600–700 people, a population that contributed the Clifton, Clarke, Crampton, Forrest, Hurst, Hymus, and Moore families, pioneers who built their own homes and established gardens and crops, and raised livestock.[11] The settlement expanded into the hinterland as far as Harvey as settlers moved north and east in search of grazing land.[12]

Arrivals in the later years of the 1800s and early 1900s added to the business, farming and timber interests. These include brewer Herman Beigel (1885); R.W. Lowe, manager of the West Australian Bank (1879) and founding member of Bunbury's Methodist Church in 1888; J.C. Port, one of the earliest timber millers; and Dr Simon Joel, health and quarantine officer.[13] Bunbury mayors, first elected in 1887, included Spencer, Mitchell, Moore, Clarke, Hayward, Baldock and Reading, all names which figure in the Snell correspondence. In 1896, three years after the completion of the Bunbury–Perth railway, Snell's father joined this dynamic community as Superintendent of Railways for the South West. Among the correspondents are two families of Haywards, one (Thomas Hayward) among the Bunbury-Australind originals and the other (Roy Hayward), coming from South Australia in the late 1800s, thus placing him in the third group.

In 1905, Bunbury, with its port, was a small country town situated between bush and sea. The local population was still responsible for almost every aspect of community development, and included early surveyors E. Clarke, John and Alexander Forrest and Newton Moore.[14] By the 1860s, the second generation of settlers held official positions, including wheelwright James Blythe (1841), now a police officer, William Spencer, a shepherd who became a member of parliament, and Joseph Hough (1842), a land developer in the 1890s.[15] Later arrivals included Thomas Hayward (1852), a farmer and merchant who lived until 1915 and William Reading (1865) and his son George who took over the *Southern Times*, begun in 1888.[16] Government appointees were few until the late 1800s: teacher Thomas Paisley was appointed in 1881 while Messrs Snell, Becher, Jefferson and Joel were among government appointees in the 1890s. The 1890–1910 group contains the Daddow, Castieau, and Fabricius families who arrived in the district from the goldfields in response to the government's closer settlement policy.[17]

Expansion in the hinterland

While the town of Bunbury was growing during the period 1840 to 1900, the settlement expanded in the hinterland between Bunbury and Harvey.[18] The district saw waves of pioneers who gradually intensified land use.[19] The villages of Brunswick, Benger, Wokalup, Burekup and

Roelands developed as settlers moved inland in search of grazing land and established farmsteads.[20] This group include Clarke, Rose, Castieau and Smith, who developed a farming system adapted to new climatic patterns, sowing crops in autumn rather than spring, harvesting in early summer rather than late, managing calving mid-year and allowing the cows to dry off in summer when pasture was scarce. Meat, butter and cheese, fruit and vegetables, wine and olives were produced for home consumption and sale, the completion of the rail link between Bunbury and Perth in 1893 providing a convenient link to the metropolitan markets.[21]

In the late 1880s, Lands Commissioner John Forrest created new land subdivisions to encourage closer settlement for citrus farming around Harvey. The Snells purchased land in the district and moved there after Snell senior's retirement in 1910.[22] Others also came from Bunbury, while a significant new population entered the district.[23] Snell senior managed several properties, a fruit packing shed and manufactured packing cases.[24]

The period 1880 to 1900 also saw the appointment of government 'experts' such as Frank Becher to promote citrus growing.[25] The introduction of milking machines, milk separators and potato harvesters, the development of subterranean clover and superphosphate, and scientific pest management were led by Frank Becher, Roy Hayward, and the Clarke, Smith, Rose and Wykes families.[26]

After leaving school, Charlie Snell gained farming experience in crops and livestock and mechanised farming systems with Harvey orchardists George Gibbs and Roy Hayward, farmers Castieau and W.H. Smith, and agricultural experts Jefferson and Abernethy.[27] George Gibbs was among the earliest settlers in the Harvey district, having come from South Australia in 1884 or 1885 to manage the estate of the first colonial Governor, James Stirling.[28]

The Wellington community was educated and cultured. The letters in the archive demonstrate a high level of literacy, and some beautiful handwriting by lawyer Kenneth Eastman, his wife, Sylvia, and Margaret Castieau of Roelands. Writers range in age from the young Marjorie Snell the elderly Mrs Buchanan, with her spidery handwriting.[29] The surname of 'Rupert', so florid as to be indecipherable, is strongly influenced by the Old German script which was still in use at the time.[30]

The high level of literacy of the Snell community can be traced to the earliest arrivals in the district.[31] The Clifton family brought their own library, and the father of John and Alexander Forrest was a qualified engineer.[32] The 1911 census reported a literacy rate in the Wellington district of 99% and even the two Snell correspondents whose mother tongue was not English are highly literate in English.[33] Welborn's claim that only officers demonstrated high literacy, is not supported by the evidence of this archive.[34] Only one letter, signed 'Brenda and her ma', possibly Brenda Wenn, suggests that her mother may have been illiterate and needed her daughter to write on her behalf.[35] Much of the schooling was done on the scattered properties by wives and daughters.[36] Small private schools such as Mrs R. Forrest's 'Torrington Ladies' College' (1878–80), taught 'written work', needlework and music to around twenty Buchanan, Gibbs, Hay, Hayward, Mitchell and Spencer children.[37]

In 1892, under headmaster Thomas Paisley, the Bunbury Boys State School had around 50 pupils.[38] The state school for girls in Bunbury opened in 1893, while the first private girls' school was opened in 1908 by a highly educated female principal.[39] Marjorie Snell attended the Bunbury Catholic school, opened in 1898.[40] The Elementary Education Act of 1871 had created a Central Board of Education with elected district boards to manage schools and administer government grants for children between ages five years and seventeen.[41] The Bunbury District Board was diligent in its management of elections and in reminding parents of their duties to their children.[42] The Wellington board operated between 1866 and 1916 under the dynamic leadership of the Reverend A. Buchanan, managing all the schools in the Wellington district, from Harvey and Cookernup in the north, mill towns including Mornington, the Blackwood district to the east, and Stratham to the south.[43] The board's monthly meetings attended to sanitation, access roads, water supply and drainage, staffing, compliance with education regulations and student matters.[44]

In 1901, when Charlie Snell and his brother were at school, the annual prize-giving ceremony at the Bunbury State School was an opportunity for reflection.[45] The prize-winners for 1898, 1901 and 1904 included many who later figured in the Snell correspondence, through their war service or as grieving friends.[46] Many of these individuals lived to fulfill their potential, and some, like the Paisleys, Frank Blythe, Norman Holtzman and Wisbey Sinclair were to live out their lives with war-caused disabilities causing endless disputes with repatriation officials.

Charlie Snell's cohort attended school between around 1897 and 1910, when schooling did not always begin at age 5 to 6, but the majority of children were in schooling at age ten. From age 13, numbers in school began to decline, to age 15, when the majority of children were not in school. In 1911, there were 39 young people above age 15 who were in some form of schooling, including Wedd Tuxford, attending Perth High School and taking the Adelaide University examinations.[47] Others, like Newton Moore, born 1870, attend Bunbury State School before spending two years at Prince Alfred College, Adelaide, while John and Alexander Forrest followed their primary schooling in Bunbury with three years at Bishop Hale's School in Perth in the 1860s.[48]

Thomas Paisley was connected with many church, cultural, sporting and community organisations and was later pivotal in wartime patriotic work. As respected schoolteacher and headmaster for 32 years, Paisley taught the Snell brothers and three generations of their fellows.[49] He believed character building and citizenship were essential elements of education, and many of his pupils later served as state premiers (Forrest, Newton Moore and Mitchell), mayors and councillors. Newton Moore, for example, grandson of John Moore (arrived 1842), married Isabella Lowrie, the daughter of a former shepherd, in 1898 and became state premier and later a member of British parliament.[50] Paisley's former pupils dispersed throughout the state, to America and the UK, and one was among the first white party to travel through Africa from east to west.[51] Paisley could not have predicted the part so many of them, including himself, were to play in the coming war.

From 1869, the Bunbury Mechanics' Institute, later the Bunbury Railway Institute was an important provider of community education.[52] Snell's father and many others were active in the institute, including Port, Eastman, Paisley, Clarke, Hayward, Forrest, Gibbs, and Dr Joel.[53] The institute was open to 'all classes of the community', promoting intellectual and physical development, teaching accountancy, mechanics, work safety, shorthand and first aid under the instruction of Dr Joel.[54] The Institute's library stocked a wide range of local and British newspapers, educational, scientific and theological works as well as works by 'popular authors' Charles Dickens, Dumas, and Disraeli.[55] Discussions 'of a contentious nature, such as politics and grievances' were forbidden: the institute was to be used only for 'recreation and instruction'.[56]

The state government became involved in post-school education from 1905, when Premier Newton Moore offered free post-school vocational education for boys and girls above fourteen years of age.[57] The men's first aid classes in 1914 included Eric Duce, Robert Hurst and Percy Smith, all country boys who later went to war.[58] Bunbury had access to the state's library system by 1907.[59]

In 1907, a call came for a literary society for the young to match investment in sporting competition.[60] The churches responded: the Anglican church offering books as Sunday School prizes.[61] The Roman Catholic Girls Literary Society held weekly meetings between 1914 and 1917, studying Shakespeare, holding mock parliaments and debates, essay competitions and publishing a magazine.[62] The girls themselves recognised the club's value in broadening attitudes and dismissed fears of members becoming 'too advanced'.[63] The 1913 inquest into the death of a 15-year-old Harvey girl in the collapse of a new hall during a severe storm was able to call on a range of expert witnesses including building contractors Gibsone, Roesner, Stewart and Ward, a lawyer and a doctor.[64]

1. Charles Snell civilian and soldier 1915.
Snell archive.

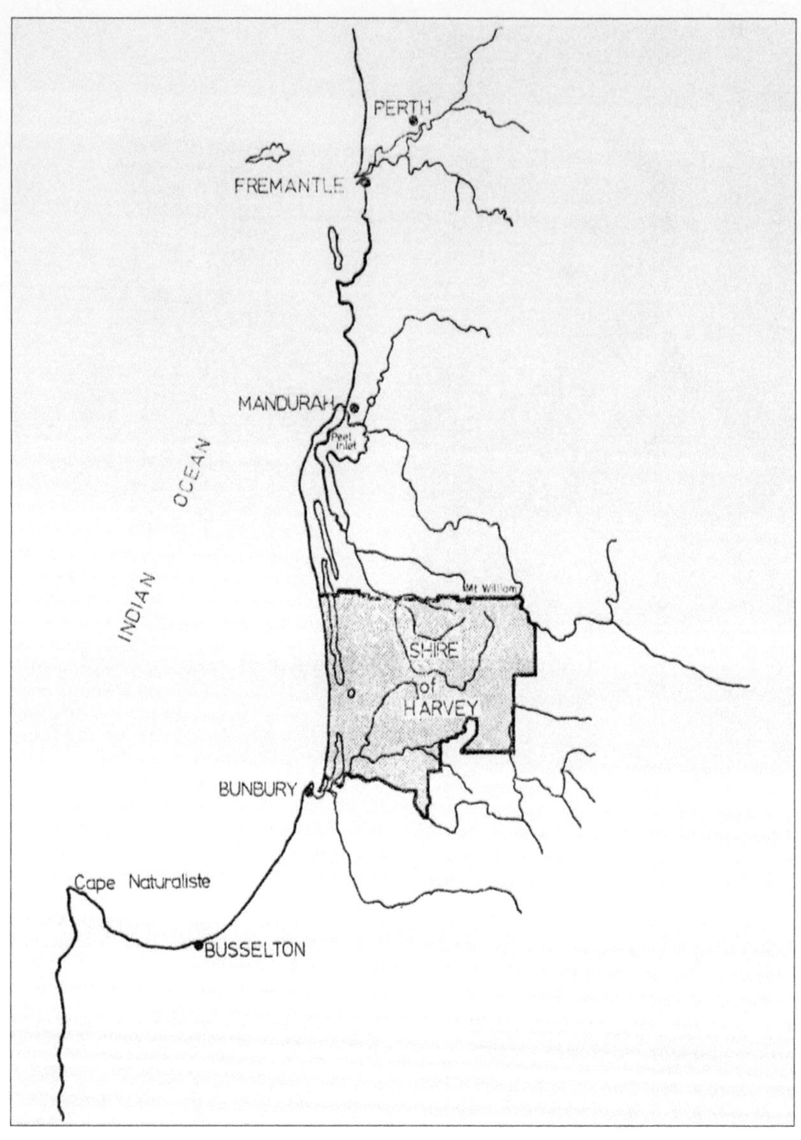

2. Location of Wellington district.
Staples, They Made Their Destiny, *Frontispiece.*

Back row:
alf, ?, Wedd
? Hemingway, Tuxford.
Middle row:
Dannell, Ida Staples, ?, Chrissie Moore
Georgie Hemingway
Marjorie "
alice Staples,
Cora Moore
KODAK PRINT
43141
Sitting at front
Mother, Marjorie +
Mrs Hemingway.

3. The Snell community, beginnings 1905. Mesdames Snell and Hemingway with Dannell, Hemingway, Moore, Snell and Tuxford children.
Bunbury Historical Society.

4. The town of Bunbury, 1905, as the young Snell knew it. Adjacent to the busy port, from left: Post Office, St Paul's Anglican Pro-Cathedral (adjacent right), Wesley Church (foreground), Bon Marché store (facing intersection), Congregational–Presbyterian church (rear), railway station (to left, rear). *Battye Library, 006101PD.*

5. Harvey 1905: the community in its setting of open jarrah–marri forest. *Battye Library, 019224PD.*

The town of Harvey 1890–1916

The Snells were part of a group of Bunbury residents who moved to Harvey to take up citrus farming. Press reports fostered links between the two towns. In 1897, the town, set in a 'dense forest of stately gums and giant grass trees', consisted of a railway siding, a few cottages, a store and post-office. By 1905, it included a railway station and goods shed, telegraph and post office, schoolhouse, hotel, three stores, butcher and baker, chapel, blacksmith, nurseries, private residences, an agricultural hall and library.[65]

The railway station remained a centre of activity for the district as visitors were greeted and farewelled. In 1906, there was an air of 'healthy prosperity' in the carefully tilled soil, the reticulated water supply for stock and a citrus nursery. The newspaper correspondent predicted that with closer settlement the area would become, like John Forrest's 1888 plan, 'the home of a peasantry as famous as those found on the fens and lowlands of the old country'.[66]

Australian country towns such as Harvey were home to a population which was neither exclusively rural nor urban, 'but something in between'.[67] A town address did not signify 'urban' in the present sense of the word, and was far removed from the industrial cities of Sydney and Melbourne and the sprawling cities of England. This reinforces Devine's view that 'even those who came from the towns were not city-bred in the sense in which the term is generally understood ... the life of the bush was in their blood'.[68]

An image in the Snell archive of the Harvey Christmas party of 1912, seated in a field next to a haystack, is evocative of the rural surroundings of Harvey. It includes some who went to war, and some who stayed at home and worked to provide 'comforts' for those at the front. Charlie himself is second from left in the back row, with Guy Gibbney on his left. Both would die at war. Reg Ibbotson, who would return, took this photograph, while another exists, taken by Charlie, with Reg standing in his place. Charlie's brother, Alf, is second from the right in the back row, standing next to his father. Alf was rejected for service three times. Second from left in the middle row, with Caroline Snell on her right, is orchardist, Bessie Lambert, who supported patriotic funds while in Harvey, before sailing to London to work in an aircraft factory. The other adults, the Johnsons and the Campbells, and their children all played their part in the war effort.

Letters from two of Charlie's childhood friends provide clues as to the childhood experiences which contributed to this identity. Maud Dunlop, the daughter of Bangkok friends, visited Harvey and enjoyed hunting frogs, when 'Alfie you and I made a little boat and paddles out of kerosene tins and it sank in the swamp at the back of your garden'.[69] The children 'had to cross a railway line before getting to town, and your father kept bees and grew tomatoes'.[70] Wedd Tuxford, wrote of fishing and football.[71] A Miss Moir, another friend, 'when cantering into Bunbury, and about six miles distant', had an accident when her horse went into a hole in the road.[72] These memories, and photographs of 1905 and 1912 showing picnic parties in the paddocks, reflect the natural surroundings in which the children grew up.[73]

Bean attributed the 'common sense, courage and leadership ability' of the Australian soldier to life in the arid outback.[74] Yet in the Wellington district, which was neither remote nor arid, rural dwellers made up around half the population.[75] Townspeople also raised stock, kept horses, grew fruit and vegetables and had frequent contact with farming families.[76] In 1911, Australia was a nation of country towns. In the agricultural districts, there were around 450 towns like Bunbury, with populations of between 1,000 and 4,000, each catering for around ten smaller centres in its hinterland.[77] Bunbury's population was around 4,000 in 1911, with a slight female dominance.[78] It was an agricultural service centre and port with strong municipal structures, newspapers, lawyers and doctors, hospitals and churches. Among Bunbury's smaller centres, Brunswick had a population of 323, Harvey 256, and Wellington Mills 676. Despite these small populations, each was significant: Brunswick, central to the district, was the location of Road Board meetings; Harvey was the centre for a number of agricultural societies; and Wellington Mills had its own church and sporting groups. The mining district of Collie and its associated settlements had a population of nearly 3,000, around 18% of the total Wellington population.[79] The Collie community consisted of miners, farmers and associated service providers and their families and maintained a strong connection with the Bunbury community through the railway and the port.[80]

The occupation data for both the Snell population and the Wellington district as a whole had a relatively even balance of urban and rural pursuits. The 1911 census shows that the Snell population was concentrated in the managerial class, at 31%, compared to Wellington as a whole at around five percent, while the percentage of farmers is more than double that of the district as a whole, at 39%.[81] Wellington farmers took a highly professional approach to their occupation, bringing them into frequent contact with the professional class. Many of the townspeople also participated in small-scale agricultural production, reflected in reports for agricultural shows. The occupational categories of commerce, transport and communication, industrial and domestic workers are somewhat reduced in the Snell population. The occupational structures of women will be examined in a later section.

The dominance of the railway is indicated by the more than 400 men identified in the census as railway employees and working under Mr Snell. The Bunbury–Boyanup railway, the first railway in Western Australia, built to serve the agricultural district, was opened in 1887, and operated by a private contractor as a horse drawn railway. The government later took it over, rebuilt and reopened it using steam engines in 1891, pre-dating the opening of the Perth Bunbury railway by two years.[82] The large number of people employed in the railways highlights the role of rail as the major form of transport before motor cars became dominant. The rail network significantly increased personal mobility, with special trains for public and private events.[83] As railway superintendent for the district until 1910, Mr Snell's position was onerous, involving 'the administration of many hundred employees, supervision and arrangement of time-tables and general traffic and the profitable handling of the business'.[84]

In Bunbury, the Misses Cons and Bayliss and Mrs Devereaux were independent women among twelve in the district. Significantly, there were seven female and 47 male breadwinners among the Snell population. The dependents are either the wives and children of Snell correspondents or young women who have left home. Although urban-dwelling wives did not generally contribute to the family income, the wives of farmers participated in farming activities and catered for farm labourers. Among the Snell correspondents, more than 20 women were the wives of farmers.

In the Wellington district, occupation was an ambiguous indicator of social class since many who had come to the district as labourers or tradesmen went through numerous changes of occupation and status, becoming landowners, professionals and administrators. The Hymus, Hurst and Forrest families, for example, all came as tradesmen or servants and gradually expanded their business interests. Conversely, those who came with capital had to engage in physical work in order to establish a livelihood.[85] In many cases, young men such as Charlie Snell were the sons of neighbours learning the skills needed to manage their own properties, yet his family sat among the higher social levels with the Forrest, Mitchell and Moore families, who all produced state premiers.

Mrs Snell shared in the workload once the family moved to Harvey.[86] Both sons moved through multiple classes of employment. Alf, the elder, trained as a railway mechanic later managing a mechanics business in Harvey and also travelling the state as the 'expert' (mechanic) for shearing teams, collecting natural history specimens during his free time. Following his retirement, he manufactured metal suitcases for shearers and became well-known as a naturalist. Charlie Snell expected to eventually take a managerial role in the New South Wales Department of Agriculture.[87] Marjorie did not undertake paid work, and married Thomas Pollard, a surveyor and prominent mining figure in Bangkok.[88]

The occupation data also demonstrates the fluidity of the rural-urban distribution of the population. Plumber, Norman Holtzman, lived in Bunbury yet much of his work was carried out on farms, while a farmer,

W.J. Sutton lived in a town house from 1913, and orchardist, George Gibbs also worked as an 'agent'.[89] The Snell population, equally divided between rural and urban dwellers, reflected connections made through living in both Bunbury and Harvey.[90]

The population was strongly influenced by British family ties and traditions, well educated, adaptable and innovative in their response to life in an alien environment. The rural and urban populations were relatively evenly balanced in an economy based on farming, orcharding, mining, and the port of Bunbury. Country towns provided the basis of community life for a population that was strongly connected to the natural environment. The Snell community was representative of the Wellington community as a whole with concentrations in the professions and farming. The next section examines the community cohesiveness which enabled the rapid transformation of community structures into patriotic committees to send men to war and support them through the home front war effort.

The pre-war Wellington community: cohesive and mutually supportive

A strong sense of community permeates the letters in the Snell archive. Participation in local affairs was the norm since the establishment of the Bunbury Town Trust in 1842. Fostered initially by the need for the settlers to collaborate in the establishment of farmsteads and infrastructure, community-mindedness was perpetuated through road boards, farmers' associations, lodges, newspapers, sporting associations, churches and social events. Often coming from rural villages in England, the settlers brought the community-mindedness with which they later supported the war effort. Snell's own letters demonstrate the strong connection he felt with his community through neighbourly interactions and workplace associations.[91]

David McMillan's concept of 'sense of community' involves the feeling of belonging and a shared commitment to fulfilling members' needs.[92] It is based on shared history, as in the pioneer experience, an understanding of reciprocity and a commitment to group problem solving. As early as 1840, just as the European settlement of the Bunbury–Harvey was beginning, Alexis de Tocqueville described the way that pioneering Americans formed associations for the construction of homes and infrastructure, for education, the development of agriculture and for entertainment.[93] There were many parallels with the American experience in the Wellington district: in the leadership of public men such as Baldock, Hayward, Paisley and Reading, in the development of intellectual and moral associations and in the close association between the public groups and the newspapers.

Large families also helped to promote connectedness. Weddings and funerals hosted large numbers of individuals from interconnected families, and community cohesion was further promoted by multiple families residing on farming properties.[94] Mrs William Logue, née Clarke, for example, who died in 1914, was a member of a large family and herself had many children, who married into other large families, spreading links throughout the district.[95]

While large families enhanced community connections, fictive kinship relationships developed between those who, like the Snells, had no local relatives. Snell referred to Daniel Harrington as 'Dad Harrington', E.M. Clarke spoke of Thomas Hayward as 'almost an elder brother', and George Clarke spoke of Thomas Paisley as 'a brother rather than a schoolmaster.'[96] Wedd Tuxford, in his letter to Mrs Snell from Sheffield, England, referred to himself as: 'your foster son (as you used to say)'.[97]

While the concept of sense of community partially accounts for the feeling evoked by the letters, the concept of social capital provides a more concrete measure of the civic engagement in the community. The outcomes of community participation are measurable in pre-war community structures and in the wartime output of goods, funds and community support for the soldiers, to the families of the soldiers and to the surviving soldiers who returned to the community.

Alexis de Tocqueville's 1840s concept of social capital, systematised by James Coleman in 1988, is currently used as an aid in addressing social, economic, educational and political issues, and disaster relief, especially in developing countries.[98] The World Bank defines social capital as 'the glue that holds society together'.[99] Social capital is found in the norms of trust and reciprocity that guide collective social behaviour to achieve outcomes beyond what individuals acting alone could achieve. Community networks and structures based on communal attitudes, behaviours and shared interests, provide order and predictability.

In pioneering communities such as the Wellington district, where central government interference was minimal, the social capital embedded in the local associations enabled the community to solve local problems and advance the economic development of the district. In 1909, for example, the Brunswick Road Board managed roads, bridges, fences, land allocations and rates, with Sutton, Logue, Reading and Staples among its members.[100] This helps to explain local resentment at the growing government interference in local affairs after the 1890s.[101] School celebrations, public entertainments, agricultural shows, and annual ploughing and pruning competitions promoted community spirit and encouraged progress.[102]

In Harvey, the Agricultural Alliance, begun 1894 and the Harvey Citrus Society, 1904, were important generators of social capital. The Harvey Agricultural Alliance managed matters of general importance as well as agriculture, such as its efforts to establish a post office in Harvey.[103] Associated social functions united the community and promoted 'good fellowship and kindly feeling'.[104] The Alliance sought upgrades to railway station facilities, extension of the train service to enable people to travel to Perth and back in one day and protest at the removal of the station master from Harvey in 1903.[105] Many of these requests were directed to the Minister for Works, W.J. George, who took a personal interest in the community. Mechanisation of agriculture was promoted through the introduction of mechanised ploughs, seed drills, milk separators and potato planters and provision for agricultural education.[106] In 1900, following a return visit to England, Thomas Hayward senior reported on the latest trends in mechanisation there.[107]

The Harvey Citrus Society, of which Snell senior was a member, active between 1904 and 1924, also concerned itself with local infrastructure, including telephone and postal services, the Harvey irrigation scheme and later, the Anzac Memorial fund.[108] It advocated for improved marketing and shipping of fruit, labour needs and the efficient use of fertilisers.[109] By 1914, through the influence of Bessie Lambert, daughter of a wealthy South Australian pioneer family, and now farming in Harvey, a meeting sought ways of increasing the involvement of local women in the society's activities.[110] The society promoted community events such as produce shows, dances and picnics which attracted people and parliamentarians from Bunbury and Perth.[111]

Under the increasing influence of state government regulation and management of the rural sector, social capital was diluted. Once the district needed to look outwards for markets, and as infrastructure needs grew beyond the resources of the district, the Wellington delegates at a Department of Agriculture conference were forced to consider their farming activities in a broader context.[112] The conference considered the possibility of manufacturing farm machinery in Western Australia, improving livestock infrastructure at Fremantle port and stock breeding.

The Korijekup Drainage Board managed early water supply and drainage problems in Harvey.[113] However, a major irrigation system was beyond local resources and calls for government intervention in 1907 resulted in the Harvey Irrigation Scheme, the product of consultation between the Minister for Works, W.J. George, and the Harvey Citrus Society.[114] The proposed scheme was made public in 1913, and construction of the main dam began in 1915 with water first flowing over the crest on 16 July 1916, just one week before Charlie Snell's death.[115] Debate on the rating system for the irrigation water between Minister W.J. George and the Harvey Citrus' Society was finally resolved in 1917.[116]

Agricultural shows, first held in 1854, promoted the district's economic activity and enhanced urban-rural interactions. Displays of commercial and domestic crops, fruit and livestock, and home produce such as butter, bacon and jams were accompanied by luncheons and social evenings.[117] The Snell community was highly visible among officials, judges and exhibitors.[118] While Harvey's focus was on citrus fruit, Bunbury emphasised livestock and wine production, Duce and Clarke dominating.[119] Special trains and visits by government ministers signalled the significance of the shows.

By the end of the 19th century, the community had a strong sense of its past. In 1890, a dinner speaker described Thomas Hayward's decades-long connection with ploughing competitions.[120] At a 1913 reception for Thomas Paisley, Mayor E.M. Clarke commented on their three-decade connection, and named Bunbury families, Clarke, Forrest, Hay, Hayward, Mitchell, Moore and Spencer which had persisted in the district since the Australind settlement in the 1840s.[121] Premier Sir John Forrest often referred to Bunbury's past and the men who had come out from England with his father, uniting the community and embracing new 'settlers' in its shared history.[122]

Return visits to England by Thomas Hayward, the Jeffersons, the Paisleys, and Bessie Lambert, despite strong identification with relatives 'at home', highlighted their Australian identity.[123] For Hayward in particular, who had emigrated 50 years earlier, it was an opportunity to distance himself from his past as change in the home country had not increased prosperity to the level enjoyed in the Wellington district. J.S. Jefferson declined a position in the British Agricultural Department, saying 'I've had enough departmental tyranny and rottenness', with England's 'great wealth, great poverty, and rigidness (sic) of class distinctions', concluding, 'on the whole I like the colonials best'.[124]

The Bunbury–Harvey community was acutely aware of the qualities needed for cohesiveness, articulated at a Clifton funeral in 1905. The deceased had taken

> *a prominent and active interest in the advancement and benefit of the district, was always willing and ready to help his neighbour, genial, kind and courteous to all, and in the time of grief or trouble – one whose hand-grip conveyed more comfort and sympathy than any form of speech.*[125]

Thomas Paisley was also a 'force for good', speaking his mind 'without fear of consequence', seeking to build character among his charges and training them to become good citizens.[126] The Bunbury press was proud of the community's output of public citizens, describing how John and Alexander Forrest, Newton Moore, and James Mitchell, all Bunbury boys, had risen to the highest levels of state government.[127]

When a suicide attempt left the Johansen family in difficulties, local people offered support with a fund-raising concert and dance.[128] In a major community effort, the 'Fresh Air League' hosted children from the goldfields during the summer, emulating a movement begun in Scotland in 1874.[129] On the initiative of Mayor Newton Moore and his wife, the first children arrived in Bunbury for the summer of 1901.[130] The railways department arranged special trains and offered concession fares, enabling children to come from as far away as Laverton, 730 miles (more than 1,100 kilometres) away.[131] Administered for some years by the town clerk, the ladies' committee arranged accommodation with local residents, who organised swimming, boating trips and concerts for the children.[132] The doctor provided free medical care, farmers donated milk and meat, merchants offered groceries and the caretaker of the swimming baths allowed free use of the facilities. By 1910, more than 4,000 children had been hosted and a permanent home able to accommodate more than 100 children was opened by Premier Newton Moore.[133] The effort continued during the war as the community found time and resources for needy children in addition to their work for their fighting men.[134]

Music played an important part in maintaining community cohesion, as almost everyone could play an instrument and volunteered their musical talents to fundraising concerts in support of community causes, and later, the war.[135] Vocal and instrumental solos, duets and trios, formed part of community events, the Sailors' Rest, dinners, 'smoke socials', welcomes and farewells.[136] The Cliftons had brought a piano with them in 1840, and by the 1900s, high-quality musical instruments were sold in Bunbury.[137] An extended visit in 1869 by an Italian-American musician had long-lasting consequences for the musical life of the district. Signor Raffaele Abecco (1836–79) settled in Bunbury and collaborated in concerts at the Mechanics' Institute.[138] 'The Professor' asserted that, 'in this little district, he had found more musical taste and talent than in Perth or Fremantle'.[139] Abecco's sojourn was long remembered, his death announced in a local paper, and reminiscences in 1920 and 1938 described how his performances had inspired Cecil Clifton to build, with scavenged materials, a violin, a cello and a series of pipe organs.[140]

The Bunbury Amateur Orchestral Society operated from 1889, and a 1903 concert featured Snell's father playing the viola.[141] The press noted Bunbury's 'enviable position as a centre of musical culture', and in 1913 the Bunbury Musical Association was formed to oversee local musical activities by the town band, the orchestra and choral societies.[142] The participation of Mayors Newton Moore, E.M. Clarke and J. Baldock and delegates from the Municipal Council, the Railway Institute and the Lumpers' Union acknowledges the contribution of music to community wellbeing.

London's Trinity College of Music examiners visited Bunbury from 1899.[143] In 1913, for example, 60 local candidates were examined in piano, voice and violin.[144] Highly qualified local teachers such as Isabel Rhead, principal of Malvern Music College from 1913 to 1920, had studied at the Elder Conservatorium in Adelaide.[145] She and her sister, Muriel, a London-trained violinist, played major classical and contemporary concert works.[146] Miss Rhead also taught in Harvey, where Marjorie Snell was a pupil.[147]

Comment that musical performances served to promote 'good feeling among all classes', from the 'leading residents' to the 'working classes' and timber workers who 'flocked in from the bush', hints at class divisions in the community.[148] Snell himself reported that certain families disapproved of his working his passage to Sydney, contrary to his social position.[149] In letters to his father he mentions an episode of orange stealing in Harvey and names an employee who should be carefully watched while in the house.[150] Commenting on the planned irrigation scheme he wrote, 'I see you have more faith in those around Harvey than I do'.[151] Hints of class distinction also appeared in the 1903 decision of the Harvey Agricultural Alliance to form a debating society as a means of 'bringing settlers more together, and doing away with the numerous cliques'.[152]

Drunkenness was the target of the local Temperance movement, the Salvation Army and other ministers of religion who promoted abstinence.[153] A Temperance cricket team played in the local competition, while the Harvey Total Abstinence Society organised socials and debates.[154] The Misses Bayliss and Cons, sisters of Lillian Bayliss and Emma Cons, who ran the Old Vic theatre in London, were active members of the Women's Christian Temperance Union (WCTU), attending conferences and promoting temperance through the Bunbury Sailors' Rest.[155] Temperance people endured some derision, being sometimes referred to as the 'cold water brigade', however, there was widespread community support and respect for the movement.[156]

Leading the community: 'public men'[157]

In country towns like Bunbury, where life revolved around mutual help, 'great men' were a source of social capital and civic engagement across all social classes.[158] The district's churches too, were effective sources of social capital, and churchmen from a range of denominations held positions on the local school board.

Among the public men was Simon Joel, the local doctor who was dispenser of justice, authority on pests in citrus crops, and patron of the cricket club.[159] He had studied medicine in Melbourne, the UK and Europe before practicing in Bunbury, where he was also president of the Wellington Agricultural Society, chair of the Bunbury Lodge, justice of the peace, founder of the South-West Club, a director of the South-West Dairy Farmers' Co-operative Company, and with his wife, a founder of the Bunbury Golf Club. Owner of two dairy farms, he also improved dairy stock and pasture management.[160] Husband and wife were to figure prominently in Bunbury's wartime activity.

Mayor E.M. Clarke described Thomas Hayward as 'one of the most upright and useful men in the district'.[161] Following his day's farm work, Hayward rode on horseback into Bunbury, a distance of 28 miles (45 kilometres), for meetings of the Building Society, the Mechanics' Institute, the Agricultural Society and the Chamber of Commerce.[162] Schoolteacher Thomas Paisley was another whose commitment to the community culminated in extensive wartime activity.[163] Three state premiers, all former Paisley pupils, John Forrest, Newton Moore and James Mitchell were all born and raised in Bunbury, and the community celebrated its influence in the public lives of these men.[164]

J.J. Tuxford, the father of Charlie Snell's childhood friend, Wedd Tuxford, was born in Adelaide in 1861, left school at the age of 12 and made a trip to England alone.[165] Returning to South Australia he worked in banking, land sales, share broking and railway construction before coming to Western Australia during the gold rush and working on the Midland and Bunbury–Boyanup Railway contracts. Returning east, he worked in gold mining and railway construction in Victoria before settling in Bunbury and becoming a commercial agent to the urban and rural communities. A speech in 1897 showed his understanding of infrastructure and financial management, covering roads, water supply, fire safety, drainage, sanitation and street lighting.[166] Several hundred people, including Premier Forrest, members of council, lodges, the Australian Natives Association celebrated Tuxford's contribution to the community after his sudden death in 1900. His private and public identities as citizen, 'employer who knit to himself the hearts of his employees and a promising public man' were extolled in the local press.[167]

The correspondence between W.J. George and Snell's father concerning their respective losses during the war, are intensely personal and demonstrate a keen mutual understanding.[168] George was another who pursued multiple occupations and public positions and was closely connected with Bunbury and Harvey as a government minister.[169] He studied mechanical engineering in England before working in Victoria, Tasmania and Western Australia on railway construction and on the Victoria Reservoir, the first permanent water supply for Perth city. A member of the Legislative Assembly from 1895, and later, as Commissioner for Railways, he expanded the state's rail network. In 1907, he briefly took up farming, but returned to parliament and from 1916 to 1930 held the portfolios of Works and Water Supply.

Ethel Forrest, a childhood friend of Charlie Snell and niece of Premier John Forrest, married Fred Roberts, a son of the Chief Traffic Manager of the Railway Department. Possessing 'more than ordinary business ability, and an exceptional degree of energy', he worked for a city newspaper before moving to Bunbury in 1906 as chief goods clerk for the railways under Snell's father.[170] Moving into business, he became a member of the Harbour Board and Chamber of Commerce, took part in the military and many sports, and was largely responsible for the establishment of the swimming club in Bunbury.

A 1901 visit to Bunbury by the Minister for Lands highlighted the influence of local men in connecting local and state agencies as population growth began to outstrip local resources.[171] The schedule included a public meeting, meetings with heads of government departments including Snell senior (railways), Captain Abrahamson (harbour) and Thomas Paisley (finance). He attended a council meeting where discussion covered infrastructure, land reclamation, sanitation and health, land grants for local organisations, the establishment of government agencies and fire-fighting. It also included visits to local farms, vineyards and orchards, and a mill town.

Many more men of the Wellington district contributed to the community in similar fashion. Harvey pre-war public men such as Kenneth Gibsone, the 'financial genius' who managed the rebuilding of the Harvey Hall, which had been destroyed by severe weather, were joined by others who rose to prominence in wartime.[172] Men of vision and energy such as these worked together for the advancement of the Bunbury-Harvey community and raised the young men of the district who were to contribute to Australia's military effort. A later section will demonstrate how the women, who were largely absent from public view, found public voices and managed the home front effort in wartime.

As a unifying force, social capital can be created and strengthened, weakened or destroyed, and it can be transformed, as it was in the Wellington community when war came.[173] It also provided a survival mechanism on the battlefield as soldiers encountered friends and relatives from home, among the different battalions.[174] Despite some social division in the Wellington community, it was never strong enough to cause serious disruption, and the community retained its remarkable cohesiveness despite the strain of war. The letters of Bunbury and Harvey friends writing after Snell's death convey the strong sense of community connectedness and provide a window on the community relationships which supported the Snell family in a time of bereavement.

From the earliest European settlement of the district in 1838 until war broke out, the pioneering Bunbury–Harvey community was being formed and transformed through processes of community evolution by individual and combined effort in a population that combined the attributes of town and country in a community that was cohesive and mutually supportive. The next chapter will show how existing associations and social groups were appropriated for a new purpose to address wartime needs.

3

THE WELLINGTON COMMUNITY AT WAR: CIVILIAN AND MILITARY EFFORT

The countryside best represents the true heart of Australia[1]

Civilians at War

When war broke out, the Wellington community quickly reorganised its civic and social structures to the purpose of fighting the war on the battle front and the home front. Munitions and patriotic committees managed recruitment and repatriation, relief for the Belgians, fundraising, parcels for the men at the front as well as ongoing community needs. Scott recognised the close relationship between the fighting front and the home front work of organisation, reinforcement and supply, providing a model for later scholars, including McKernan (1980), McQuilton (2001), Payton (2012) and Beaumont (2013).[2] The Wellington community's war effort confirms McQuilton's conclusion that the women's contribution on the home front was far from passive, as Shute and others have suggested.[3] The Wellington community personified Scott's observation that World War I evoked 'the deepest feeling of patriotism and the most eager desire for service,' prompting non-combatant men and women to channel their patriotic feelings into work at home.[4]

When war erupted on the other side of the world, the local press eloquently expressed the mood of the moment:

> *War has broken out. Europe is ablaze; we in Australia as a patriotic portion of the Empire are endeavouring to assist the Mother Country in her time of need. We are now passing through a state*

of affairs which has not happened before in the world's history, and we desire the hearty cooperation of all our fellow citizens in Bunbury and the surrounding districts. We have formed ourselves into committees ...[5]

While the organisation of the military effort was largely invisible due to censorship, Wellington's civilian war effort was vividly depicted in local press reports, as the district's leadership group took charge of the local war effort, fulfilling Brigadier General Sir William Birdwood's 1920 claim that the Australian soldier was the best-cared-for soldier in the war.[6] Individuals used their many skills and connections to support the soldier in the field, working at home in Australia and nearer to the fighting front in England, at the same time supporting each other as private war-time tragedies unfolded.

Wellington citizens were well placed to deal with the crisis. Patriotic activities operated through social circles and more than 60 Snell correspondents were identified in reports of wartime events. Early wartime work emphasised gendered divisions as individuals took on multiple roles in support of sons and brothers, cousins and neighbours at war. Enthusiastic reporting of early patriotic events, such as a fête for the Belgian Fund, was replaced by more subdued accounts as reality struck.

Local Road Boards provided the foundations for the war-time committees that managed manpower and munitions needs, and for the practical needs of the men which the army would not supply. At a 'large gathering of leading citizens', Mayor Clarke became Chairman of Committees and Honorary Treasurer, the local public men dominating among the organisers.[7] The duties of committees were wide ranging: the munitions committee, for example, investigated the munitions capacity of Germany, promoted the purchase of shares in the Western Australian Munitions Company, and supervised the production of sandbags and fund-raising.[8] In October 1915, the committee reported that Germany, was much in advance of Britain in terms of munitions capability.[9] The production of ammunition in Australia was quickly abandoned once its inefficiency due to distance and the rapid evolution of weapons technology were recognised.[10] However, fund-raising for munitions continued, and when initial enthusiasm waned, citizens were exhorted to practice self-denial and save a small amount each week for the purpose.[11]

The Wellington recruitment effort

At the commonwealth government's prompting, recruitment dominated community activity throughout the war, press reports documenting the ebb and flow of local efforts. Wellington did not experience the resistance to war and recruiting by feminist groups such as the Women's Peace Army in Victoria and New South Wales.[12] World War I recruiting followed on from Australia's existing system of military service. During the nineteenth century, militias operated in all states, transferring to the Commonwealth at Federation in 1901.[13] Lord Kitchener's 1910 visit to Australia included Bunbury and led to the passage of the *Defence Acts* of 1910, 1911 and 1912, providing for compulsory military service from 1911.[14] A core of trained officers existed in Bunbury in 1900 under area officer Captain Newton J. Moore of the Bunbury Rifle Volunteers, while Captain Thomas Paisley was in charge of the cadets at the time of Kitchener's visit.[15] Kitchener's system comprised junior and senior cadets, aged from 12 to 18 years and citizens forces aged 18 to 25. A permanent professional officer in command of military reserves also had the task of registering all eligible men in the district. In the early 1900s Bunbury's Forrest Military camp housed the militia, and light-hearted military drills, skirmishing in the sand hills, and mock courts martial took place.[16] Charlie and his contemporaries did their military service, taking part in the military displays which were a regular feature of the agricultural shows. Reviewing a parade in 1911, president of the local agricultural society, W.B. Castieau, remarked on the 'excellence and high quality of the horses and the fine bearing of the men', highlighting Australia's 'national service' to the Empire.[17]

Soon after war broke out, local military officers were instructed to begin recruiting.[18] The Bunbury Recruiting Committee represented the civilian-military interface, providing the link between the community and the government, and responding to requests and instructions from military authorities and relief organisations.[19] In the early days of the war, men flocked to recruiting centres, Wellington's Ray and Dick Clarke and Tom Rose among them, resulting in an excess of enrolments, and for a time, it seemed that only single men would be needed, and local authorities felt no need to campaign for recruits until late 1915.[20]

In the early stages of the war, fitness requirements were high, resulting in many rejections, lapel badges worn to show that the men had offered themselves. By May 1915, the arrival of casualty lists caused recruitment to fall, prompting calls for systematic recruitment and suggestions of compulsion. For the remainder of the war, the Commonwealth Government renewed its pleas for volunteers though acts of parliament and personal invitations to men who remained at home. The first of these was the *War Census Act* of 23 July 1915, when census papers were sent to all males aged between 18 and 60 years of age requiring them to report their personal details and military training.[21] Then, in December 1915, under the *War Precautions Act,* these men were further asked 'are you willing to enlist now?' and if not, to explain why.[22] In January 1916, a personal appeal from Prime Minister Hughes, the 'Call to Arms', was sent.[23]

An official recruiting sergeant was appointed to assist Municipal Councils.[24] Extreme pressure was now put on men as appeals were made to their 'imagination, patriotism, reason, sentiment and manhood'.[25] At a public meeting in October 1915, Councillor Baldock identified three classes of men who had not gone to war: those whom the military had rejected due to physical incapacity; men who were willing to go but were prevented from enlisting through family and other ties; and men who simply 'would not go'.[26] Quoting a letter from the front, he said, 'If any young man in Bunbury is out of work, send him here and we will give him plenty.' As an incentive to enlistment, the military authorities provided free meals to those attending the Bunbury enlistment office, 'to add to Bunbury's roll of honour by going to Blackboy Camp'.[27] By December 1915, the White Feather movement began stigmatising men who did not enlist, adding a note of dissention to the community. An anonymous protest, written perhaps by an individual who felt unable to enlist, pointed out the opportunities that existed at home for war service.[28] In a small community where everyone was known, shirkers were conspicuous, so men rejected for service found highly visible and acceptable ways of participating on the home front, such as through the 'Ugly Men's Association' and 'The Rustics' which were widely reported in the local press.[29]

During 1915, 425 recruits enlisted at Bunbury, with another 60 in January 1916.[30] Thomas Paisley, secretary local recruiting committee, condemned as 'unpatriotic' the eligible men who were choosing to ignore the Commonwealth 'Call to Arms' appeal, pleading with them to report to the local recruiting committee and warning of penalties for failure to comply.[31] Visits to surrounding centres, 'canvassing the men to join the colours' resulted in a further 200 men enlisting at Bunbury in February 1916.[32] A newspaper report of August 1916 names 101 Harvey men who had gone to war, with three reported killed, although there were at least five by this time, including Charlie Snell and Guy Gibney.[33] Although these numbers appeared healthy, by the end of the following month the Bunbury recruiting committee was advocating compulsory military service, citing the 'unjust and inadequate' voluntary system. [34] The committee pointed out that, despite a 'systematic and thorough canvass of this district which had secured a large number of recruits, the supply of volunteers is now exhausted, and any further appreciable number of men can be secured only by compulsion'. Local campaigning had focused on single men since the committee considered it 'unjust and economically unsound' to call on married men while many single able-bodied young men ignored calls to enlist. The committee reluctantly admitted that such men lacked the foresight to recognise that the war might ultimately affect them personally, reflecting the experience of south-eastern Australia.[35] Perhaps Thomas

Paisley had sufficient knowledge of men who had passed through his school and the military cadets to realise that the supply of suitable men really had been exhausted.

The Commonwealth Minister for War demanded the formations of separate local recruiting committees for Harvey early in 1916 and in Bridgetown early the following year.[36] The Harvey committee comprised eight members of the Snell community.[37] In a major reorganisation, a Director General of Recruiting was appointed and a new state committee, with a committee for each Federal Electorate. In recognition of the increasing difficulty of finding recruits, these new committees now had paid organisers, often discharged soldiers or rejected applicants, and women were invited to join in the recruiting effort.[38] The Bunbury committee was now known as the Central South-West Recruiting Committee, with a local recruiting officer.[39] Voluntary personnel remained, and local organisers, Septimus Shaw for Busselton and W.J. Sutton for Harvey, hard-working older men whose enlistment attempts were unsuccessful, were employed.[40] Despite earlier fears that the source of reinforcements was exhausted, recruits were still being found. Speaking to the people of Bunbury, the recruiting officer emphasised the responsibilities of all individuals to support the patriotic cause, and impressed upon eligible men the urgent need for them at the front.

During the February 1917 'Call to Arms' campaign, the Bunbury organisers interviewed nearly 200 men, of whom nearly half applied for service, 68 going into camp and 25 being rejected. Some men accepted at their local centres were later rejected at Blackboy Camp, which the local committee considered prejudicial to recruiting.[41] Bart Ziino notes a range of medical issues which resulted in men being sent home within three months of arrival in camp, evident among the military records of Wellington men who went to training camp.[42] His examination of responses to the 1916 'Call to Arms' appeal in Victoria and New South Wales resonate with the Bunbury evidence.[43] Men were forced to weigh their personal and family duties against the demands of the government:

wives and children, ageing and infirm parents, and siblings, especially in farming communities where family labour was essential. Financial issues, the sacrifice of income on enlistment, debts and investments in homes, businesses and farms added to their dilemmas.

The 1916 and 1917 conscription referenda

As casualties mounted and war-weariness caused a diminishing supply of volunteers to satisfy British calls for reinforcements, the Australian government was forced to consider conscription.[44] Australia's existing compulsory military service was never intended to include overseas service. Prime Minister William (Billy) Hughes had promised not to force men to fight overseas, and in the absence of parliamentary support to enact conscription, a referendum was needed.[45] The two referenda over the conscription of men to fight overseas are recognised as among the most divisive debates in Australian history, but the debate in Western Australia was more subdued.[46] The Wellington experience was different from that of regional Australia in general, but in line with Western Australia as a whole. The two Bunbury newspapers and Perth's *West Australian* were staunchly in favour of conscription, although they dutifully presented both sides of the argument.[47] Bunbury and Harvey public men, Mayor Baldock, E.M. Clarke, MLC, Castieau, Clifton, Eastman, Joel, Logue, Mitchell, Paisley, Reading, Rose and Trigwell figure prominently in the debate. In public meetings chaired by the mayor or another local dignitary, visiting speakers addressed knowledgeable, articulate and predominantly peaceful crowds, with two notable exceptions. The principal arguments in Bunbury included the universal cry of support for the men at the front, the principles of democracy and freedom, and the protection of Australia.

Until this time, censorship had remained a minor issue in debate surrounding the war. The *War Precautions Act* of 1914 aimed to prevent the spread of reports 'likely to cause disaffection or alarm', and in 1917, a Bunbury labourer was fined £5 for 'disloyal utterances', having claimed he had worked with Germans and would do so again, but with fifteen relatives at the front, he was hardly a significant threat.[48] However, newspapers were now 'deluged with instructions' about what they could and could not publish'.[49] In late 1917, George Reading, editor of Bunbury's *South Western Times*, commented that all reports and editorials relating to Federal politics, including the conscription referenda, would henceforth be signed by the author, a notable departure from existing journalistic practice.[50] Reading was vocal in his support for conscription, his name dutifully attached to many reports and editorials. In November 1917, the prime minister sent a memorandum to major eastern states newspapers, stating that the editors of 'responsible press' were to be 'unrestricted', and 'purely political' matters left to their judgement.[51] No mention was made of the requirement that the author's name should be attached to any editorial. However, in 1916, a Perth man was prosecuted for circulating leaflets without 'the name and address of the person authorising it, contrary to the *Military Service Referendum Act 1916*'.[52]

In Britain, following fierce debate, the conscription of single men aged between 18 and 41 was introduced in January 1916.[53] The Bunbury press recognised the gravity of the military situation, but feared the weakening effect of division, believing the Australian people capable of an 'intelligent adjustment' of the issue.[54] Although Charlie Snell was killed before Australian conscription referenda were held, he saw it as a possibility by mid-1915, when he expressed a preference to go to war as a volunteer rather than as a conscript.[55] By the time he reached Egypt, 'judging by talk, conscription will come in', providing, he believed, a means of dealing with the 'loafers around the capital cities'.[56] However, despite his enthusiastic descriptions of his wartime experiences, as the conscription debate intensified he became more cautious, commenting that of 'the Lowe boys', one was 'lost' and the others could stay at home, having 'done their bit'.[57] He was sorry the Gibbs boys were not accepted for military service, but their mother had already lost one son, and he did not think they 'could stand' the war.[58] Moreover, when his brother reiterated his desire to be with him, his response was blunt: 'take a fool's advice and stay away'.[59]

The *Bunbury Herald* began 1916 with a reminder of the citizens' duty to Empire, and that 'national service' was 'the highest duty and obligation of the citizen'.[60] At that time, with victory seeming remote, it was 'hard to believe that even one capable man would not rush to the colours'.[61] When the first referendum was called for 28 October 1916, the newly formed Bunbury referendum committee chaired by George Clarke, MLC, held an 'orderly' meeting, despite strong feeling on both sides.[62] Sir John Forrest's call for conscription received a 'splendid hearing from conscriptionists and anti-conscriptionists alike'.[63] At the Anglican cathedral, a sermon on, 'National Service – our duty in the present crisis', sought to demolish 'some of the conscientious and domestic objections to conscription'. Although conscription was strongly supported by Bunbury people, opposition was ever present and the debate became heated at two meetings, one for and the second against, shortly before voting day. Both degenerated into 'seething uproar' as the 'most rowdy and disgraceful meetings ever held in Bunbury'.[64]

Anticipating a 'yes' vote, in early October 1916, Prime Minister Hughes ordered all single men aged between 21 and 35 to register and submit to a medical examination, threatening imprisonment for non-compliance.[65] In Perth, 840 men were examined in the first round. Of these, only 40% were found fit for service, 70% of whom claimed exemptions.[66] Of the Wellington men examined, only 26% were deemed fully fit, most claiming exemptions.[67] The proportion of eligible fit men claiming exemptions in Western Australia is therefore almost double the Victorian figures quoted by McNeice, adding weight to claims that most eligible and available men had already gone to war.[68] Existing regulations allowed for exemption for only sons or sole surviving sons, for families where other sons were serving and for men supporting aged parents, widowed mothers or under-aged siblings. In Western Australia, metropolitan exemption courts held in October examined 206 applications, of which around 40% were successful.[69] Only one exemption court was convened in Bunbury, the outcomes giving a clear picture of the eligibles who remained in the district.[70] The fact that these men came forward is an indication of their confidence that they should be exempt from service.

Ten men (around 30%) were granted permanent exemptions, three were denied and the rest, around 60% were given temporary exemptions. Half claimed dependent parents and siblings, three of whom were Greek or Italian men sending money to family in their home country. Just under one third claimed exemption on grounds of siblings at war, among whom five had died, including two in one family. Only two of the applicants eventually went to war. Farmers and labourers each comprised nearly half the applicants.[71] There were two schoolteachers, and the three Greek fishermen mention above, who may have had little attachment to the British Empire. McQuilton finds that, in rural Victoria, labour shortages were evident in the farming shires by late 1916, and that 64% of exemption claims came from the farming districts.[72] In Wellington, where so many local farmers had already enlisted, similar claims were made, but the presiding magistrate granted only temporary exemptions. In Wellington, farmers, labourers and others were fairly evenly represented. Two men who claimed exemption had already failed the medical examination. Only two of the claimants eventually went to war, both surviving, but one returning with TB.[73] One man who was granted exemption to be near his dying mother, himself died of 'pneumonic influenza' (Spanish flu) in 1919.[74] The fact that most of these men never went to war again suggests that the pool of available men was indeed exhausted.

The regulations were repealed in December 1916 after the defeat of the referendum.[75] Enlistments temporarily increased after the referendum, but again declined, amid feelings that Australia was being drained of its young manhood.[76] The Labor party split after the referendum, expelling Hughes, who joined the Liberals to form the National Labor Party and was reappointed as Prime Minister on a platform of winning the war. The Bunbury community was brought close to the drama of Federal politics when the (Labor) Assistant Minister for Defence visited the town in early 1917 to address the community on the state of the Labor Party following the post-referendum split.[77] McQuilton has noted that at this time, Victorian community leaders often shunned visiting speakers whose opinions they did not support, however, Mayor Baldock introduced the speaker despite their differences of opinion.[78] The minister reassured the audience of Labor's commitment to winning the war, and of the adequacy of voluntary enlistment. While the Bunbury audience expressed disapproval of some of the minister's claims, he was given a fair hearing. Across Australia, returned men who had been in favour of conscription often interrupted 'no' speakers, and here, Bunbury was no different, as a man in uniform was ejected from the meeting, followed by a group of his friends, despite appeals from the minister that he be allowed to remain.[79]

The assistant minister's urgent appeal for recruits was supported by the local recruitment officer, who advised citizens to approach eligible men in a 'manly way', and persuade them of the 'urgent necessity' for them to enlist, but his comment that in Bunbury, 'one did not see many eligible young men about', contradicted his claim that there were 150 eligible men at the meeting.[80] There is a sense that this officer was speaking from a prepared script which was less applicable in a district so strongly committed to the war. State Recruiting Committees were now using recruiting handbooks produced by J.B. Castieau of Victoria, very likely the brother of local farmer W.B Castieau, with calls for married men to now come forward. The meeting produced two volunteers.[81]

While government calls for local councils to reconstitute themselves as recruiting committees were rejected in some districts, the existing Wellington committee renewed its efforts at a March 1917 Recruitment Conference.[82] Recent figures showed local rejection rates of 30% and high rates of men from other districts who were rejected once they reached Blackboy Hill training camp indicated that the pool of suitable men was near exhaustion. Mayor Baldock blamed government inattention for recruitment difficulties.[83] Motions calling for the reduction of height and chest measurements and increasing the military age were passed. A call for distinguishing badges for rejected men was dismissed amid concern that it might lead to assumptions about the man's employability. Such men, it was felt, 'knew that they had done their best' and were unconcerned about the opinions of others. Delegates noted that excessive alcohol consumption amongst troops influenced some parents to prevent their sons enlisting. The conference called for military authorities to rectify the situation whereby railwaymen, who represented a significant pool of likely recruits, were hindered from volunteering by the failure by the military to rank men according to their experience and seniority. Motions called for Federal and State Governments to refuse employment to men otherwise eligible for war service. A similar motion directed at private employers was watered down on the grounds that men were needed at home for the production of basic necessities. Serious concern was expressed shortly after the meeting when a council position was filled by an 'outsider' rather than a local returned man.[84] Conference delegates remained mindful that the Australian people had voted against compulsory service, so were reluctant to recommend measures that could be construed as compulsion. Looking to the future, the meeting presciently noted that nine-tenths of the fighting men would be changed by the war.[85]

A visit around this time by suffragette and anti-war campaigner, Adela Pankhurst, was an opportunity for Bunbury residents to demonstrate their open-mindedness as well as their commitment to the war. Although Pankhurst, like anti-conscriptionists, had been refused a hearing in other centres, a large Bunbury audience was asked to acknowledge her right to speak and offer her 'British courtesy'.[86] Her claims that the war was a capitalist enterprise, and criticisms of Sir John Forrest, were heard politely, despite a steady stream of perceptive questions and accusations of 'scare mongering' and being anti-war.[87]

During 1917, send-offs for enlisted men provided further opportunities for impassioned recruitment speeches, and further proof that there were 'not many shirkers in Bunbury'.[88] The enlistees were now older men who were 'sacrificing much to go to the front'.[89] When two older men enlisted, both with sons at war, the Military Registrar bluntly called on eligible men to get out from behind their 'mothers' apron strings' and picture the 'bespattered bodies' of these older men. Of these recruits, one was repatriated from England and discharged with 'senility'. Of his three sons, one served as a runner and won the military medal, while the others were both repatriated from England without seeing service, one with 'deformities to hand and debility' and the other for 'defective physique and mentality'.[90] The second elderly enlistee served in England and France and was discharged unfit on his return, while his son was killed in Belgium.[91] In Harvey, a 45 year-old sawmill manager and chairman of the Harvey Road Board, who also had a son at the front, was fêted by a large crowd.[92] Both served in the Light Horse and survived the war.[93] By December 1917, more men were being rejected than passed fit for service: in one instance, five out of seven volunteers were rejected.[94]

Prime Minister Hughes unsuccessfully proposed deferring a scheduled Federal election in May 1917 to prevent further factionalising the people.[95] Sir John Forrest once again addressed Bunbury electors, calling on loyalty to the 'gallant fighting men' and political unity in the task of defeating the enemy.[96] Referring to the conscription referendum, Forrest accused the opposition of telling lies and working 'against the welfare of the boys at the front'. However, he knew he was preaching to the converted as he finished with a plea: 'above all, vote!'. The visiting Minister for Defence mesmerised the Bunbury crowd with details of Germany's strength and ambitions towards Australia, receiving no questions during his long speech, but loud applause at his final comments.[97] Framed as a 'Win the war' election, the people were again promised no conscription without a referendum. The election result was in line with Bunbury and Western Australia as a whole, the Hughes's Nationalists winning by large majority.[98]

Recruiting remained a priority at public events, such as the August 1917 ceremony to mark the anniversary of the war's outbreak, attended by 'all classes' of the community, who were reminded of the fathers and mothers, wives and sisters who had 'given their dearest' to the cause.[99] Although almost everyone in Western Australia seemingly had a loved one at war, and recruitment from the district had remained strong, the local recruiting officer was still appealing for recruits and encouraging single women not to socialise with eligibles. He indicated an enlistee in the audience who had tried multiple times and had undergone surgery before he was finally accepted, but it was increasingly evident that the pool of suitable recruits was exhausted.

The second referendum, scheduled for 20 December 1917, was held against a background of the greatest casualty rates of war, and around Australia the violence of the second exceeded that of the first.[100] Speakers at rallies were shouted down, jostled, pelted with foodstuffs, and women attacked other women.[101] Although in Bunbury campaigning was again intense, there was no repeat of the 'rowdy and disgraceful' meetings of the earlier campaign.[102] The 'no' case in Bunbury stood little chance. An anti-conscription speaker, addressing a supportive crowd, was simply reported as presenting a poor argument.[103] Campaigners themselves inadvertently hinted that supplies of eligible men were indeed exhausted. The campaign played on fears of Germany's aims, and of the 'grim necessity' to do our duty for the brave boys at the front.[104] One plea for the 'yes' case came in the form of a lament from an Australian soldier, supposedly written after the 1916 referendum:

... There must be an error or something ...
A country go back on her soldiers:
That's more than a German would do ...
'We're tired, we're wounded, we're Weary,
With death up above and below,
But we'd sooner be here with the Heroes
Than back with the cows that said 'No!'[105]

Voters were warned against the claim that conscription aimed to cripple trade unions, and farmers were urged to vote 'yes', amid promises that labour supplies would be maintained.[106] A visiting Senator promoting the 'yes' vote, told of a painful experience in Collie, where he met six families, each of whom had lost two sons, and fourteen families which had lost one son each.[107] This again demonstrated that the district was 'doing its bit'.

The Minister for Defence, returning to Bunbury, was again greeted enthusiastically.[108] He compared the imbalance between recent recruitment numbers and the thousands of casualties recovering in England, in transit or returned to Australia. He reported 380,000 single men of serving age in Australia, but conceded that only 40% of them were thought to be fit. Emphasising the 'tired boys in the trenches in France', he claimed that women preferred a hero's death for their sons to a coward's life. The Minister concluded his speech to shouts of affirmation: 'Is it a just fight?', 'Do the boys in the trenches need help?', 'How are you going to vote on the 20th?' The 'yeses' 'nearly lifted the roof'.

When interim results were published, Bunbury and Perth were two to one in favour of conscription, anticipating the final results for WA, while Tasmania had a small 'yes' majority and other states had a clear 'no' majority.[109] George Reading wrote a bitter editorial on the referendum result, deriding Prime Minister Hughes's deviousness, 'stupendous folly', and a government shirking its responsibility and 'not playing the game'.[110] Reading believed that it was 'asking too much of the masses' to decide 'so vital an issue', in 'an appeal from those who know to those who do not know'. Reminding readers that some Labor parliamentarians had 'worked so splendidly for conscription', helping to produce the 'magnificent majority in favour of conscription by all classes of the Western Australian community', he remained critical of the State Labor Congress when it resolved that members must obey its 'autocratic dictates'.[111]

The Bunbury clergy also supported recruitment to the end. In April 1918, the Anglican rector of South Bunbury told of a Western Australian soldier in France whose dying words expressed regret that there was no one to take his place.[112] He told of the admiration and respect shown by a Bunbury wife to her 'returned wounded brave', and exhorted reluctant men to 'go through the streets of our conscript-free capital city and read the signs … that loss of self-respect means demoralisation'.[113]

Efforts to stimulate recruiting continued into 1918, despite a recruiting sergeant's observation that Harvey had sent so many men to the front that recruitment efforts would face 'hard work to find eligibles'.[114] The final meeting of the Bunbury Recruiting Committee was held in December 1918.[115] The Bunbury Recruiting Committee in its various guises applied its managerial skills and community connections developed during the pre-war settlement period to send nearly 2,000 men to the war, including its own sons, relatives and friends, some never to return, others to return changed forever.[116] By early 1919, unlike in other parts of Australia, where the rifts caused by the referenda were slow to heal, the community remained united, and when the Minister for Repatriation visited Bunbury, he was greeted enthusiastically by the Mayor, state parliamentarians, E.M. Clarke and Edwin Rose, the local Repatriation Committee, the Traders' Association, the Lumpers' and Tally Clerks' Unions, councillors, and leading business and shipping men.[117]

Wartime fundraising and patriotic work

While Bunbury's public men focussed on recruiting, the 'first great impulse' in women's wartime fundraising was to assist the Belgians, invaded by Germany. Belgian 'days' and others like them are estimated to have raised 100,000 pounds in Western Australia.[118] Contemporary reports estimated amounts raised, but at a time when one quarter of one penny was significant, such figures are almost incomprehensible to modern readers except as a means of comparison between different funds and different states. Figures will therefore be noted sparingly.

In November 1914, a circle of women including Mesdames Eastman, Spencer and Fabricius appealed for parcels of warm clothing for the Belgians, and held a grand garden party at the Eastman home, attended by 300 people, and raising nearly £150.[119] Reported in the effusive style of pre-war weddings and dances, it was opened by Mayor Clarke to the singing of the

Belgian National Anthem, and assisted by girls dressed in white uniforms to represent nurses at the front.[120] Donated items, including Belgian laces donated by Mrs Fabricius and foodstuffs were auctioned. The children of Wesley Church sacrificed their annual Sunday School prizes, commemorated by George Draper with cards inscribed 'For God and the Empire'.[121] Amy Mitchell conducted a house-to-house canvass for monthly subscriptions.[122] Harvey citizens held a concert by local children organised by Olive Roesner, traditional items being supplemented by patriotic songs and military drills.[123] The appeal continued through 1915 with clothing and funds donated by Isabel Rhead's music school, the Bunbury State School, municipal employees and local businesses.[124] The fund was discontinued in May 1916, transferring its attention to local unemployed men and their families.[125]

More broadly, community activity shifted to the relief and comfort of Australian soldiers in the field and in hospital. Melanie Oppenheimer has documented the leadership of the Red Cross in supplementing government provisions for the soldiers and Scott describes how 'everyone got knitting and spinning, collecting food, literature and medical equipment'.[126] The 'skilled, sympathetic and capable direction' needed for such a vast effort was readily available in Bunbury, where Red Cross activity was well under way by 1915, and Charlie Snell regularly reported on parcels he received at the front.[127] Money and goods were sent to prisoners of war, to hospitals and rest homes in Australia, to the British Red Cross, while Red Cross volunteers provided transport for sick and wounded soldiers. Tradesmen and manufacturers assisted with the packing and distribution of the goods. Bunbury's effort was led by Mesdames Eastman, Spencer, Joel and Miss Isabel Rhead, while Harvey's contribution was led by Bessie Lambert and Mesdames Hurst and Johnson.[128] Existing community organisations became involved, including the churches, Bunbury railway workers and the military.[129]

Community groups received instructions from the head office in Perth. In late 1915, 'sheets, pyjamas, milk covers or rolled bandages' were no longer needed, but 'shirts, sox, (sic) large (coffee dyed) handkerchiefs, scarves, face washers and long swabs in 4-fold butter muslin, with narrow tape attached to one end, are urgently required'. Bunbury's efforts attracted specific praise from the state president. Amy Mitchell and Isabel Rhead organised a concert which included a patriotic song composed by Rhead, 'The Appeal of the Red Cross Nurse', in response to the state president's request for funds for surgical equipment.[130] The concert raised almost £100 and planning for the next entertainment began immediately.[131]

A Red Cross tea-room at the reinstated agricultural show in 1915 was a lucrative fund raiser. Mrs Joel organised an army of helpers who constructed the booth, donated food and furnishings, and cooked, served and cleaned.[132] Once the show was over, she took charge of sewing groups. At the 1915 annual ratepayer meeting, Mayor G. Clarke reported that during the previous year, Red Cross funds raised £900, the South Bunbury Girls Guild had collected £12, the Belgian Relief Fund, £500, while Mrs Eastman had raised more than £400.[133] A concert had raised £55 for Bunbury's returned soldiers and their families, the Sandbag Fund had raised £110, the Munition Company had sold £430 worth of shares, while the emergency fund created to relieve distress locally and find work had raised £275.[134] In total, Bunbury had so far raised £3,000, including £1,200 during the previous six weeks. Contributions by individuals remained a feature of the civilian wartime support: Teesdale Smith, for example, donated 40 pack camels and water canteens for the use of the troops in Egypt, and T.T. Moore donated two cases of books and a cage of five canaries for raffle.[135]

In Harvey, Red Cross activity was initially under the direction of Bessie Lambert, Mrs Hurst, and Mrs Snell and their friends.[136] The women canvassed the district for a weekly subscription of threepence for the purchase of materials and took instruction from the Victoria League in Perth on patterns and materials. They dispatched completed items and funds for the purchase of surgical instruments and Christmas gifts for the soldiers.[137]

By mid-1916 exhaustion was setting in, with the weekly Red Cross 'sewing bees' discontinued due to falling attendance.[138] However, a handful of overworked individuals and groups such as the 'Well Wishers Sewing Circle' and the 'Florence Nightingale Sewing Circle' continued the work, supervised by Mrs Joel.[139] Enthusiasm was restored as Christmas approached, when Isabel Rhead's Trench Comforts Fund received more than 200 Christmas boxes from local individuals and groups, as well as knitted items and reading materials. Packing cases were donated by local men and transport was provided free of charge by a local company.

Red Cross Society constantly appealed for 'anything that will contribute to the comfort of the brave men who have gone to fight for us'.[140] During 1918, large quantities of foodstuffs such as eggs, honey, tea, cheese, jam and fruit as well as funds were sent to the Fremantle hospital, which housed 500 soldier patients, and to hospital ships passing through the port. The campaign for Christmas 1918 focused on soldiers in hospital, transport and quarantine. The Florence Nightingale Circle provided dozens of Christmas cakes, plum puddings, tins of biscuits and packets of cigarettes. Again, the packing was carried out by local men with the assistance of local businessmen. The South Bunbury Sewing Circle had a short break over Christmas, before continuing its activities 'as vigorously as ever, as comforts are still urgently needed for the boys'.[141] Red Cross work continued until mid-1919 when the last soldiers were repatriated. The Wellington community's war effort was equal to any in Australia.

A range of other activities contributed to the well-being of the soldier. Physical and mental recreation were provided by the YMCA in centres run by Australians in Australia, Egypt and France. Charlie Snell frequently visited YMCA centres and many of his wartime letters were written on YMCA letterhead. For him they represented a haven of tranquillity where he could rest, read and write, free of alcohol-fuelled interruption, although he was not himself a total abstainer. A former Bunbury friend of Snell senior, John Beecham, worked in the YMCA in Perth, fielding enquiries from anxious relatives as to the fate of their sons and giving public lectures to raise funds for the YMCA at the front.[142] In one month alone, Beecham investigated 100 cases, some of them 'intricate and delicate', including

Snell's own, in the hope that among conflicting messages there was still cause for optimism.[143] As well as official correspondence, Beecham sent handwritten letters to Snell's father expressing his personal condolences to the family. In the course of his work, Beecham came in contact with shell-shocked and other psychiatric cases, leading to his creation of the West Australian Lunacy Reform League.[144]

An offshoot of the Bunbury Munitions Committee was the Sandbag Committee, which administered the manufacture of sandbags by local groups under instructions from the state committee.[145] Snell's mother took over the management of the Harvey group from the local road board, and eventually produced 120 sandbags, enough to support a few metres of trench wall.[146] Charlie commented on it in his return letters.[147] This was an important means by which the family could participate vicariously in their son's wartime activity, but it must also have reminded them of the reality of his situation.

The Bunbury community had a tradition of religious tolerance and was free of sectarian divisions, such as those noted by McQuilton in rural Victoria, and by General Birdwood when he visited Australia in 1920.[148] The church men of the Bunbury-Harvey district were integral to all aspects of the community's wartime participation, with Dean Smyth of the Catholic church, Rev. Stanley Edwards of Wesley church and Reverend Whalley of the Congregational church figuring prominently, both on committees and with their own individual efforts, alongside other local church people. In March 1916, for example, the Reverend Edwards was among the speakers at a recruitment rally in the city and raised funds for the Red Cross in Bunbury, while the Roman Catholic Boys' Club made sandbags under the direction of Archdeacon Smyth, who noted the spirited conversation of the boys as they reflected the importance of their wartime contribution.[149]

The Bunbury Catholic church mobilised its own community structures in the service of the war, making it the scene of feverish patriotic activity.[150] Dean Smyth was a charismatic leader who had an enthusiastic ecumenical following among the soldiers in the Bunbury camp.[151] Masses were well-attended by the soldiers, and on Saint Patrick's Day, in the absence of uniforms, a Military Church Parade was held wearing the Irish green and gold. Schoolchildren sang for a Military Mass, and an enthusiastic committee of men and women organised a ball in the evening.[152] The Girls Literary Society organised a concert for the soldiers.

One fundraising effort which escaped Scott's notice was the so-called Queen Carnivals campaigns which 'caused some wrangles around HRV (Harvey, sic)'.[153] Wartime Queen Carnivals were held in England, France, America, New Zealand and Australia, initiated by a professional organiser, merging existing fundraising techniques to raise spectacular sums of money within a limited time-frame.[154] Giving was promoted as a national duty and a means of assuaging non-combatant guilt.[155] The organiser, in this case, 'Professor' Owen Cardston, mobilised government and community organisations, incidentally encouraging military recruitment. In January 1916, he was invited to Western Australia by the State War Council to establish a Queen Carnival 'for the extension of the patriotic and charitable funds'.[156] The campaign aimed to raise £150,000 for patriotic funds, the retraining of disabled soldiers, the various children's funds and to supplement the weekly payment to the wives of soldiers. For the duration of the carnival, no collections for other funds was permitted. A queen was to be nominated by local committees, the candidate of the committee which raised the most money being pronounced state winner. By early 1916, thirty-two queen candidates, each backed by a committee, had been nominated around the state.[157]

Bunbury's nomination day was set for early February 1916, but it was not until March that the 'professor' visited Bunbury and surrounding centres, to a lukewarm reception.[158] The Queen Carnival did not eventuate in Bunbury, but Harvey citizens embraced it enthusiastically, and two candidates were nominated, each with her own committee.[159] During the following weeks, amid good-natured rivalry, serious fundraising activity took place.[160] By early May the Queen Carnival drew to its conclusion with a grand concert.[161] The Minister for Lands announced the winner:

Miss Hurley, who had raised over £200 pounds, with her fellow-candidate raising £161, a total of £366.[162] Many substantial items were donated for raffles, including a horse, a case of wine and a phonograph, the last item being donated to the YMCA soldiers' hall by the winner.

In spite of the differing outcomes for the Queen Carnival in Bunbury and Harvey, each community was united in its own way. It could be that in Bunbury the fund-raising effort was functioning so efficiently that any outside interference was superfluous, while in Harvey, the smaller centre, the additional impetus from outside the district was useful. Later in the year, however, concerns were raised at a South West repatriation conference over the financial burden on a generous few and the way Queen Carnival funds had been disbursed by Perth organisers.[163] Ever the peacemaker, Thomas Paisley pleaded for co-operation between the country contributors and the Perth organisers. By late 1916, there were fears that the obligation to send locally-raised funds to Perth was contributing to the movement of soldiers' dependents to the city in search of assistance.[164] This reflected the tension between pioneering self-reliance and the increasing dependence on central government for large infrastructure projects and for repatriation funding.

The Snell population's patriotic effort in the United Kingdom

Expatriate Wellington residents, the Newton Moore family and Bessie Lambert in London, and the Jeffersons in Devon, also contributed to the comfort of Australian troops abroad. On the outbreak of hostilities, a group of several hundred West Australians and their friends formed the 'Australian War Contingent Association' to 'watch over the interests' of Australian troops coming to Britain to serve in the war.[165] Its aim was to relieve the British Red Cross Society of any responsibility for the Australian troops, and over £8,000 in cash and goods were quickly collected. With Sir Newton Moore, the West Australian Agent-General as chairman, and his wife, a large group of mostly Western Australian women was ready to welcome the Australian troops and attend to their needs in camp and at the front.[166] A grand concert was planned, dampened only by concerns that the public might be reluctant to attend performances in the present circumstances.[167] Donations of £25,000 came from Australia and Sir Newton negotiated with the British Red Cross to ensure that any goods or funds sent to it by Australians were directed to the Australian troops.[168]

The Association, of which Bessie Lambert was also a member, visited wounded Australian soldiers in hospital and arranged hospitality for hundreds of troops on leave.[169] Letters to the newspapers, despite some class-consciousness, expressed the grateful Britons' willingness to entertain the Australian men, who basked in the recognition. Lady Moore and her daughters, and the Jeffersons in Devon, entertained Bunbury men such as Dick Clarke.[170] Charlie Snell had maintained his connection with the Moore family, with his own expectations of being entertained by them when he made his visit 'home' to England.

The organisation expanded and in August 1916 opened a hostel for 300 men in Horseferry Road, with the prospect of more such centres.[171] The group also coordinated the receipt and distribution of huge quantities of donated newspapers for men in the trenches, for men in camp at Salisbury and in hospitals in England and France.[172] The War Contingent Association was wound up in July 1917 and its responsibilities transferred to the Australian Red Cross.[173] During its existence it had received and disbursed around £20,000. The closure provoked protests to the Australian Government but it seems likely that the Red Cross had expanded, through the work of Vera Deakin, to such an extent that the London organisation unnecessarily divided resources.[174]

Several Snell correspondents travelled overseas to contribute to the war effort. Aside from the nurses mentioned elsewhere, Bessie Lambert and Wedd Tuxford both worked in munitions factories. Lambert had worked tirelessly on the home front but decided to move closer to the action. In Harvey, she had led support for the Minesweeper Fund due to family connections at its London headquarters.[175] She also contributed to sandbag days, the Red Cross and fundraising for ambulances at the front.[176] In 1916 Miss Lambert left for England, where for more than three years she worked in an aircraft factory.[177] At war's end she worked in the Inquiry Department of the Australian Red Cross in London.[178] In her off-duty hours, she worked at the Church Army rooms, packing parcels of food and clothing for British prisoners of war in Germany, one of which was received by Harvey man Keith Johnson.[179] As well as her work with the Australian War Contingent Association, she spent her Sundays visiting Australian soldiers at the Wandsworth Military Hospital where she met, among others, Harvey man Roy Charman.[180]

McQuilton has emphasised the intense wartime activity against a background of daily life which was not without problems caused by the war.[181] Newspapers reported on the 'great upset to all conditions of life by the war' and here again Bunbury's public citizens combined their talents to address war-caused problems.[182] The war caused the diversion of local funds away from the Bunbury District Nursing Association, despite the continuing demand for its services.[183] Similarly, although the port of Bunbury suffered a downturn in activity during the war, the town's community-minded men continued to support the Sailors' Rest in addition to their patriotic duties.[184] Wartime conditions caused unemployment in the timber industry, as falling international markets and oversupply in the east put about 50 hewers out of work and closed mills.[185] As a consequence, 180 remaining Collie sleeper hewers suffered a severe reduction in wages.[186] Economic stagnation was accompanied by a significant loss of shipping throughout the war. At the same time, although the German ship *Emden* and others menacing shipping lanes in the Indian Ocean had been sunk, shipping activity in Bunbury had not returned to normal, putting 280 shipping employees out of work.[187] This produced severe hardship, as women were forced to sell valuables to buy food for their families, causing a flow-on effect for local business. Local brewer, Max Beigel led a committee of already over-committed men seeking solutions to the problem.[188] In a time of increasing government intervention, the committee initially focused on ways of obtaining money: borrowing from the government, or raising public subscriptions to be matched pound for pound by the government. Although the government was seeking sleeper contracts it still could not find work for the more than 300 unemployed men. The committee sought free railway passes for single men seeking work. Other options included redistributing available work, giving preference in employment to married men, putting men on half-time, limiting earnings to £2 per week, employing 60 men on harbour construction on two-thirds time instead of 40 on full time, and encouraging single men to go to the wheat belt or to the front. Possible new projects included road-work and drainage projects and the subdivision of land into partially-cleared farming blocks with cottages on each. Beigel offered £50 to a relief fund if nine others would contribute the same, which some did. The committee resolved to send a deputation to the Government and to divert Belgian Fund contributions to local needs.

Children also played their part in various patriotic activities. While in a pioneer area such as Wellington, children were often required to help on the family property, the war forced children to see the world beyond the confines of the local community. The wives and daughters of fruit growers in the Bridgetown district worked in the packing shed.[189] Children were thrown into more egalitarian relationships with adults. Snell's young sister, Marjorie, took part in the making of sandbags, and children's participation in concerts now assumed a higher purpose in raising money for their 'soldier heroes'. Children also became bearers of bad news which passed around the school playground.[190] The Wellington Agricultural Society had abandoned its annual show in 1914 due to the shadow of war and the withdrawal of Government financial assistance.[191] However, attitudes changed, and the show was reinstated as a means of maintaining an economy for returning soldiers, and providing enjoyment for children.[192] Ultimately, children like Marjorie Snell never recovered from the personal losses they endured.

Bessie Lambert and Thomas Paisley were seemingly indefatigable, yet they were not alone in devoting all their waking hours to the service of the men at war. Many Wellington residents whose names appear in this account operated in so many patriotic activities that it seems impossible that they could have managed all these commitments as well as maintaining their family and work responsibilities. Aside from General Birdwood's acknowledgement of Australia's home front activity in support of its men at war, they seem to have received little lasting recognition. Thomas Paisley's tireless wartime work was not mentioned in his 1928 obituary.[193] His most lasting memorial was his role in unveiling a Bunbury war memorial in 1920, having 'educated 75 per cent of the lads whose names appeared on the monument, as well as a great number of their fathers and mothers'.[194] Perhaps so many people had worked as relentlessly as he that his contribution could not be singled out. It is possible too, that the wartime period had been so traumatic that it was best forgotten. The Wellington population possessed a wide array of management skills and community connections that they were able to mobilise in response to the wartime situation. The community's cohesiveness enabled it to contribute significantly in many fields, in manpower, financial, material, and humanitarian resources, all the while against a background of their own personal anxieties and losses.

Wellington's military contribution

The Western Australian military contribution has been examined by Suzanne Welborn, and while around 300 men in her sample were from the South West district, her focus is the men of the wheat belt.[195] Battalion histories by Belford and Hurst (11th), Devine (48th) examine the military contribution of Western Australians, Anstey has compared the Murchison and the Beverley's contributions, and local histories mention their wartime contribution.[196] Jeff Pierce has compiled a database of the war service records of men identified with the Wellington district in his *ANZAC Heroes* website.[197] However, there has been as yet no comprehensive study of a regional West Australian community at war.

My summary of the war service and outcomes of the Snell community is based on a search of names from the Snell archive and a selection from

Pierce's database, supplemented by a search of the National Archives database for names not identified by Pierce. The large families of the early settlers have complicated the task, so next of kin and searches of the birth, death and marriage records help to identify individuals known to the Snells to produce a 'best guess' population.

Of the approximately 32,000 Western Australian men enlisted, I estimate that nearly 2,000 were from the Wellington district, over 45% of the eligible age group.[198] By February 1916, the mining district of Collie, with a population of 4,000, had sent more than 600 to war, and in 1918, the Wellingon organisers had enlisted 1,000 men.[199] However, this does not account for the many who enlisted in Perth or, like Charlie Snell, in another state. Of the Wellington men who embarked for overseas, an estimated 462 were killed, including 93 at Gallipoli and seven at Fromelles, 66 were prisoners of war, and around 1,500 or 77% returned to Australia, nearly half of whom were unfit.[200] Wellington men and women served as infantry, snipers and gunners, tunnelers and miners, drivers, railway men and medical personnel in infantry battalions, the Light Horse and Camel Corps.

Among the Snell population, 49 families sent 77 men and four nurses to war, as well as Wedd Tuxford to work in a Sheffield munitions factory, and Bessie Lambert to work in a London aircraft factory.[201] Two men were rejected for service: Snell's brother Alf and David Breen, the Harvey orchard inspector. Four men died at Gallipoli, one died at Fromelles and three were prisoners of war. Overall, by the three methods included here, the death rate ranged between 22% and 26%, while the survival rate ranged from 73% to 78%. The Wellington community therefore made a significant military contribution to the war, and, as will be seen, the return to Australia marked the beginning of a lifetime, whether short or long, of suffering for the veterans and their families.

Six thousand Australians were recruited for munitions work, first by the British government and later the Australian government.[202] Snell's childhood friend, Wedd Tuxford, a mechanic, was employed in Sheffield from November 1915 to April 1917, with railway manufacturers W.S.

Laycock, who moved into the manufacture of aircraft engines in wartime.[203] Wedd suffered chronic bronchitis, possibly Spanish Influenza in 1918, and returned to Australia in June 1919.

While most of Snell's cohort had spotless military records, one stands in contrast to the rest. Mervyn Bailey Wenn, born 1896, was a brewer's labourer before enlistment.[204] At 17, while in senior cadets, he was fined and imprisoned for being disorderly on parade.[205] He was one of Stanley's 'bad characters' throughout the war, losing gear, going absent without leave, twice hospitalised with VD, twice court martialled and imprisoned, escaping confinement and forfeiting nine months' pay.[206] While recovering from wounds, he married in London in December 1916.[207] Post-war, he caused several years' consternation to the Repatriation Department.

Events at the Liverpool training camp in Sydney where Snell spent several months demonstrated the contrast between the Wellington population and the predominantly urban population at the Sydney camp. The indiscipline and larrikin behaviour of some of the men of the 1st Australian Imperial Force was described by war correspondent Charles Bean as early as December 1915 and later examined by Stanley.[208] Charlie Snell brought it to the attention of his family through wry comments in his letters from training camp in Sydney.[209] As the son of a railway man, he spoke with authority in his description of a railway accident which occurred when he and 700 fellow soldiers were returning from musketry practice near Sydney.

> *We came through Liverpool station at about 20 miles an hour and there was a terrific crash as we banged into a stationary carriage and truck and went through the dead end. The distance between the engine and the edge of the embankment was barely six yards. When we hit the second time the lights went out and windows smashed and glass was flying around. We were sent head over heels. I lost no time in getting out as I expected to see a big explosion from escaping gas. The engine was buried half way up the wheels in the dirt. What with escaping this time and surviving the lightning at*

Glen Innes I'm beginning to think I'll go through anything and come out safely.[210]

Newspaper reports described how a late-evening military train failed to stop at Liverpool platform and collided with a carriage and truck before crashing through the buffer stops, the engine and one carriage coming to rest part way down the embankment above the Georges River.[211] Investigations revealed that the train's air brakes had been tampered with, presumably by railway men.[212] Two soldiers were admitted to the camp hospital, while many others did not report injuries since they were absent without leave.[213] The collision with the stationary trucks, one laden with coal, reduced the force of the moving train, but the barriers were hurled more than 50 metres over a 15-metre embankment. A section of the railway lines was torn up and the engine and first carriage of the train were derailed. Had the train gone over the embankment, the results would have been catastrophic.

The records of the two injured soldiers suggest that they were among the larrikin element in the AIF. The first, an engine driver before enlistment, had been fined in the magistrate's court for disobeying orders while in cadets.[214] He did not embark for overseas and was discharged as medically unfit in mid-1916.[215] The second, a labourer, was punished for absconding while serving overseas.[216]

Charlie made frequent reference to the poor behaviour of the men around him in camp and was regularly selected to help round up drunken men in Sydney hotels. Newspaper clippings among his letters describe how rail traffic was disrupted by the breakdown of two Liverpool trains when several thousand soldiers returning to camp overloaded the trains, causing gear failure.[217] One train was so overloaded that the springs were straightened and the brake system damaged, forcing the train to travel at reduced speed. Another article describes how, near the Liverpool camp, the soldiers held up trains, reminding one old driver of the bushranging days of Cobb and Co. Two stations served the military camp, but rather than use either, the soldiers formed gangs on the rails at a strategic point and forced the driver to slow down so they could jump on the moving train. One attempt to hold up a fast train failed, causing a narrow escape for the men.[218] When large numbers of men wanted to leave a train, many climbed through windows and jumped to the ground, causing minor injuries and a fatal accident when a soldier was cut to pieces by a train. Soon after Snell's departure for the front, dissatisfaction over conditions at Liverpool culminated in rioting by several thousand soldiers at Central Station and looting in Liverpool.[219]

There was little similarity between training facilities in New South Wales and Western Australia. Around 32,000 men passed through WA's training camp, Blackboy Hill, around 1,500 men at one time.[220] In contrast, by September 1915, Liverpool camp in New South Wales housed nearly 17,000, with up to 15,000 visitors on Sundays.[221]

In Western Australia, attacks on businesses owned by foreign residents brought some disrepute on some recruits, but reports on the camp were overwhelmingly favourable.[222] Any poor behaviour arising from the camp was blamed on visiting 'easterners'.[223] The Western Australian recruits were 'active men', who did not 'hang round street corners or frequent the race grounds, men who have lived an untrammelled life in the bush', the far north, the goldfields, the timber belts, or even city offices.[224]

Five Bunbury women known to the Snell family served as nurses. Their service will be discussed in a later section. The community cohesion which led to the significant contribution of the Wellington district to the war produced consequences beyond the imagination of the far-sighted community leaders. The war's outcomes would test to the limit the community's physical, social and emotional resources, and force acceptance of conditional assistance from the higher levels of government. Even a community as resilient as Wellington struggled to cope with the demands of its wounded veterans and their families in the post-war period.

4

THE WELLINGTON COMMUNITY AND THE AFTERMATH: MEN ON THE LAND, THE PUBLIC AND THE PRIVATE

I thank God every morning that I don't owe any money to the Agricultural Bank[1]

The Bunbury repatriation committee formed early in the war interpreted state and commonwealth repatriation policies on behalf of returned men and their families. Local-state conflict was an ongoing problem as local committees complained of injustice and hardship inflicted on the returned men and their dependents by government agencies, however, they recognised that 'no responsible minister could give them a free hand'.[2]

The National Archives files held in Perth record individual experience in the war's aftermath, some veterans moving to the city or interstate in search of employment, while opportunities to take up land attracted some Wellington men to farming areas beyond the district. The Bunbury repatriation committee therefore expanded its understanding of the 'local area' in its work on behalf of Wellington veterans. The work of Bunbury repatriation committees was well-documented in the contemporary press, and while reports suggest that women reverted to social roles in community activities for returned men, their reappearance in repatriation files suggests that they remained as articulate as they had been in wartime. Census data suggest that the post-war needs of the men caused some women to return to the domestic sphere.

Bunbury's repatriation effort was truly an 'emanation from the heart' in its work for returned men and their families.[3] Local-state tensions was a recurring theme in the repatriation story as community groups and individuals negotiated official repatriation structures. Much of the existing literature focuses on agricultural settlement, yet the Bunbury repatriation committee was committed to placing returned men in urban settings. Since the financial aspects of post-war repatriation have been explored by researchers such as Scott, Lake, and Scates and Oppenheimer, monetary amounts will not generally be mentioned.[4]

The Australian government's 1917 repatriation system was designed to repay the community's debt to the men. Repatriation involved 'placing the returned man in civilian employment and life generally', ideally restoring him to an economic condition comparable with his pre-enlistment life.[5] By June 1920, 60% of the 167,000 working-aged men, and 14,000 English wives and fiancées, were placed in employment or training.[6] Pensions were granted to the men according to degree of incapacity, to their wives or widows for up to twelve years after the war, and children up to the age of 16. Pensions of £4 weekly were paid to 136 blinded soldiers and to 983 tuberculosis sufferers. Payments quickly outstripped projections and became the source of much of the conflict between Repat and the men.

The original Bunbury repatriation committee

A repatriation committee was among the war committees set up in Bunbury on the outbreak of the war.[7] The committee anticipated that 10% of returned men would go on the land or take up their old occupations, so it worked with the local traders' association to reinstate men in their former positions or find other suitable employment.[8] In a bid to ensure that their returned men remained in the district, Messrs Clarke, Baldock, Paisley, Rose and Foreman convened a meeting in mid-1916.[9] Anticipating peace in 'three on four months' time', the community had a 'solemn duty' to the 30,000-strong war contingent who would 'come back in droves' to Western Australia. The South West was well placed with its reliable rainfall and ample cleared land along the railway lines, and by expanding the irrigation scheme, land could be farmed more intensively.

Mindful of failures in the wheat belt, soldier resettlement in the South West aimed to place the men on established farms where, assisted by neighbouring farmers, they could immediately make a living. The 'best and fairest' opportunity would be afforded by the 'Ready-Made Farm', a cleared, fenced, watered and stocked dairying property, with a 'decent and comfortable' house, funded by a low-interest loan. A local board would select the most capable men, allowing them five years to become established, after which they would have three or four years to repay their debt and 'either get on or get off'.[10] Keen to place men in urban positions, the Bunbury committee sought to increase local processing of farm produce, setting 'the best brains of the most practical men in the South-West' to the task.[11] The committee hoped to re-establish the local tanning industry and employ men in fruit-canning in the Bridgetown district. Although slowing markets were pushing Harvey citrus producers into dairying, the Harvey Fruitgrowers' Association hoped to attract men to the industry through a short course at the fruit packing shed.[12]

By 1916, the Bunbury committee was thinking beyond the local area to the south coast and into the wheat belt region, known as the 'Great Southern' where some Wellington men established themselves. Post-war repatriation policies helped to produce a diaspora of men from the Wellington district to the Great Southern, the Murchison district, to the capital city, Perth, or even interstate.[13] At the same time, there was a movement of new men into the district, some filling the community roles of the departed men, while the men who moved to the Great Southern became active in their new communities.

The Bunbury committee felt unwelcome pressure to conform to the 'bald official programme laid down in Perth', even though Industries Minister James Mitchell was himself a Bunbury man.[14] His 'comprehensive scheme' contained elements of the Bunbury proposal, with groups of 20 men on properties accessible to water, roads and railways.[15] Local knowledge would guarantee the suitability of land for semi-intensive mixed farming in the South West and 1,000-acre properties in the wheat belt, where Bunbury's Paisley brothers were to settle. The Lands Department would allocate the land and the Agricultural Bank would provide loans for clearing, fencing, stock and water supply, however, unlike the Bunbury plan, repayments would begin immediately. Local management would be facilitated by Agricultural Bank inspectors, selected from among experienced farmers. Scates and Oppenheimer made extensive use of inspectors' reports in their study of repatriation in eastern Australia, yet comparable files from the 300 Western Australian inspectors have not been located.[16] Minister Mitchell optimistically stated: 'we can absorb soldiers as settlers as fast as farms can be prepared', employing 8,000 waged men for land clearing, while Minister for Works, W.J. George planned further extensions to the railway network.

The scheme was reported approvingly in Bunbury, and expectations were high that men would flock to the district.[17] Mitchell assured critics that safeguards were in place to protect the 4,000 men who were expected to take up land in the Wellington district. He grandly promised that the debt to the soldiers would be repaid by 'the most experienced men in Australasia' who would guarantee the efficient and sympathetic management of the scheme. By 1918, nearly a thousand men were settled in the South West and further afield, some share-farming like the Paisley brothers and Reg Ibbotson.[18] Despite the optimistic plans, local returnees soon complained that they were not receiving the support they anticipated.

The Bunbury committee was impatient at government delays which prevented them accepting offers for factory and housing sites and proposals for co-operative industries.[19] The Bunbury committee and the Returned Soldiers' and Sailors' Association (RSSILA) were concerned at the risk of losses and discredit falling on soldier settlers through lack of local advice and a probationary system for new settlers.[20] They soon concluded that farming in the South West and the wheat belt was too demanding for returned soldiers suffering war-caused illnesses or wounds.[21] In fact,

Snell's cohort suffered the full range of war-caused health issues: embedded shrapnel, scarring, heart and lung, and mental problems.

There was further local-state conflict over the decision to subdivide the Brunswick State Farm into lots for soldier settlement.[22] Administrative delays led to criticism over the 'iniquitous policy' of letting the farm run down and reducing the numbers of milking cows and teams of horses.[23] Instead, its 'magnificent farm buildings' could have been converted into an Agricultural College offering training in dairying, horticulture and irrigation.[24]

Soldier Settlement in the Great Southern

The Paisley brothers took up wheat farming in the Tambellup district in the hinterland of Katanning, the major centre for the region known generally as the Great Southern, the Stirling Range forming a natural southern boundary to wheat growing. To the north of Katanning, the next major centre is Narrogin, while Gnowangerup, Wagin, Cranbrook and Broomehill were all connected by rail, to the main Perth-Albany line.

The first wave of settlement had arrived in the district in 1907, followed soon after by interstate migrants who raised wheat and fodder crops alongside sheep for high quality wool and meat on farms of around 1,000 acres.[25] Local business was conducted through a farmers' co-operative store in Tambellup, situated by the Gordon River, which had pools of fresh water for boating and swimming. A progress association was the equivalent of Wellington's pioneering road boards. The district had rifle clubs, children's day at the seaside and a camping reserve on the river.

In 1917, the Lands Department inspected land around Tambellup with a view to soldier settlement, hoping to settle 4,000 men.[26] 'A man who has been willing to fight for the Empire's defence will be equally ready to work for it as a producer,' said Minister Mitchell, comparing the financial security of the man on the land to the precarious position of a wage-earner in a town.[27] When Mitchell visited Katanning in 1917, twelve 'suitable' returned men, financed by the Agricultural Bank for clearing, fencing, housing and water supply, were already settled on wheat farms.[28] Assistance for wheat cropping included horses, funds to employ a man and a living allowance of nine shillings per day paid monthly by the visiting bank inspectors.

Two years later, now Premier, Mitchell reaffirmed his belief in the district's contribution to agriculture, which, by then, surpassed gold, pastoralism and manufacturing as the means of repaying the state's wartime debt.[29] Progress in the district was reflected in requests for extensions to roads and water supply for newly settled land and a new hospital to cater for the expanding population. The local medical officer, a wartime medic, reported insufficient beds for women, lack of an isolation ward for diphtheria and scarlet fever patients, and the urgent need for a motor ambulance.[30] The Returned Soldiers' Association, with more than one thousand local members, requested land for a club house. Losses to the district through local men moving elsewhere were compensated by the arrival of newcomers such as the Paisleys. As in Bunbury, the local repatriation committee requested that land valuation and the selection of men should be carried out locally to reduce delays for returned men whose cropping activities were dependent on seasonal conditions. The premier assured the community of his sympathy, but admitted to being overwhelmed by a backlog of 1,200 applicants for land.[31]

Meanwhile in Bunbury, the Agricultural Bank reported that 281 returned men had settled on re-purchased estates in the South-West in recent months.[32] Forty men were placed around Harvey, the remainder around Boyanup, Brunswick and Dardanup, the original plan for men to be settled in larger groups now abandoned.[33] While these men were placed on repurchased estates where some improvements had been carried out, a government gang was clearing land around Boyanup for further settlement.[34] The subdivided Brunswick State Farm, was now occupied by eighteen soldiers.

The strain was beginning to show. In Harvey, Roy Hayward,

Charman, Castieau and Driscoll of the Harvey Road Board reported that roads, drainage and bridges were coming under pressure from the increasing population.[35] Requests also came for police in Harvey, sanitation improvements at a new school and a local hospital to cater for diphtheria, maternity, pneumonia and scarlet fever cases.[36] A soldier settler's property mortgaged to the Board was foreclosed and in Bunbury, local soldier settlers complained over the dismissal of Agricultural Bank inspectors too sympathetic to returned soldiers.[37]

In the Great Southern in 1920, water supply problems resulted in complaints that returned soldiers were being 'thrashed with the whip they had taken from the Germans' hands'.[38] Other grievances included the inadequacy of sustenance payments, the seizure of income from the sale of live-stock to cover debt, the burden of debt from previous landowners and the taxing of produce consumed on the farm. The inspectors, in turn, reported a lack of motivation in the men, prompting calls by the Returned Soldiers Association for a Royal Commission to examine complaints.[39] There were reports of inflated land prices which left the soldiers little chance of success, along with the recurring complaint that local committees were ignored by the government. In 1922, despite the 'great difficulties', the Tambellup press reported 'steady progress' in the district.[40] The hard-working soldier settlers had adapted to soil conditions ranging from 'loose sand to stiff clay and from deep loam to shallow pin-grass country,' and, assisted by the Agricultural Bank, had created a 'sound, self-contained community'. A boating club held regattas, and scattered residents were brought in by train.[41] Although women were less visible in the context of land settlement, women were considered an asset on a farm due to their home management skills.[42]

In Boyanup a labour force of returned men improved drainage on Trigwell estate and while turnover of men was a problem, the locals viewed the new arrivals as a 'good strong set of men', and held social events to welcome them into the community.[43] Throughout the south west and the wheat belt, there was a ready acceptance of the soldier settlers, reminiscent of pre-war times when new settlers were arriving constantly.

The community remained conscious of its debt to the returned men and there was a sense of a new pioneering era.

By 1923, a Royal Commission was appointed to assess soldier settlement.[44] The press closely followed its deliberations as it identified 'maladministration and incompetency' by government, wasted money and excessive interest charges.[45] Poor supervision, inefficiency and inexperience inflated land clearing costs and farmland purchased at unrealistically high prices resulted in high interest charges, leaving the settler with a crippling debt burden. Men taking blocks abandoned by other veterans were burdened with pre-existing liabilities. Wheat belt witnesses reported lack of sympathy from government, inadequate railways, roads and water supply and marketing difficulties. The commission recommended writing down the cost of clearing, deferring interest payments and special consideration to settlers planting new orchards or vineyards.

The 1923 Royal Commission provides evidence for comparing Soldier Settlement in Western Australia with other states of Australia.[46] In 1923, Western Australia had 4,665 soldier settlers, third after Victoria and New South Wales. Western Australia had the lowest rate of abandonment, the next lowest being Victoria at 7%, the highest being Queensland at 16%. In this respect, Western Australia was the most successful of the states, an outcome consistently reported throughout the period. Signs of optimism appeared in the Balingup RSL's 1924 report on its support for its 38 soldier-settlers, including improved road and rail services for dairy farmers and extra railway vans for transporting meat and cream.[47] Lectures examined fruit growing, cattle management and efficiency on small farms and members attended soldier settlement conferences at Bunbury and Perth. The branch had lost four members: one had died and three had left the district.[48] The report suggested that although conditions were difficult, a strong sense of community empowered the men to address challenges.

In the same year, however, settlers in nearby Capel were battling a mysterious disease killing young cattle, and in Bunbury, a soldier settler was on trial for having sold some Agricultural Bank-funded machinery.[49]

Neighbouring farmers reported purchasing items on the defendant's assertion that he was free to sell them. The bank claimed it had 'dealt very leniently' with the former dock worker, provoking one court official to comment, 'I thank God every morning that I don't owe any money to the Agricultural Bank'.[50] The defendant claimed he had purchased the machinery with his own money and that he and his son had made many improvements to the property during their five-year tenure.[51] It was unclear whether the accused had abandoned the property or had been evicted by the bank. Ultimately, the evidence was contradictory, the bank claiming the man was not farming wisely, that he owed arrears of interest and threatening foreclosure. In the light of the problems faced by soldier settlers, and the defendant's lack of prior farming experience, he may have been guilty of the alleged crimes, despite his evident improvements to the property. Ultimately, the jury found the defendant 'not guilty', reflecting a general feeling of sympathy with the soldier settler in the district.[52]

In Harvey in 1925, a dispute arose over the government's failure to fulfil a commitment to buy clover seed locally instead purchasing it from the eastern states, leaving settlers holding 'anything from one hundred to a thousand bags' and ultimately affecting the Agricultural Bank.[53] The South-West district was already suffering the failure of the potato crop, and the sale of the clover may have enabled them to meet 'at least some' of their liabilities. Settlers had been 'humbugged, fooled and callously treated by the Department', which had instructed them to grow clover at the expense of pasture for their cows, thus reducing their milk and cream supplies, with further loss of income. Additional costs were incurred through the purchase of bags and fertilisers and employing outside labour and they now risked losing their farms. The dispute raged over lack of co-ordination, affecting both the struggling soldier settlers and the Bank to which the settlers were indebted.

The Harvey irrigation system also experienced problems, provoking a deputation from the RSL and local dairymen to W.J. George MLA to discuss water costs and payment problems caused by a bad season.[54] George's observation that there were 'problems with the scheme since its inception', unwittingly echoed Snell's earlier doubts surrounding the ability of Harvey people to manage the scheme.[55] A soldier settler reminded the minister of the 'very hard struggle' of the veterans, while a long-term resident cited the Soldier Settlement Scheme's failure to ensure the promised 'level footing' for the irrigation scheme, which favoured some at the expense of others.[56] Despite these difficulties, the establishment of the Harvey Co-operative Milk Supply Company through Commonwealth initiative fostered the integration of existing settlers and veterans.[57]

The Balingup Road Board reported difficulties in collecting rate moneys from soldier settlers, who claimed they were unable to pay as they had 'no certainty of tenure'.[58] In the previous year, around 25% of settler properties had been abandoned, an unusually high number in the light of the 1923 Royal Commission report mentioned earlier. This left the Road Board unable to carry out necessary works or continue to employ an 'Inspector of rabbits'. It complained that while 'old settlers always pay their rates', none were received from soldier settlers.

The situation appeared more optimistic in the southern wheat belt where the Paisley brothers were farming, making 'big improvements during the last two years'.[59] Farmers were increasing productivity by integrating sheep raising and fodder crops with their wheat crops, and farming was becoming more business-like, in line with government policy.[60] Flock quality was improving and rams were being bred for the North West, a trend which has continued to the present day as the area regularly produces the finest wool in the state.[61] By 1928, there were reports of 'Soldier Settler's Success' in dairying at Wokalup south of Harvey.[62] A field day on the dairy farm of 'an Agricultural Bank client' attracted more than 100 farmers and highlighted progress in the dairying industry.[63] Workshops on crop and milk production, breeding and complementary pig-raising gained approval from the district's Agricultural Bank Inspector. Harvey stalwart Roy Hayward was one of the speakers, and as in pre-war days, the ladies provided refreshments. In 1929, interstate tourists were taken to a local estate which had become an exemplar for soldier settlement, with nine prospering settlers and no abandonments.[64] However, south of Bunbury, in the Manjimup district, holdings had been abandoned and soldier settlement pronounced a failure, since 'Government assistance had encouraged irresponsible settlers' while local knowledge could have prevented some of the problems.[65]

In Harvey in 1929, despite complaints of holdings being too small, soldier settlement was prospering, with 100 soldiers occupying repurchased blocks on the former Korijekup and Uduc estates served by the Harvey irrigation scheme.[66] There were three apiaries, four poultry farms, two turkey farms, 500 acres under potatoes and other crops and two nurseries for fruit trees. Refuse from dairies was sold to a piggery and a third dairy factory was under construction. In ten years of soldier settlement, 'large areas of bush have been changed to a countryside of meadows and homesteads', dairy farms and factories, and fruit, dairy produce, cattle, sheep and pigs supplied the metropolitan market.

East of Tambellup, where the Paisley brothers were farming, mixed farming of wheat and sheep was well established, although farmers were still struggling.[67] Appeals to the Premier in 1925 and 1926 and to the Controller of Soldier Settlement and parliament in 1930 called for the revaluation of land to address debt problems as even 'capable, practical and industrious' men risked foreclosure.[68] Of 5,300 original soldier settlers, 50% had left the district and 'about 90% of the soldier settlers were labouring under conditions which made farming impossible'. Complaints of new settlers having to take on debt incurred by former settlers and demands for increased local management reiterated problems ongoing since the Royal Commission in 1923.

Collie Leitch, one of few soldier settlers remaining in home territory, was cited as a success story when Premier Mitchell visited his Trigwell Estate property in 1931.[69] One of the nine soldier settlers on the estate and with a wife, a son and six daughters, he successfully integrated pigs and dairying and was repaying his debt. He managed the clover harvest 'with two of his daughters, his son and one man, the girls building the stack using two sledges, three horses, one engine and elevator, hay rake and mower, achieving vastly improved output'. Stock numbers on the estate had increased and milking machines, motor cars and trucks had been purchased.

The Harvey River Diversion Drain (1931–1936) was one of a number of government projects designed to provide relief work for unemployed veterans during the Great Depression.[70] Constructed to reduce winter flooding and open up new farm land, it employed 1,300 men working two days a week each.[71] Beset with indiscipline and dissent over the intense manual labour and the part-time nature of the work, the men called for increased work days and meaningful activities to occupy their spare time.[72] The project had a significant impact on Harvey, through the efforts of Messrs Lowe, Hanks, Johnstone and Aubrey Smith, and its completion was celebrated by the now Lieutenant Governor, Sir James Mitchell, with a guard of honour by the local troop of the 10th Light Horse.[73]

Between 1934 and 1938, on the former Brunswick State Farm, finance concerns and weed problems were replaced by optimism.[74] The farm now hosted 20 successful settler properties, the 'richly fertile area' producing whole milk and cheese for the metropolitan area and promoting town growth. An exemplar of 'high production by intense culture', one farmer had achieved an eight-fold increase in carrying capacity since 1919.[75] Local subterranean clover seed now supplied the whole state, with a surplus for export. The local school was experimenting with fodder crops and fertilisers and the old farm hall was used by the RSL. In 1938, alongside complaints that farms were too small, the Government threatened to subdivide and sell the Harvey Commonage if the Harvey Road Board did not meet its interest charges.[76] Jack Lowe, supported by an RSL petition, cited locally-funded improvements to water supply and stressed the importance of the commonage to settlers.

Fifteen years after the 1923 Royal Commission, the outcomes of the soldier settlement scheme were published.[77] In the Great Southern, the RSL had secured the revaluation of a local soldier settlement estate, the Agricultural Bank implementing debt adjustment schemes on twenty repurchased properties and suspending arrears payment for three years, thus reducing settlers' liabilities by nearly £1 million.[78] In all, loans totalling nearly £10 million had been made to nearly 9,800 men. Abandoned properties numbered 2,100 and the loss from the scheme was £6,000,000, but more than 400 properties were free of debt and 2,600 no longer required inspectors' supervision.[79] The dairying industry in the South-West was considered the greatest beneficiary of the soldier settlement scheme and the Minister for Lands claimed that Western Australia had accomplished more in debt adjustment than all the other states combined.[80]

Although repatriation planners had anticipated men returning to their home communities, this did not often occur. Communities willingly absorbed returned men, quickly adopting them as their own as they had done before the war. Civic structures remained, augmented by new organisations such as local repatriation committees and the RSL which were active in the cause of returned men. There was continuing tension between local committees who believed they were best placed to support the men and the state and federal authorities who provided the bulk of the money, albeit under punitive conditions. Women have largely, though not totally, disappeared from these narratives, although the repatriation files show that the wives and daughters who supported war-damaged men were assertive when necessary as they shared the legacies of war.[81]

Lake has shown that many of the problems faced by the returned men were a result of the conflation of post-war settlement with the imperative of settling the land under a yeoman model.[82] While eastern states planners optimistically placed men on small properties, Western Australian planners gave careful thought to the amount of land needed for successful farming in varying environmental conditions.[83] Lake and others have mentioned the Depression in their studies and Beaumont is currently assessing its impact through her own examination of repatriation files. However, apart from the Harvey River Diversion scheme discussed here, the impact of the Depression was not evident in the press or in the Repat files examined.[84] While soldier settlement remained in the public discourse long after the war, 1938 seems to mark a natural closure, with government reports and a final summation of the new patterns of agriculture that had emerged. However, the repatriation files demonstrate that private battles were not over, as men carried the scars of war throughout often long and painful lives.

Urban resettlement had continued in Bunbury throughout the war. In 1918, the Bunbury repatriation committee which included Mayor Baldock, Robinson, Beigel and Eastman was placing returning Bunbury men in urban positions similar to their pre-war occupations.[85] The committee was highly critical of the federal authorities' failure to support new industries and impatient at government delays which prevented them from taking up offers of factory and housing sites, electricity and water supply, and plans for the establishment of co-operatives.[86] The 'returning men were not additions to the population' they said, 'but were part of it temporarily withdrawn for war service', therefore, places must be made available to them.

The local committee attempted to offer preference to returned soldiers and was critical of the federal government paying sustenance to 'men below normal efficiency as a result of their war experiences', thus forcing them to be 'involuntary paupers', rather than establishing industries where they could 'earn their daily bread by the sweat of honest toil'.[87] The theme of avoiding any hint of charity wherever possible permeates the post-war repatriation discourse.

The establishment of an axe handle factory during 1918–1919 was one of the successes of the Bunbury Repatriation committee, the result of the persistence and commitment of 'prominent businessmen' Beigel and Baldock, although the plan provoked criticism that the committee was doing too much and allowing federal authorities to 'shirk their duty'.[88] Appeals for state and federal funding were unsuccessful, and eventually Beigel and Baldock augmented state finance with their own personal funds.[89] Two eight-hour shifts operated, enabling a weekly production of over 800 handles, increasing to 3,000 with upgraded machinery. By December 1919, the factory was showing a profit and was unable to keep up with demand.[90] The tireless efforts of men such as Beigel on behalf of the returned soldiers were recognised by General Birdwood when he visited the factory in January 1920.[91] By June of that year, the initial four-man workforce had increased to sixteen men on day and night shifts, with 40 foresters cutting the raw timber.[92] Local innovation further increased the output of handles, which were exported to the eastern states and New Zealand. In the 1920s a box factory operated in Boyanup and press advertisements confirm that furniture, beverages and tailoring provided significant manufacturing work in Bunbury in the post-war period.[93]

Several of Snell's cohort returned to urban occupations, although only one returned to Bunbury. Norman Holtzman, gassed and wounded at war, worked as a plumber in Bunbury after the war.[94] His case is discussed in the next chapter. Others, such as Len Gibbs, a farmer's son, worked as a salesman in Perth and never received a pension.[95] Richard John Moore was blinded in one eye and suffered additional post-war health problems. He worked in various occupations in Carnarvon and Collie, near Bunbury, before eventually running a knitting mill in the city. He appealed unsuccessfully several times for a pension and died in 1947, his wife dying two years later.[96] Three of Snell's cohort moved interstate. Reg Hemingway, a bank clerk who lost a foot in the war, transferred to Melbourne in 1924, and died around 1950. His wife received a pension until 1973.[97] A brother, Grosvenor Hemingway, moved to Adelaide in 1920.[98] Another brother, Herbert had been killed at Gallipoli. Their mother applied unsuccessfully for a pension in 1930.[99] Leonard Baldock, received vocational training in a Bunbury hardware store before moving to Adelaide, where his record ends in 1922.[100] No two stories are the same.

The private lives of men on the land: new light on old themes

Studies of post-war repatriation focus on the hardships of soldier settlement (Lake, Scates and Oppenheimer), on issues such as grief and loss (Damousi) or on caring for war-damaged veterans (Crotty and Larsson).[101] Thomson and Straw, basing their studies on small populations, have explored specific issues affecting individuals.[102] Researchers can obtain their samples by random sampling or recruiting. Lake, for example, selected 100 cases per settlement district in Victoria, ensuring examples of successes as well as failures. Garton used government reports for his analysis of soldier settlement and reports, journal articles and hospital records for his discussion of shellshock.[103] For their analysis of the neuroses of past conflicts, Jones and Wessely selected every 50th file from archives to obtain a 2% sample.[104] Larsson sought the children of veterans through newspaper advertising and through her own family and friendship networks.[105] Thomson recruited his oral history subjects through the RSL, seeking working-class participants in particular.[106]

This study of the Wellington district uses names found in the Snell archive to reconstruct the post-war experience of the men and women represented by repatriation files held in Western Australia. Many are compiled from multiple files, hence referencing will appear confusing. The post-war experiences of individual men and women and their families were lived in the context of the state and community policies described earlier. None of these individuals returned 'hale and hearty'; all were 'blighted by the war'.[107]

Returned soldiers fell into several categories: those few who returned to pre-war occupations, those who became and remained soldier-settlers, those who initially settled on the land but later moved into other occupations, and those who returned to new occupations in an urban setting. Veterans struggled with war-caused disabilities, often suffering increasingly with the passage of time, and many faced an ongoing struggle for acceptance of their claims by the authorities. Despite their problems, they often raised large families and lived long lives.

The repatriation files attest to the financial, medical and emotional difficulties experienced by almost all the men, and the contribution of wives and families to their care. Two Wellington women who served as nurses are the subject of repatriation files and one in particular was to test the limits of the resources and medical understanding of the period. Several other women, wives of the veterans, also figure in the Repatriation files. Each file points to some unique experience and some hint at mysteries which could only be solved by the most painstaking research. The files demonstrate that the Western Australian authorities did their best to accommodate the needs of the men.

Claude Clifton: Becker muscular dystrophy

Claude Clifton should never have been accepted for military service, but went to war and returned to Australia to take up his life where he had left it, as a farmer on the family property at Brunswick Junction. Grandson of Marshall Waller Clifton, commandant of the West Australia Company settlement at Australind, Claude was born at 'Alverstoke', the family farm in 1894, son of Algernon Francis Clifton and Augusta Dorinda Ker.[108] Single, he was working as a farm hand at the time of enlistment. In September 1916, Claude was rejected for military service on account of 'abnormal enlargement of leg muscles', but two months later was accepted and served in England, Belgium and France as a driver in the 8th Australian Field Artillery Brigade.[109] A fall from a horse resulted in hospitalisation with a septic knee and in 1918, unfit for driver's work, he became a gunner.[110] Throughout his service, he was unable to march and he was eventually found permanently unfit for general service on account of 'muscular hypertrophy both calves with consequent muscular weakness', in mid-1918.[111] He filled in the time until his return to Australia as a traffic controller.[112]

On his discharge from the AIF in March 1919, Claude was unable to 'walk any distance', his condition variously described as 'dystropia', 'muscular atrophy' and 'suppertraphy' (sic).[113] Claude was among the many returning men who did not seek repatriation assistance on discharge, although he reported weakness in the legs and 'some mental impairment'.[114] In April 1919, when he suffered tonsillitis, his underlying condition was described as 'Oppenheim's disease' or 'amytonia congenita'.[115] In June 1919, Claude became a soldier settler on the family farm under the supervision of the Brunswick Repatriation Committee.[116] For the next three years, he received a 20% disability pension for 'amytonia congenita' and 'sustenance awaiting productivity' of the land.[117]

In 1920, through the Harvey Repatriation Committee, Claude politely requested a medical examination. He was:

> *going to Perth Thursday, and must be back in Brunswick Saturday evening. Please make the necessary arrangements and advise me as to where and at what hour I am to be examined. Also, please advise as to whom I am to apply for travel expenses.*[118]

The examining doctor noted that Claude had been closely observed in camp in England and during his three years' 'strenuous' service, suffering leg cramps on exertion. On discharge, his disability was not deemed to be due to war service.[119] Claude's pension was cancelled in 1922, his condition described as 'enlarged calves, power not proportional to size. Power in arms also impaired, will likely get worse.' His claim for continuance of his pension was rejected on the grounds that he had been 'amply recompensed'.[120]

There is a hiatus in the record until 1929, when Claude was still working the farm but appealing for assistance, reporting 'loss of power' in his legs.[121] A testimonial from a neighbour described Claude as sober, a sportsman and a cricketer.[122] A search of his military records by Repat noted that while carting ammunition at Shellfire (sic) Corner, Ypres, he was 'blown up' and 'never the same afterwards'.[123] The Brunswick RSL reported that Claude had enjoyed good health before the war, but had 'returned a cripple, sometimes unable to get about'.[124] He was now socially isolated, he played no sport and led a 'sober and straight forward life'. Claude's medical report noted that he had been gored by a bull in 1924, resulting in adhesions from a perforated intestine, he had appendicitis in 1926 and was obese.[125] His case was difficult to determine 'because the disability was related to a pre-war condition' and when he had been found fit for the land, his disability was not considered serious.[126] Repat rejected Claude's claim.

Claude immediately announced, 'I intend to call evidence.'[127] Encouragingly, Repat suggested that as Claude had received a pension for three years from discharge, it should be continued.[128] Now aged 36, his spidery and irregular writing resembled that of an elderly person. Another search of his history was carried out, the medical notes claiming 'amyotonia' more detailed than for the earlier appeals, now noting pneumonia in 1915, and an uncle who had died at 28.[129] His discharge as 'permanently unfit for general service', and the fact that he was self-employed and did not seek assistance despite the weakness in his legs were again reported, as well as 'mental impairment', tonsillitis in 1919, and Oppenheim's disease (amytonia congenita).[130] The case was finally referred to Melbourne. Here, the repatriation record ends. Claude did not die in a military hospital as did many of his comrades. When he died in Bunbury in 1932, aged 38, the local press, ignoring his military service, reported simply that his was one of few recent burials in Australind Cemetery, where his grandfather lay.[131]

Claude Clifton's condition, now diagnosed as Becker Muscular Dystrophy, came through his mother's line.[132] Augusta Dorinda Ker was the daughter of Henry T. Ker, customs officer of Busselton and Dorinda Guerin, the daughter of an early Busselton police officer.[133] Augusta Ker had three brothers, Robert (1853– ?), Charles Buchanan, 1855–86 and Claudius Buchanan, 1859–88.[134] Claude in fact had two, possibly three uncles who died young, one at 31 and the other at 28 years of age, not one, as the repatriation records indicated.[135] He outlived his longest-living uncle by seven years.[136] Claude himself had three sisters and no brothers – sisters who could themselves pass on the condition.

Claude's disability would have been obvious to recruiting officers and he should never have been accepted for war service.[137] As a young man, he would have been able to play cricket, to ride horses and engage in farm work where he could manage his own activity levels, although the pneumonia he suffered in 1915, prior to his enlistment, would have weakened his condition. The intense military training would have exacerbated his condition, producing intense pain and contributing to muscle breakdown and damage to his heart. He would not have been able to participate in the long marches with full pack so thoroughly documented by Charles Snell. It is surprising that Claude was not returned to Australia as unfit on his arrival in England, as were 16,000 of his compatriots.[138] The fact that he was assigned to driving duties illustrates his tenacity and a degree of humanity in his superior officers, but driving under conditions such as those at Hellfire Corner presented its own physical challenges, the area necessarily crossed 'with the accelerator pushed to the floor'.[139]

Claude Clifton's post-war experience ranks among the most trying, not because he suffered new hardships in settling the land after the war, but because he was accepted for war service when his physical condition should have precluded it, and was then exacerbated by his war service. Having accepted him for war service, the repatriation authorities should certainly have supported him for the rest of his short life, as the DC noted in March 1930.[140] They should also have paid for his funeral.

Amputees

Butler briefly discusses provisions for limbless men and the heroic post war lives of two in particular.[141] Dugald Leitch was one of around 4,000 amputees in Australia after the war.[142] When the Boer War veteran enlisted in 1915, he was a widower with a dependent daughter. On repatriation to Australia in 1917, after six months' hospitalisation, he returned to farming. He remained a crack shot well into his nineties and at the end of his life, many of his friends were unaware that he had an artificial leg. Yet his repatriation file shows that he suffered considerably over the years and received little help from Repat apart from new artificial legs every ten years.[143] In a 1950 survey of amputees, he reported pain in the missing limb at night and recurrent 'stabbing pains' in the 'foot that isn't there'.[144] Volunteer effort provided considerable support for amputees. In Western

Australia, the Maimed and Limbless Association, with a membership of more than 400, raised funds, operated a city hostel for its members and supported the work of an artificial limb factory.[145] The Bunbury community held sporting and social events on behalf of the association.[146] In his final years, blind and deaf, Dugald was cared for by his daughter and her husband, who unsuccessfully appealed to Repat for assistance.[147] He never received a pension, he received no assistance with general medical expenses in later life, or funeral expenses. He simply got on with his life despite his disabilities.[148]

Another Harvey amputee, Martin Myatt, had come with his family from England in 1906 to take up citrus farming.[149] Brothers Frank and Martin, with Guy Gibney, left for the front in mid-1915.[150] Frank Myatt and Gibney were both killed at war, and Martin, who served in the Camel Corps in Egypt, suffered a severe gunshot wound to the thigh in mid-1917.[151] This resulted in amputation and nearly three years' hospitalisation, before Martin returned to Australia in late 1919.[152] Martin married in 1920 and did not return to the land, but worked as a public servant, living in Peppermint Grove, Perth's most prestigious suburb and able to purchase further property.[153] Martin must have spent considerable time in hospital in Perth because he was among hundreds of mourners at the funeral of a 'most loving and devoted' nurse in 1936.[154] Martin died in 1940 aged 50.[155]

Tom Rose: struggles on the land

Thomas Hayward Rose, 1888–1973, served in Gallipoli and France, married in England and came home with disabilities caused by gun-shot wounds in the shoulder, injuries which were still evident when he later presented with age-related illness.[156] He had his own farm, but at the end of the war, needed loans to restock and renovate his property. His application was considered 'a manifest absurdity. His position is so sound compared with probably 90%' of the men seeking help from Repat, echoing observations that the repatriation system discriminated against established farmers.[157]

Assistance from the Bunbury Repatriation Committee secured him a loan, but poor seasons and instalment due dates which did not accommodate the harvest and sale of potatoes soon resulted in overdue repayments. This provoked stern warnings from Repat: 'the leniency shown to you has not had the effect anticipated'. Tom responded: 'it has been a bad year for all of us here on the land. My wool has not been sold yet, the sheep have not done any good, I had a bushfire through my property and it burnt all the grass'.[158] Problems throughout 1924, exacerbated by an attack of influenza, led to the plea: 'I am doing my level best to get this matter squared up'.[159] Finally, in 1925, after a struggle lasting seven years, his debt was repaid.[160] Tom Rose was a victim of the unrealistic conditions set by the Repatriation Commission and their relentless efforts to recover money loaned to veterans. Application of the Bunbury committee's original proposal of a five-year grace period before repayments were due would have significantly eased his burdens.[161]

Ray Clarke: war torn man on the land

Ray Clarke, served in the 11th Battalion for nearly four years in Gallipoli and France, and was awarded the Military Cross, presented personally by General Birdwood while on his post-war visit to Bunbury.[162] Caught in a bomb blast in 1917, he suffered severe abdominal wounds which left serious scars. Discharged unfit, he resumed dairy farming with a loan of £700 to restock the farm.[163] He married Marjorie Clifton in 1918 and they had seven children, two of whom died in their first year and one at 25.[164] In 1919, Ray's scars seemed well healed and he was initially able to supervise farm work.[165] However, in 1920 he underwent major surgery for abdominal adhesions, and in 1925 they were again causing pain.[166] In 1921, he received a 60% pension, reduced to 30% in 1931.[167] Over the years, he repeatedly failed to keep repayment deadlines, claiming disruption by the birth of children, and he was unable to continue payments on insurance policies during the Depression.[168] By 1938, he was incapacitated. He unsuccessfully appealed for a pension increase in 1952.[169] His wife nursed him at home from the age of 65 and he died of heart disease on the Busselton Rifle Range in 1959 five years later.[170] His wife unsuccessfully claimed that his death was war-caused, but she was granted a pension in 1960 until her death in 1990 aged 96, after a widowhood of thirty years.[171] Ray's extensive abdominal wounds caused problems throughout his life, and work must have been a struggle, added to financial worries and a large family, yet he was unusual in that there is no hint of war neurosis in his notes. He was fortunate compared to Les Paisley.

Les Paisley: a man broken by battle

Les Paisley is the first of four siblings whose post-war experiences will be examined. As he was battling on the land, his siblings were having problems of their own, some of which Repat came to see as a family failing, to the detriment of all its members. Les suffered the after-effects of war wounds, war neurosis and battles with Repat throughout his post-war life.[172] At the same time, he and his wife were supporting other family members from a distance. Les epitomizes Bruce Scates' 'man broken by battle ... whose body gaped with wounds'.[173]

A station overseer in the Kimberley on enlistment, Leslie William Paisley served from late 1914 to 1919, as lieutenant in the 10th Light Horse, Camel Corps. He served at Gallipoli and the Middle East, and in August 1915, suffering gun-shot wounds, he spent 51 days in hospital in Mudros and the UK.[174] He later received a shrapnel graze over the eye at Hill 60, Gallipoli.[175] In Egypt, he suffered influenza and in 1918, malaria, which resulted in many weeks in hospital.[176] On discharge, he was suffering headaches and his general condition was described, strangely as 'nervous, but no sign neurasthenia'.[177] Although classed as permanently unfit, he was given no pension. Instead, he received sustenance while awaiting income from his Soldier Settlement wheat-sheep farm at Toolbranup via Tambellup, obtained with the assistance of the Bunbury Repatriation

Committee, which he worked with his brother, Selwyn.[178] Like his brothers, he married late, at age 39, to Ethel Grace Foreman, a Bunbury girl, in 1928. The hardship of life in the Great Southern required that when Ethel was expecting a child, she spent several months with her parents in Bunbury, returning to the farm two months after her confinement.[179]

Les ran the Tambellup troop of the Light Horse after the war, and on ANZAC Day 1923 spoke of his experiences at Gallipoli: four or five months there were 'enough to last a life time', and 'the great day of the Light Horse was 7 August when they lost 75% of their strength'.[180] In 1924, the Tambellup Troop won the award for the 'smartest and most soldierly turnout' at the annual training camp.[181] In 1930 the Paisley brothers were represented at Perth wool sales and in 1943 Les and his wife attended community, RSL and Soldiers Aid Society events.[182]

Les first appealed for a pension in 1927, suffering arthritis in his right shoulder which necessitated employing a labourer to manage the wheat harvester and carry bags of wheat.[183] Witnesses, including a former commanding officer, testified to his serious wartime head wound, for which he 'could not be persuaded to see a doctor'.[184] Others reported a 'shaking' from an exploding shell, for which he again refused medical aid, stoicism which was to cost him later.[185] According to testimonials, Les was an 'honest, straight and sober man' from a 'a very fine family', and he was a 'very decent fellow, who lived a good clean life'.[186] He was 'not a strong constitution, particularly since the war,' and was 'deserving of assistance'. Repat awarded a 33.3% pension. [187]

Ongoing problems with his old wounds during the early 1930s were not accepted as due to war service.[188] In 1938, he was suffering from arthritis and vomiting, but his doctors found him difficult to treat because of the 'rarity of his visits'.[189] In 1940 his old gun-shot wound to the forehead was causing problems and he was diagnosed with 'neurasthenia', which remained an issue for the rest of his life.[190] By 1945, Les was too weak for light manual labour, and in such pain he needed bed rest, reducing his work to less than one day a week and forcing him to give up farming.[191]

Disconcertingly, the doctor could not find much wrong despite the pain he was experiencing.

After leaving Tambellup, Les took up 'light work' with J. Duce in Boyanup, near Bunbury.[192] In 1949, his bomb wound to the temple was again under investigation.[193] In 1950, aged 62 and living in Bunbury, he appealed unsuccessfully for a pension increase, saying he could do little work and was unable to sleep despite medication and weekly physiotherapy.[194] By 1951, he had not worked for 12 months due to pain and could not dress himself or 'even fish' (sic).[195] He spent time in Hollywood hospital suffering 'very much an anxiety state' and unsuccessfully claimed war causation for a duodenal ulcer, and assistance with vehicle costs.[196] He appealed, saying that during service in Palestine, a stomach ulcer was aggravated by the worry of war service, and protesting at pain caused by 'pulling about by the medical board!!! (sic)'. [197] After further deliberation, his duodenal ulcer was accepted as war caused, and in 1952 he was again hospitalised with vomiting and backache. [198]

For the next five years, Les again worked as a farmer until in 1957, and now 69, he claimed for treatment and sustenance for a hernia.[199] A family history was now produced, which noted three brothers with war neurosis and a 65-year-old sister, Vera, with a nervous disorder. Another sister, Ivy, had died at 64 of a heart attack, and a brother, Tom, had died at 27 after a motorcycle accident. Their father had died at 67 of a stroke, and their mother at 82.[200] Les had four children aged 21 to 29 who were all well. The hernia was accepted as war-caused and costs were awarded.[201] Improbably, Les was now classed as 'very fit', despite spondylitis, a duodenal ulcer, two hernia operations, and 'paralysis of the legs when vomiting'.[202] A flurry of correspondence, including a letter written by his wife, 'Ethel G. Paisley', suggests that Les may have hoped to visit South Australia in 1958.[203] Another stay in hospital, and medical opinion that 'this is a most unusual sequence of events', seems to have prevented the trip.[204] He had periods in hospital in 1935, 1950, 1951 and 1958. [205]

For the last 15 years of his life, Les suffered a series of age-related conditions, always involving Repat. Increasingly, his wife Ethel advocated for him. Regular physiotherapy over many years seems to have been beneficial, as he endured further abdominal conditions, skin cancer, and a tumour behind the knee.[206] A non-smoker, he nevertheless suffered chronic bronchitis and emphysema and, unsurprisingly, clinical depression.[207] He now referred to himself as a retired farmer, and at 78 years old he was 'still a fit looking man for his age'.[208] In 1971, his daughter began managing his affairs and that year, at 83, he suffered a stroke. He made a good recovery, 'a man of remarkable determination who has made a great effort to overcome his disabilities, with gratifying success.'[209] Around this time, his wife died, leaving him lonely and depressed.[210] Family and community organisations provided support for him to remain at home, and RSL functions maintained old friendships. However, an application for a Recreation Transport Allowance was denied on the grounds that his inability to walk was not war-caused.[211] Despite his old bullet wounds giving trouble, he remained a 'real trier' but eventually he was admitted to a nursing home where he died in 1974 at age 86.[212]

Les was remarkable for his return to farming after long periods of hospitalisation and incapacity, and for his resilience under the trials of ill-defined illness which left authorities sceptical, despite testimonials as to his strength of character. Rae notes the slow recognition by authorities that men of good character also succumbed to post-war neurosis.[213] He endured a long and painful post-war life, fortunately supported by family and community who were able to provide the long-term care he needed. While Les lived long after the war, his brother Selwyn's post-war life was relatively short and marred by war neurosis and malaria.

Selwyn Paisley: Malaria and War Neurosis

Selwyn Addey Paisley was a station hand in the far north of Western Australia, and 'very active' before the war.[214] He served in Egypt in the Camel Corps and as a gunner in France from 1915 to 1918. In 1918, he was hospitalised in Leeds War hospital, London, then Harefield Hospital, Weymouth, with attacks of malaria, although the medical record also notes 'NYD' (not yet determined).[215] He returned to Australia in August 1918 and was discharged medically unfit with 'malaria in the heart, lungs, and spleen, anaemia and debility'.[216] His condition was accepted as being aggravated by war service, and he was classed as unfit for six months, with 'neurasthenia' causing 20% disability. He took up a soldier-settlement block near Tambellup in the Great Southern district with his brother.[217] In 1920, there was some seemingly trivial confusion over his address when he applied for rail fare to Perth from Tambellup. It was refused on the grounds that he had 'always lived at Bunbury'.[218] Selwyn was to endure disputes and appeals with Repat over his condition and his pension throughout his remaining years.

In 1921, he was described by a doctor as 'spare, sallow, and nervous'.[219] A breakdown in his health in 1924 elicited advice from his brother, Les, that Selwyn's breakdown was the result of gas in France.[220] He 'reluctantly' claimed a pension, stating that his health had broken down as a result of being 'frequently blown up and gassed', and suffering malaria in France.[221] For much of 1926 he received a pension, but for 'neurasthenia' rather than malaria.[222] He was now described as 'neurasthenic, introspective and despondent', thin, sleeping badly and nervous.[223] Blood was detected in his sputum, he looked ten years older than his stated age and suffered nervous twitches.

In 1925 Selwyn's brother Cyril suffered symptoms of tuberculosis, which caused Selwyn to worry that his gas-related lung trouble was TB.[224] The doctor concluded that his 'health was definitely impaired by war service' and that he had 'some neurasthenia', and ordered six months holiday with 100% pension. During the latter part of 1926, Selwyn spent six months with his parents in Bunbury and consulted a private specialist in Perth who found no TB.[225] He continued to worry about TB, but returned to 'light' stock work, remaining very nervy, sleeping poorly, and vomiting if overworked, while his pension was gradually reduced.[226] His brother Les married in March 1927, and Selwyn's plan to marry in April 1928 seemed to his doctor 'incompatible with serious anxiety over his general health'.[227] His wife, Hilda, a schoolteacher, was to share the burden of his illness and suffer the loss of several babies, which does not appear in the records until it haunts her during her long widowhood.[228]

The latter part of 1929 was another trying period, and Selwyn appealed for a pension increase. 'I am a shell-shock case and can't work properly'.[229] Despite his nervous condition, Selwyn remained articulate and assertive in his letters: 'I consider very unfair …'[230] However, to his doctor, he was a 'typical neurasthenic, complaining of symptoms in every part of body'. He was too nervous to pass urine, 'never sleeps before 3.30', and he 'seems a bit of a "wreck"'.[231] 'His wife gives a poor account of his condition' and a few months later, his 'wife and brother were in despair over him'.[232] With regard to the pension application, the doctor did not 'feel competent to give a final decision', suggesting a trial of psychiatric treatment, but there is no evidence that this eventuated.[233] Selwyn is the only individual among the cases examined here to have a doctor suggest that psychiatry may be applied. Butler uses the term 'psychiatry' quite liberally, characterising it as the study of insanity.[234] In terms of using 'psychiatric analysis' as a treatment of mental illness, it appears rarely, although Butler did believe in the 'curability' of psychiatric illness 'if treated properly'. Butler quotes figures which show that in Victoria in 1935, 66% of psychiatric in-patients were 'cured', without directly stating that they were treated by psychoanalysis, however, in 1940, Butler still saw work as the best cure for mental illness.[235] In Western Australia, around 1930, public opinion was still ambivalent about the value of psychiatry, and a former patient of Lemnos Hospital for mentally-ill soldiers in Perth emphasised the care and attention of the female staff of the hospital, rather than any scientific treatment, in facilitating his cure.[236] Psychotherapy may have helped Selwyn, however, according to Fassin and Rechtman, even after psychoanalysis and the role of the unconscious were accepted, suspicion of nervous veterans did not disappear.[237]

Selwyn's symptoms continued during the 1930s, and since no symptoms of neurasthenia had been reported on discharge, his 'post war anxiety neurosis' was attributed to fear of TB and 'an inherited disability found in other members of the family'.[238] Officials were frustrated because his 'unrelated complaints smack of mendacity', he was 'unduly obsequious' and 'tremulous throughout the examination', and 'it is extremely difficult to get this man pinned down to a definite statement'.[239] The authorities found Selwyn's urgent need to return to the farm 'most unsatisfactory', hinting that he was exploiting his nervous problems to avoid work. [240]

Selwyn's records for 1931 and 1932 depict constant struggles with Repat over the reduction or cancellation of his pension. According to officials, in early 1931 his 'only disability was neurosis' and it was not war caused.[241] His pension was cancelled, and then restored on appeal, since his 'constitutional neurasthenia was aggravated by war service'.[242] His wartime medical history was again re-examined, and the violent shaking that had him admitted to hospital was attributed variously to shell shock and malaria. Although it was conceded that he had often been gassed, his increasing disability could only be due to 'constitutional factors', that is, an hereditary condition.[243] Selwyn's pension was again cancelled, prompting further correspondence from Selwyn, his brother and his wife. His doctor commented: 'I have no doubt that he has quite a degree of neurasthenia', however, pension disruptions and appeals continued.[244]

The record now becomes spasmodic, with a curt note in 1938 that Selwyn's pension was not to be increased.[245] Around 1945, Les left the farm. In 1946, Hilda's pension was transferred to Gnowangerup where she taught for eleven years until September 1957 when she left work to care for Selwyn until his death six months later, 'after much suffering'.[246] Selwyn's death did not provide release, as Hilda then managed the farm alone and began caring for her 92-year-old mother in South Perth, regularly making the 200-mile journey until she moved to South Perth in 1970.[247] After her mother died in 1974, Hilda cared for a sister in Harvey for some years.[248] Although articulate and assertive, Hilda was to sign herself 'widow of

Selwyn A. Paisley' for many years after his death until in her final years when she became 'vigorously independent'.[249] Her last years were marred by sadness and 'deep grief' over the loss of several stillborn babies, her husband's early death and the struggle to run the farm alone, until she died at 95 in 1995.[250] To her friends, she was a 'dedicated community minded citizen, reunited with her loved ones'.[251]

Selwyn and Hilda struggled throughout their post-war lives against illness, uncertainty surrounding Selwyn's illness, and Repat who tried to balance the care of returned soldiers with the need to expend taxpayer funds efficiently. Hilda was married to a sick husband for 30 years, and then a widow for nearly 40 years, battling the illness of her husband, the loss of her babies, then caring for mother and sister, with no children of her own to support her in later years. That task fell to Les's children.

While the Bunbury Repat committee originally envisaged that the men (and women) would return to the community, and indeed, many did, this was not the rule among the population studied here, except for the pre-war land-owning farmers: Ray Clarke, Tom Rose, Claude Clifton, Dugald and Collie Leitch and Percy Smith. Les and Selwyn Paisley, who worked in the Kimberley district before the war, but did not own land, took up soldier settlement land in the Great Southern, while Reg Ibbotson, an orchardist, made several unsuccessful attempts to work the land after the war. These men were all severely affected by war wounds, many having relatively short working lives, while Dugald Leitch and Les Paisley, despite their war-caused disabilities, worked into old age. Among the town-dwellers, only Norman Bird, a timber worker, plumber Norman Holtzman and Dick Clarke returned permanently to their former homes. Of the rest, the majority made their way to the city, with a small number moving interstate.

These movements represent a diaspora from the Wellington district. This may have been a result of the natural attraction for the city during the Depression and beyond, which was also seen among the young women.[252] The concentration of medical services in the city may have attracted the ailing men. Individuals who moved away from Wellington after the war did not have access to support from the extended family, although returnees formed new social networks among neighbours, the RSL and community organisations. In their later years, Les Paisley returned to Bunbury and Reg Ibbotson and Hilda Paisley both made regular visits to Harvey, demonstrating enduring connections with the district.

Researchers focus on criticisms of the repatriation system. Garton points out that the system was naturally adversarial and that officials had a reputation for being 'harsh', 'miserly' and 'abusive'.[253] Despite occasional sceptical comments by medical and administrative officials, the files examined for this study provide ample evidence that Repat officials were sympathetic to the plight of the men. Lake, on the other hand, frames negative attitudes to Repat in terms of criticism of soldier settlement itself, which again, is not evident in this study.[254] Repatriation officials, whether administrators or medical officers, had to work under conflicting constraints. The Repat scheme was committed to restoring the men to lives as family men and economic producers, necessitating financial and vocational support to get the men working again, while also dependent on the ability of the medical profession to restore the men physically and mentally to productivity. The longer it took to restore the men, the more expensive the operation became. The travelling medical officers, who were closest to the source of finance, were often frustrated by the failure of the men to 'get better', their condition often exacerbated rather than ameliorated with time. However, once a man was hospitalised, judgement disappeared and was replaced by compassion. The situation of the medical officer was further complicated by the fact that he often got to know wives and siblings and sometimes friends, placing increasing constraints on his ability to remain objective. The local repatriation committees, often composed of men who had known the veterans and their families since childhood, were the direct conduit between the individual and Repat, making their situation all the more difficult. On the other hand, in the rare cases where familiarity did not breed respect, the committees were blunt in warning Repat of likely problems, as discussed in a later section.

It is impossible to generalise about the success or otherwise of post-war soldier settlement with such a small population, however, the local press considered it a success. Returning to run-down properties, with assistance from Repat to refurbish and restock, was inevitably going to test the war-damaged men to their limits. The next chapter further explores the medical outcomes of the war. It demonstrates that the veterans ultimately fought their battles with Repat as individuals and therefore alone, despite the efforts of families, local committees and communities.

5

REPATRIATION: MEDICAL OUTCOMES FOR URBAN VETERANS

While Straw and others have examined a range of medical outcomes of the war, only Butler has attempted to explore all possible outcomes.[1] The community base of the present study reveals a multiplicity of post-war medical outcomes. This chapter examines some post-war medical outcomes in Wellington men, such as tuberculosis, war neurosis and the 'war-torn soldier', which have been examined by other researchers. A blinded veteran, a trench foot sufferer, a former prisoner of war who suffered thyroid problems and neurasthenia, and several who suffered lung conditions, all endured drawn-out battles with Repat over the causes of their conditions and their pension entitlements. The repatriation files testify to the resilience of men and women, who, despite suffering severe disabilities and long absences from the workforce, remained in employment until late in life. Despite the efforts of local individuals and community groups to secure the support the veterans needed, in their dealings with repatriations officials, the veterans were essentially alone, the victims of limited medical knowledge and financial constraints.

Butler provides eloquent examples of disabled returned men who, given 'a fair go … a determined and capable man could re-educate himself to adapt to post-war life'.[2] A farmer who had lost his right arm, carried out all major tasks involved in sheep farming, and was thankful he had lost an arm and not a leg. A man who suffered chest and arm injuries, with several pieces of shell remaining in his back, studied art, leatherwork, poultry farming and accountancy, and worked for multiple soldiers' associations. Another, an artist before the war, had his right arm amputated at the shoulder, but created the symbolic windows in glass mosaic around the central dome of the Australian War Memorial with his left hand. These men had clearly defined and highly visible injuries. They did not suffer the endless battles with Repat of those who had less clearly defined conditions. Bunbury man, Dick Clarke, who was totally blinded in the war, led a fulfilling post-war life, aided by Repat, the Red Cross and family. On the other hand, veterans such as Les Paisley, returning with shrapnel remaining in his body faced increasing problems as they aged while having to deal with sceptical Repat officials.

Dick Clarke: Totally Blind

Mervyn Ephraim (Dick) Clarke, son of early settler, E.M. Clarke, was totally blinded in the war, and epitomised determination and capability throughout his long life.[3] At the time of enlistment, Dick was, like his brother Ray, a farmer. He served with the 11th Battalion as observer in Gallipoli, Egypt and in France.[4] In August 1918, he was wounded by a bullet which struck him in the nose and then exploded, 'splashing him all over the face' and causing the loss of both eyes and wounds to nose and mouth.[5] During the succeeding years, he underwent several reconstructive operations on his nose and further treatment in Adelaide after his return to Australia.[6]

On enlistment, he was considered 'one of the most popular of Bunbury's younger generation, loved for his genial, happy personality, a bright, sunny-hearted boy'.[7] Friends attested to his 'marvellous' courage since he lost his sight.[8] An emotional arrival in Fremantle was followed by a rousing return to Bunbury as friends lined the railway and the engine driver enthusiastically sounded the whistle.[9] Apart from his blindness, Dick's general health was good, and he received a special pension, reviewed annually, until his death in 1986. This pension was the subject of an unusually good-humoured correspondence, written by himself or family members.[10] Enquiries regarding his wife's entitlements should he predecease her resulted in nearly 30 pages of paperwork.[11] A trip to Sydney in 1957 with his wife and youngest child caused some disruptions to his pension, a 'missing fiver' and another enquiry. 'My visit to the mother state seems to have caused some upset. I am safely back in my home state and hope to stay put for a good many years.'[12]

Dick was loaned £500 to build a house and remained fiercely independent, refusing offers of institutional care.[13] In 1972, he declined an offer of a guide dog and/or binaural ultra-sonic spectacles with training in Melbourne (at the Department's expense, except for food for the dog), on the grounds that he was 78 years old and 'never had any desire to get around on my own'.[14] Accepted war-caused medical conditions included chronic eye socket infections, respiratory tract infections and dental problems. In 1940, 'numerous small metal fragments around mouth' caused problems.[15] From 1946 he suffered boils and carbuncles, and from 1949, heart irregularities were treated with sedatives and advice to restrict cigarette smoking.[16] In 1982, he suffered pneumonia and a heart attack. When he died in 1986 at the age of 92, he was great-grandfather of six. For the 66 years following the war, Dick was cared for by a nurse, then his wife until her death in 1971, then his daughters. Unlike Larsson's 'invisible' families, Dick's wife and daughters are highly visible in the Repatriation files.[17]

Dick wore a black patch over one eye socket and a glass eye in the other for 60 years.[18] His medical files report that he suffered endless discomfort, yet he was uncomplaining. In 1976, after an episode of choking, he was admitted to Bunbury's St John of God hospital rather than the Bunbury Repatriation Hospital. This provoked a flurry of correspondence, in which he excused himself by claiming: 'I thought I just needed my throat clearing' and St John's was closer ('excuse the mistakes, I don't use typewriter much these days').[19] Local medical staff claimed, reasonably, that in the emergency, no-one realised he was a veteran, and the authorities eventually conceded 'In view of veteran's age, disability and promise not to offend again' it could be regarded as a special case.[20]

After Dick married in 1926, his wife was the focus of social reports in the local press, just like other Bunbury women.[21] Between 1927 and 1941, she bore five children, the first three automatically receiving pensions, but when a fourth child was born in 1933, his pension claim was rejected on the grounds that children born after 1931 were ineligible.[22] In 1941, he wrote: 'I have been blessed with another daughter … Is she to go unrecognised by the Commonwealth?' And in 1943: 'I don't want to appear grasping, for we have been treated most generously', but he needed assistance for schoolbooks, and in 1951, he was 'struggling' to pay a daughter's board.[23] Ultimately, both later children received assistance. Dick owned a car from 1955 and was driven by his wife or one of his daughters and in 1963, received a life pass for the railways.[24] After his wife died, he lived alone, with daily visits from the Silver Chain, and a daughter looking after his affairs from a distance.[25] From 1975, another daughter, newly married, lived close enough to visit every day.[26] Requests for a bigger car and funds to re-carpet the house were denied.[27]

Dick had undertaken woodwork training in England, and during the 1930s and 40s he earned money for 'odd cabinet making'.[28] In 1954, though, when his youngest child was eleven years old, he was 'at a loss for something to do' and requested further instruction, perhaps in 'rug making'.[29] A period of occupational therapy in Hollywood Repatriation Hospital restored his sense of purpose, and in 1963 and 1964 he was granted first a dowelling machine and then an electric sander.[30] A letter from a friend testified to the 'beautiful cabinet work' he did, illustrating the community support he was receiving.[31] Subsequent grants came with kind letters from Repat 'trusting you will derive pleasure …'.[32] In 1973, he requested an electric planer as he was 'getting old' and planing was 'rather strenuous'.[33] His doctor supported his application, saying 'he will get much pleasure and productivity', but it was refused as too dangerous for a blind man.[34] He accepted the refusal graciously.

Equipment provided by the Red Cross immeasurably enhanced his quality of life. The first was a Braille typewriter in 1948. He was already a 'competent typist,' having learnt Braille in England.[35] He expressed his delight in the 'splendid typewriter', apologising for errors, as 'this happens to be my first letter'.[36] From 1950, he received a series of 'talking book machines' from the Red Cross in Melbourne, with books sent weekly. Over the years these machines were to provide almost as much consternation as pleasure as they needed repair or replacement. At such times, he 'missed it greatly' and was chastised by Repat when he had repairs done locally.[37] The Red Cross considered him 'one of our keenest readers', the Repatriation Department, a 'prolific reader', and the Braille Society, a 'very undemanding chap … a very good friend of ours'.[38] There were limits to their generosity though; when he was learning German, and wanted a new machine, he was reminded that he already had a new one.[39] The Red Cross also provided a Braille watch.[40]

Until her death, Mrs Clarke liaised with support organisations, providing feedback and thanking them for their interest in her husband's welfare. Dick's sense of connection with the people supporting him is evident in 'please excuse this awful typing but I just found the "wireless" stopping the carriage going full length'.[41] When there were problems, an 'evil spirit' was watching over him.[42] These comments also reveal the difficulties of an ageing blind man, now managing alone, however, his good humour reappeared with the receipt of a new typewriter: 'I'm glad my old machine caused so much merriment to the girls'.[43]

The wartime press were indeed prescient in describing Dick on his enlistment as 'a bright, sunny-hearted boy'.[44] This characteristic sustained him through his long post-war life. Although the authorities were careful in their allocation of funds to him, they only once complained about the cost, when damaged recordings had to be replaced in the United States.[45] Dick's comfort came at enormous cost to the authorities, which they bore, not only without complaint, but often with the kindest regard to his comfort and happiness. In turn, he bore his disabilities with grace and dignity throughout a long and productive life. Stories of fulfilling post-war lives among disabled veterans are rare indeed.[46] Men such as Dick were raised when community feeling and personal recognition were strong and their war service and return were surrounded by the rhetoric of heroism.[47] Dick's story also testifies to the valuable work done by the Red Cross, reported by Oppenheimer and Larsson.[48]

Reg Ibbotson: Trench Foot

Reginal Montague Ibbotson lived and worked as one of the family on the Snell Harvey orchard before the war.[49] He served in the 38th Battalion in Egypt, France and Belgium and was discharged unfit in April 1917.[50] His pension file reports childhood ear problems and post-war, he suffered deafness and trench feet, causing his toes to go blue in the cold.[51] He had a twin brother, Leslie Montague, who also enlisted, and returned briefly to Australia in 1917 and again in 1927–28 and 1932–37, before spending the remainder of his life in England.[52] Throughout his post-war life, Reg longed to be reunited with his family in England.

After the war, Reg initially sought clerical work with the support of a former commanding officer at Blackboy Hill training camp. However, he returned to farming in Harvey but found himself unable to manage the heavy work.[53] In early 1919, he applied unsuccessfully for assistance to return to England to care for his widowed mother and sister and seek medical advice which he felt was unavailable in Australia.[54] He unsuccessfully appealed the decision, reiterating medical problems and a desire to be with his family.[55] His brother, Leslie (Monty), was still in Egypt. Reg claimed he would have remained in the UK in 1917 but for a misunderstanding over his discharge. His beautifully written letters at this time reflect his intense longing to return to his family.

In 1919, somewhat surprisingly in the light of his short-lived post-war farming attempt in Harvey, Reg entered a partnership in a pastoral lease at the recently-established 300,000-acre Mooloogool Station, near Meekatharra, 800 kilometres north-east of Perth.

The Meekatharra Repatriation Committee advanced funds for the purchase of sheep, but sustenance 'awaiting production of land' was refused on the grounds that he was already getting a pension for deafness.[56] Reg worked the property with two brothers, who were from Cue, also in the Murchison goldfields.[57] He may have kept the books on the station, presaging work he eventually did for the rest of his life. He married Irene Smith, his partners' sister, in 1922 and their first child was born a year later. Reg left Mooloogool in 1925, by which time it ran 2,800 sheep and other animals, had nine watering points, 125 miles of fencing, a homestead, outbuildings and garden.[58] Reg returned to farming at 'Lyndhurst', Harvey, served as 'capable' secretary of the Harvey Agricultural Society and in 1927, a second child was born.[59] In 1928, he again applied unsuccessfully to Repat for assistance to bring his mother, brother and sister to Australia to settle on the land.[60] While brother Monty spent several years in Western Australia around that time, Reg did not visit England until 1970.[61]

It was during the 1930s that Reg, like increasing numbers of his fellow ex-servicemen, began having serious problems resulting from his wartime trench feet.[62] Causing swelling, numbness and pain, it resulted from the cold and wet conditions in the trenches, poor diet and the fatigue of battle.[63] Wartime prevention involved rubbing with whale oil to protect from moisture, but amputation often became necessary. Much was written about trench foot during and soon after the war, and it has been recognised in combat as recently as the Falklands war, however, among Australian repatriation studies, it is only briefly mentioned by Thomson.[64] Butler does not mention trench foot in his 'disease groups affecting pensions', although he does present figures for men being treated for trench foot across Australia in 1926 (69), 1933 (133) and 1939 (172).[65] Numbers increased with time, Reg figuring among the 1933 and 1939 groups. These figures are among the lowest for men being treated for war-caused conditions, suggesting that trench foot was a minor post-war problem, but, as Reg's files testify, for him it was a major problem.

In 1934, Reg was still farming, but was seeking a full medical investigation as 'I have not been satisfied with myself for a long while now'. He was 'in a very bad way financially and could not stand the strain of having to pay wages' for a caretaker while he was in Perth.[66] Now 40, his feet were 'numb and painful in winter', and he needed 'boots with no toe caps', to allow free movement of the toes.[67] He was given a daily allowance and surgical boots were prescribed, but he was to be troubled by his feet and footwear for the rest of his life.[68] In 1936, he returned some boots for repair, noting that they had hardened despite his rubbing them with fat, hoping to 'get a little comfort'.[69] A reprimand followed: although it was the 'object of the Department that you shall always be in possession of 2 (sic) pair serviceable boots' they must be used correctly, the work boots worn for work and the soft boots for 'Sunday wear' only, and they must be kept in proper repair'.[70]

Reg was farewelled by the local RSL when the family left Harvey in November 1937 to run a grocery business in George Street, East Fremantle.[71] This venture was to last only six months before he and his wife declared bankruptcy.[72] He now became a 'commercial traveller', applying for soft shoes, as boots were too heavy for 'my class of work'.[73] In 1939, he was working as a temporary clerk in the Fremantle Repatriation office, where he suffered a crushed toe, adding to his woes.[74] From around 1940, and for the next 20 years, Reg worked for Commonwealth Customs, a position he found fulfilling despite his ongoing problems with his feet and later, his hearing. In his new position, Reg was concerned for his appearance as his old shoes were 'looking shabby and not suitable for office wear'.[75] He was no longer eligible for surgical shoes and needed normal shoes that were two sizes larger than his feet. Always reasonable, he argued: 'In my position as a clerk it would look anything but nice to have my feet thus shod'.[76] At the time, Repat was reducing its assistance to ex-servicemen and Reg was among 130 men now being supplied modified ordinary shoes, in his case, simply felt insoles.[77]

Alongside his foot troubles, Reg was now receiving assistance for his deteriorating hearing, which, in a position which involved contact with the public, was 'not improving my chances of promotion in the Commonwealth Public Service'.[78] His regular work enabled Reg to move to the more prestigious suburb of Applecross in 1948.[79] His foot troubles recurred in 1952. He had 'never had any real comfort since the Department ceased making my shoes some years ago'.[80] Reg received sustenance payments while recovering from the amputation of two toes, which made him 'much more comfortable'.[81] In 1956, Reg was again supplied with surgical shoes, but his feet continued to cause problems, necessitating costly time off work.[82] A relocation into the customs residence in North Fremantle reduced his housing costs.[83]

In late 1960, at 67, Reg retired on a service pension after 20 years with the Customs branch.[84] His many letters during this period testify to his pride in his position and his concern that his work should not be interrupted by his ongoing medical problems. We can only imagine the physical pain he endured with little complaint. Reg lived for another twenty years, suffering ongoing foot and ear problems. A trip to Adelaide in 1962 was interrupted by a heart attack near the wheatbelt town of Kellerberrin.[85] Repat was concerned about the cost of the single bed ward in which he was placed, but was assured by the hospital, experienced in dealing with Repat, that he 'required complete rest and quiet', and no other was available.[86] Age-related illnesses followed, but he continued to enjoy trips to the south west, and at 73, was 'keeping and looking well' for his age.[87] Reg's wife, who never appeared in the Repat files, died in late 1969, and in 1970 he had his long-awaited reunion with his brother during a visit to England, but Repat was no longer paying his medical costs.[88] In 1971, Reg, a 'cheerful elderly gentleman', moved once again, this time into retired servicemen's accommodation.[89] He developed dementia, suffered pneumonia, bone fractures, a hip replacement, and one final bout of gangrene in the foot.[90] By 1978, his son and daughter could no longer manage his care and he was admitted to a nursing home.[91] His daughter visited regularly, but it 'tore her to pieces every time'.[92] Reg died two years later at the age of 86.[93]

Although a soldier settler for a time, Reg's story bears little resemblance to that of other soldier settlers, who either struggled on or, in abandoning their properties, disappeared from the historical record. Reg left the land after several attempts, and after some false starts, finally found a sedentary occupation which gave him fulfilment and some financial security, enabling him to raise a family in a marriage that lasted 47 years, and travel to England to be reunited with his long-lost family. He may even have visited the battlefields which had cost him so dearly and where so many of his old friends lay. His letters, while documenting his struggles, depict a character of great dignity, who, with considerable help from the repatriation department, his family, and no doubt the RSL, made a valuable contribution to his community and lived to a ripe old age despite his war-caused injuries.

W.H. Sinclair, prisoner of war, 'thyrotoxic type'

Wisbey Harrington Sinclair, born 1896 in Bunbury, left school at 14. On enlistment, he claimed that his mother was his dependent, although his father was employed on the Bunbury pilot boat for 33 years and was then lighthouse keeper before retiring in 1918.[94] When his mother died in 1927, her estate was administered by her husband, so it seems strange that Wisbey claimed her as a dependent.[95] Sinclair's case is interesting for two reasons: firstly, as a returned prisoner of war, whose wartime and post-war experiences are only now coming to light; and secondly because he was a sufferer of mental illness 'of the thyrotoxic type'.[96] Butler places this condition among nervous symptoms of organic rather than emotional origin. Unfortunately for Wisbey, once his organic illness was diagnosed, his significant mental suffering was discounted by the medical authorities.

A butcher by trade, Wisbey enlisted aged 19 in the 28th Battalion, serving in Gallipoli and France, and was one of 3,800 Australians taken prisoner on the Western Front.[97] His detailed yet dispassionate POW statement describes horrific experiences. Captured at Pozières Ridge in July 1916 after lying in no-man's-land for two days, passing Germans rifling his pockets, and rescuing him when they realised he was alive.[98] He survived nine months in hospital and four internment camps, where the food was often inadequate and treatment harsh. Knowing that officers' lives were more comfortable than other ranks, he 'promoted himself to corporal' but did not escape the forced labour he resisted whenever possible.[99] Red Cross parcels, sent weekly from London but received intermittently, provided relief.[100] He was returned to England in August 1918 after two years in captivity.[101]

Wisbey married in 1919 and assisted by the Bunbury Repatriation Committee and the RSL, he received vocational training in a department store.[102] Ongoing medical treatment caused disruptions to his pension, resulting in frequent correspondence with Repat. Initially unable to lift heavy weights, by 1920, he was 'doing his very best' and by the end of that year was '100% efficient'.[103] In 1921, he underwent surgery to remove infected shell fragments, resulting in further disruptions to his pension, and subsequent appeals.[104] A gap in the record suggests that Wisbey struggled on with metal fragments in his back, but problems persisted. In 1934 his wound was re-examined and further fragments found, but were impossible to remove.[105]

Twenty years after the war, in October 1941, Wisbey became seriously ill: his 'nerves had gone to pieces' and he wept during medical appointments.[106] Surgery revealed a 'large number of widely scattered metallic fragments' but it was 'hopeless to try to remove all fragments'.[107] He remained highly emotional, weeping 'on any provocation', upset by current war news, and sleeping little, causing 'severe nerve strain' to his wife and disconcerting doctors who expected stoicism in dealing with private emotions.[108] His 'neurasthenia' was accepted as war caused and he returned to work.[109] However, he soon broke down again with a 'coarse tremor of the whole body' and severe weight loss, and six months later, a thyroid condition was suspected.[110] Holidays in Margaret River and Kalgoorlie and rest under the care of his wife did not help.[111] Attempts to return to work as a shop assistant failed.[112] The RSL and his doctor advised Repat that his condition was urgent, and criticised delays in treatment resulting from disputes over the cause of his problems, now diagnosed as thyroid dysfunction. Repat responded by deleting neurasthenia from his entitlement and refusing thyrotoxicosis as a war-caused condition[113] In July 1943, 18 months after his symptoms first appeared, a thyroidectomy was performed, his condition normalised and he resumed work.[114] Appeals ultimately induced Repat to accept his thyroid condition as war-caused.[115]

Wisbey was working as a commercial traveller in 1946, receiving a pension and living in the northern suburbs of Perth.[116] He died in 1967 of heart disease and arteriosclerosis, his funeral expenses paid by Repat after a successful appeal by his widow and the RSL.[117] Unusually, Mrs Sinclair remarried, six years after her husband's death, the only one among the population examined here.[118] Although it is unlikely that his thyroid problem was war-caused, Wisbey suffered the after-effects of war for the rest of his life, whether through his experiences as prisoner of war or because of the metal fragments he carried in his body. He was certainly deserving of any assistance he received from the RSL and the Repatriation Department.

On the evidence of other veterans, in dealing with the authorities it was preferable to have an easily defined condition. Dick Clarke, who was blinded in both eyes had a long and happy post-war life, despite his disability. However, when Wisbey presented with symptoms of neurasthenia and was eventually found to have thyrotoxicosis, his problems continued. Nevertheless, despite contemporary limitations in medical knowledge and the financial imperative of minimising repatriation spending, the records of Wellington men provide ample evidence of compassion and careful consideration of each case by both the state Repatriation Department and local authorities.

Cyril Paisley: Tuberculosis.

Although tuberculosis was one of the two conditions (alongside mental illness) which 'dominated the history of the aftermath', Butler devotes relatively little space to discussion of lung conditions, due principally to the difficulty of associating lung conditions with warfare.[119] Alongside TB, chronic bronchitis, 'fibrosis of the lungs' and emphysema figure prominently in the Repat files. Butler pays even less attention to these.[120] This section first examines Cyril Paisley's post-war struggle with TB, followed by discussion of other lung conditions suffered by Wellington men, to the consternation of the doctors trying to treat them. Straw is the only contemporary researcher who provides a detailed study of TB among returned men.[121]

Cyril Paisley, brother of Les and Selwyn, served in the AIF in Egypt and France from 1915 to 1919, and on discharge at age 24 was considered fit for work.[122] He had suffered multiple gun-shot wounds (to the right arm, left thigh and left hand) and appendicitis on service. He undertook a correspondence course in accounting and returned to his pre-war occupation as a bank clerk, at York and later Kalgoorlie and Menzies in the goldfields.[123] Although receiving medical treatment, his employment rendered him ineligible for a pension. When his appendix problem recurred in 1923, he unsuccessfully applied for a pension.[124] In 1924, the Bunbury press reported: 'Mr Cyril Paisley's many friends will be pleased to hear he is recovering from his recent illness and is now enjoying a lengthy holiday in the hills'.[125] This was a euphemistic reference to the Wooroloo Sanatorium, where TB cases were treated, yet it was not until late 1925 that tuberculosis appeared in Cyril's Repat file. He was coughing and 'rather thin and introspective', had lost six months from work with TB 'due to war service', and was receiving a full pension.[126]

Butler places TB second to mental disorders in its post-war public profile due to its extreme complexity and the community's fear of it.[127] He considered TB sufferers among the most tragic because of their 'hopeless outlook and miserable death' and because of the slow recognition of the illness. Nearly 300 men died of TB prior to discharge and 2,000 men were discharged with the disease, although Cyril was not among them. In fact, TB ran in his mother's family. Cyril's uncle, Daniel Wallace McGregor, was diagnosed with TB in 1950 after many years of treatment for 'chronic bronchitis'.[128]

Cyril's TB forced his resignation from the bank in late 1926, and he took up outdoor work as a 'tally clerk' at Northam.[129] Suffering a 'slight cough' and depression, he was granted several months' treatment in a Toowoomba (Queensland) clinic which produced some improvement, but he was still unwell.[130] One year later, his 'cough was less troublesome since giving up smoking,' but his new job had caused his condition to deteriorate.[131] Early in 1929, he appealed to Repat: 'during last 3 years I have expended over £1,200 of my own savings in trying to recover my health but without success and now my resources are practically exhausted'.[132] Repat doubted that he had 'complied with 2nd Schedule' for TB cases, and feared that assisting him 'might establish an undesirable precedent'.[133]

The Schedule 2 pension for servicemen and their dependents, was created in 1922 for men who had chronic illnesses necessitating ongoing medical treatment, to enable the patient to receive treatment without financial worries.[134] The Schedule 2 pension required a treatment regime of 'graduated exercises in six progressive grades' learnt in the sanatorium. Only a minority of men systematically followed the program on returning home, authorities conceding that the war-time experience itself was 'detrimental to recovery', as well as a 'lack of co-operation by the tubercular soldier himself'. Cyril's case presented a clear diagnosis, so it seems strange that he had to fight for his pension. In 1922, 520 Australian men were on the special pension for TB, and Cyril was among the 1,047 men in 1927, when numbers peaked, the numbers declining to 716 in 1941.[135]

Cyril reiterated his claim in 1929, when all his resources were exhausted, but two doctors found him a 'healthy looking man despite his breath sounding harsh. His present physical condition is excellent, he is introspective and neurotic – a family failing exhibited by two other pensioners in the same family'.[136] Repat noted that, since giving up work, Cyril had 'done nothing', but, curiously, had not been 'laid up'.[137] So despite his positive test results for TB, his application for a special pension was rejected.[138] A hospital outpatient in 1930, Cyril was suffering 'marked wasting of the lungs' and severe attacks of coughing, but was still smoking a packet of cigarettes a day.[139] He began working intermittently as a clerk in a dairy company to augment his pension, hoping to 'live outdoors a bit more'.[140] He had given up all outside interests and felt that he could not 'keep going much longer'. A new claim for a pension increase was rejected because he was employed.[141] Test results remained inconclusive, as pneumococci were detected and X-rays showed TB, but, unaccountably, doctors did not diagnose TB.[142]

Cyril had his appendix out in 1934, causing consternation when the procedure was conducted at a private rather than a public hospital, but he felt 'much better'.[143] The improvement was of short duration, as, in August 1936, aged 42, influenza and pleurisy forced him to give up work. [144] He was sleeping for most of the day, feeling like a 'wet rag', his war wounds aching, and he was looking grey haired and anxious.[145] He recovered sufficiently to take an extended trip to the eastern states later in the year.

Cyril married quietly in 1938, twenty years after the war and after years of poor health, fruitless pension appeals and two years' unemployment.[146] His wife, whom he may have met while working in Northam after his discharge, was from a pioneering family.[147] Although Cyril was playing bowls, he was losing weight, nervy and 'upset by excitement and noise' and having 'frequent dreams about war'.[148] The considerable deterioration of his handwriting was a visible manifestation of his condition, but this appears to have been overlooked by the authorities.[149] Cyril now claimed exposure to gas during the war but his condition was classed as 'quiescent TB'.[150]

In early 1940, Cyril again took up clerical work, the further deterioration in his writing suggesting declining physical condition, and he was soon off work again, nervy and depressed.[151] Apart from a stay in hospital in 1942, he appears to have worked full-time in the Taxation Department for the next four years, the civil service's policy of giving preference to returned men overriding fears about his TB.[152] A pension claim for a son born in February 1943 was rejected as being too long after the war, the provisions of Schedule 2 notwithstanding.[153] The birth of a child must have brought great joy to Cyril and his wife after the dismal years since their marriage, however, it was to bring fresh worries for Cyril. After three anxious weeks with pleurisy, an x-ray report found 'fresh signs and symptoms' of TB and now, emphysema.[154] He continued working at the Taxation Department with regular checks on his now-acute TB, but he was smoking again.[155] In 1949, the family moved nearer to his work, but Cyril was haunted by the death of his mother.[156] His 'terrible cough' soon rendered him unfit for work as a threat to public health and he was ordered to repay an over-paid pension.[157] His request for a 'not a menace' certificate from the Repat Hospital was denied as, according to his doctor, he was, in fact, 'a menace to public health'.[158] Hospitalisation naturally conflicted with his desire to be with his seven-year-old son.[159]

Cyril was to live one more year, in and out of hospital and still smoking.[160] When he was in hospital, he wanted to go home, despite fear of infecting his wife and son, and all the authorities could do was to check his wife for TB and immunise his son. In May 1951, he was declared totally and permanently disabled, but incredibly, he still had to claim sustenance for time spent in hospital.[161] He was finally awarded 100% pension and he died in hospital in late 1951, among the longer-lived TB sufferers.[162]

Two months after Cyril's death, his wife Edith sent a plaintive note to the hospital requesting her husband's personal belongings.[163] This seems a long time since his death, and suggests that apart from the harrowing years she had spent during Cyril's long illness, she may well have undergone some type of nervous collapse of her own after his death. She was now a 'war widow' and 'rather worried about her child's schooling'. The son suffered the usual childhood injuries and illnesses, all the more difficult for his mother to deal with alone, but the authorities responded sympathetically.[164] By 1978, Edith was a 'pleasant older lady' who suffered age-related illnesses which, however, did not prevent her taking an Asian tour.[165] Edith died in 1990 after a widowhood lasting nearly 40 years.

Cyril was remarkable for his determination to work after several years' absence, in the face of serious illness and scepticism from the authorities.

At work, his cough must have caused concern, and, on the evidence of his handwriting, he must have appeared frail. His case illustrates the determination of the authorities to keep men working in the face of conflicting priorities regarding public health and finance.

Alf Gray: Chronic Bronchitis

Just as Thomson's subjects usually operated in urban settings, a high proportion of Charlie Snell's friends returned to urban employment.[166] Alfred Clifton Gray endured chronic bronchitis, a crippling lung condition with a chronic cough which kept even his neighbours awake at night. Bronchitis, fibrosis of the lungs and various other 'lung conditions' affected nearly 12,000 men in 1931, yet these conditions rated only passing mention by Butler. Chronic bronchitis has largely escaped scrutiny in the repatriation literature, although Scates writes of men 'who coughed their lives away'.[167]

A painter and decorator before enlistment, Alfred Clifton Gray was accepted for service on his second attempt in late 1916, having been rejected earlier that year for 'faulty teeth and painful varicocele'.[168] In France, in 1918, he spent 70 days in hospital with VD, yet soon after his return to battle, he was awarded the Military Medal for 'conspicuous gallantry, pluck and endurance' while acting as battalion runner at Belléglise (Peyronne).[169] His citation noted that despite heavy casualties among runners, he repeatedly carried 'important dispatches under intense enemy bombardment', and several journeys guiding food wagons to the troops.[170] After war's end, he spent one month in hospital with probable Spanish influenza, returning to Australia on a hospital ship. [171]

Alf's discharge report in October 1919 after six months in hospital stated that he was well, was gaining weight and suffering no disability, and would received medical benefits for ongoing treatment.[172] He returned to work with his former employer and was married at St Georges Cathedral in 1920.[173] He applied for assistance for his dependent mother and for purchase of tools of trade and furniture.[174] He was regarded as a 'good type of man' who had developed 'a good little business by his own efforts since his discharge'.[175] His wife bore children in 1921 and 1924.

In January 1921, the appeals and medical investigations which he was to endure for much of the rest of his life began. His background as an athlete, his 'chronic bronchitis', and discharge medically unfit were noted.[176] Despite his incessant night-time cough that kept the family awake, he worked part time as a 'jobbing contractor'.[177] There is a gap in the record from March 1925 to January 1931, when he described himself as a 'master painter' with 20 employees.[178] He had been receiving medical attention privately, but now needed assistance from Repat, and for the rest of his life, 1931–48, he endured monthly medical examinations and multiple hospitalisations.

In 1931, Alf was investigated for pulmonary TB and despite 'frothy blood-stained sputum', tests were negative.[179] By this time, X-rays could distinguish between TB and types of 'pulmonary fibrosis' such as emphysema and cancer.[180] When asked about his treatment for VD, he was 'certain in my own mind I only had scabies', and his Wasserman test was negative.[181] Testimonials from neighbours and friends supported his claims of coughing and spitting blood.[182] A female neighbour described him as a 'respectable citizen who coughs all night'.[183] Others referred to his 'indifferent health from the war', stating that he was a 'temperate drinker', 'battalion runner', and his '"cobbers" have known for years that he is a very sick man'.[184] His wife provided a record of times she had to call the doctor and remedies Alf had tried, and appealed to his lodge for extra benefits, but while one doctor described him as 'deserving every consideration', another could not support his appeal.[185] At this time, his disability from chronic bronchitis was deemed 20% due to war service.[186] In January 1932, Alf applied for sustenance for the pneumonia he developed whenever he worked hard. He was granted 30 days and in 1933 his incapacity was considered to be 30%.[187]

There is a gap in the record from April 1935 to October 1939, by which time he was 'no good at all, his coughing at night enough to send anyone to the grave'.[188] In February 1944, all his illnesses were accepted as war caused. [189] He then applied unsuccessfully for the funds to build a home near the sea.[190] He was now totally disabled due to war service and his pension was increased to 100%, with medical expenses.[191] At around this time, feeling 'rotten', he stopped smoking.[192] In the light of current medical knowledge, it seems incredible that Alf should have continued smoking throughout most of his life. When Alf died in August 1948, his wife received financial benefits from his lodge, his insurance fund, and funeral expenses from Repat.[193] The post-mortem autopsy revealed emphysema. [194]

Alf Gray was one of many WWI veterans who, suffering Spanish influenza, but with no record of wartime gassing, suffered chest problems. He was investigated for TB, with negative results. He is one of many who returned from the war a heavy smoker, and, post-war, worked as a painter. It is possible that, in the absence of Occupational Health and Safety regulations, his occupation, as well as his smoking contributed to his disease. Whatever the causes, he endured a relatively long and miserable post-war life, affecting family, friends and neighbours who witnessed his cough and debility. His wife was among the women who bore the brunt of the care of the ailing veteran.[195]

Norman Bird: War-torn Soldier and his Wife

Norman Bird and his wife fit into multiple narratives: he in the context of the soldier who never recovered from the war and as a victim of difficult-to-diagnose post-war lung disease, and she in the context of the wife advocating for her wounded soldier, caring for veterans of two world wars and pleading for justice for herself and her family. Norman was born in Victoria in 1889.[196] A 'timber getter' before enlistment, he served with the 44th Battalion in England and France for the last two years of the war. Working in traffic control, he was never in the trenches, but during his service, he was hospitalised with tonsillitis, measles and pneumonia, and was 'never right since'.[197] He came home on a hospital ship, and on discharge was described as a 'thin delicate youth' suffering from 'toxic myocarditis' and other 'heart symptoms', the result of 'stress and strain of service'. He was awarded a 40% pension for 'effort syndrome' on the basis of his heart symptoms, an unusual diagnosis given the lack of acceptance by authorities at that time that the general conditions of war could produce such symptoms.[198]

Norman resumed work at Mornington timber mills suffering chest pain, heart and lung problems and losing weight, his incapacity deemed at 25%. He married in 1921, and for the next 24 years his wife cared for him as he struggled to work with gradually deteriorating health, and fought endless battles with Repat for pension increases and medical assistance. Until 1931, thin, pale and debilitated, he continued working at the mill, 'helped by his mates' and suffering heart, lung and increasing gastric problems. Sometimes unable to work for months at a time, he endured six-monthly interviews and medical examinations by Repat, and seemingly the only assistance they could offer was cod liver oil.

After the mill closed, and now diagnosed with chronic bronchitis, Norman worked intermittently through the 1930s, variously as a labourer, 'relief worker' and forestry worker, 'crook in the stomach' and vomiting repeatedly.[199] Incredibly, in 1934 Repat recommended discontinuing his meagre pension entitlement, causing his wife to write to Repat on his behalf, demanding, 'can it be definitely said that effort syndrome is his only disability due to war?'[200] Repat replied curtly that his condition was not organic and that he needed reassurance.[201] Bird's pension remained at 25% from his discharge until his death. In 1945, now diagnosed with Hodgkins disease, he was working as a night watchman, vomiting, and in pain. He died in October 1945, the post-mortem showing lung cancer as cause of death. This led Repat to reject the war as cause of death, since there was 'no connection between war and lung cancer'.[202]

Dorothy Bird appealed for a pension, demonstrating a clear understanding of medical reports and a woman's sense of injustice.[203] She was now caring for a son suffering the effects of WWII service in Borneo, finding it hard 'to give my husband stuff to keep him going, all the extras I could afford and some I couldn't'.[204] She described the futility of applying for pension increases:

> *the many tiresome journeys to Perth waiting in cold halls. Women are pleased to do all they can for their men. It's very hard after all the struggle to lose them and live the later part of their lives thinking what might have been. It's time some of the wives and mothers were put on these medical boards. The mill manager will give you some idea of how my husband suffered. I only want what I think is due to me as these two wars have robbed me of my husband and put a sick son for me to look after (sic) doing his share at Balikpapan.*[205]

In another appeal, 'I was married to my husband for 23 years 10 months. I think I am entitled.'[206] The doctor who replied to her claim was sympathetic, but

> *medical science at the present time cannot be definite about the cause of cancer. I'm afraid I have not been very helpful, but it is no good telling you there is hope if I cannot see it. The Repat know what a hard trail they have set you on.*[207]

In 1948, Bird's death was finally accepted as war-caused. He is another whose death was likely due, at least in part, to the wartime enthusiasm for sending cigarettes to the men at the front. At the time, in ignorance of the link between smoking and a range of medical conditions such as lung cancer, it must have seemed like a simple thing to do for their men. Dorothy Bird lived for another 45 years until her death at 86, presumably in paid employment in the twenty years between her husband's death and receipt of a pension in 1967.[208] Her later years were beset by health issues but she remained at home with a daughter to look in on her.

Norman was not exposed to gas in the trenches, and although there is no reference to cigarette smoking in his files, it is almost certain that he was a smoker. Until the 1920s, lung cancer was relatively rare, but was becoming increasingly common and was often blamed on poison gas exposure in the war or the global influenza pandemic.[209] Between the 1930s and 1950s, combined evidence from population studies, cellular pathology, animal experimentation and the identification of cancer-causing chemicals in cigarette smoke proved unequivocally that smoking was the cause, although 'scientific' rebuttal by the tobacco companies began in the 1940s.[210] It is highly likely, then, that Bird's lung cancer was war-caused, yet it is not surprising that Repat did not make the connection.

Jack Blythe: Shrapnel Cancer

John Howard Drummond Blythe had difficulty finding his niche after the war and fought long battles with Repat over a late-onset war-related illness which captured the attention of one medical officer. Jack was a practicing Catholic, champion swimmer and football umpire before the war.[211] He enlisted in Queensland and served at Gallipoli and France, winning the Military Medal and returning to Australia in 1918.[212] Jack's failure to go before a medical board on discharge was to have long-term consequences.[213] His first pension claim soon after his return to Australia cited nervous debility and a bomb wound in the back which rendered him unfit for heavy work, and made it difficult to find suitable work.[214] His mother and sister were dependent on him and he never married.

Jack's selection by the local RSL to accompany Generals Hobbs and Birdwood on a visit to the district was a mark of respect, and with the support of the Bunbury Repatriation Committee, he successfully applied to take over the local swimming baths.[215] This venture did not last and after retraining in the sawmills, in 1922, he worked as a farm manager at Tambellup, later spending three years as foreman at a group settlement in the South West until he was dismissed for absences from work and drinking bouts at weekends.[216] In 1927, while working as a telephone linesman, he applied for a pension, citing testimonials regarding his good character and the fact that he 'would not apply for a pension without reasonable justification'.[217] In 1928, he pleaded: 'I worked myself to a standstill in

ANZAC, France and England for king and country'. A Repat official retorted, 'it is all bosh that it was war caused' and he was again refused a pension.[218]

Blythe returned to Queensland where he worked in a meat factory and underground mining, before taking clerical work.[219] In 1942 he served in New Guinea and Queensland.[220] In 1953, a tumour was removed from his lung and a further shadow on the lung was detected during a routine TB survey in Bunbury.[221] He unsuccessfully appealed for a pension, despite assistance from Gordon Freeth MHR, and worked until 1955.[222] Between 1957 and 1960, Blythe appealed repeatedly for a pension, claiming his condition was war-caused, with doctors bemoaning his 'pathetic efforts to get help'.[223] When in 1959, a metal fragment was found in his lung, his doctor cited an article describing a similar case, and a 40% pension was granted.[224] His case was taken up again in 1960 by a doctor who had seen cases in London where foreign bodies had migrated and produced cancers in unusual positions, and in 1961 Blythe was finally granted a full pension and a rubber mattress after further appeals from Gordon Freeth MLA and Blythe's sister, who was caring for him.[225] Yet still, according to Repat, he was 'making the most of his disabilities and is determined to get everything possible'.[226] Blythe died of pneumonia later that year, and after a further year, his death was accepted as war related and funeral expenses were granted.[227]

Doctors such as Bunbury's Simon Joel often went to England for some or all of their medical training, and they naturally read the British medical journals, as did the doctor treating Blythe in Bunbury during the 1950s. Despite that doctor's enlightened ideas, Repat did not support his findings. The article he cited describes the development of carcinomas at the site of foreign bodies in the lung, including shrapnel received during World War I.[228] The carcinomas developed an average of 24 years after the event, and caused chronic bronchitis in the intervening years. Patients, suffering extreme anxiety, died within months of first admission to hospital. There is no mention in that article of toxicity from the object as the Bunbury doctor suggested. However, the effects of the bizarre habit of eating cordite was first described in 1903, the affected individual appearing aged, his work 'sloppy', his speech incoherent and he suffered bad dreams.[229] Further scientific study on the effects of cordite in 1947 confirmed earlier findings.[230] Consideration of the effects of toxic exposures in war other than gas did not appear until the Vietnam war, just when Jack Blythe was in the final stages of his illness. [231]

War Neurosis and Neurasthenia: 'a silly thing to do'[232]

The term 'neurasthenia' is prominent in the repatriation files, not least those of Wellington veterans examined here. It is one of a range of terms used to describe mental illness in both the primary and secondary sources since the 1914–18 war. The evidence from the Wellington population shows that incomplete understanding of mental illness was a significant factor in the difficulties faced by veterans, compounding the isolation of the medical consulting room. Discussion of mental illness in contemporary sources shows a general understanding of related terms. However, clues left by contemporary writers, recent advances in medical imaging technology, and new psychological understandings shed light on the problem.

Important studies of repatriation in Australia, prior to the opening of the repatriation files in 2014, were made by Lake, Damousi, Thomson, Larssons and Garton.[233] Lake and Damousi make no mention of neurasthenia, Lake using the general term 'mental disorders'.[234] Thomson uses a range of terms including neurosis and shellshock, noting the acceptance of war neurosis as the official term in the 1920s.[235] Thomson reiterates the high proportion of 'mental troubles' among returned soldiers and examines debate over whether 'neurasthenia' was a 'legitimate psychological condition' or a character failing, noting that by 1940, neurosis was accepted as war caused. This understanding is not apparent in the files of the Wellington veterans. Larssons uses the terms 'shellshock' and 'mental soldier'.[236] Thomson also explores psycho-neuroses, and 'acute mania'.[237] According to Garton, 'nervous breakdown', 'shellshock', and 'war neurosis', were the most commonly-used terms in World War I, replaced by 'combat exhaustion' or 'battle fatigue' in World War II.[238]

Reporting on the newly-opened Repatriation files and influenced by Butler, Scates and Oppenheimer generally use the term 'neurasthenia', suggesting that some medical men came close to the modern concept of post traumatic stress disorder, and linking post-war struggles to mental illness.[239] As the most recent study on the post war lives of Australian veterans, Straw's findings from the repatriation files come closest to my own. Commenting on the man 'walking around with shrapnel in him', she links war-time injury to war neurosis.[240] Straw makes no reference to 'disordered action of the heart' (henceforth DAH) or neurasthenia, instead referring to war trauma and war neurosis, nervous disorders and nervous breakdown. Added to the stress of trying to do physical work with war wounds, war neurosis resulted in decades of poor health and intermittent work, as seen in the post-war lives of the Paisley brothers.[241] Straw equates war neurosis with Post Traumatic Stress Disorder, a combination of anxiety, debility and depression.

Butler's analysis of war neurosis provides the official diagnostic context into which the Wellington veterans fell, and demonstrates that official confusion is reflected in the difficulty local doctors had in defining and accounting for mental conditions. In wartime, Australian medical staff, many of them graduates of British medical schools, worked closely with British medical officials, naturally adopting the British position on war neurosis.[242] Mental illness was seen as a moral failing and equated with cowardice and malingering. The confusion over definitions of mental illness is especially evident in Butler's 'Statistics of the War', which cites a range of definitions applied between 1915 to 1940.

Butler outlines the development of terminology, from 'railway spine' in 1881 to the various types of insanity, or psychoneurosis, all considered disorders of conduct, which had been described by the outbreak of war. In military camps in Australia, mental illness was initially categorised as 'diseases of the nervous system' and 'DAH'.[243] Mentally ill patients evacuated from Gallipoli were classified into three major groups: firstly, men who wilfully disregarded accepted rules; secondly, 'neurosis' sufferers, whether 'neurasthenia', 'traumatic shock and shell-shock', or DAH, sometimes called 'heart trouble', which was replaced by 'effort syndrome' by 1918.[244] The third major group, sufferers of psychoses, dementias, delusional insanity, exhaustion psychosis, compulsive disorders and stupor had lost touch with reality. The difficulty of distinguishing between neurosis and psychosis remained. Butler notes the gradual recognition that environmental conditions could influence human conduct. Throughout the war, predisposition and family history remained important causative factors, always coloured by military concern over malingering.

At the war's end, 'war neurosis' was the overarching term applied to Australian troops suffering mental illness resulting from war service, and included 'conversion hysteria' which had visible symptoms, and 'neurasthenia', related to anxiety, with a range of nervous symptoms.[245] 'Disordered action of the heart' or 'effort syndrome' was recognised as a war neurosis, but its physical manifestation rendered it distinct from the purely mental condition. However, uncertainty continued with 'war neurosis *or* neurasthenia' and 'neurosis following "shell-shock"' persisting in diagnoses.[246] It was already noted that men could return to work after long periods of illness, a phenomenon which appears frequently in the Wellington population. By 1919, it was recognised that chronic 'shell-shock' could appear after men were evacuated from the front, and was now described as 'hysterical', 'anxious', 'neurasthenic', or 'confusional'.

The Post War Medical Advisory Boards defined 'neurasthenic' cases as those that would 'otherwise not be certifiable as insane', thereby excluding psychosis sufferers. However, confusion remained among the 'types and degrees' of neurasthenia, which included shell-shock, 'definitely neurasthenic', 'borderland (sic) mental', and neurasthenics 'of the debilitated heart (DAH) or thyrotoxic type'.[247] By 1924, wartime events and environment were accepted as causes for mental conditions, although pension claims for nervous complaints could still be considered 'neurotic embroidery' to physical damage, and self-help remained the best remedy.[248] Pension data for the period 1924–40, show mental illnesses of various types among veterans at around 20%.[249] Significantly, the 'war neurosis' group was growing: from 2,600 to 3,300, and will be discussed in a later section.

The 'K Card' enquiry of 1931, carried out by the official medical historian, with the assistance of the Repatriation Commission, covered around 40% of the men on war pensions, listing every disability as defined by doctors treating veterans, and providing a useful reference point for understanding contemporary definitions of mental illness.[250] Pensioners suffered an average of 1.46 causes of disablement, meaning that patients could be pensioned for wounds as well as a physical or mental illness. Over 400 conditions (other than wounds) were recorded, with the terms 'trouble' and 'condition' used multiple times, reflecting overlap in terminology and measurement.[251] Likely mental cases appear as 31 conditions, including four 'neurotic', and two 'nervous' conditions. Mental illness groups with 100 or more sufferers include: shell shock, neurasthenia, neurosis, nervous debility, shell shock concussion, effort syndrome (including DAH), tachycardia, insanity, and 'mental', the last two probable psychosis. However, some diseases of the heart are possibly also war neurosis, including 'cardiac condition' (mentioned twice), 'cardiac trouble' (twice), and 'heart trouble'.[252] 'Debility' also reappears. This summation produces results well above Butler's three thousand or so cases for the period 1924–40 and reflects his comment that mental illness accounted for 80% of the medical outcomes from the war.[253]

In 1936, when service pensions were awarded to all servicemen on reaching the age of 65, just two classes of mental illness were recognised: 'nervous system', and 'neurosis, psycho-neurosis and mental disorders', shell shock and neurasthenia having disappeared.[254] The rate of insanity (psychosis) among ex-soldiers remained comparable to that of the civilian population.[255] In the period 1940 to 1943, moral and mental disorders numbered three to one over all others. However, 'acute cardiac trouble', 'effort syndrome' or 'DAH', attributed to war also accounted for a large group of pensions. Although Butler still claimed a pre-existing nervous weakness in a majority of sufferers, he was beginning to recognise the post-war struggle as a cause of neurosis.

The number of patients presenting with disabilities relating to gunshot wounds (GSW) remained high throughout the period 1924 to 1940, at almost 3,000 from around 75,000 pensioners. This was also noted by Straw.[256] Besides organic diseases affecting returned men, ongoing problems related to wounds, which might have been expected to diminish with time, added considerably to their burden. Research has shown that war neurosis (other than insanity) increased during the period, after a slight decline in the 1920s, whilst problems with gunshot wounds remained relatively static.

It is possible that for men like the Paisley brothers, old war wounds, and in Selwyn's case, malaria, contributed significantly to their reported 'neurasthenia'. Butler's recognition that post-war trials created their own stressors that contributed to the increasing incidence of neurasthenia, compounded by the 1930s Depression, is supported by both statistical and anecdotal evidence.[257] Always moralistic yet genuinely sympathetic to the plight of neurosis sufferers, Butler remained torn between the reality of the suffering and his belief in the power of the Anzac spirit.[258]

Butler was not alone in his struggle to comprehend the connection between war and mental illness. Shortly after the outbreak of war, a British medical doctor on the Western Front described how an officer, 'morose and apathetic' one day, 'blew his head off' the next.[259] The doctor thought it 'a silly thing to do', but later recognised it as a new kind of illness, and examined fear as a moral and medical problem of war. Various medical conditions have been found to be induced by stress. Guillain-Barré syndrome, an auto-immune disease first described among World War I soldiers, was attributed to physical and psychological stress and the unhygienic conditions of trench warfare.[260] It has been identified recently among survivors of the Great East Japan Earthquake of 2011.[261] Similarly, a history of trauma or PTSD increases the risk of developing lupus, another autoimmune disease.[262] In 1936, a Canadian researcher found that exposure to stressors such as cold, injury, and excessive physical exercise produced physical changes in the body, independent of the damage itself.[263]

Carl May, a British researcher, reviews contemporary medical disagreement over shell shock and concludes that by 1918, most medical writers had recognised that a syndrome of 'neurasthenic and hysterical' symptoms could result from 'long exposure to horror'.[264] Van Bergen concludes that suppression of fear was the greatest cause of post-war neurosis.[265] In the Australian context, Butler, summing up the 'moral and mental lessons of the war' concluded that moral failing could be prevented by character building, through 'traditional British methods' of physical fitness and leadership.[266] English researcher Joanna Bourke associates emotional breakdown with the 'terrifying impotence and horror of trench warfare'.[267] Like Butler, she attributes some post-war mental illness to the men's fears for their pension.[268] Rae uses the term shell shock throughout her discussion, reiterating Butler's definitions of war neurosis and equating it with post-traumatic stress disorder.[269] In a 2014 re-examination of contemporary literature, Jones and Wessely describe the terms 'neurasthenia', 'shell shock' and 'war neuroses', confirming Butler's terminology and May's association of shellshock with malingering.[270] They note the recognition during World War II of the links between numbers of physical and psychological causalities.[271] Like Rae, they define PTSD as chronic war neurosis.

Jones and Wessely's claim that delayed onset PTSD is uncommon allows for the contribution of other factors in the post-war traumatic symptoms that appeared in the Wellington men.[272] Recent studies have found that veterans can be more sensitive to bereavement and disruption to family life, and that severe physical wounds 'almost inevitably' lead to psychological trauma. This supports the conclusion that the post-war disabilities of the Wellington veterans which prevented them from working and supporting their families, added to disputes with Repat, significantly increased their post-war trauma. PTSD now dominates diagnosis for mental illness associated with trauma among military and civilian patients, and includes delayed onset and the influence of life stress following the original trauma, a likely scenario for Vera Paisley, whose post-war life will be described in the next chapter.[273] Symptoms of PTSD such as insomnia, irritability, hypervigilance and startle reaction repeatedly appear in Repat files. Only Straw's and the present study have identified injury as a predictor of war neurosis in WWI survivors.[274]

Studies of survivors of bombings in France between 1982 and 1987 showed PTSD rates of 31% two to three years and 18% eight years later, also consistent with Butler's figures.[275] Disordered action of the heart has disappeared from discussion of PTSD, but heart irregularities in otherwise healthy individuals are now attributed to anxiety, depression or physical causes including excessive intake of nicotine, a significant factor among World War I soldiers.[276]

Studies of the catastrophic September 11 attacks in New York in 2001 make a useful comparison with the Great War.[277] Outcomes shared by survivors of war and 9/11 include the consistency of neurosis symptoms at around 20%, similarity in the types of symptoms, the co-incidence of respiratory and gastric illness, and the delayed onset of symptoms, whether psychological or organic, such as cancers. These modern studies also consider exposure to dust and chemicals emanating from the collapsing buildings. The only reference to chemicals as a hazard in World War I is in discussion of gas warfare, yet any eye-witness report of the war, including Snell's own, comments on smoke, smells and 'fireworks'. Like World War I survivors, late-onset PTSD and cancers have developed eight to ten years after the event among exposed individuals.[278] Researchers have found that among survivors who suffer PTSD, 32% sustained an injury, comparable to the high incidence of injury among Wellington veterans.[279] The strongest demographic risk factor for 9/11 surviviors was low income, which echoes the post-war financial problems faced by Wellington veterans.[280] The absence of moral judgements of 9/11 survivors, such as malingering or exaggerated reporting is notable. It seems unimaginable that authorities would question the moral fibre of survivors in diagnosing the effects of a catastrophe such as 9/11.[281]

Recent medical research has also identified biological markers for PTSD.[282] Among Gulf War veterans, 30% experience multiple symptom conditions such as major depressive disorder and chronic fatigue syndrome, alongside PTSD.[283] Neurological testing has found abnormal responses to painful stimuli in Gulf War illness sufferers and researchers are now focusing on exposure to toxic agents and brain – body connections.[284] Acevedo reviews recent research on sensory processing sensitivity (SPS), found in roughly 20% of humans, concluding that high SPS is associated with greater than average sensitivity and responsiveness to environmental and social stimuli.[285] Genetic markers such as serotonin transporters become depressed in response to stressful life events in high-SPS individuals, suggesting that greater sensitivity to stress is not a weakness of character, but an inbuilt characteristic in a significant proportion of the population. It helps to account for those whose neurosis developed after the war in response to the endless confrontations with Repat. This is evident in the letters of the veterans, their families and the doctors treating them. While post-war medical staff intuitively looking for physical clues to the illnesses confronting them lacked modern diagnostic tools, in future catastrophes, the new diagnostic tools will enable sufferers of psychological distress to receive early treatment.[286]

Norman Holtzman: Chronic Bronchitis and Depression

Norman Guy Holtzman perhaps comes nearest of the Wellington veterans to a clear case of PTSD, despite his situation being complicated by chronic bronchitis. Norman was unusual in being specifically diagnosed with depression by several doctors, who noted that he 'appeared' depressed, and he was also unusual in that his wife figures only marginally in his repatriation files. Norman, a classmate of Snell's, fought with the 11th Battalion in Egypt and France.[287] He suffered gunshot wounds and gassing, resulting in around five months in hospital, and on discharge, pulmonary fibrosis, bronchitis and oedema in the right arm and hand were recognised as war-caused.[288] Norman returned to his pre-war occupation as a plumber in Bunbury and to the social life of the town, however he was far from well.[289] Throughout the 1920s, he suffered pain from his war wounds, chronic bronchitis and the 'depression', which was diagnosed soon after the war. In 1919, he was prescribed a 'tonic for depression', and he lost several months from work each year due to 'depression and weakness', which his doctors ascribed to his wounds and cough.[290] With the support of testimonials that he was a 'clean living good type of man in a good family situation and entirely to be trusted', he was awarded a minimal 10% pension in 1926.[291]

Norman's irritability, depression and difficulty concentrating continued, although, unlike Selwyn Paisley and others, he never reported sleep problems.[292] While his doctors noted that he 'suffered severe mental strain the last time he was wounded' and had suffered 'impaired mental faculties' since, they felt that his 'neurosis' was due to post war worries.[293] This too was unusual, in that doctors usually equated depression with malingering. In 1929, unable to work for seven months in the previous year, claiming that with his 'nerve and lung trouble', his pension was 'inadequate to provide for wife and family while he is confined to bed', his pension was increased to 25%.[294] Norman spent late 1929 in hospital for his depression, a chronic cough, pain in old wounds, and a metal fragment was found in his skull.[295]

Although she bore three children, Norman's wife is surprisingly absent from the record, with only a wartime letter enquiring about his injuries, and his children do not appear to have received pensions. Norman was apparently unscathed by a fall from a windmill in 1931, but his symptoms continued, keeping him from work for days at a time.[296] His doctors were unsympathetic, describing him as a 'neurotic type of man', now suggesting that he was 'lazy', certain that his condition was 'post-war caused', and 'neurosis' was questionable.[297] His chronic bronchitis was investigated periodically, but since his wartime gassing was well-documented, it is not frequently mentioned, as it was among men whose exposure to gas was questionable.[298] Norman was at least able to enjoy the companionship of his mates on occasions, although the newer arrivals in the district could lead him astray.[299]

Norman's two sons served in World War II, one spending more than two years as a prisoner of the Japanese in Thailand.[300] This must have caused distress, and in 1943 he unsuccessfully appealed for assistance for ongoing stomach complaints and fainting.[301] In the 1950s, Norman's 'mental depression' continued, although he enjoyed companionship at bowls.[302] By 1957, at age 66, climbing on roofs in the course of his work was becoming difficult, so he was taking light work with other plumbers, and he felt entitled to retire on a pension.[303] Although the scars of war were still visible, his health was considered good for his age, and he was granted 80% pension for his war-caused fibrosis and chronic bronchitis.[304] Around this time, he gave up smoking.

In 1960, although women were hitherto absent from Norman's record, it was noted that his wife and two sisters were still alive.[305] He continued working until he was hospitalised for bronchitis.[306] He made five trips to Victoria and one to New Zealand, which must have provided some pleasure after a life of unremitting work and sickness.[307] Eventually, a doctor in Victoria suggested that he should be entitled to a full pension, for which he appealed, claiming that having to 'clear his throat up to 30 times per day' caused him 'discomfort when in company'.[308] The doctor confirmed the diagnosis of 'mild chronic bronchitis and emphysema'.[309] In view of his age, he should have received a service pension, yet it is unclear whether this appeal was successful.

Norman made his last visit to Victoria in 1971, and in 1972, his right leg was amputated above the knee and a prosthesis fitted.[310] He unsuccessfully claimed that the problem was war-caused.[311] However, he was still able to enjoy outings to the races, reunion dinners and Christmas at home, although he lost contact with his Victorian friend.[312] In 1976, we read that his daughter in Harvey was caring for him following further surgery.[313] Back in Bunbury in 1979, 88 years old and 'very independent', Norman was showing signs of dementia, applying for ambulance benefits because taxis were overcharging him and 'I do not like to be robbed'.[314] Once placed in permanent care, his serious disagreement with room-mates caused disruption at the hospital.[315] After Norman's death in September 1979, the Department of Veterans Affairs paid just 15% of his funeral costs.[316]

Until the formulation of diagnostic criteria for PTSD, sufferers of war neurosis, like Norman Holtzman, when seeking treatment and assistance faced diagnostic confusion and scepticism about their motives. However, even with PTSD as a diagnosis, some war veterans still face problems of acceptance of their disability. It is possible that with new diagnoses based on neurological imaging and genetic decoding, survivors of trauma will have more ready access to treatment and will never again experience the additional post-war suffering of veterans of WWI. These narratives enhance the findings of Garton, Scates, Larsson and others who have highlighted the painful outcomes of war for veterans, complicated by battles with doctors and Repat for assistance for themselves and their families. In their dealing with Repat officials the men were seemingly alone, yet they all had wives, sisters or daughters who tended them in their illnesses. The next chapter will examine interactions between women and the repatriation department.

6

WOMEN AND REPATRIATION

Vera returned from the war a nervous wreck … her three brothers are wrecks from the war.[1]

Women as carers and advocates for their veterans

We have seen how men tried to negotiate with Repat for better post-war outcomes for themselves and their families. Women too were forced into advocacy roles, for themselves and for ailing veterans. Women caring for disabled veterans sought better treatment for their men. Bunbury's wartime nurses were also dependent on Repat throughout their post-war lives, some leading productive and relatively untroubled lives, while extreme suffering of one nurse was to test family and Repat resources to the limit. There were a few assertive women who may have taken advantage of Repat for their own ends, adding to the already complex task of the local repatriation committee.

The wives and other female relatives of war veterans were forced to renegotiate gender roles in caring for shattered bodies as men struggled to re-establish themselves in civilian occupations.[2] Larsson has described this process as 'invisible', since the term 'caregiver' was not yet defined, yet many Wellington women were highly visible in the repatriation files.[3] Repat awarded pensions on the basis of percentage disability, and only the blinded Dick Clarke received a full pension. The partially disabled struggled to undertake paid work in an attempt to supplement the pension and support a family. Wives or other family members shared the burden, as they themselves were unable to participate in the paid workforce. The repatriation files reveal the women's perspectives on the struggles of their husbands, fathers, siblings, sons and neighbours. The invisible woman is rare, and the women's testimony speaks eloquently of the intertwined emotional, social and economic costs of war.[4]

Claude Clifton never married, and must have been cared for by his mother and sisters for the fourteen years he lived after the war. While testimonials from long-time friends bear witness to his struggles, much of his suffering and physical deterioration occurred in the privacy of the family home. For men who married before or during the war, the wife inevitably took on the caring role.[5] War-caused problems would already have been evident to women who married returned soldiers, yet many Wellington men married ten or more years after the war. By this time, for Selwyn Paisley's doctor, for example, marriage seemed incompatible with his physical and mental condition.[6] When Selwyn's brother Cyril married Edith in 1938, he was already a semi-invalid.[7]

The wives of Wellington veterans tended to infected shrapnel wounds, trench foot, pain from abdominal adhesions, frequent vomiting, interminable coughing, and post-operative care. There were constant reminders of the physical traumas the men had suffered in the visible scars of men like Les Paisley and the Clarke brothers.[8] Added to this was the shame of male dependence that many of the women would have encountered.[9]

Many of the Wellington men lived long enough to develop age-related conditions, adding to the war-caused problems the women were already dealing with. Reg Ibbotson and Norman Holtzman's leg amputations late in life increased the burden on their long-suffering wives and, later, daughters.[10] These men, and Dugald Leitch, a war-time amputee, became unmanageable in old age, forcing family members to consign them to professional care, a process fraught with emotional pain.[11] Blinded, Dick Clarke lived for 66 years after the war, and although independent-minded, was cared for by his wife for 45 years, and after her death, by his daughters.[12]

Women also cared for men who suffered mental illness, sharing the social and emotional burden as officials made moral judgements about family traits and mental weakness, even the 'mendacity' of veterans, and noted the despair of wives and siblings.[13] The stigma of mental illness was exacerbated as women endured the humiliation of their husband's having to obtain character references from friends and employers.[14] Cyril Paisley's wife must have been aware of official scepticism over Cyril's compliance with instructions, and the doctor's linking of Cyril's neurotic tendencies with family failing.[15] We can imagine the trials Wisbey Sinclair's wife endured as doctors struggled to separate his neurosis symptoms from his thyroid problems, or Reg Ibbotson's wife sharing in Reg's nostalgia for family in England.[16] Norman Holtzman's wife had to endure the indignity of having her husband labelled as lazy and neurotic, while privately enduring his irritability, depression and periods of incapacity.[17] Yet she would also have been aware of dangers inherent in his work: climbing windmills (in 1931), and roofs (until 1957), hardly the habits of a lazy or neurotic man.[18]

We can imagine the sense of helplessness and the emotional strain on women as they shared their husband's battles with Repat. Technically, a pension was a recognition of disability, yet Wellington men were forced to work so long as their pension was less than 100%, and sometime as low as 10%. Pensions were subject to regular review, entailing medical examinations and often resulting in reduction or cancellation. Ray Clarke's initial 60% pension was gradually reduced to 30%, even as his incapacity increased.[19] Some appointments were held locally, either with Repat doctors or the local committee. However, Selwyn Paisley frequently had to travel to Perth, causing interruptions to work and leaving his wife alone on the farm. Reg Ibbotson's wife shared the emotional and financial impact of bankruptcy, while Tom Rose's wife shared Tom's seven-year financial battle with Repat. The early deaths of men such as Alf Gray, Selwyn Paisley, and Norman Bird must have provided some justification for the years of appeals to Repat, yet wives suffered the final indignity of fighting for reimbursement of funeral expenses.

Where the veteran's life was short, women were left with the struggle to bring up children and manage businesses alone. Women with large families had to care for and educate children while tending to the needs of a sick husband. Ray Clarke's wife had seven children, hospital costs adding to their financial difficulties, while the loss of two children in their first year was an additional emotional burden.[20] For Hilda Paisley the loss of several babies increased the loneliness of farm life.[21] As Cyril Paisley's condition worsened, his wife's fears for him were complicated by fears for a vulnerable young son.[22]

Some men struggled to settle down. Amputee, Reg Hemingway, moved to Melbourne in 1924, dying around 1950, leaving his wife to a widowhood of nearly 25 years.[23] Reg Ibbotson moved around the state, from a remote pastoral station to a Harvey farm, then Fremantle, to work in a business and then a government department. Richard Moore, with ongoing health problems, worked in various occupations in Carnarvon, several hundred kilometres north of Perth, then Collie, near Bunbury before finally settling in the city. The wives endured social dislocation as well as years of caring for a sick husband.

Women such as Ethel Paisley also wrote letters, pleading their husbands' cases.[24] Dick Clarke's wife maintained contact with the Red Cross, providing feedback and thanking them for their interest in her husband's welfare.[25] Selwyn Paisley's wife, Hilda, had to deal with employees during the periods when she managed the farm, or to work alone when she could not afford help.[26] Alf Gray's wife kept a record of all the times she had to call the doctor and all the remedies he had tried, demonstrating a business-like approach to managing his condition.[27] Others, like Dorothy Bird, pleaded hardship and a sense of injustice in their appeals.[28] She became increasingly assertive in her communications with Repat. After her husband's miserable post-war life, during which he never received more than a 25% pension, she reasserted her entitlement in claiming funeral costs.[29]

The post-war experiences of Bunbury nurses

Several Bunbury women entered the war thanks to their nursing skills, and Jessie Clifton and Vera Paisley, with brothers and cousins at war, may have wanted experiences which were denied to them at home.[30] Rae and McQuilton have shown, how they received recognition for their professionalism despite gendered challenges to their position by their medical superiors.[31] While Butler makes brief reference to nurses' entitlement to repatriation benefits, their post-war lives are only gradually being documented.[32] Williams has researched the small percentage of nurses who took up land in New South Wales and Victoria.[33] Bassett focuses on illness and poverty among former nurses, while Harris has researched their immediate post-war lives, exploring how some survived on pensions while others were forced to keep working.[34]

Jessie Christina Clifton had an eventful four years at war. Born in 1877, and a cousin of Claude Clifton, she was appointed to the Australian Army Nursing Service in 1910.[35] Aged 41 on enlistment, she served as matron in the Sea Transport Corps, making three trips between the UK and Sydney, on a troopship going out and a hospital ship on the return journey. She served on a hospital ship at Gallipoli and was on a ship that was torpedoed in 1915.[36] She had a heart attack in Fremantle while awaiting her next voyage to England, resulting in six weeks in hospital, and six months' home service.[37] In September 1918, on a return trip to Australia, she suffered severe food poisoning while at Sierra Leone. After the war, Jessie worked for some years at Beverley in the wheat belt, before becoming an itinerant nurse in South Perth. In 1956, at age 79, still working and suffering from angina and bronchitis, she claimed a war pension. Officials variously described her as 'a forlorn case' and a 'sprightly old lady', and doubted that her condition was war-caused, rendering her ineligible for a pension.[38] A service pension was suggested, but both were rejected.[39] It is possible that, for some years at least, Jessie was happy to continue working, but to be denied a pension at 79 seems harsh.

The case of another Bunbury nurse raises further questions about the post-war treatment of veterans. Victorian-born nurse Kate Bruton was matron of the Kookynie Hospital north of Kalgoorlie in 1902 before transferring to the Bunbury Hospital in 1903.[40] In England to attend a nurses' conference in 1914, she volunteered, serving in the British field hospital run by the Red Cross in Antwerp, Belgium. Originally intended to accommodate 60 to 80 patients, it housed 160 wounded after an early battle between Belgian and German troops.[41] Serving alongside the wives of well-to-do British farmers and officers, she was one of the few trained nurses in the hospital. She served throughout the war and was awarded the Mons Star for services abroad.[42]

Kate was involved in a controversy over her war service in 1920, when her RSL membership was cancelled and her employment at the Kalamunda Convalescent Home terminated by Repat because she had not served with the AIF, as the position required. A meeting of the RSL executive deplored the 'bad mistake' and 'grave injustice done to her'.[43] Australian nurses who had served with British organisations were eligible for Australian repatriation services, but were often not invited to be part of the local RSL.[44] However, she was strongly supported by the RSL, in this instance, and she returned to the Bunbury hospital for a time and later transferred to Perth Hospital.[45] When she died in 1943, she was fondly remembered by many former colleagues.

Despite some seemingly callous treatment from Repat, these post-war lives were relatively untroubled compared to that of Sister Vera Paisley, who lived long after the war, suffering severe mental illness. Daughter of Thomas Paisley, Vera Agnes Margaret Paisley enlisted in the Australian Army Nursing Service in mid-1917, serving in India and Dartford, England, until she returned to Australia in June 1919.[46] Vera's files demonstrate the concern of her family, themselves suffering war-caused disabilities, local authorities, to whom the family was so well-known, and the difficulty that medical officers had in diagnosing her condition. She is remembered by my mother as an old lady who wandered the streets of Bunbury in shabby clothes and worn-out slippers.[47]

No clues as to the origins of Vera's mental illness appear in accounts of her early life. Like other young people of her class, she was reported in the press from her first years at school, winning certificates and attending weddings, balls and fetes, later competing in rifle shooting and golf and attending the races.[48] Recognised for her 'untiring and unselfish good work for the Church and the community', she commenced nursing training at the Perth Public Hospital in 1913.[49] Return visits to Bunbury and her appointment to Fremantle Hospital were noted by the press.[50]

Vera was the fourth member of the Paisley family to go to war, when in June 1917, she and three nursing colleagues of the Australian Army Nursing Sisterhood (AANS) sailed 'for one of the fighting fronts', accompanied by good wishes for a 'pleasant and enjoyable trip' from their military comrades.[51] Although she expected to go to France, and was reported serving at the Military Hospital in Bombay, India, she was in fact appointed to the Deolali 34th Welsh General Hospital.[52] Vera was among 560 members of the AANS who served at Deolali, 250 kilometres from Bombay, where they encountered smallpox, plague, cholera, venomous snakes, cultural differences, primitive nursing conditions and a trying climate.[53] Spanish influenza swept the hospital, claiming the life of one nurse, and leaving another dangerously ill for five weeks.[54] This may have been Vera, as her record and her own testimony show that she was ill with influenza for many weeks, also suffering 'DAH' (disordered action of the heart), then considered a psychosomatic condition, perhaps a hint of her later mental health problems.[55]

Vera returned to Australia in June 1919 to a warm welcome from family and friends and a public celebration with her three brothers.[56] She worked for several months at Fremantle hospital before discharge from the Army in November 1919.[57] What Vera's family and friends could not know was that she was to be 'forever affected by accusations of immoral behaviour' levelled at the Australian nurses at the Deolali hospital, which cared for patients of mixed ethnic and religious groups evacuated from the Middle East.[58] Holmes has explored the sexual dilemmas of women caring for wounded men, showing how the nurses positioned themselves as mothers and sisters in order to reduce this tension. [59] They were not always successful, as Rae has shown. When some Muslim patients, who had assumed that the nurses were married, discovered that they were single, they made accusations of immorality against several nurses. These accusations were rigorously investigated, some nurses submitting to physical examinations and ultimately being exonerated. The events were never made public so the doctors treating Vera would not have known of them.[60]

Post-war, Vera lived mostly in Bunbury until she was appointed district nurse at Dongarra (sic), 350 km north of Perth, in 1935.[61] The press reported her comings and goings, including medical treatment and holidays at the military nurses' home in Perth, her brothers' farm at Tambellup and the Eastern states.[62] She was close to her brothers, especially the youngest, Tommy, as well as Les and his future wife, and she remained a competitive golfer.[63] In 1925, she attended a dinner for the Tenth Light Horse Bunbury Troop, and 'very suitably' responded to a toast to the nurses, and, accompanied by Cyril, she participated in the Bunbury centenary celebrations, in 1929.[64] Vera was last mentioned socially in 1932.[65]

Vera's Repat files tell a different story of her post-war life. She presents as a trauma victim who was torn between trauma and ordinary life, in a kind of 'parallel existence'.[66] Her wartime experiences, traumatic enough at the time, were, in retrospect, relived time and again.[67] In early 1920, with 'slight tachycardia' and with the support of the RSL, Vera resumed private nursing.[68] She soon began exhibiting symptoms of neurasthenia, feeling a 'wreck', with headaches, sleeplessness, memory loss and debility. She was to claim several times that she had malaria in India, but had been unable to take leave due to pressure of work.[69] Her father claimed that her breakdown was caused by her war service, but doctors expected improvement with time, prescribing six months rest.[70] Vera was unable to resume nursing, again blaming the stress and climatic conditions of India, but her pension was reduced to 80%.[71] Her 1921 appeal for a full pension until she was fit for work, was rejected.[72] By mid-1921, she was 'thin and debilitated, neurotic, introspective and emotional', her doctor commenting perceptively that it was 'not unlikely' that there was 'some repressed experience, which was also responsible for her condition', but 'she should recover'.[73] Later medical reports were to recount her complaints in detail, but at this point we can only guess what she might have revealed to the doctor.

Vera's condition remained unchanged, and in 1926 a medical officer who had examined her brothers suggested a 'neurotic strain in the family'.[74] Her mother's own concerns at Vera's condition did not help her case, and Vera tired of being told by doctors there was nothing wrong with her. By 1927, she was 'a querulous person, in bed unnecessarily' and her incapacity was 'imaginary'.[75] Neurasthenia was her 'only' disability and her pension remained at 50%.[76] Vera nursed her father until his death in 1928, and in 1929, did very little work.[77] In 1930, while Cyril's TB was in remission, her youngest brother, Tommy, died of head injuries as a result of a motor cycle accident, after which she remained with her mother. [78] These periods spent nursing family members may have enabled her to avoid returning to work outside the home.[79]

By 1931, Vera was attending a few private patients, and was now considered fully fit for work; in Repat's view, any 'grievances and symptoms' were 'baseless'.[80] She spent much of 1931 training in obstetrics at the state's major maternity hospital, but after a short period of casual work at Bunbury, was unable to work for the following two years.[81] She spent three months in Cue in early 1934, finding work beneficial, but that year she underwent two major operations, including a mastectomy. Her doctor, unusually, suggested that she was 'cracking hardy', that is, putting on a brave face.[82]

Vera returned to work at Bunbury Hospital before being appointed District Nurse in Dongara in 1935. She participated in community life there, playing golf and bridge.[83] The Boy Scouts assisted her by 'cleaning up her yard, repairing fences, burning rubbish, and cleaning out tanks and gutters'. [84] Her first year in the town was 'very successful' due to her 'hard work and efficiency', and despite being a 'very nervous woman', Vera was happy.[85]

Vera attended to the victims of two fatal accidents within two weeks of each other, and this, added to the death of her brother, may have provided the tipping point for her mental health. The first involved a man being dragged under a moving train, severing one hand and crushing the arm and a leg.[86] Vera accompanied the victim on the several hours' journey to Geraldton hospital, during which time he remained conscious.[87] The second was a fatal motorcycle accident, the victim 'taken to the quarters of the district nurse, Sister Paisley, who attended to his injuries'.[88] Vera left Dongara shortly after these events, amid eulogies for her work and popularity in the district from the Country Women's Association and community residents, to which she responded appreciatively.[89] In one year, Vera and her successor treated 360 patients and made 1,200 visits, an average of three to four visits per patient, but it seems the CWA could no longer afford to employ a nurse at Nurses' Union rates.[90] Vera was again suffering nervous symptoms, which Repat attributed to 'neurasthenia, with a strong family connection through her brothers'.[91] Worse, her doctors believed that the time on a pension had exacerbated her symptoms.

Vera left Dongara in February 1937, around the time her sister Ivy moved to Busselton. By mid-1938, she was suffering horrifying delusions and hallucinations.[92] Her mental condition was now diagnosed as 'paraphrenia', and, on a 20% pension, she was managing some nursing in Bunbury despite her fragile condition.[93] Later that year, no longer simply 'nervy', Vera was diagnosed with 'mild involutional insanity' at age 45, the 'critical age' for this condition.[94] Appeals for pension increases in 1938 and 1940, even though supported by the RSL, were disallowed.[95] Her condition was now described as 'involutional insanity' and the influence of war service on her condition was 'absolutely nil'.[96] Her sister, Ivy, having returned from Busselton, was now caring for Vera, and she and her mother were supporting her financially.[97] In 1946, Ivy approached a visiting federal senator, who appealed to Repat for increased financial assistance for the family who were 'finding the financial worry, added to 30 years (sic) of constant attention and nervous strain, almost beyond their capacity'.[98] Repat courteously reminded the Senator that Vera was not entitled to free medical treatment for conditions such as psychosis, that were not war caused.[99]

Ivy Paisley died suddenly in 1947 and Martha, their mother, in 1949.

Vera was admitted to Perth hospital in 1949, 'not bad enough for Heathcote' (mental hospital), and a further application for a pension increase was denied.[100] Strangely, her *Guide to Nursing* was published by the hospital in that year, a pocket sized, hard-cover book of instructions for nurses for preparation for minor surgical procedures, likely distributed in hospitals throughout WA.[101] This may have been assigned to Vera as occupational therapy, which appears often in veteran files.

There is a gap in the record from late 1951 until early 1959, when a Bunbury doctor applied for a service pension for Vera, who was now suffering 'delusional insanity, which is quite harmless'.[102] Vera's parents, two brothers, and her sister all predeceased her, leaving her to the care of two brothers who themselves had serious war-caused disabilities and injuries, and their wives, already burdened with the care of their husbands. There is another gap in the record until 1968 when, nearly 20 years after the deaths of Vera's mother and sister, matters became 'most delicate', and Social Welfare, the Bunbury council and the RSL worked with Les and his wife to try to improve Vera's position.[103] She was living in 'indescribable squalor' in a house that was a 'fire trap' and she needed care, but was uncooperative.[104] She was admitted to hospital with 'neurasthenia accepted as war caused, not involutional insanity', minor surgery was performed and some of the effects of personal neglect were remedied.[105] Letters and reports from family and authorities, including the police, attest to the genuine concern that surrounded this World War I nurse. Vera was discharged from hospital, angry and confused, sometimes uncooperative, but still interested in current events.[106] This was a difficult time for everyone concerned for Vera's welfare, when they were themselves suffering. Vera remained able to write letters for herself, although the problems she described were often of her own making, and, now in hospital in Perth, even more difficult for Les to attend to.[107] Her remaining years until her death in 1974 at the age of 82 were spent in a nursing home in Perth.[108]

In 1944, when Vera's mental illness was becoming apparent, bipolar disorder, or 'involutional melancholia' which doctors considered to be her condition, was attributed by one researcher to 'recent prolonged severe mental stress', where the mechanism of 'crowding out' of 'melancholia' operates to keep 'unpleasant thoughts out of consciousness by occupying the mind continuously and completely with other matters'.[109] Formerly active patients were considered vulnerable to it as they aged, due to 'remorse for long past sins that are nearly always sexual'. The illness is 'reactive and not constitutional', caused by events rather than inherent weakness, and further attacks could be caused by 'trivial misfortunes'. The author claimed that he was usually able to identify the origin of the illness and recommended drugs or electric shock rather than psychological treatment.

Doctors and nurses suffered the effects of mental strain caused by inadequate facilities and pressure of war work, and while the term 'shell shock' was rarely applied to them, AANS nurses were often diagnosed with 'debility' or 'neurasthenia', caused by 'exhaustion of the nervous system'.[110] The general belief among medical practitioners that post-war mental health problems resulted from a predisposition is repeatedly reflected in the files of the Paisley family.[111] Doctors had difficulty in differentiating between wilful behaviour and neurotic or psychotic conditions. It was common for wartime nurses to have difficulty returning to civilian life, and Vera's relative isolation in Bunbury as other local wartime nurses went elsewhere made her condition more difficult for doctors to comprehend.

It was not until 1980, eight years after Vera's death, that the term 'Post Traumatic Stress Disorder' (PTSD) was officially recognised as an outcome of war, and diagnostic guidelines developed.[112] War zone stress involving repeated, indirect exposure, as in nursing, can remain a dominating experience through intrusive recollections, nightmares and flashbacks. The hypervigilance characteristic of PTSD sufferers may resemble paranoia. After World War I there was not the debriefing which routinely occurs today for defence personnel. This may have compounded the risk of 'delayed expression', where symptoms do not fully appear until years after the events, when a situation reminiscent of the original trauma appears, as occurred in Vera's case. There may also be remissions and relapses, which Vera also experienced. If war could produce total amnesia in an individual, then it is probable that Vera's almost total mental collapse was war-caused.[113]

Vera's files make painful reading indeed. Only the broadest outline of the suffering that she and her family experienced is given here, enough to show that this is one of the saddest cases because each individual's own trials compounded the problems of other family members. For a family who had been pillars of the community, the effects were widely felt. Local and state, private and government organisations all sought to assist Vera. Her mental condition was not accepted as war-caused, but considering the events of her life, we must conclude that Vera's war service in India influenced her post-war mental deterioration. The accidental deaths of her brother and the two men in Dongara probably revived memories of her time in India.

The belief by Repat officials that family failing caused the mental suffering of her four children who had gone to war, compounded by the early death of her youngest son, must have been severely distressing to their mother. Their father, too, had previously suffered a breakdown in his own health in 1913, a likely consequence of his untiring professional and civic work.[114] The fact that he recovered and became a stalwart of the home-front community testifies to his innate strength rather than any moral weakness. In his years as a schoolteacher, one of his principal aims was to inculcate in his pupils a sense of civic duty. It must have been a bitter blow that his children, through following his principle of duty to king and country, were prevented from full civic participation in their own post-war lives. The frequent references to 'malingering' in the files of all except Cyril, had they been seen, would have added distress to the already painful situation in which this respected family found itself after the war. While we can sympathise with the authorities in their attempts to limit public spending on returned men and women, in retrospect, we can deplore the additional suffering they caused. That the individuals whose post-war lives described here could return to paid employment after long periods of incapacity and endless battles with Repat, testifies to their innate resilience and desire to be useful members of their community.

Women and the moral economy

While many women negotiated with Repat on behalf of other family members, some women, in advocating for their men and for themselves, caused more than the usual headaches for the Bunbury Repatriation Committee. Members of two extended families, these Bunbury women exerted a strong sense of entitlement when they and their large families were themselves eligible for pensions.[115] Messrs Beigel, Eastman and Paisley of the Bunbury repatriation committee, who knew the families well, penned many letters on their behalf.

When William Henry Wenn, a private in the 51st Battalion died at Gallipoli in 1915, his mother, Selina Wenn claimed he was her sole support since her husband had recently died.[116] She received pensions for herself and two daughters under the age of 16 until 1920.[117] Her son Clarence Ross Wenn, a blacksmith before his three years' war service, had difficulty settling into work after the war, however his wife, 'a very illiterate woman indeed' managed her finances carefully.[118] When Clarence applied for a loan to purchase furniture, Beigel, on behalf of the Bunbury committee, wrote that 'they wouldn't get what they were asking for if they had to pay for it themselves'.[119] Wenn's character was 'fair to good', but 'this appears to be a case where the department will have difficulty obtaining repayments without pressure' and would need to be 'very strict'.[120] Problems soon arose, both with his work and with loan repayments.[121] After working for six months as a postman, Wenn had to relinquish the position to the previous incumbent on his return from war service.[122] This provoked an angry letter from the younger Mrs Wenn:

> *I would like to know why my husband has been refused sustenance. I consider it a base act of injustice considering there are single men in Bunbury who have made it a boast that the Repat are keeping them, in fact one went as far as to refuse work, some of them never*

saw a shot fired at the front, where my husband saw three years of service, lost 2 fingers and shot through the knee. I have just stated my case. We have hardly sufficient to maintain ourselves.[123]

Mrs Wenn later informed Repat that her husband was working on the wharf and she would make loan repayments as soon as possible. The Bunbury committee agreed that the family were having 'a very rough time' and reluctantly deferred payments.[124] In July 1922, Wenn himself wrote that repayment was

utterly impossible, I will pay what I can on payday. I haven't earned enough in the past six months to by (sic) food, but you will get your money in time, I know I have had a good run, but the work here is dreadful. I am not pleading poverty, but telling you plain facts.[125]

In 1924, there was still money outstanding.[126]

Clarence Wenn eventually worked on the waterfront for 40 years, and his wife bore ten children. However, in 1942 Mrs Wenn divorced her husband and to her dismay, found she was no longer entitled to a pension.[127] Matters must have settled down, but when, in 1973, she enquired about an age pension for herself and her husband, Repat naturally asked questions about the divorce. It transpired that they had only separated for six weeks and Mrs Wenn had destroyed the papers. The 'fiery tempered' Mrs Wenn continued: 'I didn't ask for this third degree. When I married him in 1919, I became and still am Mrs Alma Irene Wenn.'[128] Both lived past the age of 90 and died just a year apart in 1986 and 1987, outliving Paisley, Eastman and Beigel by decades.

Another Mrs Wenn, the wife of Mervyn Bailey Wenn, a cousin, was to cause four years of consternation of a different kind to the Bunbury committee after the war as Mervyn tried to persuade her to come to Bunbury as she had promised when she married him in London during the war.[129] As mentioned earlier, Mervyn had a troubled military career, and, with a wife and child, he was discharged with a 15% disability pension. Although he applied to remain in London after the war, in 1920 he was back in Bunbury, owing money on loans for furniture caused by interruptions to his work on the wharf by a railway strike.[130] In 1921, he applied for a free passage for his wife to come to Australia and a third-class passage was approved pending enquiries to the High Commission in London.[131] Cables and letters flew between Bunbury, Perth, London and Melbourne for the next two years as Wenn pleaded for his wife to come to Australia and she vacillated, until the application was finally cancelled in 1923 and Wenn disappeared from the repatriation records.[132] He eventually remarried in 1936 and was working on the Fremantle wharf in 1945.[133] Nothing more is known of the London Mrs Wenn, or whether her life was the better or worse for not having come to Australia.

The women of another Bunbury family were to add further to the workload of the Bunbury committee. While Jack Blythe was fighting lung disease and struggling to find support from Repat, his mother and sister were fighting their own battles. Mrs Blythe had married James Drummond Blythe in 1885, had five children, was widowed in 1897 and lost a young son in 1900.[134] Of her three sons who went to war, two died, Drummond James (Gallipoli) and Francis Albert, (France–England).[135] Mother and a daughter, 'Queenie', were nominated as dependents, but by 1919, were dependent on the surviving brother, Jack.[136]

By 1916, the women were having financial difficulties and Mrs Blythe wrote long and eloquent letters to Mayor Clarke and to Repat, appealing for the assistance to which she felt entitled.[137] She was not seeking charity, she said, but 'only a fair and just treatment'.[138] When her husband and a young son died, she said, she had mortgaged the house in order to obtain money for medical bills. She had taken in boarders for a time to feed and educate the children, but could barely earn enough. She had hoped her sons would be able to help her, but only Jack, in Queensland, had sent her money. Queenie had worked in a fruit shop but had given up work to keep her company when her two other sons enlisted. When the first son died, his money stopped and now a second son had died and Repat had ruled she was not entitled to assistance. Lamenting the 'awful sorry strain of money worries', she pleaded: 'now that I have given my all for the Empire, must I go to the wall or old women's home? God alone knows if I'll ever get the third one home again.'[139]

Mayor Clarke wrote to the War Council of the 'pathetic case', detailing her property and meagre income, and suggesting that the daughter was 'something of an invalid'. He continued, 'Mrs Blythe is of a peculiar temperament, somewhat soured by her many misfortunes, and laments the treatment meted out by the authorities to dependents of those who have fallen in the defence of the Empire'.[140] As already described, Jack survived the war, to fight his own post-war battles and support mother and sister as best he could. After his death in 1961, Queenie enquired whether she was eligible for a pension.[141] She had cared for her mother until her death in 1930 and now called herself a 'war old maid', reflecting the diminished marriage prospects of young women following the war.[142] She applied again in 1965, saying that after her brother served in World War II, he was 'very sick for a considerable time', reminding Repat again that she was a 'war caused old maid'.[143] Exasperated, the Repat official noted that her lack of entitlement had been 'carefully explained in 1962'.[144]

It is hard to know how these women survived financially. Perhaps they took in laundry or became home help for women slightly better off than they. Although Queenie cared for her mother and brother until their deaths, she and her mother, and the Wenn women, unlike the other women described here, appear to have expended considerable effort to obtain their own entitlements.[145]

These narratives show that the post-war lives of veterans cannot be neatly classified, but were complex and nuanced. The injustices suffered by individuals must be balanced against the sincerity of the local officials who tried to support them, with their imperfect understanding of the conditions they were dealing with and the financial imperatives of a country struggling to manage the catastrophic effects of the war. We cannot doubt the good intentions of men such as Beigel, Clarke, Eastman, Paisley and many others, who worked so hard on behalf of returned men and their families. The files also contain a whole population of medical men, whose skill and good intentions must also be recognised. Another population, of high government officials like Ministers Mitchell and George, and Commissioner McLarty were themselves part of the Bunbury and Harvey communities and well known to the Snell family.[146] There remains a population of Repat officials in Perth who might seem to be unknown, yet letters in the files shows that veterans and their wives were personally acquainted with some of them and were able to appeal directly to them. In Western Australia at least, community connections were so strong that it is unlikely that officials could deal dispassionately with the veterans.

7

GENDER AT WAR IN THE WELLINGTON COMMUNITY: THE PUBLIC AND THE PRIVATE

Mrs Joel desires it to be notified that she will be at Mr George Clarke's office between three and four o'clock on Wednesday afternoon to receive contributions as usual.[1]

Prior to the war, men dominated public life in the Bunbury community. However, change was already occurring and the war added impetus to this process. Explorations of gender and World War I revolve around the question of work. There were three distinct groups of women who 'worked' during the war: the middle-class women who 'worked' to support the men at the front, the women in paid employment and the feminists who 'worked' towards political goals. The Wellington community included women from all three groups.

When hostilities erupted, women were immediately plunged into the context of war, increasing their visibility and mobility, and ultimately adding impetus to pre-war developments in feminism.[2] While the war highlighted the differences between the masculine battle front and the feminine home front, it also blurred gender identities and roles. This section examines the gendered aspects of patriotic work during the war, feminist influences on the Wellington population, census data on women in the workforce and the life-narratives of four Wellington women.

In the Bunbury district, war brought irrevocable change to the lives of women once they demonstrated competence in the public sphere.[3] Both publicly and privately, the lives of men were also altered by the war. The public discourse surrounding feminist issues in the Bunbury press also shows that feminist influences were aired and were taken up by local women before the war and increasingly after it.

While the discussion surrounding women in the paid workforce has been largely based on anecdotal evidence, the data from the 1901, 1911 and 1921 census allow us to identify trends relating to working women. According to the statistics, the war did not push women into the workforce. Neither was there increasing acceptance of married women in the workforce as claimed by Kingston and Murray *et al.*[4] The workforce participation of Western Australian women followed a different pattern from women in the rest of Australia. Although overall trends remained largely unchanged, there was significant readjustment of the place of women in the workforce between 1901 and 1921.

The life narratives of a number of Wellington's public women whose wartime and post-war activities were reported in newspapers suggest how far they were changed by the experience of war. Although feminist historians have discounted women's wartime contribution on the grounds that women did not create rhetoric to promote their work, women adopted masculine language, and press reports of the changing lives of women were full of rhetoric.[5] Feminist rhetoric was applied to women aviators in the inter-war period, illustrated by the flying career of a Harvey woman, Janie Sutton. The discourse surrounding so-called 'flappers' and whether they had any part to play in understandings of wartime and post-war gender roles and behaviour is also examined.

The public and the private in the Wellington district

The experience of the Wellington community during and after the war demonstrates a significant redistribution of gendered activity. Shute argues that the Great War entrenched the idea of separate spheres for men and women.[6] McQuilton, and more recently, Payton, conclude that women's patriotic work was merely an extension of the domestic sphere and produced little change.[7] While the essence of these arguments cannot be disputed, a closer examination of women's and men's home front activities, elicits a more nuanced picture. Through the widespread press reporting of women's activities, women became visible as actors.[8] Scates concludes that the work done by women during the war 'both challenged and reinforced traditional gender roles', through the vast quantity and economic value of material produced and by the size of the workforce.[9] In so doing, 'women renegotiated what had been men's and women's traditional roles and blurred the boundaries between the public and the private'.[10] Sharp and Stibbe remind us that in 'total war', the mobilisation of the civilian population pushed women into the public sphere and previously masculine roles.[11] This resulted in the 'renegotiation of gender roles' in the war's aftermath.

The foundations for the Wellington community's gendered responses to the war were laid in the pre-war period in the men's civic activities and women's social circles. The influence of gender on pre-war life was evident in the separate spheres of men and women, as public masculine identity was created through men's occupations, while women's identity existed largely in the private sphere of family and social activities.[12] Contemporary writer, E.C. Buley, noted in 1905 that women's identities were changing, confirmed by local press reports of the four Harvey women among the local land-owners or managers.[13] Their acceptance in the male domain was reflected in Snell's comments on a friend working for 'Miss Lambert' and by her part in local infrastructure development.[14] Bessie Lambert later worked in an aircraft factory and the Red Cross in London, as we have seen.[15]

In Bunbury by 1901, W.J. George was actively seeking the female vote in the coming state elections.[16] Women were already involved in activities that provided the organisational and public relations skills needed in time of war. They participated in the education system, either in association with the men or by running their own schools.[17] The wives of male school officials made presentations and speeches at school celebrations, emphasising the importance of education for girls as well as boys.[18] Girls had equal access to post-school education in Bunbury and while some courses were gendered, others, such as commercial courses, provided both males and females with managerial skills that supported their wartime activities.[19] In the domestic sphere, women were employers of domestic staff, also giving them managerial skills.[20] Men also moved between the masculine and feminine spheres. The pre-war Bunbury Nursing Association and the Sailors' Rest, which gave women autonomy and organisational skills were supported by men in organisational roles.[21]

While many wartime activities were carried out within the existing domestic and public spheres, boundaries were stretched as men and women collaborated in new ways. As in earlier times, men went to war and women stayed home, but, as Garton points out, within those spheres there were dilemmas, contradictions and negotiations.[22] Women produced comforts, first aid materials and sandbags, and raised funds, often stepping into masculine spaces in the process. Men ineligible for war managed recruiting and repatriation, thus maintaining their masculine roles, but also collaborating with the women in these endeavours.

Patriotic activity was a means of managing the suspense of war as the Bunbury-Harvey community waited while their men were at war, crossing gender boundaries in the process. The early wartime activities in the community were highly gendered, with the creation of the war committees by the men and a garden party for the relief of the Belgians organised by the women.[23] Although men assisted with the project, reporting of this event was highly feminised, but similar events later in the war were reported in gender-neutral tones. When, for example, the Bunbury Red Cross held a social evening to collect foodstuffs and gifts for returned men in city military hospitals, although women's participation outnumbered the men's, the reporting of the event was concise: 'the second gift evening for soldiers at the different military hospitals was held with a very satisfactory result'.[24]

The public men who remained at home were already active in civic affairs and swiftly adapted their activities to fighting the war, but ultimately, the majority of activities involved both men and women. 'The Rustics', men who had failed the medical examination worked with women to raise funds for the district nursing association and the families of the men at war.[25] The scale of patriotic work compelled men to allow women into their spaces and to accept a subordinate role in some of the women's activities, Mrs Joel, for example, operating out of the Mayor's office and men assisting the Red Cross with the packing and transport of comforts.[26]

Wartime dissension was muted in the Wellington community. While in other districts, non-serving men could be harassed by young women, transgressing the boundaries of good behaviour, in Bunbury such women were simply 'frivolous young ladies' who could be more profitably employed volunteering as nurses or joining a sandbag committee.[27] Women were frequently reminded that the men remaining at home had been rejected or exempted from service and were playing their part on the home front.[28]

Nearly two million pounds was raised by Western Australians, that is approximately £3 for every man, woman and child in the population of 323,000, at a time when Charlie Snell considered £200 per year a sufficient income for marriage.[29] While Scott identifies sixteen individual funds in the state, many administered by women, such as the Red Cross, the Patriotic Funds, and the unemployment relief fund, a randomly selected Bunbury newspaper refers to eight such organisations, including the Sandbag Fund, the Benevolent Fund, the Australian and French Red Cross, War Loans and the Roman Catholic Entertainment Committee. [30]

One of the most diligent (male) wartime workers wrote to the press at the time: 'When the history of the war came to be written it will be found that the women had done as much war work as the men'.[31] Although he emphasised the role of women, participation in the war on the home front was promoted as a national duty, and both sexes could face accusations of failing to contribute to the war effort.[32] Brigadier General Sir William Birdwood summed up this vast effort in his assessment that 'the Australian soldier was looked after better than any other man in the field'.[33]

Wartime committee work enabled women to expand their skills and influence. At least 20 women in the Bunbury – Harvey district took on major organisational roles. These women, working through their pre-war social circles, knitted, sewed, spun, cooked and packaged items to send to the men. They manufactured sandbags and bandages and collected funds for the purchase of surgical equipment. The manufacture of sandbags involved sourcing materials and donations and sewing them by the hundreds. Women collected reading materials for soldiers and money to be sent to higher authorities for disbursement, and organised entertainments and sports days for men in training and for returnees. Women also participated in recruitment campaigns and carried out house-to-house canvasses for subscriptions to various funds. Organisers of the comforts groups sourced materials and patterns and gathered women to do the sewing and knitting of items for soldiers.[34] The collection of funds for the purchase of Christmas gifts for the soldiers was a huge logistical exercise.[35] One Christmas, more than 200 Christmas boxes were made up, involving extra men and women to receive and forward them. Men, working for the Red Cross, set up a Soldier's Institute, entailing further fund-raising and sourcing of items for the comfort of soldiers, assisted by women.[36]

While major fund-raising events raised large amounts of money, it took many smaller ongoing activities to raise the final totals. A major event such as the Belgian fete or the Queen Carnival involved organising and decorating venues, soliciting donations and enlisting assistance to prepare and conduct activities and publicity. The various fund-raising activities involved the administration of large amounts of money; by November 1915, for example, Bunbury had raised £3,000. Regular concerts were held as entertainments and fundraisers, involving helpers to cook, serve and clean, arrange furnishings and collect donations of funds and goods. There were collection centres where tradesmen, directed by women, packed and forwarded goods to individual soldiers, prisoners of war, hospitals and rest homes in Australia, the British Red Cross, the War Contingent Association and to hospital ships at Fremantle.[37] War work continued until mid-1919 when the last soldiers had been repatriated. Normal activity had to continue as families and the sick needed care and children had to be educated, always against a background of grief and loss.

The W.A. Soldiers' and Sailors' Relatives Association, active during and after the war, saw women serving as committee members and in supporting capacities, and in 1921, for the first time, women were invited to the social function at the conclusion of the agricultural show.[38] In Harvey, women were now well-represented on local management committees.[39] In the process, women undertook new roles and activities, collaborated as equals with men and adopted a new professional language. During volatile wartime community meetings women's voices were well-represented, especially those of women whose husbands were serving. When Adela Pankhurst visited Bunbury, a soldier's wife interrupted to query Pankhurst's opposition to the war and the first question at the end of Pankhurst's speech was from a 'lady', who claimed that failure to support the war would result in Germany taking over the country.[40] For George Reading, Pankhurst set back the cause of feminism, and in an editorial on her visit, he called her an 'interesting but delightfully irresponsible female who strained the chivalry due from man to woman and whose sole aim was to create unseemly squabbles'.[41] He accused her of speaking half-truths regarding the employment of women, claiming low wages paid to some women when, he said, it was well known that British female munitions workers were well-paid. At conscription referendum meetings, women were again a vocal element in the audiences.[42] Although interruptions were so frequent that the reporter found it impossible to mention individual incidents, one example was of a woman holding a baby saying to another woman, 'send your husband to the war, as I sent mine'. Some women did not meekly step into the background and return to their former passive roles after the war, but maintained their position in the front line of community activity, as will be seen.

Wartime letters: stretching the boundaries of gender

The letters in the Snell archive demonstrate gender shifts in the private lives of individuals, the creation of fictive kin relationships and reversals of feminine and masculine expressions of emotion. Against the background of feverish public activity, private tragedies were unfolding. Roper discusses ties that bound immediate family, especially mothers, to men at the front, but letters to Snell's family from absent relatives show that the war extended the idea of family, dissolving gender boundaries in the process, as when Charlie's uncle in London wrote of how the family 'missed the dear boy's letters' and an aunt wrote of 'that darling boy of yours'.[43]

Outside the family, fictive kin relationships, served to blur the boundaries of intimacy between men and women in wartime.[44] These relationships already existed in the pioneering Wellington community where relatives were absent. A school friend of Snell's was a 'foster son' to Mrs Snell, while an elderly neighbour was 'Dad' Harrington, a surrogate grandfather.[45] When Mrs Snell, the 'sacrificial mother', was hospitalised, the (male) clergy, were able to visit her in their role as fictive kin.[46] Snell's Glen Innes employer, wishing him goodnight in the familiar manner he adopted with his daughters, welcomed Charlie into the feminised space of the family.[47] When war came, these fictive kin relationships intensified as Snell's Glen Innes friends began calling him by his first name and offered him a home whenever he should be in the district.[48] Women abandoned accustomed reticence in expressing their affection for Charlie: Blanche Martin of Glen Innes writing of his 'dear bright face', while Miss Treloggen in Sydney, who had met him only once, wrote of her 'motherly interest' in the 'dear brave boy'.[49] The Paisleys in Bunbury recalled sharing Charlie's childhood, writing: 'how well we all remember him!'.[50] Jefferson, a former employer, writing that he would be pleased to hear what Charlie had for breakfast, evoked a feminised and nostalgic image of the two sharing a meal.[51] The Camerons in Glen Innes reported having Snell's photograph among those of their 'soldier friends'.[52] Some male correspondents, although claiming fictive kinship, retained masculine forms. For example, W.J. George, wrote to Mr Snell as 'one who like yourself has the cloud of sorrow hovering', offering a handshake from 'brothers and sisters in one common grief'.[53] Fictive kin relationships enabled non-family members to relax the boundaries of intimacy with gifts which might otherwise have been considered too personal, such as pyjamas and hand-knitted socks, scarves and gloves.[54] Mrs Dunlop in Bangkok, whose ladies' guild was sending clothing items to Egypt, enquired whether 'thick or thin' clothing was needed.[55] A khaki-covered pillow from Snell's fiancée seems an intimate item, but was mitigated by its practicality and military colour, and Charlie's frankness in reporting it to his family.[56]

Women also presented themselves in new ways, as Snell's photographs of Glen Innes girls dressed in soldiers' uniforms indicate blurring of boundaries between the sexes. They suggest a female desire to identify with the men, but at a time when young women still wore long skirts for picnics and sports, it would have been daring. Before war, even family members did not kiss in public, yet at his farewell from Glen Innes, Snell was kissed at the station by eight women, and on visits to his fiancée, her mother pointedly left them alone at home.[57]

Gendered language and emotional expression altered in wartime. While at home, the male role was simply to bring the girls home safely after outings, in the context of war it became 'preserving the honour and purity of our womanhood'.[58] Emphasising the masculinity of war, writers described Snell as a 'fine manly boy' and a 'noble young man,' who 'did his duty right manfully'.[59] To Snell's English grandparents he was 'a good and brave man among brave men who have gone forth to fight for the old country'.[60] Others wrote of a 'clean souled young man', 'fighting for his country as any man should', or 'a man grown he felt he must do a man's work'.[61] All agreed that 'none displayed a cleaner and truer manhood than the dear lad'.[62]

The war induced men and women to modify their normally gendered behaviour in a counter-current of emotion which both men and women could express privately.[63] Women could express anger and indignation which would have been unusual in a peace-time context.[64] Writing of the conscription plebiscite, Sydney feminist, Miss M. Treloggen, contrasted Western Australia's 'splendid result' with the 'lasting disgrace' to states that voted 'no', at the same time apologising for her strong language.[65] Charlie's childhood friend, Maude Dunlop, wrote angrily from Scotland, comparing the sadness of families who had lost men in the war with the greater sadness for the families of men 'too cowardly to fight'.[66] Women could also expose the emotional state of the men at war. Bessie Lambert wrote from London of men who could not speak of the horrors of the battlefield, 'it is so awful to see their dearest friends falling in the most terrible agony,' while Mrs Jefferson would have liked to send Charlie's last letter to his mother, but 'my husband will not part with it'.[67]

Just as war helped to define masculinity, it also served to transform it, as men more freely expressed emotion in their writing. Roper explores the proportions of letters written by mothers and other women, whether relatives or friends, compared to letters written by men, showing that letter writing itself was gendered.[68] In the Snell archive, apart from letters written by Snell himself, 63% of the letters were written by women, while 61% of the individuals named in the letters were men, as might be expected in the wartime context. [69] With the wartime focus on the 'sacrificial mother', most letters were addressed to Snell's mother, but it was his father who answered them.[70] While Jalland points out that men were expected to remain stoical when confronted by death, we can see grieving fathers moving into emotional spaces previously occupied by women.[71]

Letters in the archive show men and women employing both masculine or impersonal, and feminine or more emotional voices in different contexts.[72] In condolence letters, when men expressed opinions or reminisced, they used more masculine styles of writing, for example, Thomas Paisley's masculinised: 'I always looked on him as a good and promising lad'.[73] When expressing grief, men adopted a more feminine style, their writing almost indistinguishable from that of the women. Snell's own writing combines the masculine with the feminised. For example, the masculine 'military training will make a man of me' contrasts with the feminine 'she's one of the dearest little kiddies I've ever struck' and the gentle tone he adopted when writing to his young sister.[74] The emotions of the farewell from the Glen Innes community evoked strong feeling: 'my heart was too full to make much of a speech in return'.[75]

The masculine identity of Snell's father in his former position as railway superintendent in the Malay States and in Bunbury was eroded by the war as he moved between masculine and feminine forms.[76] The home, as the private sphere, was the domain of women, yet it was also the space where men recognised and verbalised their own femininity.[77] This masculine statement of facts to the doctor: 'Mrs Snell went to Nurse Brown's Hospital this morning. Please use your discretion informing her Charlie died of wounds', was followed shortly after by this feminised plea for support in dealing with his grieving wife:

> *since my efforts to keep her from doing unnecessary work are ineffective, I beg of you to insist upon her remaining in Bunbury. I can't make her do it and if you can't, there'll soon be another calamity.*[78]

Masculine writing is evident in the terse official report of Snell's death: 'died of wounds received in action at No 44 Casualty Clearing Station. GSW face, skull, foot, thigh' or the listing of casualties among Snell's company: '4 killed, 6 wounded, and 2 missing, of 16 men'.[79] A letter from a male correspondent to Snell at the front also adopts a distinctly masculine tone: 'I have no doubt that when the opportunity comes the Western Australian contingent will do well'.[80] A letter from Snell's commanding officer, however, combines a formulaic structure and masculine tone with a sincere expression of sympathy:

> *I feel duty bound to write you concerning the end of your nephew. He was always formost (sic) in matters of duty, his character was exemplary. I regret having to open what must be a most painful wound, still it is respect to your nephew or son that it is done.*[81]

Letters from male community organisations remain impersonal, calling on ideals of heroism, masculinity and Empire, however, the writer of one letter softens the impersonal tone by adding: 'I may add my tribute of respectful sympathy and condolence'.[82] Another letter that adopts a masculine tone manages, by its eloquence, to convey a personal sense of loss:

> *The war is indeed leaving its terrible toll in our bright young promising lives and shrouding with sorrow, this district of ours. All the nation mourns with you … the great heart of the people is full of gratitude.*[83]

Male voices became feminised when expressing their own pain. W.C. Robinson wrote: 'I have felt it and still feel it and may again through this war as my eldest is in Mesopotamia', the same writer using the feminised 'dear old Australia'.[84] However, the most emotional letters were from childhood friend, Wedd Tuxford and a Bunbury businessman and neighbour, Max Beigel. Wedd wrote of the 'sad task' before him:

> *expressing my sympathy to you in the loss of poor old Charlo (sic). I can't think of anything else but the years and years of happy outings … can't imagine I'll never see him again. Believe me, my regret is that I was not with him at the last.*[85]

Beigel wrote:

> *I have been sitting over this sheet of paper for half an hour. Your heart has been rudely lacerated and is sore and broken. The shock of the ghastly news is almost beyond one's strength to bear. My whole heart goes out to you and yours in your sad loss – I am deeply grieved and sorry.*[86]

These men have shed any mask of masculinity, exposing raw and heartfelt emotion almost as freely as the women, whose writing is discussed below. This was matched by Snell's father's response as he described his surprise at the strength of his own feelings:

> *our hearts are very sore. I never credited myself with much sentiment, but I've a very strong conviction that when my own time*

comes it will be eased by the thought that Charlie is waiting, my dear old friend … [87]

Recognising the significance of the men's change of position, he later wrote: 'the greatest consolation came from the fellow feeling shown by so many friends, many of whom had themselves sore hearts from a similar cause'. [88]

Women too could adopt both masculine and feminine forms. The masculine tone was adopted by Mrs Dunlop, commenting on Charlie's soldierly appearance:

you look just splendid – I sincerely trust you will be spared to come safely through whatever dangers you may have to face to save the country and people from the tyranny of the Hun and it's the brave and strong who are going to do it. [89]

Despite the sincerity of the men's messages to Snell's father, none of their writing matched the empathy and emotion of the women's messages to his mother. Lorrie Clark did not try to be evasive when she wrote: 'your dearly loved Charlie is dead oh my own poor darling friend, how my heart aches for you'.[90] Nellie Gibbs cried:

my own dear girl, so brave, so dear, nothing would ease the pain in my heart for very sorrow for you – and for us – and I know Mr Snell is just full of sorrow.[91]

Eva Withers mourned:

The very mention of your dear son must reopen the wound – but I feel I must tell you how very much I feel for you and Mr Snell. I know, dear Mrs Snell, how your heart must ache … perhaps it is cruel to write to you.[92]

Although none of these women addressed Mrs Snell by her first name, the most intimate being 'my dear friend', these women, unlike some, did sign themselves by their first name, another sign of relaxing of the boundaries of intimacy in the wartime context.

The gendered activities carried out by men and women on the home front during the war had their foundations in the separate spheres of men and women before the war. However, there was much blurring of the boundaries as men assisted women and women supported men in their wartime activities. The formation of fictive kin relationships in the support of soldiers heading for the battle-front was also an extension of relationships that existed prior to the war. However, the war also provided incentives for the blurring of the boundaries of intimacy that went beyond what had existed in pre-war Australia. New ways of expressing emotion were found by grieving men as they reported feelings that were previously suppressed, and by women who were able to give free reign to their emotions. We can also uncover some contradictions in the community's response to war. When a collection of war photographs depicting the Australian Light Horse at Beersheba was brought to Bunbury in 1923, to let 'mothers know what their boys did and where they lived a portion of their lives', the masculine was emphasised by the removal of images of wounded men from the exhibition.[93]

Gender influences on the Wellington community, before, during and after World War I

Press reports suggest that feminist influences in the Wellington community were already producing change before the war which accelerated post-war, alongside new attitudes towards women and increased participation by women in public life. The term 'feminist' was first reported in the Australian press in connection with the *Congrès Feministe* in Paris in 1892, which aimed to improve the working conditions of women and increase female participation in municipal councils.[94] The *Sociétés Féministes Françaises* was frequently reported in Australia, with only hints that similar organisations existed there.[95] In 1895 a Tasmanian (male) parliamentarian who supported the vote for women was derided as a 'feminist', however, it was soon accepted that some Australian women were feminists, equated with the English 'Woman's Right Movement'.[96] The term first appeared in Western Australia in 1896 in reporting of the Paris feminist conference.[97] In 1898 women declared that they were no longer going to demean themselves to please men, and in 1899, 'the feminist movement and the equality of the sexes' was cited by the Western Australian press as the 'greatest event' of the nineteenth century.[98]

American Jessie Ackerman, a first-wave feminist and the founder of the Women's Christian Temperance Union, travelled widely in Australia, lecturing and publishing and advocating for the rights of women.[99] She visited Bunbury in 1910 and 1911 on behalf of the Australian Women's National Liberal League, and was hosted by Bunbury feminists Eliza Cons and Violet Bayliss.[100] Ackerman's impressions of Australian society, published in 1913, note that women made their political decisions independently of their husbands, and that while upper class men considered women to be economically unproductive, working men recognised the contribution of their wives.[101] Bunbury women were reported at political meetings as early as 1900.[102]

Campbell points out that the art of persuasion was considered to be a masculine skill, so women were initially censured for entering the public sphere.[103] Victorian Vida Goldstein (1869–1949) was among the Australian First Wave Feminists who were profoundly influential in Western Australia, setting the scene for post-war reforms for women. Goldstein was associated with suffrage, feminism, anti-conscription and pacifism, and made several visits to Perth.[104] While reports of her early speaking engagements in Melbourne focused on her dress and the fact that she was the 'pretty daughter' of a military man, she was soon taken seriously.[105] In 1906, as president of the Women's National Political Association of Victoria, Goldstein spent two months lecturing in Western Australia for the Women's Australian Natives Association and the Women's Social and Political Crusade.[106] Her 1911 speech at the Karrakatta Club on social problems affecting women was attended by a large audience from the Women's Service Guild, of which Bunbury's Ivy Paisley was later a member.[107] Although during the pre-war years, the discourse on feminism seemed well established, local news reports suggest that, after the war, it was necessary to redefine feminism and restate its aims of promoting social responsibility and equality of the sexes.[108]

Women and work in the press before and after the war

The pre-war nursing experience of two Wellington women who moved into the domestic sphere after marriage remained largely hidden from view. When, in 1911, W.J. George, MLA, was being driven around the 'orangeries' of Harvey by a local man, the horse driving the trap they were in bolted, causing injuries to both men. Mrs Charles Shenton, a nurse prior to her marriage, was called to assist the wounded.[109] It was not until 1938, however, that a press report revealed the extraordinary background of Mrs Margaret Castieau, wife of public man, W.B. Castieau. In 1894, two years after the discovery of the Coolgardie goldfield, the arrival of the first nurses, matron Margaret O'Brien (c. 1870–1950) and a friend took the total number of women to twenty-five.[110] Trained in Adelaide, they came armed with a purse of one hundred sovereigns, letters of introduction to the Lieutenant Governor of Western Australia, and hospital equipment which included beds and mattresses and a specially designed tent. After the fortnight's journey from Perth to the goldfields, the sight of 200 men in their rough mining clothes at breakfast evoked panic; however, protected by their uniforms, the nurses commanded respect among the miners. At the rudimentary hospital, they found men who had been lying 'sick unto death for weeks with their boots on'. Faced with scarce water, expensive and inadequate food, swarms of flies on the medical utensils, and the constant turnover of cooks and orderlies, they battled typhoid, dysentery and scurvy. Their first hospital was a tent, later replaced by an earthen floored, iron and hessian structure; pillows were sugar bags stuffed with newspapers, and bedside tables were grocery boxes. Surgery was conducted in a tent, or in the open if the wind was not stirring up the red dust, and if their ministrations failed, they carried out undertaker's duties. Margaret O'Brien married Victorian, Walter Buckley Castieau in 1895, remaining on the goldfields for a further four years until they moved to Bunbury in 1899. In her work in Coolgardie, she ministered to three lords, author and explorer, David Carnegie, and G. Casey, father of the early Federal Treasurer, later Governor General of Australia, Gavin Casey.[111]

Notwithstanding these hidden examples, Bunbury press reporting of women's work prior to the war shows that local people were aware of the growing acceptance of women in the workforce. The completion of the Perth-Bunbury railway in 1893 brought the Perth daily newspapers, increasing the availability of news on women's interests. In 1901, several women attended a meeting to form a Bunbury branch of the Political Labour League, which advocated improved working conditions for both men and women in factories.[112] The league expressed its willingness to support a female candidate for parliament and its confidence in women's political capacity.[113] Conditions for women in factories and canvassing the support of Bunbury women remained on the agenda and by 1909, the conference of the Women's Labour League included one Bunbury woman delegate.[114] While there were still women who disapproved of married women in the workforce, the conference again called for improved pay and conditions for women and recommended having women in parliament as a means of raising its moral tone and improving law-making.[115]

The movement of women into public spaces was occurring before the war, with women accepted at the Bunbury Mechanics' Institute from 1913.[116] The Bunbury press kept the community informed of employment trends for women in other countries. In 1911, for example, women in France were appointed as magistrates and assisted in cases involving juvenile offenders and two years later, a major British scientific association appointed its first woman president.[117] Reportedly, in 1912, there were nine million women working in Germany (14% of the population), of whom 20,000 worked in the mining industry.[118]

6. Harvey's public men: one of Harvey's two important Agricultural Societies.
Battye Library, 019138PD.

7. Snell in the military: it was an honour to be selected for a firing party at a military funeral.
Snell Archive.

8. The first men to leave Bunbury for World War I, 17 August 1914.
SLWA, slwa_b1953321_4.

9. Welcome home parade in Bunbury, 12 January 1919.
SLWA, BA444/14.

10. Tambellup 1907: the cleared townsite, a cluster of businesses and some remnants of the original woodland vegetation.
SLWA, 009855PD.

11. Hidden suffering: the Paisley siblings in uniform for their homecoming celebration, 1919. Standing, from left: Les (gunshot wounds), Selwyn (malaria and shellshock), Cyril (TB) and Vera (trauma-induced psychosis).
Bunbury Historical Society.

12. Reg and Irene on their wedding day, Mooloogool Station, 1922.
Snell archive.

13. Glen Innes girls in uniform: Nona Gennys (rear), May Gennys (seated).
Snell archive.

14. Bernice Taylor (left) and Janie Sutton (in VAD uniform) at the presentation of a fully-equipped ambulance to the Royal Australian Navy, funded by the Boans Red Cross committee, *The West Australian*, 29 July 1941: 3.
Courtesy Murray Ryall.

Significant state legislation increased women's rights during and after the war.[119] Jean Beadle, first president of the Women's Labour Conference, was known in Bunbury from 1910.[120] She campaigned for improved divorce laws, better working conditions and wages for women, and child endowment for mothers. Beadle came to Bunbury in 1918 to address the Shop Assistants' Union which supported the many young Bunbury working women.[121] Perhaps in recognition of women in the workforce, the Cathedral Ladies Guild changed its name to 'The Guild of Women Workers' in 1913.[122] Although nursing was still a gendered occupation, in 1914, Thomas Paisley was the 'gentleman Treasurer' of the Bunbury District Nursing Association, and male members of the town council, the Traders' Association, the friendly societies and unions attended meetings.[123] Perhaps feeling under pressure, several public men stated that they did not attend the meeting as its activities were 'purely women's work'.

The Bunbury press valiantly promoted women's interests and recorded the increasing visibility of women in public life. The Roman Catholic Girls Literary Society that met between 1914 and 1917 gave Bunbury girls the opportunity to examine community issues: in 1914, a member spoke eloquently of the 'chaotic' effects of the war in Bunbury and in state politics.[124] The group held mock parliaments, debated the placement of a road, discussed gender issues and organised concerts for soldiers, all aimed at broadening girls' participation in public life.[125]

Perth feminist Bessie Rischbieth, a major force for social, political and legal equality for women, visited Bunbury in 1917 as a representative of the Citizens' Anti-shouting League, then seeking the support of electoral candidates who would promote ways of reducing alcohol consumption.[126] The Women's Service Guild, which she founded, was the most important feminist organisation in Western Australia between the wars, its membership overlapping that of the Women's Christian Temperance Union.[127] The organisation's shows of home produce, farming, textile and pottery industries aimed to educate women in the broader aspects of economic production.[128]

The women of the 1920s, rather than demanding the right to speak, acted in their chosen field, opening up the 'rhetorical space' and allowing women to be heard.[129] Dr Roberta Jull was another feminist influence in Bunbury. She advocated for social reforms which would enhance communal life, and promoted the removal of barriers which restricted women to domestic roles.[130] Trained in Glasgow, married, and one of the first Western Australian women to practise as a doctor, Jull lectured on child health in Bunbury and Collie between 1917 and 1927, advocating medical examinations for school children and the provision of public playgrounds.[131] In 1920, as Medical Officer of Health and Schools, she gave a public lecture in Harvey, supported by Harvey public man, A. Clifton, who used a new language of respect for women.[132] Jull's work in Bunbury culminated in the opening of an Infant Health Centre in 1927.[133]

Marriage and motherhood generally were seen as a means of restoring order to a war-torn community.[134] Marie Stopes, birth control advocate, offered an alternative perspective in the *Bunbury Herald* between 1922 and 1927. Stopes suggested that the 'enslaved woman of the past' would be replaced by the woman who would choose her own mate and would continue her occupation after marriage. She would choose how many children she would have, would be paid wages for her services as a mother and would share domestic duties with her husband.[135] Stopes also urged men and women to adopt more relaxed clothing in the summer months and gain the benefits of sunlight.[136] While finding a husband remained a priority, Stopes identified a 'fever of reaction after the war' as women sought to replace old standards with new and to enjoy as much freedom as men.[137]

In 1928, Miss Maude Royden, feminist lecturer, preacher and writer came to Western Australia as guest of the Women's Service Guild.[138] Royden was the subject of more than 200 articles in the Western Australian press, although a proposed Bunbury visit did not eventuate. The press emphasised her femininity, which contrasted with the stereotype of the feminist as a 'masculine man with a scorn of feminine characteristics'.[139]

Although she spoke with 'ferocious conviction', her 'artistic excellence in speaking, her learning and her gift of shaping words', combined with a sense of humour made her a highly influential speaker.[140] Royden deplored the 'denial of woman's humanity', and campaigned for women to be a 'free agent in deciding her own life'.[141] These women who either lectured in Bunbury or were reported in the press spread feminist rhetoric, persuading the community to look anew at the status of women.

During the 1920s and 1930s, women were remaking the political, scientific, and cultural landscape in an international movement that was not lost on the Bunbury press.[142] Although in pre-war years the Bunbury press had reported the activities of women in employment, in public advocacy of women or in activities previously considered the domain of men, this trend accelerated after the war. Reports appeared of the election of the first British woman as a Member of Parliament, framed as improving the manners, morals, and efficiency of parliament; the appointment of China's first female chief judge, and the graduation of a woman from the National School of Engineering in Italy.[143] In Germany, a woman parliamentarian was asked to form a government, while a woman became a minister in the Congregational Church in Birmingham.[144] In Britain, Mexico and Puerto Rico women were granted the vote and in Turkey, government educational programs for women were implemented.[145] In 1925 there were around eight million female wage-earners in the United States, (around 7% of the total population), nearly half of whom were under the age of 25.[146] As in Australia, the largest number were in domestic service. Of the rest, in American towns, most young women worked in lighter manufacturing, while in large cities the majority worked in department stores and offices. These reports from afar suggest the increasing acceptance in Western Australia of women in public life and encouragement for local women.

In 1924 the first female jockey competed in Bunbury, with only slight condescension from male jockeys who made 'chivalrous concessions' to her.[147] A Ladies Surf Life Saving Club was formed in 1928, with formal arrangements such as a club uniform, membership fees and the election of club officials.[148] In Bunbury in 1923, six women were named as chief mourners at a funeral, formerly an exclusively masculine domain.[149] In 1926 a Victorian woman was appointed solicitor to her local shire.[150] At the same time, women became accepted as authoritative reporters of international affairs. When a Sydney woman toured Syria, the United States and South Africa on behalf of the (Australian) Armenian Relief Fund, her activities in refugee camps and an Australian orphanage in the war zone in Syria were reported in detail. The head-mistress of the Sydney School of Science reported that in the USA, men and women teachers received equal pay for equal work, and that girls in an all-girls college achieved better educational outcomes than those in coeducational schools. In America, the International Council of Women and the Medical Women's National Association, addressed matters of 'social hygiene', perhaps a euphemism for venereal disease, in order to reduce its impact on women's health.[151]

While there is much evidence that women's position in society was changing, it is more difficult to directly attribute the changes to the war. However, the discussion emerging from the 1920 Lambeth (London) conference of the Church of England hierarchy suggests recognition that the war itself had produced change in the lives of women.[152] The conference passed resolutions that directly affected women, including equality of men and women in church councils.[153] Although women were not yet admitted to the priesthood, the order of deaconesses was revived, enabling women to take a leading role in worship.[154] The conference acknowledged the 'tremendous changes made in recent years in the position of women in public affairs', with women in parliament and local government contributing to debate on social, economic and political questions.[155]

As a result, a petition signed by 86 women, requesting the admission of women to council, was presented to the Bunbury Church of England Synod the following year.[156] The preamble stated that women were now 'emancipated', were permitted to own property and enter the professions and universities, and, in many countries, to vote. The formal debate on the motion included censure of opponents who cited the 'distinct spheres' of men and women. In support of the petition, Western Australia's highest-ranking military officer reported that seeing women working long hours and 'proving themselves to be the equal of men' in wartime had changed his attitudes to women.[157] Others, noting the fundamental differences between men and women that made their participation desirable, claimed that women should no longer be 'kept in the background'.[158] The proposal was carried conclusively, on the grounds of justice, equity, common sense and reward for women's hard work during the war.

Despite this support for women, the conference remained emphatically opposed to birth control, an attitude that was not supported by the press.[159] The *West Australian* reported that the King's physician, although believing motherhood was good for women, supported birth control as an economic necessity.[160] The Lambeth Conference in London had conflicting outcomes in Australia, the appointment of women to church councils being quickly implemented, but the condemnation of birth control being out of touch with local opinion. In both cases though, the war was cited as a reason for changing the position of women, who, although entitled to a voice in decision making, were not yet entitled to control over their own bodies in the eyes of the church.

News reports showed a new awareness of the roles women could play in achieving world peace through the League of Nations.[161] At a Bunbury thanksgiving service for the end of the war, the speaker looked forward to the league preventing future wars and diverting money spent on armaments to improving the living conditions of oppressed people.[162] Women were quick to denounce ironies contained in ANZAC Day sermons on peace, as military authorities espoused disarmament while continuing to build battleships.[163] In 1929, a feminist writer encouraged the community to recognise the common humanity of all people and remember the German and French mothers and wives who had also lost their loved ones at war. The writer called on schools to include the League of Nations in the curriculum, and to teach that war was not a 'glorious adventure but a sordid business', to ensure that 'bright bonny boys would not face death and mutilation on the battlefield'.

The public discourse on women in post-war Western Australia raises the question as to whether 'flappers' were part of a larger women's movement. References to flappers appeared in the Bunbury press in 1912 and 1913, as 'flighty and fickle' young women between the ages of 13 and 18 who wore their long hair loose.[164] The term gained popularity with the young women themselves, as one of the Foreman girls organised a 'flappers' dance at the Bunbury Tennis Club.[165] Flappers were not mentioned again until the final year of the war, when their 'swanking around' the district with returned men provoked censure.[166] The 'demure' behaviour of nurses was contrasted with 'the antics of a flighty flapper who is insinuating herself into the picture'.[167] Post-war, flappers were seen as a moral blight on the town, 'parading the streets' unchaperoned at night and being ordered home by the police.[168] The saga continued as the local press reported the Pope exhorting women to give up 'scandalous and indecorous' fashions and return to 'more moderate ways'.[169] In 1919, concern for the 'short-frocked flappers' who stayed out late in unsuitable parts of Perth led to calls for women police.[170] The Bunbury press had first reported a uniformed women's police force in London and New South Wales in 1915.[171] Requests for specially trained mature women to work with 'unfortunate girls' in Western Australia soon came from the Labour Federation, the Temperance Union and the women's branch of the Liberal Party.[172]

By the mid-1920s flappers were firmly entrenched in films such as *What Fools Men Are* and were satirised as lazy, self-indulgent and ill-mannered:

> *Do nothing all the morning, and then rest. Don't be a household drudge. Dance all night. Don't say 'Thank you' to a tired man in tram if he gives you his seat; say 'thank you' if he doesn't and watch him wriggle!*[173]

Maude Royden, the English feminist, noted that the vote for women was sometimes erroneously called the 'flapper' vote.[174] The Bunbury press later associated the social upheavals after World War II with the 'flapper period' that coincided with women's emancipation during the earlier war, implying that women's emancipation by the war had negative consequences.[175] The frivolous behaviour of the young women may have been a reaction to the sombre wartime period, and although some writers equated the flapper movement with the emancipation of women, it had little in common with the high-minded activities of the feminists or the diligent patriotic workers of World War I.

Wartime patriotic activity and bereavements challenged gendered patterns of community participation by men and women and demonstrates that both men and women stepped outside previous gender roles. Private writings illustrate the emotional work done by women in a time of communal grief and the growing awareness by men that they could express emotion in new ways. The public discourses surrounding women show that the press played a significant and supportive role in shaping gender patterns, before, during and after the war.

8

WAR, WOMEN, WORK AND THE CENSUS

Although Marilyn Lake claims that the history of Australian women at work has been documented and analysed, census data have been used sparingly, Kingston, for example, quoting from the 1947 census.[1] The *Bunbury Herald*, however, observed midway through the war that:

> *In quite a number of industries women will have proved their worth in such positions as to defy displacement, and in other cases organisation of works and factories and offices will have been modelled on lines preventing their replacement.*[2]

Commonwealth censuses conducted in 1911, three years before the war, and in 1921, three years after the war, provide an opportunity to test the long-term influence of the war on women's lives. Comparison with the 1901 census results identify existing trends in order to isolate war as the cause of change.

Bolton's claim that trends in Western Australian social history followed a different pattern from that seen in other parts of Australia is supported by census data.[3] Utilising data for 'classes' of employment, that is, whether it is professional, domestic, or commercial for example and for 'grades' of employment, whether the individual was an employer, self-employed, or worked for wages enables us to check the validity of the results for one type of data against another. Data on married women in the workforce support the findings of the other types of data. Western Australian women lagged behind their compatriots in their workforce participation at the beginning of the period, the gap narrowing during the period 1901–1921. Some women moved out of domestic work into clerical positions, while the war forced some women out of paid work into caring roles for wounded veterans. Subtle adjustments in the status of men and women as breadwinners are also discernible.

One challenge is the lack of local data on war service pensions or on women engaged in home nursing. Butler provides data on pensions only for Australia as a whole.[4] The need for women to care for disabled veterans caused some Western Australian women to leave the workforce after the war.[5] The 1933 census data suggests that 2% of males in the Wellington SD were receiving pensions, which could also reflect the 1921 situation.[6]

In 1911, secondary industry, such as food, textile and clothing manufacture provided employment opportunities for women. Bunbury had four breweries and at least one manufacturer of soft drinks as well as newspapers, which could have employed women in clerical positions.[7] Hotels and boarding houses, and the wives of the professional classes offered paid domestic work for women. Mrs Joel, the wife of a Bunbury doctor, for example, employed three domestic staff.[8] Western Australia's rural population at 41% of the total suggests opportunities for women working unpaid on family farms.

The 1916 Snell population provides a small sample for a study of women and work in Western Australia over the wartime period. In 1915–16, midway through the census period, there were 21 women who worked, alongside 90 men whose occupations are known, with women making up a high 18.7% of this workforce, perhaps skewed by their position as the leadership group of the community. The largest number of women, eleven, were in the professional class, which included several high-profile charity workers, as well as teachers and nurses, with two women in domestic service, one in posts and telegraph and four in farming. Mesdames Hymus, Stanford, Mayne and Misses Lambert and Charman all managed orchards.[9] Many of the wives and/or daughters of the farmers provided unpaid assistance on the family property. Two other married women worked: Mrs Middleton who taught music, and Mrs Taylor, who was home help to Mrs Buchanan.

For the Wellington district in 1911, women made up 13% of the workforce and 13% of the breadwinners, significantly lower than the proportion of working women in the Snell population.[10] For the district as a whole, the largest proportion of working women was in the domestic class, whether providing accommodation or domestic service. Among the professional class, which includes nurses and teachers, women comprised 42% of the workforce. The commercial and industrial classes also employed significant proportions of women, at 14% and 12% respectively. The majority of women in these two classes were involved in the manufacture and sale of clothing and textiles or in general merchandising. In commercial enterprises, relatively large numbers appear to have worked in banking, and 13 women worked in communications (posts and telegraph). Bunbury was a significant commercial centre and port, and women of the town worked in stores and hotels which catered for the ships and their crews, although this is not evident in the Snell population. Secondary industries which employed women are harder to identify. Bunbury had two newspapers and four breweries, and while breweries may have employed women as clericals, newspaper publishing, which employed women as journalists, is not identified among the occupational classes.[11]

A randomly selected Bunbury newspaper of 1911 contained advertisements that illustrate employment opportunities for women. Firms such as dentists, architects, veterinary surgeons and a jeweller-optician-watchmaker all employed women.[12] Bunbury Girls' Grammar School was headed by a London-trained female principal, and a 'highly qualified staff' that included a woman who also offered art classes to the public. Department stores such as Hayward's and Clarke's sold a full range of goods including 'groceries, drapery, ironmongery and crockery', providing employment opportunities for women, and at least one women's outfitter employed a milliner and dressmakers.[13] Miss McCallum, matron of the

Bunbury Fresh Air League hostel, had been president of the Tailoress's Union in 1900.[14] Advertisements for three hotels indicate where paid domestic staff were employed, catering for boarders such as Snell family friend George Goss, who spent an extended period in a hotel and a 'lady with three daughters seeking one month board'.[15] At this time, when the wearing of corsets was obligatory for 'ladies', a maid was employed to fasten the garment, to spare her unwilling husband.[16] The type of unpaid work done by wives and children is suggested by an advertisement for a milk separator, which contains an illustration of the machine being operated by, presumably, the children of the dairy farmer.[17]

In 1921, the paid domestic workforce contained the largest proportion of female workers as compared to males, at 73%, with the professional class at 44%, the commercial class at 20% and the industrial class at 8%. Women made up a very small proportion of the transport and communication class (<3%) and were less than 1% of the primary class. Women made up 12% of the total workforce as well as 12% of breadwinners, as opposed to the 13% and 13% respectively that they made in 1911, representing a slight decline. Some of this may be accounted for by the needs of the estimated 1,500 Wellington men who returned from the war, many of whom needed home nursing care, and, unfit for work, were supported by pension and sustenance payments.[18]

In 1921, 12.7% of Wellington women of working age were working and comprised 13.9% of all workers, with the majority of the female workforce on a wage or salary. The proportion of female employers had halved, while the proportion of women working for a wage or salary had risen by 6 percentage points to 78%. The proportion of women who reported working without pay had declined from 19% to less than 1%. In Harvey at least, there were no women who declared themselves to be unpaid workers. This contradicts Mr Snell's comments in his letters that his wife did 'not spare herself' during busy times in the orchards, suggesting that she was, in fact, an unpaid worker.[19] It is likely that many more women fit this category, working but not reporting as such. Reports on the agricultural shows also indicate the degree of participation of women in farming activities alongside their unpaid domestic activities.[20] Overall, it is clear that little change had occurred.

Women working as a percentage of all women remained the same, while women working as a percentage of all workers rose slightly. Although percentages are small, the war is a possible cause for the increase in numbers of women as a percentage of all workers. This could be explained by the need for women to work in the place of men who were no longer able to undertake paid work.

A different view of the workforce is given by the data 'grade not applicable' and 'not stated'. According to the 1921 statistician's report, 'not applicable' refers to women who were either dependents or were 'not engaged in gainful occupations'.[21] The proportion of women assumed to be non-working remained almost unchanged at 67% and 68% respectively between 1911 and 1921. This suggests that 33% and 32% respectively of women were working, a slight decline in the proportions of women working between 1911 and 1921, but overall, a much higher participation rate for women than is suggested by other data. This represents a discrepancy of around 15% compared to the data for women in the workforce, which could represent the proportions of women who were caring for disabled returned soldiers, or working unpaid on family farms or businesses.[22]

Butler provides war pension data for the whole of Australia for 1931.[23] They show that the number of men receiving pensions in Australia rose from around 3,000 in 1916 to around 79,000 in 1921, falling to around 75,000 in 1931. Dependents also received pensions, around 143,000 in 1921, and around 207,000 in 1931.[24] Although the figures were substantial, the amount received could be paltry. The pension, combined with the need to care for disabled soldiers, must have influenced women's workplace participation rates and status as breadwinners.

The data showing the causes of male unemployment for the Wellington SD 1921 also have implications for the employment of women. Causes of male unemployment were classed as workplace-related, old age, or illness and accident.[25] Discounting old age or workplace-related unemployment, illness and accident account for 2,399 out of 7,671 individuals, or 31.3%. In addition, there were 1,576 given as 'other cause' and 384 not stated, a total of 1,960 out of 7,671, making another 25.5%. Adding the 'illness/ accident' group to the 'other cause/not stated group' produces a figure of around 57% of the unemployed. This could be war-related unemployment. Around 800 Wellington men may have been on war pensions since at least that number returned unfit from the war, however, the census reports in general ignored the impact of the war on the population.[26]

Paralleling the increase in female workforce participation was the movement of women to the cities.[27] In 1911, 58% of the state's total population lived in the metropolitan area, a figure that increased to 62% by 1921. Opportunities for clerical and manufacturing work, and education increased for women such as the Misses Paisley, Mitchell, Baldock and Sutton who moved to the city. For Janie Sutton, this meant office and dental training as well as the opportunity to fly. For Greta Baldock, it meant teacher training, while Vera Paisley pursued nursing training and wartime service. However, as we have seen, the Misses Baldock, Mitchell and Paisley returned to Bunbury.[28]

A major goal of the first wave feminists was to improve the economic status of women and their right to self-determination, so it is possible that changes in the proportions of women in the workforce occurred because women continued working after marriage.[29] The West Australian female workforce included 14% of married women in 1911, declining by two pp to 12% after the war. The two pp decline in married women in the workforce in Western Australia over the period may reflect the number of married women who were obliged to leave the workforce in order to care for husbands who had returned disabled from the war.[30] Welborn notes the high casualty rate among West Australian soldiers, leading to the conclusion that West Australian families suffered disproportionately from the war.[31] Here again, local data on the numbers of men receiving war service pensions would be useful.

The 1921 census reported on the 'conjugal condition' and grade of employment of Australian women, providing a more nuanced view of the female workforce. For Australia as a whole, predominantly single women were working, yet, of the female employers, 30% were married. Many of the married women employers were hirers of domestic staff, as we have seen. Of the females who were self-employed, 74% were single and 26% married. These women were often laundry women or dressmakers, and some were nurses who ran their own small hospitals, such as Nurse Brown of St Clair Hospital in Bunbury. Of the females who were receiving a wage or salary, 93% were single and 7% married. Many of these were young women working in shops or young teacher-monitors such as Greta Baldock, whose life story will be examined. Of the females who were assisting but unpaid, 88% were single, 12% were married, many of whom were daughters or wives helping on the family farm or business. The participation of women in the workforce in the Wellington district fell from 13% in 1911 to 12% in 1921.[32] It is possible that this again was related to the need for women working outside the home to cease work to care for ailing veterans.

The participation of women in the professional classes demonstrates another trend, possibly related to the availability of higher education.[33] The Wellington district was above the rest in both 1911 and 1921, reflecting the educated nature of the population from the earliest days of European settlement. Schooling statistics in Australia over the period shed some light on the overall pattern of female participation in the workforce, and in particular on participation in the professional class. There are significant differences between Western Australia and the whole of Australia with regard to technical and university education. While the 1911 figures for university participation in Western Australia are insignificant since the University of Western Australia did not take its first students until 1913[34], the comparison between Western Australia and the rest of Australia in 1921 shows Western Australia to be far ahead of the Commonwealth in the participation of women in both university and technical education at 41 and 42% compared to 29 and 28%.

The figures, when linked to female workplace participation data, suggest that while Western Australia was behind in female workplace participation in 1901, some other factors, such as feminist influences, may have increased women's workforce participation. Western Australian women were perhaps at a critical stage of workforce participation which enabled them to continue to move into the workplace after the war, despite losses of women caring for veterans. We have noted the diligence of the Western Australian press in promoting the cause of women. These efforts may have increased the numbers of women working before the war, allowing them to catch up with the proportions of Australian women in the workforce. Higher education levels may have made Western Australian women more receptive to new ideas, while the Labor Party and feminist groups were certainly influential.

In Western Australia, despite the tapering off of the increase in the post-war period, the increase in female participation was still higher than the Australian average after the war, albeit from a lower starting point. Western Australian soldiers had higher casualty rates than the other states, preventing some women from working outside the home because their men needed care. The inadequacy of pensions provided an incentive for women to seek paid work if they had been able to leave their husbands at home.

Despite the evidence of workforce data which shows Western Australia in a different light from the rest of Australia, the war changed little for working women. We must conclude that the women who did patriotic work were most changed by the war. The life narratives of four Wellington women before and after the war reflect trends in the workforce data and public influences reported in the press.

9

FOUR WELLINGTON WOMEN: CHANGES WARTIME AND BEYOND

The repatriation files of Wellington men show how some women became carers and shared their men's battles with Repat. Contemporary reporting of feminist influences in the Bunbury press highlighted changing attitudes to women. Wartime conditions encouraged both men and women to step outside their traditional gendered spheres in both their public behaviour and their private emotions. The population was strongly influenced by pre-war public discourses which had begun in Australia and beyond in the 1890s. Census statistics on women and work shows that the war did little to increase the participation of Australian women in the workforce, although there was significant movement of women between workforce classes. Western Australian workforce trends were different from those of Australia as a whole, and there was a significant movement of women into the workforce over the period 1901–21.

Change begun pre-war accelerated during the post-war years, resulting in new attitudes towards women and increased participation by women in public life. The women whose lives are examined here did not, initially at least, become carers of disabled veterans after the war, but their lives followed new trajectories after the war. Ivy Paisley (1886–1947), eldest child of Thomas and Martha Paisley, was the only one of five siblings who did not go to war; doctor's wife, Kate Joel, (c. 1880–1950) led Bunbury's patriotic effort; Greta Baldock (1893–1980), daughter of Bunbury public man John Baldock worked as a teacher for many years; and Janie Sutton

(1910–49), daughter of Harvey farmer William Sutton became famous as a female aviator.[1] The first three would have known each other personally, and Janie Sutton would have been well known to them all by reputation. These women, all related to public men and inculcated in the community service traditions of the middle class, all led public lives, enabling us to examine the factors which influenced their life-courses.

Ivy Paisley, 1886–1947, a single woman before and after the war

Ivy Paisley's life was neatly bisected by the war. As daughter of a civic leader, she did not need paid work or marriage to provide respectability. Although not the wife of a wounded veteran, she was to share in the care of shattered lives towards the end of her own life which had, until then, seemingly flourished in the post-war period. Six years older than Charlie Snell, her brothers figured in his reports from Egypt and France. More than 250 references in *Trove* document her place in the community from her earliest years. At the age of six she was contributing to church funds, at sixteen, she was organising her own fundraising stall.[2]

Although the family was Anglican, Ivy, like Marjorie Snell, received her general education in the local Catholic school, whose public image was enhanced by the study and performance of music, at which Ivy excelled.[3] Published examination results and repertoire played by pupils at Bunbury music schools indicate that both children and adults could perform at a high level. At seventeen, in 1903, Ivy began her long association with the new sport of hockey.[4] At 21, she was secretary and player in the local croquet club, and a prize-winning riflewoman.[5] Rifle shooting was a relatively short-lived activity, but she was a long-time competitor in the 'ladylike' sport of croquet.[6] In 1907, fourteen women, both single and married, competed in a rifle shooting competition, the scores suggesting that while some women were novices, others were experienced riflewomen. The press commented that there was 'no reason why ladies should not be as good as men' at rifle shooting, reflecting contemporary debate on women's place in society.[7] Ivy attended her first wedding in 1901 at the age of fifteen, and throughout her life attended and organised major social events for community leaders.[8] In 1909, she made a three-month trip to the Eastern States, where Wellington residents such as Doctor Joel had connections.[9]

Ivy was noted for her organisational skills: at the age of 20: 'with Miss Ivy Paisley as chief organiser, the arrangements are sure to be in perfect order'.[10] Her official positions included secretary of the Anglican Ladies Guild, organising events known as 'continentals', that included musical items and croquet tournaments.[11] In 1910, representing the Bunbury branch of the Australian Women's National League, she organised a civic reception for Sir John and Lady Forrest.[12] Subcommittees were needed for a reception for Premier Sir Newton and Lady Moore that aimed to include the whole community.[13] Ivy often shared committee work with her mother, in women's associations which, as George *et al.* point out, 'gave women public voices'.[14]

The Australian Women's National League operated from 1904 to the mid-1950s, promoting loyalty to the throne, resistance to 'state socialism', political education for women and the protection of home life.[15] The movement also coincided with increasing government intervention in local affairs. With the support of Sir John Forrest, a Bunbury branch was formed in 1909 and became a forum for visiting speakers.[16] Ivy Paisley was still active in the organisation in 1927, timing her Perth holiday with the visit of a high-placed League official.[17]

Unusually, Ivy was not noted for her wartime activity. However, with four siblings at war, sending letters and parcels to them all would have kept her occupied. It is also possible that her interests did not incline towards the domestic pursuits that were integral to home-front activity. Already active in her community, Ivy took a different wartime path from the majority of her contemporaries, yet her life also exhibits a change of direction during and after the war. The Great War disrupted the idea of universal marriage for women, although, for Ivy, the war came when she was already around

30 years of age, past the then accepted age of marriage for women. In wartime when so many men were away, most women were 'single', all, like Ivy, impatiently waiting for mail from their men-folk. While war offered women like her sister Vera independence and the opportunity to be at the centre of events overseas, it is likely Ivy felt pressure to remain with her ageing parents.

Alongside the intense patriotic activity of the Wellington community, local needs remained, and here, Ivy Paisley was a major contributor.[18] In 1916, for example, she organised a major fete to raise funds for renovations to the community hall and Bishop's House.[19] This was well-supported by the local community, unlike the Sailor's Rest which languished in wartime. In 1917, Ivy became 'lady librarian' and member of the municipal library committee, 'advising' the Bunbury Council on the management and promotion of the library.[20] She received her certificate of technical studies at Continuation and Technical evening classes, which was now supported by the Bunbury Traders Association, possibly with post-war needs in mind.[21] The preponderance of girls was notable; fifteen girls as against three boys received certificates. Like its predecessor, 'continuation school' taught English, mathematics, sciences and humanities, while 'technical school' included business, manufacturing and domestic subjects. Ivy, recipient of a 'technical' certificate, probably studied business subjects such as typing and accounting.

The war ended with loss at home as well as in battle, with the 1918 death of Caroline Mitchell, public woman and mother of later premier Sir James and two unmarried daughters, Kate and Amy, Ivy's associates.[22] In 1919, a public gathering celebrated the seemingly safe return from overseas of all four Paisley siblings.[23] At war's end, with so many men lost, marriage became even less likely. However, Ivy's life continued as actively as before, and new challenges beckoned. Ivy held a paid position as municipal 'lady librarian' for 20 years, her holidays now 'annual leave', after which she ran her own library.[24] In 1926, she became social correspondent for the *South-Western Times*, possibly also in a paid capacity.[25] While Ivy used her clerical skills in a voluntary capacity prior to the war, her further education and move into paid work during and after the war is consistent with Kingston's observation that the war precipitated women into white collar jobs.[26]

Moving in the same social circle as Bunbury feminists Eliza Cons and Violet Bayliss, Ivy encountered feminist influences. In 1929, a branch of the Country Women's Association was formed in Bunbury, Ivy serving as treasurer and her mother as a vice president.[27] The CWA, originating in New South Wales, was formed in Western Australia in 1922 by Perth political activist Bessie Rischbieth, to promote the health and welfare of women and children, especially in country areas.[28] The CWA was supported in Western Australia by the National Council of Women and the Karrakatta Club, of which Edith Cowan, MLA, was a member.[29] The CWA was promoted in Bunbury as a 'non-political and non-sectarian body' with facilities for recreation, 'bush nursing and cooperation among country people'.[30] Members came from Bunbury and the surrounding districts including Burekup, Dardanup, and Brunswick. Demonstrating support for women's causes, the Bon Marché department store, which already served the association's members, strategically provided the necessary facilities. Ivy was instrumental in organising Bunbury's Centenary of Western Australia celebrations and the Anglican Archbishop's retirement fund.[31]

Ivy's prominent social position is reflected in reporting of her postwar activities, which included receptions in 1934 for Sir James Mitchell and for the leading Wagnerian soprano of her day Madame Florence Austral, née Florence Mary Wilson, and shipboard receptions on the SS *Clan Matheson* in 1924, HMAS *Canberra* in 1929 and in 1934 HMAS *Australia*.[32] Sport remained a serious pursuit and, in 1929, Ivy became Bunbury singles champion in croquet after intense competition with a local male member of parliament. In the same year, at the age of 43, she became the president of the local hockey association.[33]

In 1937, Ivy, now 45, 'decided to branch out from a life of domesticity and social activities' to farm with her uncle, having 'acquired' her grandfather's Quindalup property west of Busselton, where her mother had been born.[34]

Interestingly, on her departure from Bunbury, the press referred only to her absence from her social circles in Bunbury rather than her public activity, suggesting a lack of language able to encapsulate the new directions being taken by women. However, the same report detailed the farming activities of four other single women of the Busselton district, aligning her with them.[35] Ivy may well have been acquainted with these women, as newspaper reports from 1911 and 1937 show them associating at balls and funerals.[36] Ivy probably managed the farm accounts and correspondence, but she may well have participated in farming activities such as milking, butter and cheese making, and attending to newborn calves. In 1943, after six years, Ivy leased the farm and returned to Bunbury.[37]

We can only speculate as to the reasons why, relatively late in life, Ivy took up farming. However, two of her brothers had taken up soldier settlement properties, and her uncle, who was later found to have TB, may have needed assistance. It was a significant change in direction, and if, as suggested by Kingston, 'war exacerbated divisions between married and unmarried women', the fact that she was unmarried would have simplified the transition.[38] However, she was living independently of her parents.[39]

It is easier to account for Ivy's return to Bunbury. It might have been simply a desire to be closer to her then 80-year-old mother, however, the Repat files suggest a more compelling reason.[40] Ivy's sister Vera left Dongara in February 1937, just as Ivy moved to Busselton, perhaps expecting Vera to be company for their mother. By mid-1938, however, Vera was seriously ill, although doing some nursing in Bunbury.[41] She was soon diagnosed with 'mild insanity' but her appeals for a pension increase were disallowed as Repat were adamant that her mental condition was unconnected with her war service.[42] Ivy was now advocating for Vera, caring for her and their distraught mother, and both were supporting Vera financially.[43] Meanwhile Cyril, suffering from TB in Perth, became a father, with all its attendant joys and fears.[44] Les and his wife, farming in Tambellup, were still taking part in community life, but farming was becoming increasingly difficult as Les battled old wounds and neurasthenia.[45] Two years after Ivy's return to

Bunbury, Les and his wife returned there themselves, soon to take up the fight on Vera's behalf.

Ivy now faced pressure from all directions. Having blossomed into the public domain following the war, she must now be considered a victim of the war. In a district which sent so many to war, few families carried such heavy post-war burdens. Ivy died suddenly in 1947, four years after her return from the farm and two years before her mother's death.[46] Ivy had not participated in public patriotic work during the war, yet the feverish activity around her must have contributed to her increasing public activity in the post-war period. Her obituary referred to her as a 'social worker' and celebrated her paid and unpaid community work, her organisational skill and her sporting achievements, presenting her as a 'public woman' who used her talents fully for the benefit of her community.[47]

The sense of purpose that women experienced during the war made it difficult for them to return to empty socialising after the war. George *et al.* argue that after World War I, women entered the public domain in increasing numbers, but cultural conditioning that placed women in the home prevented their words and actions from being translated into the 'rhetorical memory'.[48] The failure of individual women's successes to translate into institutional success was the result of cultural limitations that in the 1920s and 1930s led to an undervaluing of the actions of successful women. These perceptions are equally relevant to Wellington women in the post-war period, despite press efforts to promote women's interests, as the lives of Greta Baldock and Kate Joel illustrate.

Two Married Women: Greta Baldock and Kate Joel

Charlie Snell mentioned meeting Greta Baldock during his stopover in Fremantle on his way to the front. She was in Fremantle to farewell her sister's husband, Henry Foxworthy.[49] Greta Baldock was one of nine surviving children and, like Ivy Paisley, daughter of a Bunbury public man.[50] Born in 1893, she was a regular prize-winner at school and became a proficient musician.[51] In her youth, she was a member of the Women's Christian Temperance Union, and in 1911 aged nineteen, she gained the English prize at the Bunbury technical school, some years before Ivy Paisley studied there.[52] For two years, she was head teacher of a small school near Mandurah, closer to Perth, before returning to teach in South Bunbury, where she also held the 'purely woman's' position of secretary of the Bunbury District Nursing Association for at least three years.[53] During the war, with two brothers serving, she worked with the Red Cross, bringing her into contact with public women such as Edith Cowan.[54] In 1924 she made an extended trip to England, Europe and Norway where her sister lived with her sea-captain husband.[55] Greta married in 1926, aged 33, moved to the city and was never reported in the press again.[56] However, in her later years, she returned to teaching, in Waroona north of Harvey, from 1953–57.[57]

Greta was in the paid workforce for eighteen years. Coming from a prosperous family, she might have remained in the domestic sphere, but as one of six girls, this was less likely, and being bright, teaching was a suitable option. Greta may have been conscious of accusations of selfishness of women who rejected childbirth, but her late marriage naturally delayed the arrival of children. Her mother had given birth to eleven children in fifteen years, which may have provided her with an added incentive to delay marriage and children. In the event, she had only one surviving daughter.[58] Greta was a middle-class woman, who took part in patriotic activities, was in the workforce and certainly experienced feminist influences, yet feminist writers are unlikely to have considered her important to the feminist agenda.[59]

George *et al.* point to a perception that women failed to leave a lasting mark on the public imagination because they did not write about their experiences. The local conscription debate was also muted and not conducted along gender lines.[60] This may help to explain why feminist historians have dismissed patriotic activities as not creating any lasting change in the lives of women. Although the women consciously adopted masculine/professional language, the work was voluntary, another reason why it has been ignored by feminists. All the wartime press rhetoric devoted to the patriotic work of women has thus been discarded as unimportant. However, the life of Kate Joel, a married contemporary of Ivy Paisley, illustrates MacKinnon's argument that the war caused 'irrevocable changes' to the lives of women, as those with 'newly developed capacities' used them 'in ways which separated their generation from those who had gone before'.[61]

London-born Kate Davis married Dr Simon Joel in 1902 and was the mother of a young family in wartime.[62] As the wife of a Bunbury professional man, her pre-war life was devoted to child-rearing and social activities, but she was instrumental in a range of patriotic organisations during the war. Instead of retreating into domesticity after the war, she remained in the public sphere, directing her energies to the needs of the poor, especially those affected by war. Her post-war meetings continued to be held in public spaces and her public rhetoric remained militarised and masculine.[63]

Scates has pointed out that organisations like the Red Cross served to 'militarise charity' and offered women a chance 'to share in the great struggle', yet the military language adopted during wartime did not simply go away once the war was over.[64] In 1920, the Red Cross, of which Mrs Joel remained a member, determined that the Red Cross 'machine' should be 'kept going with all pistons working', raising funds for a local ambulance service.[65] Mrs Joel worked with a 'battalion' of middle-class ladies of the Bunbury Benevolent Society, more visible than ever after the war.[66] In masculinised language, the 1923 committee was now 'the Executive', meetings were held in a public library and although under a male chairman, the committee was dominated by women, and men and women acted as equals.[67] In a report on the society's activities, 'applicants for relief' were 'interviewed' and assistance in the form of funds, firewood and rail fares was 'issued' to indigent and invalid women and 'penniless girls'. Moreover, the (female) secretary was 'instructed' to canvass the mostly male business managers for donations. This use of masculine language enabled women to assume the position of men's equals and assert themselves in the public sphere. Mrs Joel was also active in the Save the Children Fund, the Seamen's

Institute, the Wellington Agricultural Society and the Harbour Lights Guild while maintaining social activities such as bridge, golf, tennis and rowing.[68] Like most middle-class women of her time, Mrs Joel had several staff to manage home and family while she was engaged in her public activities.[69]

When Dr Joel retired, the family returned to his birthplace in Melbourne, where he died as a result of a road accident.[70] After her husband's death, Mrs Joel enjoyed the social life of Melbourne, but maintained her interest in public affairs as president of a local Zionist organisation during World War II and as a member of the Liberal Party and charity organisations.[71] She made regular return visits to Bunbury, where she was part owner of a hotel, and attended an anniversary celebration for the Bridgetown RSL Ladies' Auxiliary with its state officials.[72] For her 1941 visit she flew to Perth and in 1950 made a visit to the UK.[73] Mrs Joel was a wealthy woman by this time and could have slipped into a life of ease, yet she maintained her interest in public affairs and took a leading role in the organisations she supported. Her World War I activities were clearly a turning point in her life.

The increasing acceptance of women after the war was in the public sphere rather than in the workplace. Mrs Duce and Mrs George Clarke, the mayor's wife, similarly maintained a wide range of public activities after the war.[74] Mrs Duce assumed the position of 'superintendent' of the Sailors' Rest when Miss Cons resigned in 1924, showing that, while in pre-war years public philanthropy was largely the domain of unmarried women such as Eliza Cons and Violet Bayliss, post-war, married women were moving into these roles.[75] Around this time, a Mrs Clark of Mount Lawley, who may have been a Snell correspondent, was active in an astonishing array of public positions.[76] She was vice-president, chairman, secretary, treasurer or board member of no less than six organisations serving soldiers and their dependents, as well as the Perth Hospital Board, the Westralian Industries League, the Women's Immigration Auxiliary Council and National Council of Women, activities which encompassed repatriation, health, education, immigration, industry and politics.

Janie Sutton: Gender and the Aviatrix

Janie Sutton was not the first Wellington woman to take flight. Doctor Elsie Port was reported flying as a passenger in the mail plane from Perth to Adelaide in 1932.[77] Born in Bunbury in 1883, and in the public eye from early age, Elsie left Bunbury for Perth in 1902 and San Francisco in 1916 to study chiropractic medicine.[78] She spent her life lecturing on women's health, in Australia, the UK, China, South Africa and America.[79] For her, a healthy body was essential for women, now that they were 'taking their place in every walk of life'.[80]

Janie Sutton, a close friend of the Snell family, operated in the masculine sphere during the post-war period. Sutton epitomises George's post-war woman who, rather than demanding to be heard, simply acted in her chosen field.[81] The recognition of pioneering women aviators by feminists resulted from their ability to disconnect gender from their activities, successfully 'disrupting culturally constructed norms of womanhood'. Gendered rhetoric surrounded women's exploits from the earliest reports of women in flight, and post-World War I, women aviators provoked further discussion around whether women could perform as well as men. The Western Australian press created its own rhetoric surrounding women in aviation, qualifying them to change the way women were perceived by society.

The world of the aviatrix provides a window into the interwar discourse surrounding gender. The term 'aviatrix' as the designation for a female pilot appeared in the Western Australian press between 1921 and 1954.[82] The narration of 'firsts' and other events involving women in aviation, included the first reported women's air race (1929, USA), an altitude record set by a woman, and the record-breaking flight of Amy Johnson to Australia. At the same time, the debate about the place of women in the public sphere in general and in aviation in particular was being played out.[83]

While there are no references to female aviators in the pre-war Western Australian press, the first Australian news items on women in aviation appeared in a Sydney newspaper in 1911 with another seven until 1914, after which no more appeared until 1921.[84] Facing opposition from men, women who did take up flying had to have the 'determination to overcome the prevailing mentality' that women should not be in the air.[85] The need to maintain the craft, either employing (and trusting) a mechanic, or doing it themselves, and the expense were added impediments for women fliers. However, men soon noted that women were quick to learn, dexterous, conscientious and compliant, and made good fliers. Lebow characterises early female aviators as confident individuals from childhood, flying because they had ridden bicycles and driven motorcycles and cars and now wanted to fly planes.[86] Fliers were either independent women who had the time and money, or working women who made sacrifices for their hobby. There was a hiatus in women's flying during World War I as women fliers served as ambulance drivers and mechanics. By the end of the war, former fliers were confronted with new technology and the expense of retraining, so a new cohort of women took up the challenge.

During the interwar years, female aviators 'presented a popular image', yet, despite the fact that women were welcomed and even encouraged to take to the air, the language used to describe their achievements remained highly gendered.[87] A two-stage process was at work: having first liberated the women from their previous domestic bonds and accepted them into the male sphere, it was then necessary to develop a non-gendered language to describe women in their new role. Only through the work of scholars such as Ann Summers and Germaine Greer in the 1960s and 70s was there a serious effort to apply non-gendered language to women.[88]

Female aviators, especially America's Amelia Earhart, created a significant body of writing.[89] Although Amelia Earhart (born 1897) did not make an official visit to Australia, she was extensively reported in the Western Australian press, in more than 800 articles from 1928 until long after her death in 1937.[90] As a new career, aviation provided a 'hospitable climate' for women, although they were denied access to commercial and military aviation.[91] Earhart's own scrapbooks of women in public life, recording women overcoming barriers and combining careers and marriage, show that by the early 20th century, opportunities for women were already expanding. As a tomboyish child, Earhart enjoyed outdoor pursuits and struggled against restrictions, growing into an adulthood characterised by self-control and courage.[92] Earhart's war work as a volunteer nurse (Voluntary Aid Detachment or VAD) in Canada placed her in contact with aviators, awakening her interest in flying. Working to pay for lessons, Earhart learnt to fly in 1921 and specialised in long-distance flights, which ultimately resulted in her death in 1937. Janie Sutton, born in Harvey in 1910, began flying in 1937, around the time Earhart disappeared.

Two members of the Sutton family figure in the Snell archive. The first, Janie's sister Florence (Flossie), was listed on Snell's dance card for a private dance at the home of Thomas Hayward in August 1913, and Snell's wartime letters home from New South Wales and France made reference to Janie's father.[93] William John Sutton and his wife, Florence Cecilia Logue, were both from local pioneering families.[94] He was unusually old at 48 years of age on enlistment in the Light Horse in 1915, and served for just eight months.[95] In the five months he spent in Egypt, he was admitted to hospital multiple times for measles and bronchitis. Returning home, he became an official recruiting organiser for the Harvey district. [96]

Janie Sutton's childhood was typical of life in Australia's country towns. Days were spent wandering through the bush and around the water holes, collecting flowers and observing the birds, with a baby kangaroo or goanna for a pet and helping on the family property.[97] Her education at the local school instilled in her a sense of loyalty to Empire and included community picnics and concerts and agricultural shows. Surviving memories of her dictate that 'if she were a boy, she would have been called a larrikin', a term later applied to the hard drinking, hard fighting, and wild living Australian soldiers at war.[98] Sutton's childhood experiences helped to qualify her for later enlistment in the Women's Auxiliary Air Force.[99]

Janie worked alongside her mother in patriotic activities during the war, and at the age of eight, she became a correspondent with the children's column in the *Western Mail,* developing skills and attitudes that she later applied to wartime fundraising.[100] At the age of ten, when her sister married, the men were still identified by their wartime battalions.[101] In 1925, at the age of 15, Janie moved to Perth to attend business college before working as nurse/receptionist for a Perth dentist and later joining the staff of a department store in the city, where she worked until 1941.[102] From November 1934, on her departure on a trip to the Eastern states, she was represented by the press as a vibrant young woman about town.[103]

Janie's association with the flying community began in 1937, when she gained a flying scholarship with the Royal Aero Club, and from August 1938, she was 'the only woman in Western Australia now qualified to hold a Commonwealth "A" pilot's license'.[104] In World War II, as a VAD, she worked with her local Red Cross committee to raise funds for an ambulance for the Royal Australian Navy.[105] In 1942 she joined the Women's Auxiliary Air Force as a radio operator and telegraphist.[106] Post-war, she flew throughout Western Australia for a local airline in multiple roles, including wireless operator/navigator and flight attendant, reflecting the forces which kept women out of the pilot seat in military and commercial aviation. She tested radio equipment for the United Nations Relief program and taught Morse telegraphy to 70 civil air pilots who later served throughout Australia and overseas. Although twice engaged, Janie never married and died in 1949 at the age of 39 years.[107]

By 1930, Western Australia had two licensed woman pilots, and Janie gained her pilot's license as a result of a general policy of encouraging women to fly. The local press welcomed the fact that 'throughout the Empire the "fair sex" was being encouraged to fly'.[108] At this time, the British Air Ministry offered flying scholarships and subsidised flying lessons to women, and a British law which prohibited women from holding a commercial pilot's license was rescinded, enabling 'women of all ranks' to take up flying. The visit of Amy Johnson to Australia in 1930 also boosted the number of Australian women seeking instruction.

From 1932, the Western Australian branch of the Australian Aero Club offered flying scholarships for men and women over the age of 17.[109]

The most promising candidate in a trial lesson was offered free flying instruction leading to the 'A' class license. The club held regular flying races, and the women's race in 1932, 'The Oaks,' attracted four entrants, three flying club craft and one flying her own plane.[110] Janie Sutton was awarded a flying scholarship in 1937, from a small number of female entrants among the 'swarms of mechanical minded men'.[111] That year, after the initial enthusiasm of Western Australian women for aviation, there were no longer any active licensed woman pilots in the State.[112] Two had left the city, one moving to New Guinea with her aircraft-inspector husband, while another left to manage the family farm in her husband's absence. While the Depression partially explained the decline in interest in flying among women, marriage was the major cause:

> *A girl who devotes much enthusiasm to flying has not much time to think of marriage. And most women want to marry. And most husbands hate their wives to fly.*

Marriage and a future in aviation were therefore mutually exclusive, as women left flying seemingly without reluctance on marriage. However, by the 1920s and 1930s more women were combining marriage with a flying career.[113]

The flying scholarships continued until 1947, after which there were sufficient wartime pilots for the needs of commercial aviation. Although women were being enticed into aviation, press reporting did not treat them as equals: they remained the 'fair sex with a helmet for every frock colour'.[114] While Janie Sutton broke gender barriers, she too was a victim of this gendered reporting, despite being a qualified member of the flying community.

While Janie was 'solidly plugging away at her flying hours', she remained 'a very attractive and vivid young woman, with the long lines, clear-cut features and fine skin one would want to find in a good-looking young airwoman'.[115] Despite her ability, enthusiasm and dedication, her appearance, 'tall, slim, pretty and young', dominated reporting.[116] Although Amelia

Earhart, learning to fly in 1921, immediately adopted masculine dress, it was not yet universal, nor even the female version of military dress that was 'permitted' to the Red Cross in wartime.[117] Masculine dress was eventually to become 'part of the performed rhetoric' for female fliers, archival images showing English aviator Amy Johnson wearing masculine flying dress in 1930, with jodhpurs, shirt, tie and helmet – complemented by the occasional fur.[118] Western Australia's isolation must have played its part, Janie's nod to professionalism simply 'a very becoming scarlet leather flying hat with a scarlet cardigan over a bright blue frock', contrasting with 'amateurs' who wore their 'oldest and least romantic clothes'.[119] By 1938, Janie was known as the 'Gadabout girl', 'Perth's one and only licensed flying woman', and associating with sportsmen such as Empire (later Commonwealth) Games rowers and athletes and later, sailors and golfers.[120] In 1939, as 'pretty' Miss Janie Sutton, she was moving comfortably among the top echelons of the flying community, including the founders of civil aviation in WA, the Royal Aero Club and military personnel at Pearce Air Base.[121]

When Janie presented for enlistment in the RAAF in January 1942, the military took a balanced view of her, assessing her on qualities useful to the forces: her education and skills, her leadership qualities and her adaptability. Her qualifications included 'Junior certificate, business subjects, driver's license, (car and wagon), First Aid and Home Nursing, (Saint John Association), six years dental nursing, telegraphist, and an 'A' class Pilot License'.[122] The enrolling officer commented: 'A neat appearance, clean, a good intelligent type, well mannered, officer type, can rough it'. Her country childhood gave her the skills needed to cross gender barriers and take to the air.

Women in aviation became a catalyst for discourse on the changing place of women in society, in the professions and in government. While gendered language and traditional stereotypes of women as wives and mothers remained prominent in the public discourse, there had been significant change in attitudes to women. A writer in 1927 noted women's political influence through the National Council of Women, the

Housewives' Association, the labour movement and the League of Nations, and the ability of the single female member of State Parliament to relate to her fellow members on equal terms.[123] Noting the presence of women in the traditionally male fields of commerce, the law and medicine, the author patronisingly described the female government psychologist, an aviator in her spare time, as 'a quiet … cheerful *little* lady'.[124] The 'higher status of women in public, professional and commercial life' raised women beyond the status of 'dutiful housekeeper and mother' to a position of near-equality. Just as women's entry into the workforce had eroded barriers between the public and private spheres, their entry into the world of aviation caused further disruption because in command of an aircraft, men and women were equal.

Reporting on British aviator, Amy Johnson's visit in 1930 highlighted the way women operating in a masculine world adopted their style, even as some women also exploited their femininity.[125] Observed by 'hundreds of men', Johnson was 'a smiling goddess with the pleased smile of a conqueror and the slim form of the beautiful young lady who had so ruthlessly shattered man's ideas about the superiority of the sterner sex'. This proves, remarks the author, that

> *if they are given equal opportunity, we can look to women to provide not only the brain power required in medical, legal, political, judicial, journalistic and other fields, but acts of heroism and gallantry, regardless of their sex.*

Reports on the community response to Johnson's visit show women taking control of public events. The National Council of Women, the Women's Service Guilds and the national Labor Women's organisations, represented by a female member of the Legislative Assembly, led the proceedings, while a woman directed the musical items.[126] While the mainstream press emphasised women's part in the event, the Australian Labor Party's *Westralian Worker* gave equal weight to both sexes.[127] In Labor's terms, the event was run by the female 'officers' of the Labor

Women's central executive, with male members of the Labor movement playing subordinate roles, selling tickets, acting as door keepers and generally assisting the women, showing that Labor already accepted women in leadership roles.[128] When a female speaker expressed her pride in the achievement of the young aviatrix as a woman, Johnson, in turn, recognised the speaker's pioneering place in politics.

Amy Johnson's visit also provoked further debate on marriage. A 'Mere Man' opined that despite the achievements of individual women, marriage should still be their goal, and that by taking to the air, women were making themselves unmarriageable.[129] Such a woman would 'overshadow her husband with her money, fame and flying record, overturning ideas about the traditional roles of men and women'. The writer feared that women would no longer be satisfied with marriage and family, thus threatening the future of the human race.

Aviation provided a space for the development of suitable language to represent the changes in the relative position of men and women in society. A 23-year-old Sydney airwoman took the Minister for Defence to task for his comment that he had a 'fatherly' talk with her over the airworthiness of her aircraft.[130] She reasoned: 'I'm not a child. We spoke on a business matter in a business-like way. I've a father of my own who is quite capable of giving me all the paternal advice I need.' She refused to allow the Civil Aviation Department to dictate whether or not she should fly her plane from Mildura to Sydney, a distance of more than 500 miles (840 kilometres) stating: 'I'm going to fly that bus to Sydney whether the authorities pass it or not'.

Although British and Australian female authors had long since created articulate heroines in the domestic sphere, the placing of women in new social contexts necessitated the negotiation of a new language for dialogue between the sexes.[131] It now seems natural that a higher authority should decide such matters as airworthiness, however, the foregoing debate occurred when gender roles were being contested, creating new opportunities for women, the press documenting and critiquing the process.[132]

In contrast to the gendered language used by British Australians, the Chinese Consul-General of Sydney, speaking on behalf of Chinese Australians, referred to Johnson simply as one who had 'achieved greatness by sheer force of personal effort, an act of gallantry which will enrich the history of our great country.'[133]

There was widespread acceptance, at least in the Western Australian press, that women's position in relation to work and politics had changed. Post-World War I aviators like Sutton flew across continents and oceans, not only flying but contributing to the development of aviation in areas such as communication and navigation.[134] Janie Sutton, and other women like her, who participated in patriotic activity as children during World War I, and learnt to fly in the inter-war years, created a direct link between the wars which saw them also serving in World War II.[135] In her wartime teaching role and through the press adulation that surrounded her during her flying years, Janie Sutton created her own form of rhetoric. She embodied the new perceptions of women created by those who came before, but like many other female aviators, did not live into a full maturity which may have given her further opportunities to influence later generations of women.

Ivy Paisley and Janie Sutton, born 25 years apart, both remained single, died around the same time, Sutton just two years after Paisley. Paisley's childhood was more urban than Sutton's and both were sports minded, yet the pattern of their lives was almost reversed, with Ivy's later years spent in farming. Both were public women and both trod new ground post-World War I, especially Sutton, in taking to the air. For both, there are strong indications that the war influenced the directions their lives took, with Sutton playing an active part in World War II.

The four women considered here, two married and two unmarried, two decidedly 'working' women, one more ambivalently and the fourth definitely non-working, illustrate a continuum of workforce participation and life in the public domain before and after World War I, which strongly suggests that women's lives moved away from the domestic towards the public as a result of World War I. Whether women retreated towards domesticity as a result of World War II remains a separate question.

10

CONCLUSION

The Wellington community was one of hundreds across Australia that responded to the call to war. Individual and collective narratives highlight the Bunbury–Harvey community's pioneering history, its participation in the war and its response to the aftermath.

The search for meaning in a trunk of old papers has revealed the Snell population in Western Australia's Wellington (Bunbury–Harvey) community, identifying the connections and interactions that defined the community's modes of operating in wartime and beyond and an assessment of the impact of World War I on the community. The Snell population was defined by the 200 names contained in the letters of my great-uncle, Charlie Snell. Around these names emerges a longitudinal study of the community from the earliest days of European settlement, through the pioneering period, World War I and the post-war period. Contemporary sources have revealed the lives of individuals and families, identifying personal narratives, community relationships and social structures, showing how a dynamic community developed social capital, fought the war and coped with its aftermath. In a close-knit community, the editors and contributors to the local press were also personal friends of the individuals reported on, making the reports all the more personal. The individuals and families named in the letter archive formed a significant part of the leadership group of the Wellington community. When war came, the enlistment and war-time experiences of the men, their wounding, illnesses, deaths and captivity were documented in the press alongside meticulous reporting of the patriotic effort on the home front by parents, friends and siblings. The National Archives of Australia and the Australian War Memorial hold the records of the military cohort, conveniently summarised for Wellington men and women by Jeff Pierce in his *Anzac Heroes* website. Post-war newspapers are muted with regard to private struggles, but repatriation files document in harrowing detail the trials of returned men and women.

The Wellington community which sent its sons to war was fortified by its connection to the British Empire and strong social capital created during the pioneering period. Led by its public men, the community grew, adapting British civic structures and occupations to feeding the population, educating the young and maintaining their culture in an alien environment. In a community of farmers, agricultural societies promoted education and experimentation and interactions between rural and urban dwellers, thereby creating social capital. Local government was implemented by leading men who managed community needs, and increasingly interacted with state government in Perth. The women created homes, nurtured the young and managed social events. Marriages and funerals united family and community. The young lived in harmony with the environment, learning survival skills and adaptability that later served them on the battlefront but often eluded them in their post-war struggles.

Interacting with the farming communities were the timber-getters and miners, facilitated by the railways focussed on the port of Bunbury. The later connection of the district to the capital city brought the Snell family to the district. Through rural-urban interactions, the population was neither bushman nor city-dwellers, but something in between as residents bridged the gap between the rural and the urban in their daily lives. Three 'Bunbury boys', John Forrest, Newton Moore and James Mitchell, all raised in Bunbury, developed the civic engagement needed to enter local, state, federal, and even British parliament. Return trips 'home' to England allowed Wellington people to record the changes that had taken place since they had emigrated. The longevity of many settlers gave the community a strong sense of history, local identity, and connection to Empire which heightened their understanding of the threat of war. Class consciousness was evident but relaxed at community events.

The Wellington community's wartime contribution used pre-war community structures and their embedded social capital to fight the war on the home front and the battlefield. Masculine community structures were transformed into munitions committees to recruit men, raise funds and manage repatriation. The wives and daughters of the public men rose to prominence in their own committees, raising funds for the Belgians, manufacturing sandbags, medical aids and comforts to their soldier heroes at the battle front. Community spirits intensified as men, women and children collaborated in wartime ventures, while social capital helped to assuage the grief and loss of war.

Recruiting difficulties in 1916 and 1917 led to the two conscription referenda, which, although disruptive, did not cause the divisiveness which appeared over much of Australia, because the Wellington community, like much of Western Australia, had already concluded that compulsion was needed. Disappointed by Australia's rejection of conscription, the community nevertheless quickly refocussed attention on the needs of soldiers. More than 1,900 men and several women went to war, of whom around 450 died. Some men suffered the indignity of multiple rejections to their applications for enlistment while men who had gone to school, worked, played and celebrated with their community became casualties of war. Few who returned were untouched by its effects.

The public discourse on repatriation and the private post-war narratives of the men and women who settled the land, show that the efforts and good-will of local committees could not match the needs of the returned men, whose problems far exceeded even the most far-sighted projections of the Wellington committees. Newspapers documented the public lives of returned veterans and their families, yet the official repatriation files contain often confronting material on the private lives of the returned men and women and their families. Disfigurement, pain, frustration, self-justification and determination appear on the part of the men, concern and sense of entitlement on the part of the women, and a combination of compassion and perplexity on the part of the Repat officials who tried to balance material assistance to the veterans and their families with the limited financial resources of the government.

While the Bunbury community was proactive in its wartime planning for returning men, the imperatives of state and commonwealth repatriation policies took precedence and ultimately disempowered existing community efforts despite the fact that some of those in power were Wellington men. Returning men embarked on new occupations, married and raised families, struggling against war-caused disabilities and new traumas in their battles with Repat officials. Soldier settlers faced overgrown land, environmental problems, war wounds, neurasthenia, malaria and chronic bronchitis, while their families suffered with them as they fought with Repat for recognition. Financial constraints led to confrontations with a medical profession which had to balance compassion against limited knowledge and lack of diagnostic techniques for the ailments suffered by their 'pensioners'. Government repatriation policies also created a diaspora of returned men and their families from the Wellington district, and brought new settlers to the district. The exchange of population resulting from the loss of well-known individuals from the district and the arrival of new settlers diluted the social capital of pre-war times.

Medical officers were faced with new kinds of trauma which they were only beginning to recognise as something other than character deficiencies. Many Wellington war veterans suffered throughout long lives from the effects of war and the ongoing struggle with Repat for the medical, emotional and financial assistance they needed. In their dealings with officialdom, they were effectively removed from the support of their communities. Contemporary literature on war neurosis with current understanding of post-traumatic illness arising from recent wars and catastrophes enables a reassessment of the range of symptoms reported by Wellington veterans. Current policy aims to destigmatise trauma and increase access to support for survivors, offering new perspectives on the sufferings of World War I survivors. A tuberculosis sufferer raised a family and worked in the civil service despite his illness. A former prisoner of war unaccountably developed thyroid problems. Amputees and a trench foot sufferer eventually led productive lives, while a chronic bronchitis sufferer and a man already stricken with Becker Muscular Dystrophy had their lives cut short. A blinded veteran led a fulfilling life due to the unmistakable nature of his disability, unlike those whose disabilities were less recognisable.

Wives struggled to care for their disabled veterans and men sometimes had to advocate for sisters suffering their own war wounds. Wives, daughters and sisters who advocated for ailing veterans, became increasingly assertive in their dealings with officials. Many wives endured long and trying widowhoods, still needing to deal with Repat. Wellington nurses too, often battled the effects of wartime trauma, and, like the men, struggled for recognition of their problems and were forced to work long after the war. For many women, pre-war expectations of marriage and motherhood gave way to the post-war reality of caregiving, widowhood or solitude.

Some of Wellington's repatriation stories confirm the findings of earlier studies. However, new stories document the lives of men who took up land, changed occupations and endured setbacks before finding fulfilling long-term roles. Allowances made by work colleagues for disabled veterans provide a subtext to these narratives. That most Wellington survivors were affected for the rest of their lives by the war, attests to the inability of community resources developed before the war to adequately support them. Despite genuine compassion on the part of many doctors and officials, the men and women who returned from war were denied recognition of their status as victims of trauma, traumas relived and revived by the suspicion intrinsic in the repatriation process. Their stories thus did not end until the deaths of surviving family members. The eventual formalising of the PTSD diagnosis, long after the deaths of most veterans, has removed some of the stigma of war-caused mental illness for recent trauma sufferers, but too late for Wellington veterans.

Women, who had been largely invisible in the pre-war period, came into prominence in wartime in supporting roles for the men on the battle front, in caring roles in periods of war-caused grief, and as carers and advocates for their damaged war veterans. While the emotional support of women in the grieving process is well-recognised in the literature, through wartime loss, men too discovered new self-understanding in their emotional lives. The public discourse surrounding gender in the Bunbury press advanced the debate around women in the public sphere both before and after the war, showing that change was occurring before the war.

Debate on the influence of the war on women's workforce participation has generally been anecdotal. Census data shows a movement of women out of the workforce in response to the needs of ailing veterans. Western Australian women lagged behind their eastern states' counterparts in workplace participation prior to the war, but over the period examined made rapid gains, supporting Bolton's assertion that Western Australia was a state apart in its historical development.[1]

This study confirms Scates's assertion that women did real work during wartime and that the war caused subtle changes in the lives of women, paving the way for greater advancement in the roles of women in World War II. Women did not always retreat into the private sphere after the war. Life narratives of four Wellington women show how they responded to public discourses and wartime experiences, remaining in the public sphere after the war and adapting their community activities to post-war needs and entering new occupations. The lives of the non-working women underwent the greatest change as a result of the war. Kate Joel raised her children in comfortable domesticity, but, in wartime, was precipitated into the public domain as a leader of Bunbury's patriotic effort. After the war she remained active in public view. The Paisley sisters followed different paths, one becoming increasingly active in the public domain and the other going to war and suffering harrowing post-war outcomes, contested throughout her long life. The daughter of one of Bunbury's public men, who might have remained in the domestic sphere. worked as a teacher for many years. A woman who, as a child during World War I, worked alongside the women of her community, moved to the city and prominence as a female aviator who served actively during World War II, impossible for women in the earlier war.

Community-building, with the social and cultural expression which contribute to wellbeing and the management of threats and crises, can mitigate the disastrous outcomes of war, assisted by intervention from the highest levels of government. War-caused illnesses, both physical and mental, and ongoing struggles against old injuries were compounded by battles with the repatriation authorities. Efforts continue to avoid the mistakes of the past, to mitigate the effects of later wars on those who fought and to assist in their transition to civilian life.

APPENDIX: POPULATION DATA – SNELL ARCHIVE

Bunbury/ Harvey	**Name**	**Date and place of birth**	**Address**	**Occupation**	**Relationship**	**Snell Archive: source date**	**Snell Archive: type of contact**
Snell Family							
aa	Snell, Alfred James	1864–1936	Harvey	Railway superintendent, orchardist, businessman	Father to CS	1912–1920	Letters and photographs,
aa1	Snell, Caroline Amelia, née Graves	1862–1935	Harvey	Servant on marriage, housewife	Mother to CS	1905–1916	mother
aa1	Snell, Alfred	1889–1971	Midland	Mechanic, naturalist	Brother to CS	1905, 1912, 17.10.1915, 11.8.1916	Letters and photographs
	Snell, Charles	1891–1916	Harvey	Orchardist			
aa3	Snell Marjorie	1901–2001	Bunbury, Harvey	Unmarried female	Sister to CS	1905 Bunbury image	Letters and photographs,

Bunbury/ Harvey	Name	Date and place of birth	Address	Occupation	Relationship	Snell Archive: source date	Snell Archive: type of contact
Bunbury Population							
bab	Abrahamson, Capt. John George	1878–1918	Bunbury	Harbourmaster, 1900–1913	AJS Associate	August 1916	Condolence card, hospital visit
bar	Armstrong, Roy	1882–1918	Bunbury, France	Farm labourer	Bunbury acquaintance	23.3.1916	CS comment: met in Egypt
bbac	Backhouse, Miss Dorothy	1892–1966, m. 1926, Wheeler	Bunbury/ Kalgoorlie	Volunteer, Fresh Air League	Bunbury acquaintance	August 1916	Hospital visit to CAS
bbala	Baldock, Annie	1889, m. 1911, JH Foxworthy	Bunbury	Temperance, Sailors' Rest, Bunbury District Nursing Association	School friend, neighbour	18.1.1916	CS met in Fremantle
bbalg	Baldock, Greta	1893–1980, m.L. Symes 1926	Bunbury	Schoolteacher, married 1926,	School friend, neighbour	18.1.1916	CS comment: in Fremantle
bbay	Bayliss, Miss Violet	1873–1943	Bunbury	Philanthropist, Sailors Rest', musician	Bunbury friend	August 1916	Hospital visit to CAS
bbei	Beigel, Herman Max	c. 1867–1933	Bunbury	Brewer	Neighbour, close friends	8.8. 1916	Conolence letters
bbei1	Beigel, Mary Emmeline	c. 1870, d. 1932	Bunbury	Housewife	Neighbour	August 1916	Hospital visit CAS
bbl	Blythe, Mrs Eliza Louisa (Houlihan)	1860–1946	Bunbury	Housewife	Bunbury acquaintance	August 1916	Hospital visit to CAS
bbl1	Blythe, Jack Howard Drummond	1889–1961	Bunbury	Wharf labourer	School contemporaries	19.5.1916	CS comment: met in France
bbr	Bray, Albert W	c. 1860	Bunbury	Reverend, Wesley Church, 1900–1905	Bunbury friend	August 1916	Hospital visit to CAS

Bunbury/ Harvey	Name	Date and place of birth	Address	Occupation	Relationship	Snell Archive: source date	Snell Archive: type of contact
bbre	Brenda and her ma'		Bunbury	Father ran public baths	Bunbury acquaintance	August 1916	Condolence letter
bbru	Bruton, Miss Kate	c. 1880–1943	Bunbury, Melbourne	Nurse	Family medical services	7.9.1916	Condolence letter
bbu	Buchanan Mrs Catherine Ann	c. 1835–1924	Bunbury	Wife of Rev. Buchanan, public man	Bunbury friends	6.9.1916	Condolence letter
bcas	Castieau, Mrs Margaret	c. 1866–1950	Seven Hills, Roelands	Nurse, farmer's wife, pianist	Family friends	24.7.1915, 9.8.1916	CS comment, Condolence letter,
bcas1	Castieau, Walter Buckley	1866–1934	Seven Hills, Roelands	Farmer, public man	Employer 6 months	30.11.1911	Testimonial for CS
bcl1	Clark, Lorrie T		Vincent St, Mt Lawley	Widow?	Former Harvey resident?	!7.11.1915, 9.8.1916	CS comment, condolence letter
bcl2	Clark, Ronald		Mt Lawley	Schoolboy		17.11.1915	Mentioned in mother's condolence letter
bcla	Clarke George Ephraim	1880–1958	Bunbury	Mayor of Bunbury	Bunbury acquaintance	August 1916	Hospital visit CAS
bcla1	Clarke, Mrs Elsie	1881, m. 1905	Burekup	Wife of GE Clarke, farmer/mayor	Bunbury/Harvey acquaintance	14.8.1916	Condolence letter
bcla2	Clarke Raymond Arthur	1884–1959	Roelands, France	Farmer, potatoes	Rifle shooting	31.10.1915, 18.5.1916, 19.5.1916	CS diary, comments in letters re commission, home leave
bcla3	Clarke, Mervyn Ephraim	1889–1986	Roelands, France	Farmer	Rifle shooting	31.10.1915	CS comment
bcla4	Clarke, Hubert	1886–1953+	Harvey	Farmer	Rifle shooting	24.7.1915	CS comment
bcle	Clements, Mrs Rose Victoria	1861–1932	Bunbury	Housewife, pianist	Bunbury friend	August 1916	Hospital visit CAS

Bunbury/ Harvey	Name	Date and place of birth	Address	Occupation	Relationship	Snell Archive: source date	Snell Archive: type of contact
bco	Cons, Miss Eliza	1842–1924	Bunbury	Charity worker', Sailors Rest	Bunbury friend	August 1916	Condolence card
bda	Dalton, Gwen	c. 1880	Bunbury	Unmarried female	Bunbury friend	26.8.1912	CS comment, met Kalgoorlie
bdan	Dannell, Emilia Fredrikke (husband Axel Dannell)	c. 1870–1941	Havelock St Perth	Husband: contractor	Former Bunbury residents	20.8.1916	Condolence letter
bdav	Davies, Mrs HC		Bunbury	Railway superintendent	Colleague of AJS	22.8.1916	Card, telegram
bdi	Dixon, Mrs Sarah Maria (Mainwaring)	1861–1936	Bunbury	Hospital visitor	Bunbury friend	August 1916	Hospital visit CAS
bdr	Draper, Miss MM (Tillie)	1898–1960	Bunbury	Unmarried female	Bunbury friend	August 1916	Hospital visit CAS
bdu	Duce, Eric	1893–1917	Bunbury, Egypt	Farmer	Classmate	21.1.1916	CS comment, met in Egypt
bea	Eastaugh, Agnes Ada, Mrs George A	1874–1918	Bunbury	Wife of clerk of courts	Bunbury friend	August 1916	Hospital visit, CAS, card
beas	Eastman, Kenneth	c. 1875–1950, m. 1899	Bunbury	Solicitor	Family lawyer	6.11.1915	Letters, AJS, CS comment
beas1	Eastman, Mrs Sylvia	c. 1875–1946	Bunbury	Wife of solicitor	Bunbury friend	August 1916	Condolence letter
bedw	Edwards, Rev. Stanley W		Bunbury	Minister of religion	Bunbury acquaintance	August 1916	Hospital visit CAS
bfa	Fabricius Mrs Ida (Sorense)n	1873–1968	Bunbury	Widow of merchant	Bunbury friend	August 1916	Mentioned in Mrs Dannell's letter

Bunbury/ Harvey	Name	Date and place of birth	Address	Occupation	Relationship	Snell Archive: source date	Snell Archive: type of contact
bfo	Foreman, Miss Catherine Agnes (Aggie), m. Vounder Lowe 1918	1891	Harvey	Unmarried female	School friend	15.8.1913	CS Hayward dance card, hospital visit CAS
bfo1	Foreman, Miss Ethel Grace, m. L Paisley	1897–1971	Bunbury	Unmarried female	School friend	28.9.1915	CS reference
bfor	Forrest, Ethel Marion (Roberts)	1889–1986	Harvey	Unmarried female	School friend	28.9 1915, 28.3.1916	CS references to
bhar	Harrington Daniel 'Dad'	c. 1838–1927	Bunbury	Pensioner guard	Bunbury neighbour, fictive kin	4.10.1915, 18.1.1916, 14.7.1916, 16.7.1916	CS references, Christmas card, visits
bhat	Hattersley, Mrs	c. 1840, husband b. 1833	Unknown		Former neighbour	August 1916	Funeral card sent to by CAS; condolence letter
bhay	Hay, Mrs Katherine (O'Neil) (Mrs Albert or Mrs P Hay)	m 1866, d. 1933	Bunbury (Charles St)	Wife of public man	Bunbury friend	August 1916	Hospital visit CAS
bhay	Hayward, Mr T	TH Senior, 1832–1915, Jn, 1865	Harvey	Farmer/merchant	Bunbury-Harvey acquaintance	15.8.1913	Dance host
bhay1	Hayward, Mrs T, Sarah Jane Logue	1883–1964	Harvey	Farmer's wife	Bunbury-Harvey acquaintance	August 1916	Condolence letter
bhay2	Hayward, Miss (Tillie?)	1891–1920	Harvey	Unmarried female	Harvey friend	15.8.1913	CS Hayward dance card
bhay3	Hayward Mrs Nellie (Ellen Elizabeth Spencer)	1862–1951	Bundidup', Wokalup	Widow of G Hayward	Harvey friend	14.8.1916	Condolence letter

Bunbury/ Harvey	Name	Date and place of birth	Address	Occupation	Relationship	Snell Archive: source date	Snell Archive: type of contact
bhe	Hemingway Mrs Elizabeth	c. 1870–1935	Bunbury	Wife of railway official	Bunbury friend	1905 image	Beach outing with Mrs Snell
bhe1	Hemingway, Herbert	1894–1915	Bunbury, Northam	Porter	Bunbury friend	1905	Group image w CAS
bhe2	Hemingway, Reginald	1889 – c. 1949	Bunbury, France	Bank manager	Bunbury friend	1905, May 1916	Group image w CAS, CS comments, France
bho	Holtzman, Norman	1891–1979	Bunbury	Plumber	School friend	1898, 19.5.1916	School photograph, CS comment, met France
bhu	Hutch, Mrs		Bunbury	Housewife?	Bunbury friend	August 1916	Hospital visit CAS
bjoe	Joel Dr Simon Crowson	1873–1935	Bunbury	Doctor	Professional, personal friends	August 1916	Telegrams, letters SJ-AJS
bjoe1	Joel, Mrs Kate	c. 1880–1949+	Bunbury	Doctor's wife	Bunbury friend	August 1916	Hospital Visit CAS
bjoh	Johansen Alfred	c. 1880	Bunbury	Council (Water Board) employee, joined merchant navy	Classmate?	15.10.1915	CS comment: 'visiting brother'
bjoh	Johnstone, Mr J and Mrs M		Newcastle St Perth		Former Bunbury residents	August 1916	Condolence letter
bke	Kelly, Matron		Bunbury	Nursing sister		August 1916	Hospital visit CAS
bki	King, Mr Jas. A	c. 1860	Valencia, Mundijong	Orchardist	Citrus associate, Mdjg on railway.	August 1916	Condolence letter to AJS
bmca	McCallum, Miss	c. 1880	Bunbury	Tailor? Matron, Fresh Air League	Bunbury friend	August 1916	Hospital visit CAS
bmcn	McNish, Mrs Percy	c. 1880	Bunbury	Housewife	Bunbury friend	August 1916	Hospital visit CAS, card
bmit	Mitchell, Caroline, (Mrs WB)	1847–1918 m. 1865	Bunbury	Wife of public man	Bunbury friend	August 1916	Hospital visit CAS

Bunbury/ Harvey	Name	Date and place of birth	Address	Occupation	Relationship	Snell Archive: source date	Snell Archive: type of contact
bmit1	Mitchell, Ada S	1876–1944?	Mt Lawley	Unmarried female	Former Bunbury friend	9.8.1916	Condolence letter AJS
bmoo	Moore, Sir Newton	1870–1936	Bunbury, London	Surveyor, WA Premier 1906–1910, Agent-General, London, MP	Bunbury neighbours, family friends	4.10.1915	CS comments, Christmas card sent to
bmoo1	Moore, Dame Isabella (Lowrie)	c. 1875–1936+	Bunbury	Wife of public man	Bunbury neighbours, family friends	22.9.1916	Funeral card sent to in London by CAS, condolence letter
bmoo2	Moore, Christina Zoe (Chrissie)	1900	Bunbury	Unmarried female	Bunbury neighbours, family friends	1905	Image: Snell family group
bmoo3	Moore, Cora Isabel	1899	Bunbury	Unmarried female	Bunbury neighbours, family friends	1905, 27.2.1914	Image: Snell family group, letter
bmoo4	Moore, Richard John	1895–1947	Bunbury/at sea	Electrician's assistant	School friend	January 1916	CS comment: on board Troop ship 'Medic'
bno	Norrie, William J	c. 1880	Bunbury	Town Clerk	Bunbury Council Official	26.8.1916	Condolence letter, mayor and councillors
bpai	Paisley, Thomas	1961–1928	Bunbury	Schoolteacher	Family friend	28.9.1915, 13.8.1916	Hospital visit CAS
bpai1	Paisley, Mrs Martha	1864–1949	Bunbury	Wife of schoolteacher Paisley	Bunbury friend	4.10.1915, 6.8.1916, 8.8.1916	CS sent Christmas card; letter to CAS, hospital visit CAS, condolence letter
bpai2	Paisley Ivy Gladys	1886–1947	Bunbury	Librarian, 'social worker'	Bunbury acquaintance		

Bunbury/ Harvey	Name	Date and place of birth	Address	Occupation	Relationship	Snell Archive: source date	Snell Archive: type of contact
bpai3	Paisley, Cyril John	1894–1951	Bunbury	Civil servant	School friend	19.5.1916	CS: saw in France
bpai4	Paisley, Leslie William	1888–1974	Bunbury	Farmer	School friend	16.7.1916	CS comment
bpai5	Paisley, Selwyn Addey	1890–1958	Bunbury	Farmer	Schoolfriend	16.7.1916	CS comment
bpai6	Paisley Vera Agnes Margaret	1892–1974	Bunbury	Nursing sister	Bunbury acquaintance	1935, 6.8.1916	Known to Nancy Snell, mentioned by M Paisley
bpar	Parsons, Mrs	c. 1860–1915	Harvey	Widow of railway driver	Bunbury acquaintance	28.11.1915	CS comment: death
bpor	Port, Elsie Mabel	1883–1948	Adelaide Tce, Pth	Doctor, lecturer	School friend	August 1916	Condolence letter
bpor1	Port, Lily (Lillian)	c. 1890–1949	Kalgoorlie, church	Unmarried female	School friend	26.8.1912 August 1916	Chance meeting, Kalgoorlie, condolence letter
bre	Reading, George E	c. 1880–1947	Bunbury	Proprietor *Southern Times*	Bunbury friend AJS	August 1916	Condolence letter AJS
brhe	Rhead, Isabel	c. 1884–1942, m. 1917	Malvern Music College	Music teacher	Bunbury friend	9.9.1916	Condolence letter
bro1	Robinson, W I	c. 1850	Bunbury, Geraldton	Former Stationmaster, Bunbury	Former Bunbury friend	22.8.1916	Several letters with replies from AJS
bro2	Rose, Thomas Hayward	1888–1973	Burekup	Farmer	Rifle shooting	5.6.1916	CS: met in France
bsi	Sinclair, Dorothy Ringwood	1893	Bunbury	Unmarried female	School friend	18.1.1916	CS saw Fremantle
bsm	Smith, William Henry (senior)		Riverside, Boyanup	Orchardist, largest in Preston Valley	CS apprentice 2 years	20.4.1911	referee

Bunbury/ Harvey	Name	Date and place of birth	Address	Occupation	Relationship	Snell Archive: source date	Snell Archive: type of contact
bsm1	Smith, Mrs E		Riverside Farm, Boyanup	Orchardist wife	Anna Maria Smith was AM Clarke.	11.8.1916	Condolence letter
bsm2	Smith, (Walter) Percy	1891–1967	Riverside farm, Boyanup	Farmer	Son of former employer	28.11.1915 21.2.1915	CS comment, met in Egypt
bsm3	Smith, Iris F		Clooneen, ?	Farmer's wife	Former Harvey resident	8.10.1916	Condolence letter
bsmy	Smyth, Lawrence Joseph	1875–1929	Bunbury	Roman Catholic priest	Bunbury friend	August 1916	Hospital visit CAS, letter?
bsp	Spencer, Mrs William, 2nd wife? Mary Ann Oakley, m. 1901	c. 1880, UK	Bunbury	Wife of public man	Bunbury acquaintance	August 1916	Hospital visit, CAS, card
bsp1	Spencer, Miss Rosie	c. 1900 m. 1926	Bunbury		Bunbury acquaintance	August 1916	Card
bste	Stewart, James A	1890?	Harvey	Sec. Road Board, Harvey Citrus Society	Harvey friend	16.3.1916, 12.6.1916	Condolence card
bste1	Stewart, 'young Mr and Mrs' Ernest St Clair	1882–1961, m. 1912	Harvey	Wife of clerical worker	Bunbury acquaintance	16.3.1916	CS comments
btu	Tuxford, Mrs Eliza Hay	1867–1947	Claremont	Widow	Family friends, Bunbury	4.10.1915, 28.11.1915, 18.1.1916, 9.8.1916, 7.11.1916	CS visits, cards, condolence letter, etc

Bunbury/ Harvey	Name	Date and place of birth	Address	Occupation	Relationship	Snell Archive: source date	Snell Archive: type of contact
btu1	Tuxford, Wedd	1892–1952	Claremont, Melbourne, Sheffield	Mechanic	Childhood friend, moved to Claremont, for education, visited Snells in Harvey 1907	1905, image with Mrs Snell and family, 1906, 1907, 4.10.1915, 22.10.1916	Postcards, Claremont, Melbourne, condolence letter from UK
bwa	Walker, Mrs Alice Elizabeth, Mr Walter	c. 1865	Bunbury,	Carpenter	Bunbury friend	August 1916	Hospital visit CAS
bwe	Wenn (Frances) Selina (Buswell)	c. 18650–1930, m. 1885	Bunbury	Labourers	School friend	19.5.1916	CS comment: met in France
bwh	Whalley Rev D T	1880	Kalgoorlie, church	Wesleyan minister	Bunbury acquaintance	26.8.1912	Met in Kalgoorlie
bwh1	Whalley, Mrs	c. 1880	Kalgoorlie, church	Minister's wife	Bunbury acquaintance	26.8.1912	Met in Kalgoorlie
bwh2	Whistler, Fanny Evelyn Smith, Mrs Robert Blomfield	c. 1880, m. 1902	Brancaster, Dinninup	Farmer's wife	Wellington orchardist	August 1916	Condolence letter
bwi	Withers, Mr and Mrs, Eva M.	d. 1947	Williams	Farmers	Former Harvey residents?	20.8.1916	Condolence letter
bwr	Wright, Mrs C?		Australind			August 1916	Visit to CAS
Harvey Population							
ha	Abernethy, John	c. 1880 Scotland	State Farm Brunswick	Dairy expert, 1909–, Brunswick State Farm	CS apprenticed 6 months	1.8.1910	Testimonial for CS
hbec	Becher, Francis Joseph (Frank)	c. 1860–1947	Australind	Government irrigation expert, orchard manager	Friend of CS and AS	17.10.1915	AS letter to CS.

Bunbury/ Harvey	Name	Date and place of birth	Address	Occupation	Relationship	Snell Archive: source date	Snell Archive: type of contact
hbec1	Becher, Mrs	c. 1870	Harvey	Housewife	Dance, Hayward's swimming pool	CS: Hayward dance, 15.8.1913 21.8.1916	Condolence letter
hbp	Beecham, John		Perth.	YMCA official, Perth	Had lived in Harvey, close friend AJS	September-November 1916	Several condolence letters and enquiries between Beecham and AJS, after CS death 1916.
hbel	Bellamy, Miss Dora	1886–1966	Harvey	Unmarried female	Harvey friend, fellow guest	15.8.1913 August 1916	CS: Hayward dance, Hospital visit to CAS
hbi	Bird, Norman	1889–1945	Harvey	Timberman	Harvey acquaintance	May 1916	CS comment in letter: children
hbr	Breen, David Lightfoot	1876–1956	Harvey	Agricultural inspector	Married Kylie Hymus, family friend of CS	16.3.1916, 7.5.1916, 24.5.1916, 16.7.1916	CS comments in letters to family
hca	Cambell, Duncan McGregor	c. 1880–1937	Harvey	Orchardist	Harvey friends	August 1916	1912 Christmas picnic image, flowers and card
hca1	Campbell, Annie May (Steer)	c. 1880	Harvey	Orchardist wife	Harvey friends	August 1916	1912 Christmas picnic image, flowers and card
hca2	Campbell, Kathleen	1904	Harvey	Schoolgirl	friend through Mrs T Hayward	1913	1912 Christmas picnic image
hcar	Carney, Mrs	c. 1860	Harvey	Housewife	Bunbury friend	16.3.1916	CS comment

Bunbury/ Harvey	Name	Date and place of birth	Address	Occupation	Relationship	Snell Archive: source date	Snell Archive: type of contact
hcha	Charman, Lawrence Ray (Roy)	1893–1969	Harvey	Farmer	11 Battalion	31.7.1915	CS comments re military service, hospital.
hcli	Clifton Claude Algernon	1894–1932	Brunswick Junction	Farmer	Cliftons and Snells mingled at community events		
hcli1	Clifton Jessie Christina	1875–1959	Bunbury	Nurse	Cliftons and Snells mingled at community events		
hco	Connor, Mrs Alicia	c. 1860–1929	Hillside, Benger	Wife of MP	Harvey acquaintance	10.9.1916	Condolence letter
hco	Cooke, Leonard Charles (Len)	1890–1917	Cookernup	Labourer	Rifle shooting friend	24.5.1916	CS Comment, friend of AS
hco1	Cooper, Mrs Richard		Harvey	Farmer's wife	Harvey friend	August 1916	Funeral card sent to by CAS
hco2	Corker, Mrs Constance	c. 1885–1948	The Avenue, Harvey	Dairy farmer, horsewoman	Harvey friend	17.8.1916	Condolence letter
hcr	Crampton, Miss Enid M?	1893	Harvey	Unmarried female, farming family	Fellow guest	15.8.1913	CS: Hayward dance card
hd	Daddow, Mrs Emily	b. c. 1890–1942, m. 1911	Harvey PO	Housewife	Harvey acquaintance	17.8.1916	Condolence letter
hde	Dermer, William Thomas	c. 1870–1941	Fremantle	Doctor,	Former resident Bunbury and Harvey	11.8.1916	Several letters between WID and AJS

Bunbury/ Harvey	Name	Date and place of birth	Address	Occupation	Relationship	Snell Archive: source date	Snell Archive: type of contact
hde1	Dermer, Mrs	c. 1870	Bunbury	Doctor's wife	Bunbury friend	August 1916	Hospital visit CAS
hdev	Deveraux, Mrs		Harvey	Husband, building contractor	Bunbury friend	August 1916	Hospital visit CAS
hdr	Driscoll, Mrs Olive (Frank)	1888	Harvey	Storekeeper's wife	Harvey friend	1.1.1916	CS comment re family
hdu	Dunlop Miss Maud	c. 1890	Scotland/Bangkok/ Harvey	Nurse probationer	Childhood friend, Bangkok now in Scotland	9.5.1916–8.7.1916	CAS had written, reminisces re holiday in Harvey
hgib	Gibney Guy Somerville Dion	1894–1916	Harvey	Farm labourer	Harvey friend	December 1912	b. London, 1912 Christmas picnic image
hgibb	Gibbs, George Gordon	c. 1860–1921	Wanilla Orchard, Harvey	Agent, orchardist, employer	CS did spraying	4.10.1915	CS comment, Christmas card
hgibb1	Gibbs, Mrs Nellie (Ellen/Helen Holden)	c. 1865	Harvey	Housewife	Close friend of CAS	4.10.1915, 28.11.1915, 9.8.1916	CS comments, hospital visit, CAS, condolence letter.
hgibb2	Gibbs, Len	1886–1951	Harvey	Commercial traveller'	Harvey friend	January 1916, 10.7.1916	CS comments: Egypt, France
hgibb3	Gibbs, Colin George Douglas	1893–1956	Harvey	Orchardist	Friend of CS and AS	4.10.1915, 17.10.1915, 16.7.1916	AS to CS, Australiand trip, CS commenst: didn't pass for militaty, 'Gibbs boys'
hgibb4	Gibbs, Winifred Marion	1897	Harvey	Unmarried female	Harvey friend	15.8.1913, 17.10.1915, 8.12.1915, 9.8.1916	CS: Hayward dance, tennis, dinner, CS 18.1.1916, letter to Marjorie, c. 20.8.1916,

Bunbury/ Harvey	Name	Date and place of birth	Address	Occupation	Relationship	Snell Archive: source date	Snell Archive: type of contact
hgibs	Gibsone, R	1876	Harvey	Sec. Harvey Citrus Soc. and Harvey Lodge	Citrus Society colleague	24.8.1916	Condolence letter, AJS
hha	Handley, John Edward	c. 1880–1939?	Harvey	Contract worker	Harvey acquaintance	9.10.1915	CS comment
hhan	Hanks, Mrs Katherine F	d. 1952	Harvey	Husband: farmer	Harvey friend	9.8.1916	Condolence letter
hhar	Harper Walter E.	c. 1860–1928	Australind	Fruit grower, accountant	Friend of CS and Alf	17.10.1915	Letter AS to CS
hhaw	Hawter, Edith	1871–1954	Blackwood Hse, Mullallyup	Husband: farmer	Harvey friend	3.9.1916	Condolence letter
hhay	Hayward, Roy O.	1883–1964	Riverton- Harvey	Farmer and public man	Friend of AS,	9.4.1914, 4.10.1915, 17.10.1915, 16.3.1916, 7.8.1916	CS comments, condolence letter,
hhay1	Hayward, Kate A (Mrs Roy)	c. 1885–1935	Riverton-Harvey	Wife of RO Hayward	Harvey friends	August 1916	Condolence letter, visit
hhay2	Hayward, Bernie	1908–	Harvey	RO Hayward son	Friend of CS and Alf	31.7.1915, 8.12.1916	AS lto CS, CS comment, 'home for Christmas'
hhi	Higgins, Henry C	1868–1951	Harvey	Sec, Harvey Rifle Club	Harvey friend	26.8.1916 1916	Condolence letter
hhi1	Higgins, John Brooke (Jack)	1886–1968	Sydney	Harvey orchardist	Rifle club?	14.12.1915	CS met in Sydney
hho	Horrocks, George	c. 1880	Harvey	Orchardist	Harvey friend	August 1916	Condolence letter

Bunbury/ Harvey	Name	Date and place of birth	Address	Occupation	Relationship	Snell Archive: source date	Snell Archive: type of contact
hho1	Horrocks, Mrs TW	c. 1880	Harvey	Housewife	friend, fellow guest	15.8.1913	CS: Hayward dance, 15.8.1913; condolence letter
hhou	Hough, W	1895–1866	Harvey	Farmer	Harvey friend	August 1916	Condolence letter
hhou1	Hough, Mrs C		Harvey	Farmer's wife	Harvey friend	9.8.1916	Condolence letter
hhu	Hugill, Mr		Harvey	Farmer?	Friend through Mrs T Hayward	1913	Hayward dance
hhur	Hurley, Mrs Ellen	c. 1870	Korijekup Hotel, Harvey	Hotelier	Harvey acquaintance	9.8.1916	Condolence letter, reply AJS 11.8.1916
hhurs	Hurst, Rev. TO	c. 1870–1952	Harvey	Anglican minister	Harvey acquaintance	August 1916	Visit CAS
hhurs1	Hurst, Mrs Molly	c. 1880	Rectory, Harvey	Wife of minister	Harvey friend	17.8.1916	Condolence letter
hhy	Hymus, Margaret (Turnbull)	c. 1870	Yuin Farm, Harvey	Housewife, farmer, husband SF	friend, AJS purchased land from	15.8.1915, 4.10.1915, 28.11.1915, 8.12.1915, 9.8.1916	Letter to CS, CS comment, condolence letter
hhy1	Hymus, (Beryl)Kyle/ Kylie	c. 1895–1936	Harvey	Unmarried female	Family friend	15.8.1913, CS comments 16.7.1915 7.5.1916, 11.8.1916	CS: Hayward dance, many comments; condolence letter
hhy2	Hymus, Maggie (baby?)	1903 m. 1931 (J Hayward)	Harvey	Unmarried female	Hymus family	1913, 23.3.1916	Mentioned in Mrs H letter to CS
hhy3	Hymus, Jean	1900–1932 m. 1922 (Bogle)	Harvey	Unmarried female	Hymus family	1913, 23.3.1916,	CS comments

Bunbury/ Harvey	Name	Date and place of birth	Address	Occupation	Relationship	Snell Archive: source date	Snell Archive: type of contact
hib	Ibbotson Reginald Montague	1893–1980	Harvey	Farm labourer	Worked for AJS, lived with family	1912 Harvey image, 7.11.1915, 28.11.1915, 8.12.1915, 18.1.1916, 16.3.1916.	CS comments in letters, met in Egypt.
hib1	Ibbotson Leslie Montague	1893	Harvey	Farm labourer	Friend CS, AS	17.10.1915	AS to CS, Australiand trip
hje	Jefferson J S	c1860 UK	Bunbury, Devon	District Orchard Inspector, 1906–1914	CS apprenticeship	16.7.1915, 7.11.1915, 7.5.1916, 8.7.1916	Several very affectionate letters to CS at war
hje1	Jefferson Mrs Elise	c. 1860–1931	Exmouth, Devon	Inspector's wife	Harvey friend	15.10.1916	Condolence letter
hjoh	Johnson, Robert Allison	c. 1880–1947	Esperanza Harvey	Farmer, orchardist	Employer	12.6.1916	CS: crop spraying, horse mishap
hjoh1	Johnson, Mrs Marion	c. 1880	Esperanza, Harvey	Farmer's wife	Harvey friend	August 1916	Visit, letter
hjon	Jones, Taff		Collie/Sydney	Railways?	Worked under AJS	1.1.1916	CS comment
hla	Lambert, Miss Bessie	c. 1870	Harvey, London	Orchardist	Harvey friend	30.10.1916	CS comments, Funeral card sent to in London by CAS, condolence letter
hle	Leitch, Dugald	1870–1966	1912, Kings Prize, rifle shoorting Kalgoorlie,	Harvey farmer	Rifle shooting	23.3.16	CS met Egypt, France

Bunbury/ Harvey	Name	Date and place of birth	Address	Occupation	Relationship	Snell Archive: source date	Snell Archive: type of contact
hle1	Leitch, Collie	c. 1890–1934, m. 1909	Harvey	Farmer	Harvey friend	19.5.1916	CS comment, family
hlo	Logue, Miss	c. 1890	Harvey	Unmarried female, farming family	Friend through Mrs T Hayward	15.8.1913	CS dance card, Haywards, also swimming pool
hlow	Lowe boys', Jack	1890–1968	Harvey	Orchardist	Harvey friend	10.7.1916	CS comments: Egypt, France
hma	Markham, Mrs Lillian Mary	1873–1956	Wellington NZ	Former sea captain, Alfred John Markham, Harvey orchardist	Harvey resident, visiting NZ	28.9.1916	Funeral card sent to in NZ by CAS, condolence letter
hmay	Mayne, Mrs Mabel	c. 1885–1942, m. 1913, 1917	Harvey	Housewife/ orchardist	Close friend to Mrs Snell	15.10.1915, 17.11.1915; ND, 7.8.1916	2 condolence letters and poem
hmay1	Mayne, Corrie	c. 1914	Harvey	Harvey youth	Child of Mabel Mayne	15.10.1915	CS comment
hmi	Middleton, Walter	c. 1870	Wokalup	Farmer	Harvey friend	August 1916	Joint condolence letter
hmi1	Middleton, Mrs Ethel	1876–1962	Wokalup	School teacher	Harvey friend	11.8.1916	Joint condolence letter
hmo	Moore, Mrs Vera Priscilla (Roesner)	1893–1970	Harvey	Housewife	Harvey friend	15.8.1913, 6.9.1915	Hayward dance card, CS comment: marrying
hmoi	Moir, Mena (Hymus) Mrs Edward S.	1881–1927, m. 1903	Corin' Harvey	Fruitgrower's wife	Harvey friend	4.10.1915, 8.8.1916	Xmas card from CS
hmoi1	Moir, Master Lex (Sydney Alexander)	1905	Corin' Harvey	Farmer's son	Harvey friend	8.8.1916	Mentioned in mother's letter

Bunbury/ Harvey	Name	Date and place of birth	Address	Occupation	Relationship	Snell Archive: source date	Snell Archive: type of contact
hmoi2	Moir, Miss Beth	c. 1906	Harvey	Unmarried female, horsewoman	Harvey friend	16.3.1916	CS comment: 'little Beth' well again?
hmor	Morris, Mr Frank Sergeant	1894–1951	Harvey	Orchardist	Harvey friend	23.3.1916	CS comment: 'enlisting'
hmor1	Morris, Mrs Mary Louise	1888–1954	Harvey	Orchardist wife	Harvey friend	9.8.1916	Condolence letter
hmorr	Morrison Mrs Mary Jane McPherson		Harvey	Poultry producer	Bunbury friend	12.7.1916	CS: received parcel from
hmy	Myatt, Mrs Rosa	c. 1870–1923	Winchcombe, Harvey	Farming family	Harvey friend	10.8.1916	Condolence letter
hmy1	Myatt, Miss Iris	c. 1900	Winchcombe, Harvey	Farming family	Harvey friend	10.8.1916	Condolence letter
hmy2	Myatt, (Henry) Martin	1890–1940	Harvey	Orchardist	Harvey friend	17.10.1915, 12.6.1916	CS comment: commissioned
hne	Newell, Miss Mary		Park Rd, Mt Lawley	Unmarried female	Former Harvey resident	14.8.1916	Condolence letter
hni	Nicolaus, Mrs Mary Amelia	c. 1885	Jardup	Farmer's wife	Harvey friend	12.8.1916	Condolence letter
hro	Roesner, Olive	c. 1882	Harvey	Sunday school teacher, Temperance	Friend through Mrs T Hayward	15.8.1913, 6.9.1915	CS: dance card, comment: Roesner girls marrying
hse	Sergeant, Mrs		Harvey	Housewife	Friend, fellow guest	15.8.1913	Hayward dance w. CS
hse1	Sergeant, Miss Nancy L		Harvey	Unmarried female	Friend through Mrs T Hayward	1913	Hayward dance w. CS

Bunbury/ Harvey	Name	Date and place of birth	Address	Occupation	Relationship	Snell Archive: source date	Snell Archive: type of contact
hsh	Shenton, Alma, Mrs (CE)	1882–1959	Harvey	Nurse, bank manager's wife	Harvey friend	15.8.1913, 16.3.1916	CS Hayward dance; CS comment: 'starting family', condolence letter
hst	Stanford Alfred E and C	c. 1880	Harvey	Orchardist, nursery manager	Harvey rifle club	17.11.1915	AS comment, buying land
hste	Stewart, Miss Olive	1888?	Harvey	Unmarried female	Harvey friend	15.8.1913	Fellow guest, Hayward dance
hsu	Sutton, William J.	1860–1936	Jardup, Harvey	Farmer	Harvey friends	15.10.1915, 29.5.1916	CS: enlisting; 'bad in Egypt'
hsu1	Sutton, (Flossie) Florence Kate	1892 1969	Jardup, Harvey	Unmarried female	Friend through Mrs T Hayward	15.8.1913	Friend, fellow guest
hta	Taylor James (and Mrs)		Harvey	Farmer's wife, housekeeper	Housekeeper of Snell friend	August 1916	Mabel Mayne letter
htr	Trigwell, Miss Emily Violet	1893–1959	Harvey	Schoolteacher	Friend through Mrs T Hayward	20.9.1913, 17.10.1915	Hayward dance card
htu	Turner, Miss Elsie	c. 1880	Wellington Mills	Post mistress	Former Bunbury resident	4.11.1916	Funeral card sent by CAS, condolence letter
hwa	Ward, Harcourt	1875–1947	Glengarriff, Collie	Farmer, RSPCA, Collie Road Board, public man	AJS business acquaintance	July 1916	Condolence letter
hwi	Wilson, Ada Marguerite, Mrs RM	c. 1886–1940	Harvey	Storekeepers	Harvey friend	7.8.1916	Condolence letter
hwi1	Wilson, Miss	c. 1905	Harvey	Unmarried female	friend, fellow guest	15.8.1913	Fellow guest, Hayward dance

Bunbury/ Harvey	Name	Date and place of birth	Address	Occupation	Relationship	Snell Archive: source date	Snell Archive: type of contact
hwy	Wykes, Mrs Florence		Riverside Farm, Harvey	Farmer's wife	Harvey friend	15.8.1916	Condolence letter
Perth Colleagues of AJS							
pgeo	George William J	1853–1931	Claremont	PWD	Business colleague, AJS	August 1916	Condolence letters to AJS
pgo	Goss, Alfred	c. 1860–1928	Perth	Tailor, mining entrepreneur	Colleague of AJS	10.8.1916	Condolence letter
pgr	Gray Alf	1882–1948	Perth	House painter	No connection found	August 1916	Gibbs family friend, comment in letter
pgre	Greig, Henry	1889–1974	Perth	Red Cross	General Secretary	August 1916	Several letters between Greig and AJS
pro	Robinson, J M	c. 1860	Perth	Land Dept	Professional	15.8.1916	Condolence letter AJS
pru	Rupert Surname illegible		Baird Arcade Perth	Swiss? Writing illegible	Business associate AJS?	10.8.1916	Condolence letter AJS
pst	Stead, George William	c. 1860? NSW	Railway Workshops, Midland	General manager, Railway workshops, Alf's employer	Colleague AJS, employer of AS,	August 1916	Condolence letter AJS: 'son at the front'
pwe	West, AE	c. 1880	Carinyah, Helena St Guildford	Storekeepers	Former residents, Harvey 1915	11.8.1916	Condolence letter

BIBLIOGRAPHY

Archives

National Archives of Australia

World War I Service records: these are held in series number B4255, with a barcode to identify the individual service man.

Chapple, A. B. NAA B2455/3235299.

Gray, Alfred Clifton. NAA B2455/4663108.

O'Leary, S. H. NAA, B2455/8001429.

Paisley, Selwyn Addey. NAA B2455/8000688.

Parkinson, Henry. NAA, B2455, 8008346.

Robinson, W. B. NAA B2455/1905602.

Tuxford, Wedd H. NAA, MT1139/1/5910076. (Australian munitions worker)

All other summaries of war service were obtained from the Anzac Heroes website: www.anzacheroes.com.au.

Repatriation files

Each repatriation file is identified by a range of series numbers plus an 8-digit barcode and may contain any or all of the following:

- C files: Benefit (pension) files
- H files: Hospital files
- M files: Medical files
- R files: Repatriation files

Repatriation files can be accessed on the National Archives of Australia's website: recordsearch.naa.gov.au through Name Search > Repatriation cases (Boer war & WWI).

Only a few repatriation files have been digitised, some as a result of requests from the public and others randomly selected by the archives for digitization. Among my searches, only two files are digitised of these, I have referred to one of Ray Clarke's files.

Baldock, Leonard Garfield. NAA PP2/8, 32500940 R9410.

Bird, Norman J. NAA K60 30143326 WC8061; PP2/8 32485931 M8061.

Bird, Dorothy. NAA K60 32502769 MB8061.

Blythe, Jack/John Howard Drummond MM. NAA PP2/8 32489914 R1805; PB869/1 31838609 M5410; PP865/1 31846858 H5410.

Clarke, Mervyn Ephraim (Dick). NAA K60 32924219 C26047; K60 32924219 C11173; K60 32502412 H26047; K60 32502412 M26047.

Clarke, Raymond Arthur. NAA K60 10065192 C2281; PP863/1 10154948 M2281.

Clifton, Claude Algernon. NAA PP13/1 30805443 C10831; K60 10155951 M10831.

Clifton, Jessie Christina. NAA K60 32502174 M5355.

Gray, Alfred Clifton. NAA PP2/8 32485400 M14926; PP2/8 32485401 H14926; PP2/8 10081612 R14926.

Hemingway, Reginald. NAA PP2/8 10155153 R9621; Edith Hemingway, B73 20455595 MB21936; B73 20455596 HB21936.

Holtzman, Norman Guy. NAA PP946/1 31841207 M9457 Vol. 1A; 31841208 M9457 Vol. 1B; 31841209 M9457 Vol 2; 31841210 H9457, Vol. 1, 31841210; 31841211 H9457 Vol 2.

Ibbotson, Leslie Montague. NAA K60 31873175 C28591.

Ibbotson, Reginald Montague. NAA PP946/1 10065573 H769; PP946/1 10112538 M769.

Leitch, Dugald. NAA PP878/1 11545183 M23889.

Paisley, Cyril John. NAA K60 30143759 MB4981; PP18/1 31844379 R17847; K60 20423997 C17847; PP2/8 32498039 M17847.

Paisley, Edith Barbara. NAA K60 32502871 HB17847 Vol. 1; K60 32502872 HB17847 Vol. 2; K60 32502870 MB17847.

Paisley, Leslie William. NAA PP893/1 32501692 M18287; PP893/1 32501693 H19287; PP2/8 32498837 R19287.

Paisley, Selwyn Addey. NAA K60 20423414 C4981; K60 30143204 MB4981 Part 2; PP863/1 31838463 M4981.

Paisley, Hilda Gladys. NAA K60 10113873 HB4981 Vol. 1; K60 10109085 MB4981.

Paisley, Vera Agnes Margaret. NAA PP893/1 32501495 H14276; PP893/1 32501494 M14276.

Rose, Thomas Hayward. NAA PP645/1 31847238 H2478; PP645/1 5131792 M2478.

Sinclair, Wisbey Harrington. NAA PP869/1 827785 H10243; PP869/1 10082837 M10243.

Wenn, Clarence Rossmore. NAA K60 32487628 H2716; PP2/8 32492646 R2716.

Wenn, Selina. NAA PP13/1 30804625 C7525; PP2/8 32495342 R7525.

Wenn, Mervyn Bailey. NAA B2455 8381168; PP2/8 32644956 R24945.

National Archives, UK

Dunlop, Beatrice Maud Barr. The National Archives, Kew, Richmond, Surrey, United Kingdom, WO 372/23/12287. https://www.nationalarchives.gov.uk.

State Library of Western Australia, Battye Library

Paisley, Vera. *Guide to Nurses.* Perth WA.: Perth Public Hospital. Battye Library, 11994865, https://trove.nla.au/version/25992614.

State Records Office of Western Australia

SRO West Australian Government railways. *WAGR map, indicating proposed new lines.* 1921. State Records Office. AU WA S2238 cons 1781 20466.

West Australian Government Railways, 'WAGR map, sections controlled by district officers'. 1919. SRO Au WA S2238 – cons 1781 18580.

Private papers

Snell, Charles. The Letters and Diaries of Charles Snell (Snell Archive), held by M. J. Warburton.

Official Publications

1911 Census – Notes of the Commonwealth Statistician.

http://www.ausstats.abs.gov.au/ausstats/free.nsf/0/AA7CD73FF6E6374ACA2578390010304B/$File/1911%20Census%20-%20Notes%20of%20the%20Commonwealth%20Statistician.pdf

1911 Census – Volume II – Part IV Education http://www.ausstats.abs.gov.au/ausstats/free.nsf/0/7A23661EC1823B87CA25783900125D23/$File/1911%20Census%20-%20Volume%20II%20-%20Part%20IV%20Education.pdf.

1911 Census – Volume III – Part XII Occupations. http://www.ausstats.abs.gov.au/ausstats/free.nsf/0/672F01666C9728B9CA2578390013E61F/$File/1911%20Census%20-%20Volume%20III%20-%20Part%20XII%20Occupations.pdf.

1921 Census – Statistician's Report. http://www.ausstats.abs.gov.au/ausstats/free.nsf/0/13A21D5C84E44BFACA25783900180D8A/$File/1921%20Census%20-%20Volume%20II%20-%20Statisticians%20Report.pdf.

1921 Census – Bulletin No 16 – Summary for the State of Western Australia. http://www.ausstats.abs.gov.au/ausstats/free.nsf/0/82C73B5348267075CA2578F000175C53/$File/1921%20Census%20-%20Bulletin%20No%2016.pdf.

Australian Government, Department of Infrastructure and Regional Development, Bureau of Infrastructure, Transport and Regional Economics (BITRE): Chapter 4, Australia from 1911–2006. Report 136: The Evolution of Australian Towns. https://www.bitre.gov.au/sites/default/files/report_136.pdf

Australian Government, Federal Register of Legislation, 'War Precautions Act 1914' http://nla.gov.au/nla.obj-38369983/view?partId=nla.obj-38370290#page/n3/mode/1up.

Department of the Premier and Cabinet. A vote of her own. Constitutional Centre of Western Australia, 2019.

https://www.wa.gov.au/government/publications/vote-of-her-own-constitutional-centre-of-western-australia-exhibition

Royal Commission on repatriated soldiers of the A.I.F., under "The Discharged Soldiers' Settlement Act, 1918". Chair: Arthur A. Wilson. Report: http://www.parliament.wa.gov.au/intranet/libpages.nsf/WebFiles/Report+of+the+Royal+Commission+on+Repatriated+Soldiers+of+the+AIF+1923/$FILE/Royal+Commission+Repatriated+Soldiers+1923.pdf.

Personal communications

Fletcher, Sue. Principal Research Fellow, Centre for Comparative Genomics Western Australia (CCG), Murdoch University. 23 November, 2017.

McGregor Craigie, Mary. Relative of Martha McGregor Paisley. 1 January 2018.

Sherwood (Snell), Nancy. Margaret River, WA, 2014–18.

Newspapers

(accessed through Trove.nla.gov.au.)

Age (Melbourne, Victoria.: 1854–1954)

Albury Banner and Wodonga Express (New South Wales: 1896–1938)

Argus (Melbourne, Victoria: 1848–1957)

Australasian (Melbourne, Victoria: 1864–1946)

Australian (Perth, Western Australia: 1917–23)

Barrier Miner (Broken Hill, New South Wales: 1888–1954)

Bathurst Free Press and Mining Journal (New South Wales: 1851–1904)

*Blackwood Times (*Bunbury, Western Australia: 1905–20; 1945–55)

Bunbury Herald (Western Australia: 1892–1919)

Bunbury Herald and Blackwood Express (Western Australia: 1919–29)

Call (Perth, Western Australia: 1920–27)

Call and WA Sportsman (Perth, Western Australia: 1918–20)

Camp Chronicle (Midland Junction, Western Australia: 1915–18)

Collie Miner (Western Australia: 1900–16)

Cumberland Argus and Fruitgrowers Advocate (Parramatta, New South Wales; 1887–1950)

Daily News (Perth, Western Australia: 1882–1950)

Daily Standard (Brisbane, Queensland: 1912–36)

Daily Telegraph and North Murchison and Pilbarra Gazette (Western Australia: 1920–47)

Evening News (Sydney, New South Wales: 1869–1931)

Express and Telegraph (Adelaide, South Australia: 1867–1922)

Freeman's Journal (Sydney, New South Wales: 1850–1932)

Geraldton Guardian and Express (Western Australia: 1929–47)

Gnowangerup Star and Tambellup-Ongerup Gazette (Western Australia: 1915–44)

Great Southern Herald (Katanning, Western Australia: 1901–54)

Great Southern Leader (Pingelly, Western Australia: 1907–34)

Group Settlement Chronicle and Margaret-Augusta Mail (Busselton, Western Australia: 1923–30)

Harvey Chronicle (Pinjarra, Western Australia: 1915–16)

Herald (Fremantle, Western Australia: 1867–86)

Herald (Melbourne, Victoria: 1861–1954)

Inquirer and Commercial News (Perth, Western Australia: 1855–1901)

Kalgoorlie Miner (Western Australia: 1895–1950)

Launceston Examiner (Tasmania: 1842–99)

Maitland Weekly Mercury (New South Wales: 1894–1931)

Mirror (Perth, Western Australia: 1921–56)

Mullewa Mail (Western Australia: 1921–47)

Northam Advertiser (Western Australia: 1895–1918; 1948–54)

Northern Argus (Clare, South Australia: 1869–2020)

Perth Gazette and Independent Journal of Politics and News (Western Australia: 1848–64)

Perth Gazette and West Australian Times (Western Australia: 1864–74)

Primary Producer (Perth, Western Australia: 1916–21)

Queenslander (Brisbane, Queensland: 1866–1939)

Riverine Herald (Echuca, Victoria: Moama, New South Wales: 1869–54; 1998–99)

South Western Advertiser (Perth, Western Australia: 1910–54)

Southern Argus and Wagin–Arthur Express (Perth, Western Australia: 1905–24)

Southern Districts Advocate (Katanning, Western Australia: 1913–36)

Southern Times (Bunbury, Western Australia: 1888–1916)

South-Western News (Busselton, Western Australia: 1903–49)

Sun (Sydney, New South Wales: 1910–54)

Sunday Times (Perth, Western Australia: 1902–54)

Sunday Times (Sydney, New South Wales: 1895–1930)

Swan Express (Midland Junction, Western Australia: 1900–54)

Sydney Morning Herald (Sydney, New South Wales: 1831–)

Tambellup Times (Western Australia: 1912–24)

Telegraph (Brisbane, Queensland: 1872–1947)

W.A. Record (Perth, Western Australia: 1888–1922)

West Australian (Perth, Western Australia: 1879–1954)

Westralian Worker (Perth, Western Australia: 1900–51)

Williamstown Chronicle (Victoria: 1856–1954)

Image Sources other than the Snell archive

Bunbury Historical Society. Mrs Snell and friends, 1905, Marjorie Snell's annotations, c. 1980.

Bunbury Historical Society. Paisley family in uniform, 1919.

Google Maps. Meekatharra distict. Maps.google.com.

Harvey Historical Society Photograph taken by C. Snell. Harvey picnic, Christmas, 1912.

Passey collection of photographs, 1864–1933, Battye Library, 5323B. http://encore.slwa.wa.gov.au/iii/encore/record/C__Rb1763275__SPassey__Orightresult__U__X6?lang=eng&suite=def.

State Library of WA. *The first men to leave Bunbury for the First World War, 17 August 1914*. slwa_b1953321_3.

State Library of WA, Battye Library. *Bunbury 1905*. Slwa_006101PD, slwa_006220PD.

State Library of WA, Battye Library. *Harvey School piccnic 1905*. slwa_ 019224PD.

State Library of WA, Battye Library. Harvey Agricultural Alliance or Harvey Citrus Society. slwa_019138PD.

State Library of WA, Battye library. *Tambellup 1907*. Slwa- 009855PD.

State Library of WA, Battye library. Royal Automobile Club. Map showing Roads of the South West of WA, 1921. Slwa_Rb2130967.

State Records Office of WA. West Australian Government Railways. *WAGR map, sections controlled by district officers*. 1919. Au WA S2238 – cons 1781 18580.

State Records Office of WA. *WAGR map, indicating proposed new lines,* 1921. SRO, AU WA S2238 cons 1781 20466.

University of Melbourne. Outline map of WA. https://library.unimelb.edu.au.

Dissertations

Adams, F.D. A Biography of Sir Newton James Moore: with special reference to his role in Western Australian politics. PhD dissertation. University of Western Australia, 1973.

Anstey, Stephen. The Impact of the Great War on the Beverley, Toodyay and Murchison Goldfield Communities of Western Australia 1914–1917. Honours dissertation. Murdoch University, 1980.

Bassett, Janice Mary. 'Australian Army Nursing from the Boer War to the present'. PhD dissertation, History Department, University of Melbourne, 1991.

Oliver, B. War and Peace in Western Australia – the Impact of the Great War on Westralian Ideology, Politics and Society 1914 – 1926. PhD dissertation. University of Western Australia, 1990.

Rae, Ruth. Jessie Tomlins: an Australian army nurse – World War One. PhD dissertation. University of Sydney, 2001.

Warburton, M.J. The Service, Death and Memorialization of an Australian Soldier on the Western Front, 1916: An Interpretation. Honours dissertation. Murdoch University, 2013.

Secondary Sources

Adams, David. 'Moore, Sir Newton James (1870–1936)'. *Australian Dictionary of Biography*. National Centre of Biography, Australian National University, 1986. http://adb.anu.edu.au/biography/moore-sir-newton-james-7639/text13355.

Austin, Ronald J. *The Fighting Fourth: A History of Sydney's Fourth Battalion, 1914–1919*. Slouch Hat Publications, 2007.

Barker, Anthony J. and Maxine Laurie. *Excellent Connections: A History of Bunbury 1836–1990*. City of Bunbury, 1992.

Barnes, Phyllis. *Bunbury Images, People and Places*. Bunbury Historical Society, 2004.

Bean, C.E.W. *On the Wool Track*. London: Alston Rivers, Ltd, 1912.

Beaumont, Joan. (ed.) *Australia's War 1914–1918*. Crow's Nest New South Wales: Allen and Unwin. 1995.

Beaumont, Joan. *Broken Nation: Australians in the Great War*. Sydney: Allen and Unwin, 2013.

Beaumont, Joan, Lachlan Grant, Aaron Pegram, *Beyond Surrender: Australian Prisoners of War in the 20th Century*. Melbourne: Melbourne University Press Academic, 2015.

Beddie, B. 'Pearce, Sir George Foster (1870–1952)'. A*ustralian Dictionary of Biography*. Canberra: National Centre of Biography, Australian National University, 1988.

Beddoe, Dierdre. *Back to Home and Duty: women between the wars 1918–1939*. London: Pandora, 1989.

Belford, Walter C. *Legs-Eleven: Being the Story of the 11th Battalion (A.I.F.) in the Great War of 1914–1918*. Western Australia: John Burridge Military Antiques, 1940, 1992.

Bennett, S. *Pozieres: the Anzac Story*. Brunswick, Victoria: Scribe, 2012.

Binns, J.H., N. Cherry, B.A. Golomb, J.C. Graves, R.W. Haley, M.L. Knox. 'Report of research advisory committee on Gulf War veterans' illnesses'. Veterans' Affairs, editor. Topeka, KS: 2004. https://www.ncbi.nlm.nih.gov/pmc/articles/PMC3968048/.

Black, Alan W. Lowrie, William (1857–1933). *Australian Dictionary of Biography*, National Centre of Biography, Australian National University, 1986. http://adb.anu.edu.au/biography/lowrie-william-7253

Bolton, G.C. 'Forrest, Alexander (1849–1901)'. *Australian Dictionary of Biography*. National Centre of Biography, Australian National University, 1981. http://adb.anu.edu.au/biography/forrest-alexander-6208/text10671.

Bostridge, Mark. 'Vera Brittain – A Testament to War and Peace'. *The First World War: Personal Experiences*. Adam Matthews Digital, 2013, www.firstworldwar.amdigital.co.uk.

Brownfoot, Janice N. 'Goldstein, Vida Jane (1869–1949)', *Australian Dictionary of Biography*. National Centre of Biography, Australian National University, 1983. http://adb.anu.edu.au/biography/goldstein-vida-jane-6418/text10975.

Buley, E. C. *Australian Life in Town and Country*. New York and London: G. P. Putnam's Sons, 1905.

Butler, A. G. *Official History of the Australian Army Medical Services, 1914–1918, Section IV – The Aftermath of War*. 1930–1943. https://www.awm.gov.au/collection/C1416684.

Butler, Janet. *Kitty's War*. St Lucia, Queensland: University of Queensland Press, 2013.

Caddy, F. *The Rifleman: Dugald Leitch: A Pioneer of the Harvey District 1869–1966*. Unpublished Manuscript. Perth, Australia, Battye Library, 2002.

Campbell, Karlyn Kohrs. *Man Cannot Speak for Her: Volume 1. Critical Study of Early Feminist Rhetoric*. New York: Greenwood Press, 1989.

Clark, Ann, and Paul Ashton, *Australian History Now*. Sydney: New South Publishing, 2013.

Clarke, G.E. E*arly History of Bunbury*. Bunbury, Western Australia: Unpublished. 1946.

Colebatch, Hal. *A Story of 100 years: Western Australia, 1829–1929*. Perth: Government Printer, Western Australia, 1929.

Coulthart, Ross. *The Lost Diggers*. Australia: Harper Collins, 2012.

Crotty, Martin. 'The Rise of "Returned Soldiers and Sailors Imperial League of Australia, 1916–46"'. In Crotty, Martin and Larsson, Marina. *Anzac Legacies: Australians and the aftermath of war*. North Melbourne. Australian Scholarly Publishing. 2010.

Crotty, Martin and Marina Larsson, eds. *Anzac Legacies: Australians and the aftermath of war*. North Melbourne. Australian Scholarly Publishing. 2010.

Crowley, F.K. 'Forrest, Sir John (1847–1918)'. *Australian Dictionary of Biography*. National Centre of Biography, Australian National University, 1981. http://adb.anu.edu.au/biography/forrest-sir-john-6211/text10677, 1981.

Damousi, Joy. *The Labour of Loss: Mourning, Memory and Wartime Bereavement in Australia*. Cambridge, United Kingdom: Cambridge University Press, Studies in the social and cultural history of modern warfare. General editor, Jay Winter. 1999.

Davidoff, Lenore, and Catherine Hall. *Family Fortunes: Men and women of the English middle class, 1780–1850*. London: Hutchinson, 1987.

Davidson, Dianne. 'A Citizen of Australia and the World: A reappraisal of Bessie Mabel Rischbieth'. In Jenny Gregory, ed. *Western Australia Between the Wars, Studies in Western Australian History*, XI, Centre for Western Australian History, University of Western Australia, 1990.

Dawes, J. N. I., and L.L. Robson. *Citizen to Soldier: Australia before the Great War, Recollections of Members of the A.I.F.* Melbourne: Melbourne University Press, 1977.

Devine, W. *The Story of a Battalion*, Melbourne: Melville & Mullen Pty Ltd, 1919.

Earle, Rebecca, ed. *Epistolatory Selves: Letters and Letter Writers, 1600 – 1945*. Aldershot, UK: Ashgate. 1999.

Edkins, Jenny. *Trauma and the Memory of Politics*. Cambridge: Cambridge University Press. 2003.

Efthimiou, Olivia, Scott T. Allison, Zeno E. Franco (Eds). *Heroism and Wellbeing in the 21st Century: Applied and Emerging Perspectives*. New York: Routledge, 2018.

Evans, Raymond. *Loyalty and Disloyalty: Social Conflict on the Queensland home front, 1914–18*. Sydney: Allen & Unwin, 1987.

Everett, Valerie. *Blackboy Hill is Calling*. Greenmount, Western Australia: Katharine Susannah Prichard Foundation Incorporated, 2015. https://www.museumofperth.com.au/blackboy-hill-is-calling/.

Farquharson, John. 'Freeth, Sir Gordon (1914–2001)'. Obituaries Australia, National Centre of Biography, Australian National University. http://oa.anu.edu.au/obituary/freeth-sir-gordon-404/text405.

Fassin, Didier and Richard Rechtman. *The Empire of trauma: An enquiry into the condition of victimhood*. Translated by Rachel Gomme. Princeton, New Jersey: Princeton University Press, 2009.

Friedman, Matthew J. 'A brief history of the PTSD diagnosis'. National Center for PTSD, U.S. Department of Veterans Affairs, Washington DC, 2015. https://www.ptsd.va.gov/professional/PTSD-overview/ptsd-overview.asp.

Gammage, Bill. *The Broken Years: Australian Soldiers in the Great War*. Ringwood Victoria: Penguin, 1975.

Gammage, Bill and Young, Margaret (eds). *Hail and Farewell: Letters from Two Brothers Killed in France in 1916*. Sydney: Kangaroo Press, 1995.

Garton Stephen. *The Cost of War*. Oxford: Oxford University Press, 1996.

George, Ann, M. Elizabeth Weiser and Janet Zepernick, Janet, (eds). *Studies in Rhetorics and Feminisms: Women and Rhetoric between the Wars*. Carbondale, US: Southern Illinois University Press, 2013.

Gilbert, Martin. *The First World War: a complete history*. London: The Folio Society, 2012.

Gill, Ian. *Fremantle to the Front: 11th Battalion AIF*. Perth: Advance Press, 2003.

Glossop, Verna L. *Eliza Cons*. Bunbury Historical Society, 1981.

Greer, Germaine. *The Female Eunuch*. London: Paladin, 1970.

Gregory, Jenny, ed. *Western Australia Between the Wars, Studies in Western Australian History*, XI, Centre for Western Australian History, University of Western Australia, 1990.

Gregory, Jenny and Janice Gothard, eds. *Historical Encyclopedia of Western Australia*. Nedlands, Western Australia: University of Western Australia Press, 2009.

Grootaert, Christiaan. *Social capital: the missing link?* Social Capital Initiative working paper series: no. 3. Washington, D.C.: The World Bank. 1998, http://documents.worldbank.org/curated/en/1998/04/1574630/social-capital-missing-link.

Gullace, Nicoletta. *The Blood of our Sons: men, women, and the renegotiation of British citizenship during the Great War*. New York: Palgrave Macmillan, 2002.

Gurner, C.M. 'Butler, Arthur Graham (1872–1949)'. *Australian Dictionary of Biography*. National Centre of Biography, Australian National University, 1979. http://adb.anu.edu.au/biography/butler-arthur-graham-5444/text9243.

Haig-Muir, Marnie. 'The economy at war'. In Joan Beaumont (ed) *Australia's War 1914–1918*, St. Leonards, N.S.W.: Allen and Unwin, 1995.

Harris, K. 'Work, work, work: Australian Army nurses after the first World War'. In *When the Soldiers Return*. 2007 Conference Proceedings, St Lucia, Queensland, 2009. http://hdl.handle.net/11343/32510.

Hassam, Andrew. *Sailing to Australia: shipboard diaries by nineteenth-century British migrants*. Manchester: Manchester University Press, 1994.

Hassam, Andrew. *Through Australian Eyes*. Carlton South, Victoria: Melbourne University Press, 2000.

Hawkesley, Jen. 'Long time coming home: the unknown patient of Callan Park'. In Martin Crotty and Marina Larsson. Eds. *Anzac Legacies: Australians and the aftermath of war*. North Melbourne: Australian Scholarly Publishing. 2010.

Hill, A. J. 'Birdwood, William Riddell (Baron Birdwood) (1865–1951)'. *Australian Dictionary of Biography*, National Centre of Biography, Australian National University, 1979. http://adb.anu.edu.au/biography/birdwood-william-riddell-baron-birdwood-5240/text8823.

Hillin, Sara. *Sweethearts of the Skies*. in Anne George, Weiser, M. Elizabeth, and Zepernick, Janet, eds. *Studies in Rhetorics and Feminisms: Women and Rhetoric between the Wars*. Carbondale, US: Southern Illinois University Press, 2013.

Holden, Robert and Jane Brummitt. *May Gibbs: More Than a Fairytale*. Melbourne: Hardie Grant Books, 2011.

Holmes, Janet, and Miriam Meyerhoff, eds. *The Handbook of Language and Gender*. Oxford: Blackwell Publishing, 2003, 2005.

Holmes, Katie. 'Day Mothers and Night sisters: World War I nurses and sexuality'. In Marilyn Lake and Joy Damousi. *Gender and War*. Cambridge: Cambridge University Press, 1995.

Hudson, W.J. 'Casey, Richard Gavin Gardiner (1890–1976)'. *Australian Dictionary of Biography*. National Centre of Biography, Australian National University, 1993.

Hurst, James. *Game to the Last, the 11th Australian Infantry Battalion at Gallipoli*. Australia: Big Sky Publishing Pty Ltd, 2011.

Inglis, Ken. 'Conscription in Peace and War, in Roy Forward and Bob Rees (eds). *Conscription in Australia, 1911–1945*. Santa Lucia, Queensland: University of Queensland Press, 1968. 22–65.

Jalland, Pat. *Death in the Victorian Family*. Oxford: Oxford University Press, 1996.

Jalland, Pat. *Death in War and Peace*. Oxford: Oxford University Press, 2010.

Jones, Edgar and Simon Wessely. *Shell shock to PTSD: military psychiatry from 1900 to the Gulf War*. Hove; New York, N.Y.: Psychology Press, 2005.

Jones, J., Lindsay, D., Mountford, A., Repacholi, R., Waters, A. *Bunbury, 'I Remember When'.* Bunbury, Western Australia: South West Printing and Publishing Co. Ltd, 1998.

Kernahan, Coulson. *The Experiences of a Recruiting Officer,* 1915. London: Hodder and Stoughton, 1915.

Kent, Susan Kingsley. *Making peace: the reconstruction of gender in interwar Britain.* Princeton, New Jersey: Princeton University Press, 1993.

Kingston, Beverley. *My Wife, My Daughter and Poor Mary Ann: Women and work in Australia.* Melbourne, Sydney, London: Thomas Nelson (Australia) Ltd. 1975.

Lack, John. 'Buley, Ernest Charles (1869–1933)', Australian Dictionary of Biography, National Centre of Biography, Australian National University, 2005. http://adb.anu.edu.au/biography/buley-ernest-charles-12825/text23153.

Lake, M. *A Divided Society – Tasmania during World War I.* Melbourne: Melbourne University Press. 1975.

Lake, Marilyn. *The Limits of Hope: Soldier settlement in Victoria 1915–1938.* Melbourne: Oxford University Press. 1987.

Lake, Marilyn and Joy Damousi. *Gender and War.* Cambridge: Cambridge University Press, 1995.

Lake, Marilyn and Joy Damousi. 'Warfare, History and Gender'. In, Marilyn Lake, Joy Damousi, eds. *Gender and War.* Cambridge: Cambridge University Press, 1995.

Larsson, Marina. *Shattered Anzacs: Living with the legend.* Sydney: UNSW Press Sydney, 2009.

Lawrence, Carmen. 'Tangney, Dame Dorothy Margaret (1907–1985)'. *Australian Dictionary of Biography.* National Centre of Biography, Australian National University, 2012. http://adb.anu.edu.au/biography/tangney-dame-dorothy-margaret-14913/text26105.

Lebow, Irene F. *Before Amelia: women pilots in the early days of aviation.* Washington D.C.: Brassey's Inc., 2002.

Livia, Anna. 'One Man in Two is a Woman: Linguistic Approaches to Gender in Literary Texts'. In Janet Holmes and Miriam Meyerhoff (eds) *The handbook of Language and Gender.* Oxford: Blackwell Publishing, 2003, 2005.

Lloyd, Clem. and Jacqui Wright. *The Last Shilling: a history of repatriation in Australia.* Carlton Victoria: Melbourne University Press, 1994.

Luckins, Tanja. *The Gates of Memory: Australian People's Experiences and Memories of Loss and the Great War.* Perth: Curtin University Books, 2004.

Lynch, E.P.F, ed. Will Davies. *Somme Mud: the war experiences of an Australian infantryman in France, 1916–1919,* Australia: Random House, 2006.

Lyons, Mark. 'Gardiner, Albert (Jupp) (1867–1952)'. *Australian Dictionary of Biography.* Canberra: National Centre of Biography, Australian National University, 1981.

MacKinnon, Alison. *Love and freedom: professional women and the reshaping of personal life.* New York: Cambridge University Press, 1997.

Manford, Toby. 'George, William James (1853–1931)'. *Australian Dictionary of Biography*. National Centre of Biography, Australian National University, 1981. http://adb.anu.edu.au/biography/george-william-james-6297/text10859.

Maze, Paul. *A Frenchman in Khaki*. London: William Heinemann Ltd, 1934.

McKernan, Michael. *The Australian People and the Great War*. Sydney, London: Collins, 1984.

McKillop, Robert, Donald Ellsmore, John Oakes. *A Century of Central*. Sydney: Australian Railway Historical Society, 2008.

McLaren, Glen, and William Cooper. *Beverley: our journey through time: a history of the Shire of Beverley*. Shire of Beverley, 2002.

McQuilton, John. *Rural Australia and the Great War: From Tarrawingee to Tangambalanga*. Melbourne: Melbourne University Press, 2001.

McQuilton, John. 'Enlistment for the First World War in rural Australia: the case of north-eastern Victoria, 1914–1918.' *Journal of the Australian War Memorial* – Issue 33. Canberra: Australian War Memorial, 2005.

Meyer, Jessica. *Men of War: Masculinity and the First World War, Genders and Sexualities in History Series*. Basingstoke: Palgrave MacMillan, 2009.

Morison, Patricia. 'Carnegie, David Wynford (1871–1900)'. *Australian Dictionary of Biography*. National Centre of Biography, Australian National University, 1979.

Murray, Peter A., Robin Kramar, Peter McGraw, eds. *Women at Work: Research, Policy and Practice*. Prahran, Victoria. Australia: Tilde University Press, 2011.

O'Brien, Patricia. *The Promise of Punishment: Prisons in Nineteenth-Century France*. Princeton, N.J.: Princeton University Press, 1982.

Oliver, Bobbie. 'A Truly Great Australian Woman: Jean Beadle's Work among WA Women and Children 1901–1942'. In Jenny Gregory, ed. *Western Australia Between the Wars, Studies in Western Australian History*, XI, Centre for Western Australian History, University of Western Australia, 1990.

Oppenheimer, Melanie. 'Caring for severely disabled patients at Graythwaite Hostel, Sydney'. In Martin Crotty and Marina Larsson. *Anzac Legacies: Australians and the aftermath of war*. North Melbourne: Australian Scholarly Publishing, 2010.

Oppenheimer, Melanie. '"Our Number One Priority": The Australian Red Cross and prisoners of war in the world wars'. in Joan Beaumont, Lachlan Grant and Aaron Pegram. *Beyond Surrender: Australian Prisoners of War in the Twentieth Century*. Melbourne: Melbourne University Press, 2015.

Oppenheimer, Melanie, and Bruce Scates. *The Last Battle of the Great War: Soldier Settlement in Australia*. Cambridge: Cambridge University Press, 2016.

Oppenheimer, Melanie. *Australian Women and War*. Canberra: Department of Veterans' Affairs, 2008.

Papas, Chloe. 'The forgotten women of the Great War. *ABC Great Southern*. 20 August, 2014. http://www.abc.net.au/greatsouthern/topics/?ref=nav.

Payton, Phillip. *Regional Australia and the Great War: 'The Boys from Old Kio'*. Exeter: University of Exeter Press, 2012.

Payton, Phillip. *Australia in the Great War*. London: Robert Hale Ltd, 2015.

Pedersen, P. with Chris Roberts. *ANZACS on the Western Front Battlefield Guide.* Australia, John Wiley and Son, 2012.

Pegram, Aaron. 'Bold bids for freedom: Escape and Australian prisoners in Germany 1916–1918'. In Joan Beaumont, Lachlan Grant and Aaron Pegram. *Beyond Surrender: Australian Prisoners of War in the Twentieth Century.* Melbourne: Melbourne University Press, 2015.

Perlman, Sharon E., Stephen Friedman, Sandro Galea, Hemanth P Nair, Monika Erős-Sarnyai, Steven D Stellman, Jeffrey Hon, Carolyn M Greene. 'Short-term and medium-term health effects of 9/11'. *The Lancet.* 378, (September 3 2011): 925–934. www.thelancet.com.

Rae, Ruth. *From Narromine to the Nile: the impact of the Great War on one Australian family.* Narromine NSW. 2004.

Robertson, J.R. 'The conscription issue and the national movement, Western Australia: June, 1916 to December, 1917'. *University Studies in Western Australian History,* Nedlands, Western Australia: University of Western Australia, 1959, 5–57.

Roper, Michael. *The Secret Battle: Emotional Survival in the Great War.* 6 vols. *Cultural History of Modern War.* Edited by P. Gattrell, Jones, M., Summerfield, P., Taithe, B. Manchester: Manchester University Press, 2009.

Ross, Jane. *The myth of the digger: the Australian soldier in two World Wars.* Sydney: Hale & Ironmonger, 1985.

Sanders, Theodora. *Bunbury: Some Early History.* Roebuck Series. 16 Volumes. Canberra: Roebuck Society, 1975.

Scates, Bruce. 'Finding the Missing from Fromelles'. In Crotty, Martin and Larsson, Marina. *Anzac Legacies: Australians and the aftermath of war.* North Melbourne. Australian Scholarly Publishing. 2010.

Scates, Bruce and Oppenheimer, Melanie. *The Last Battle: Soldier Settlement in Australia 1916–1939.* Port Melbourne, Victoria: Cambridge University Press, 2016.

Scott, Ernest. Vol. XI. *Australia During the War.* Sydney: Angus and Robertson Ltd, 1936. 7th edition, 1941. http://www.awm.gov.au/histories/first_world_war/AWMOHWW1/AIF/Vol11/

Sharp, Ingrid, and Matthew Stibbe. *Aftermaths of War: Women's Movements and Female Activists, 1918–1923.* Leiden, Netherlands: Brill Publishing, 2014. Proquest Ebook Central, http://ebookcentral.proquest.com/lib/murdoch/detail.action?docid=717459.

Sheffield, G. *The Somme.* UK: Cassell, 2003.

Shute, Carmel. 'Heroines and Heroes: Sexual mythology in Australia 1914–1918.' In Lake, Marilyn and Joy Damousi, *Gender and War,* Cambridge: Cambridge University Press, 1995.

Skinner, Graeme. *A biographical register of Australian colonial musical personnel.* University of Sydney. 2019. http://sydney.edu.au/paradisec/australharmony/register-A.php.

Smith, Howard J. 'de Largie, Hugh (1859–1947)'. *Australian Dictionary of Biography,* Canberra: National Centre of Biography, Australian National University, 1981.

Spender, Dale. *Writing a New World: Two Centuries of Australian Women Writers*, Melbourne: Spinifex Press, 1988.

Spitzer, Alan B. *The French Generation of 1820*. Princeton: Princeton University Press, 1987.

Stanley, Peter. *Bad Characters: sex, crime, mutiny, murder and the Australian Imperial Force.* Millers Point, New South Wales: Pier 9, 2010.

Stanley, Peter. 'War Without End', in Ann Clark and Paul Ashton, *Australian History Now*, 2013, Sydney: New South Publishing, 2013.

Staples, A.C. *They Made Their Destiny: History of Settlement of the Shire of Harvey 1829–1929*. Harvey, Western Australia: Shire of Harvey, 1979.

Straw, Leigh. *After the War: returned soldiers and the mental and physical scars of World War I.* Crawley, Western Australia: University of Western Australia Publishing, 2017.

Summers, Ann. *Damned Whores and God's Police*. London and Ringwood Victoria: Allen Lane – Penguin, 1975.

Thomson, Alistair. *Anzac Memories: Living with the Legend*. Melbourne: Monash University Publishing, 2013.

de Tocqueville, Alexis. [1840] 1945. 'Of the use which Americans Make of Public Associations and the Newspapers, Relation Between Public Associations and the Newspapers, Relation of Civil to Political Associations, and how Americans Combat Individualism by the Principle of Self-Interest Rightly understood'. In Ostrom, Elinor, and T. K. Ahn. *Foundations of Social Capital*. Cheltenham UK, Edward Elgar Publishing, 2003.

Turner, Frederick Jackson. 'The Significance of the Frontier in American History', Reprinted from Annual report of the American Historical Association, 1893, https, ://archive.org/details/significanceoffr00turnuoft.

Turner, Victor. 'Excerpt from *The Ritual Process*', London: Aldine, 1969. 'Liminality and Communitas'. http://faculty.dwc.edu/wellman/Turner.htm.

Tyrrell, Ian. 'Ackermann, Jessie A. (1857–1951)'. *Australian Dictionary of Biography*. National Centre of Biography, Australian National University, 2005. http://adb.anu.edu.au/biography/ackermann-jessie-a-12764/text23023.

Udell, Hazel. *History of Gingin, 1830–1960*. Gingin Shire Council, 1979.

Wadman, Ashleigh. AWM Blog, 'Nursing for the British Raj'. 28 October 2014, https://www.awm.gov.au/blog/2014/10/28/nursing-british-raj/

Warburton, Margaret J. 'Rebuilding Lives: heroism and gender in the Great War community of an Australian soldier'. In *Heroism and Wellbeing in the 21st Century: Applied and Emerging Perspectives*. Editors: Olivia Efthimiou, Scott T. Allison, Zeno E. Franco. New York: Routledge, 2018.

Ware, S. *Still missing: Amelia Earhart and the search for modern feminism*. New York: W.W. Norton & Company. 1994.

Welborn, Suzanne. *Lords of Death: A People a Place a Legend*. Fremantle Western Australia: Fremantle Arts Centre Press, 1982.

Welborn, Suzanne. *Bush Heroes*. Fremantle Western Australia: Fremantle Arts Centre

Press, 2002.

Wellman, B. *Networks in the Global Village: Life in Contemporary Communities.* Boulder, Colorado: Westview Press. 1999.

Williams, S. '"Not Openly Encouraged" – Nurse Soldier Settlers After World War One'. University of New England. 2010. http://e-publications.une.edu.au/1959.11/7103.S

Winter, Jay, and Emmanuel Sivan. *War and Remembrance in the 20th Century.* Cambridge: Cambridge University Press, 1999.

Winter, Jay and Antoine Prost. *The Great War in History, Debates and Controversies 1914 to the Present.* Cambridge: Cambridge University Press, 2005.

Woollacott, Angela. *Gender and Empire.* Basingstoke: Palgrave MacMillan, 2006.

Wynne, Emma and Lorraine Horsley. 'Blackboy Hill training camp: the birthplace of Western Australia's Anzac forces'. ABC Radio Perth, 26 Aug 2014. https://www.abc.net.au/news/2014-08-19/blackboy-hill-perth-ww1-army-camp/5678794.

Journal Articles

Acevedo, Bianca P., Elaine N. Aron, Arthur Aron, Matthew-Donald Sangster, Nancy Collins, Lucy L. Brown. 'The highly sensitive brain: an fMRI study of sensory processing sensitivity and response to others' emotions'. *Brain and Behaviour.* Issue 4, (July 2014): 580–594. DOI: 10.1002/brb3.242.

Atenstaedt, Robert L. 'Trench Foot: The Medical Response in the First World War 1914–18'. *National Public Health Service for Wales and Institute of Medical and Social Care Research.* University of Wales, Bangor, UK. December 2006, Volume 17, Issue 4, Pages 282–289. DOI: http://dx.doi.org/10.1580/06-WEME-LH-027R.1, http://www.wemjournal.org/article/S1080-6032(06)70334-9/fulltext.

Bankoff, Greg. 'Dangers to Going It Alone: Social Capital and the Origins of Community Resilience in the Philippines'. *Continuity and Change* 22 (2), 2007, 327–355.

Bourke, Joanna. 'Effeminacy, Ethnicity and the End of Trauma: The Sufferings of "Shell-shocked" Men in Great Britain and Ireland, 1914–39'. *Journal of Contemporary History.* 35, no 1 (2000): 57–69. SAGE Publications, London, Thousand Oaks, CA and New Delhi, [0022-0094(200001)35:1; 57–69;011185].

Cahill, Shawn P., and Kristin Pontoski. 'Post-Traumatic Stress Disorder and Acute Stress Disorder I: Their Nature and Assessment Considerations'. *Psychiatry (Edgmont),* 2(4) 2005: 14–25. https://www.ncbi.nlm.nih.gov/pmc/articles/PMC3004735/.

Coleman, James S. 'Social Capital in the Creation of Human Capital'. *American Journal of Sociology,* 94, 1988. 95–120.

Damousi, Joy. 'Socialist Women and Gendered Space, anti-conscription and anti-war campaigns, 1914–1918'. *Labour History,* No. 60 (May, 1991), pp. 1–15. Australian Society for the Study of Labour History. DOI: 10.2307/27509044, https://www.jstor.org/stable/27509044.

Di Grande L, Y. Neria, R. M. Brackbill, P. Pullam, S. Galea. 'Long-term posttraumatic stress symptoms among survivors of September 11, 2001 attacks'. *Am. J. Epidemiol.* 173(3) 2011: 271–81. doi: 10.1093/aje/kwq372. Epub 2010 Dec 29.

Garton, Stephen. 'War and masculinity in twentieth century Australia'. *Journal of Australian Studies.* 22:56, 1998, 86–95. DOI:10.1080/14443059809387363. http://0-www.tandfonline.com.prospero.murdoch.edu.au/doi/abs/10.1080/14443059809387363?src=recsys.

Gopinath, Kaundinya, Parina Gandhi, Aman Goyal, Lei Jiang, Yan Fang, Luo Ouyang, Sandeepkumar Ganji, Bavid Buhner, Wendy Ringe, Jeffrey Spence, Melanie Briggs, Richard Briggs, Robert Haley. 'FMRI reveals abnormal central processing of sensory and pain stimuli in ill Gulf War veterans'. *NeuroToxicology.* Elsevier Inc. 33, Issue 3, June 2012: 261–271. https://doi.org/10.1016/j.neuro.2012.01.014, https://www.sciencedirect.com/science/article/pii/S0161813X12000290.

Jennings J. 'Cordite-Eating and Cordite-Eaters'. *Journal of the Royal Army Medical Corps,* 1 (1903): 277–285. http://dx.doi.org/10.1136/jramc-01-04-03.

Jones, Edgar, Simon Wessely. 'Battle for the mind: World War I and the birth of military psychiatry'. *The Lancet,* 384, Issue 9955, (November 2014): 1708 – 1714. DOI: https://doi.org/10.1016/S0140-6736(14)61260-5.

Kent, Susan Kingsley. 'The Politics of Sexual Difference: World War I and the Demise of British Feminism'. *The Journal of British Studies,* Volume: 27: 3, 232–253, 1988. DOI, 10.1086/385912.

May, Carl. 'Lord Moran's memoir: shell-shock and the pathology of fear'. *Journal of the Royal Society of Medicine,* 91 (1998): 95–100 http://journals.sagepub.com/doi/pdf/10.1177/014107689809100218.

McMillan, D. W. 'Sense of community'. *Journal of Community Psychology*, 24: 1996, 315–325. doi: 10.1002/(SICI)1520-6629(199610)24:4<315::AID-JCOP2>3.0.CO;2-T.

McNeice, Jennifer. 'Military exemption courts in 1916: a public hearing of private lives'. *Provenance: The Journal of Public Record Office Victoria*, issue no. 14, 2015. https://prov.vic.gov.au/explore-collection/provenance-journal/provenance-2015/military-exemption-courts-1916.

McQuilton, John. 'Gender and War'. *Journal of the Australian War Memorial.* Issue 33, 2000. https://www.awm.gov.au/journal/j33/mcquilton.

Moore, Clive. 'Introduction: Australian Masculinities'. *Journal of Australian Studies*, 22:56, 1–16, 1998, 1–16. DOI: 10.1080/14443059809387363. http://0-www.tandfonline.com.prospero.murdoch.edu.au/doi/abs/10.1080/14443059809387357.

National Academies of Sciences, Engineering, and Medicine. *Gulf War and health: 10: Update of serving in the Gulf War.* Washington, DC: The National Academies Press. 2016. https://academic.oup.com/milmed/article/182/3-4/1507/4099774.

National Institute of Neurological Disorders and Stroke. *Guillain-Barré Syndrome Fact Sheet.* NIH Publication No. 11-2902, 2011. https://www.nonds.nih.gov/

Disorders/Patient-Caregiver-Education/Fact-Sheets/Guillain-Barré-Syndrome-Fact-Sheet.

Proctor, R. N. 'The History of the Discovery of the Cigarette–Lung Cancer Link: Evidentiary Traditions, Corporate Denial, Global Toll'. *Tobacco Control* 21 (2012): 87–91. http://tobaccocontrol.bmj.com/content/21/2/87.

Rae, Ruth. 'Reading between the unwritten lines: Australian army nurses in India, 1916–1919'. *Journal of the Australian War Memorial* 36, 2002. https://www.awm.gov.au/journal/j36/nurses/.

Rae, Ruth. 'An historical account of shell shock during the First World War and reforms in mental health in Australia 1914–1939'. *International Journal of Mental Health Nursing,* 16 (2007): 266–273. doi:10.1111/j.1447-0349.2007.00476.x

Ravindran AV, Yatham LN, Munro A. 'Paraphrenia redefined'. *Can. J Psychiatry.* 1999 Mar; 44(2):133–7. https://www.ncbi.nlm.nih.gov/pubmed/10097832.

Roberts, A. L., S. Malspeis, L.D. Kubzansky, C. H. Feldman, S. C. Chang, K. C. Koenan, K. H. Costenbader. 'Association of Trauma and Posttraumatic Stress Disorder with Incident Systemic Lupus Erythematosus in a Longitudinal Cohort of Women'. *Arthritis Rheumatol.* 69 No. 11 (November 2017): 2162–2169. doi: 10.1002/art.40222.

Robson, L. L. 'The Origin and Characterich of the First A.I.F., 1914–1918: Some Statistical Evidence'. *Australian Historical Studies.* 15, no. 61 (1973): 737–749. https://doi.org/10.1080/10314617308595502.

Roper, M. 'Nostalgia as an Emotional Experience in the Great War'. *The Historical Journal,* 54. 2, (June, 2011), Pp 421 – 451.

Scates, Bruce. 'The Unknown Sock Knitter: Voluntary Work, Emotional Labour, Bereavement and the Great War'. *Labour History.* No. 81 (Nov., 2001), pp. 29–49, Australian Society for the Study of Labour History, Inc. http://www.jstor.org/stable/27516802.

Selye, Hans. 'A Syndrome produced by Diverse Nocuous Agents'. *Nature* 138, (04 July 1936) 32. doi:10.1038/138032a0.

Schroeder, Katrin; Fisher, Helen L., Schäfer, Ingo. 'Psychotic symptoms in patients with borderline personality disorder: prevalence and clinical management'. *Current Opinion in Psychiatry*: January 2013 Vol. 26. 1. 113–119. doi: 10.1097/YCO.0b013e32835a2ae7.

Siddons, A.H. M. and A. M. Macarthur. "Carcinomata Developing at the Site of Foreign Bodies in the Lung". *British Journal of Surgery*, Volume: 39, Issue: 158, 1952. 542–545, ISSN: 00071323. Obtained via ArticleReach, Murdoch University, March 7 2018.

Stern, Edward S. 'The Psychopathology of manic-depressive disorder and Involutional Melancholia'. *British Journal of Medical Psychology.* 1944. Onlinelibrary. wiley.com/doi/10.1111/J.2044-8341.1944.Tb00738.X/Full.

Tennant, Margaret, 'Fun and fundraising: the selling of charity in New Zealand's past'. *Social History,* Volume 38, no 1, 2013. DOI:10.1080/03071022.2013.755390. http://www.tandfonline.com/doi/full/10.1080/03071022.2.

Tsuboi, Hirofumi, Naoto Sugeno. 'Retrospective analysis of Guillain–Barré syndrome and Fisher syndrome after the Great East Japan Earthquake'. *Brain and Behavior,* 4, Issue 4 (July 2014): 595–597.DOI: 10.1002/brb3.234. http://onlinelibrary.wiley.com/doi/10.1002/brb3.234/full.

Warburton, M. J. 'Liverpool Troop Train Smash: the December 1915 accident and troop behaviour'. *Australian Railway History,* November 2015, Vol. 66 no 937, 4–11. http://trove.nla.gov.au/version/11363827.

Weiner, J. S. and M. L. Thomson. 'Observations on the Toxic Effects of Cordite'. Royal Naval Personnel, Research Committee of the Medical Research Council. *Brit.J.industr.Med.,* 4 (1947): 205. http://oem.bmj.com/.

Ziino, Bart. 'Enlistment and Non-enlistment in Wartime Australia: Responses to the 1916 "Call to Arms Appeal"'. *Australian Historical Studies.* Volume 41, Issue 2, 2010. DOI: 10.1080/103146110037.

Online Sources

Anglican Communion. *Lambeth Conference, 1920.* http://www.anglicancommunion.org/resources/document-library.aspx?author=Lambeth+Conference&year=1920&page=7.

Anglican Communion. *Lambeth conference 1920, resolution 48.* http://anglican-deaconess.org.

Australian Bureau of Statistics. Frequently asked questions. https://www.abs.gov.au/websitedbs/d3310114.nsf/home/frequently+asked+questions#Anchor7.

Australian War Memorial. Australian Red Cross Wounded and Missing Enquiry Bureau Files, 1914–18 War, 1DRL/0428, 3911 Private Charles Snell, 4th Battalion, 19.

Australian War Memorial. "The Battle of the Somme", Emma Campbell, 2011. https://www.awm.gov.au/articles/blog/the-battle-of-the-somme-95-years-on.

Bunbury Cemetery Board. https://bunburycemetery.com.au.

Bunbury Museum, King Cottage. 77 Forrest Avenue, Bunbury, 6230. http://bunburyhistoricalsociety.com.au.

Chester Hon. Darren. 'Veterans and Veterans Families Counselling Service'. DVA, Canberra. https://www.facebook.com/VVCSsupport/photos/a.342744625893479.1073741830.339540802880528/996062473895021/?type=3.

Cons Photographs, State Library of Western Australia, http://encore.slwa.wa.gov.au/iii/encore/record/C__Rb2083442__SEliza Cons__P0,2__Orightresult__X3?lang=eng&suite=def.

Demographia. US population from 1900. http://www.demographia.com/db-uspop1900.htm.

Department of Justice, DOTAG, Births, Deaths and Marriages, Searching Western Australian Online Indexes. https://bdm.justice.wa.gov.au/_apps/pioneersindex/default.aspx.

First World War.com. 'Hellfire Corner'. https://www.firstworldwar.com/today/hellfirecorner.htm.

Fleurbaix map. Weather- forecast.com (France). *http://www.weather-forecast.com/locations/Fleurbaix.*

Grace's Guide to British Industrial History: W S Laycock. 4 August 2015, http://www.gracesguide.co.uk/W._S._Laycock.

Harvard Health Publications. *Skipping a beat — the surprise of heart palpitations.* October 31, 2017. https://www.health.harvard.edu/heart-disease-overview/skipping-a-beat--the-surprise-of-palpitations.

Harvey Tourism: History of Harvey. http://www.southwestattractions.com.au/history.html

Harwood's Cottage circa 1860. http://www.harwoodscottage.com.au/history.htm.

John Curtin Prime Ministerial Library, http://john.curtin.edu.au/journalist/worker.html.

Mayo Clinic. *Patient Care & Health Information, Diseases & Conditions, Varicocele.* https://www.mayoclinic.org/diseases-conditions/varicocele/symptoms-causes/syc-20378771.

Mcintyre, Alistair and Donald Fullarton. *Helensburgh Heritage.* Helensburgh Heritage Trust: 2018. http://www.helensburgh-heritage.co.uk/index.php.

Metropolitan Cemeteries Board. http://www2.mcb.wa.gov.au/NameSearch/results.php.

Museums Victoria, *Education Department of Western Australia.* https://collections.museumvictoria.com.au/articles/1934.

National Archives of Australia. 'Conscription referendums, 1916 and 1917 – Fact sheet 161'. http://www.naa.gov.au/collection/fact-sheets/fs161.aspx.

National Archives of Australia. 'Censorship Referendum campaign 1917', Series number A2939, Control symbol SC147, Barcode 963795.

NSW State Archives and records, *NSW ANZAC Centenary*, 'Liverpool Riots 1916', https://nswanzaccentenary.records.nsw.gov.au/in-service/liverpool-riot-1916/.

Oxford Living Dictionaries. https://en.oxforddictionaries.com.

Pierce, Jeff. *ANZAC Heroes, Great War 1914–1918, Bunbury-Wellington District Western Australia.* Website. 2019. http://anzacheroes.com.au.

Rail Heritage WA. South-West Rail and Heritage Centre, Boyanup, Western Australia, 6237. http://www.railheritagewa.org.au/museum/pages/swrhc/

State Library of Western Australia. Post Office Directories. http://www.slwa.wa.gov.au/find/wa_resources/post_office_directories.

The National Archives (UK). 44 Casualty Clearance Station, Intelligence summary, WO 95/345/1. https://discovery.nationalarchives.gov.uk/details/r/ff1c866a18d24bc08217dbcb59981a83.

Treloggen family website: http://www.tasfamily.net.au/~meryl/trelog.htm. Meryl Yost, 1998–2012.

Trove. National Library of Australia. Australian newspapers online. http://trove.nla.gov.au.

Statistiche Bundesamt. *Germany, statistical data. https://www.destatis.de/DE/Startseite.html.*

University of Western Australia, History. https://www.web.uwa.edu.au/university/history.

US Department of Veterans Affairs. *Gulf War Veterans' Medically Unexplained Illnesses.* Washington DC. 2017. https://www.publichealth.va.gov/exposures/gulfwar/medically-unexplained-illness.asp.

Voluntary Aid Detachments (VAD) (1914 -), Australian Women's Archives Project, The Australian Women's Register, National Foundation for Australian Women (NFAW). The University of Melbourne. http://www.womenaustralia.info/biogs/AWE0491b.htm.

NOTES

Introduction

1 Patricia O'Brien, *The Promise of Punishment: Prisons in Nineteenth-Century France*, Princeton, NJ: Princeton University Press, 1982, 53.
2 Charles Snell, The Letters and Diaries of Charles Snell (Snell Archive), held by M.J. Warburton.
3 'Bunbury Police Court', *Southern Times,* 17 September 1910: 5.
4 'Personal', *Southern Times,* 20 December 1910: 5.
5 'South-Western Railway Notes', *Bunbury Herald*, 31 October 1912: 7.
6 'Personal', *Southern Times,* 4 March 1911: 3.
7 'Personal', *Southern Times,* 9 November 1911: 5.
8 'Around Harvey', *Southern Times,* 27 November 1913: 4; 'Advertising', *Southern Times*, 20 August 1914: 2; 'Advertising', *Southern Times,* 15 July 1915: 2.
9 Telegram, military commandant to AJS, 7 August 1916; Lt P. Hay to Mrs Snell, London, 8 October 1916.
10 Snell archive.
11 Bill Gammage and Margaret Young, (eds), *Hail and Farewell: Letters from Two Brothers Killed in France in 1916*, Sydney: Kangaroo Press, 1995.
12 Margaret Young, *We Are Here Too: diaries and letters of Sister Olive C. Haynes No 2 A.G.H., Adelaide.* Australian Downs Syndrome Association, 1991.
13 Ruth Rae, Jessie Tomlins: an Australian army nurse - World War One, PhD thesis, University of Sydney, 2001; The Letters of Fred Tomlins, Mitchell Library, Sydney, MLMSS 5975/Box1/Item 9; Janet Butler, *Kitty's War*, St Lucia, Queensland: University of Queensland Press, 2013.
14 Andrew Hassam, Sailing to Australia, Manchester University Press, 1994, 55-56.
15 See Alan B. Spitzer, *The French Generation of 1820*, Princeton, NJ: Princeton University Press, 1987, xv.
16 W.C. Belford, *Legs-eleven: being the story of the 11th Battalion (AIF)in the Great War of 1914–1918,* Swanbourne Western Australia, John Burridge Military Antiques, 1940, 1992; W. Devine, *The Story of a Battalion,* Melbourne, Melville & Mullen Pty Ltd, 1919; H.G. Hartnett, H. G. *Over the Top: A Digger's Story of the Western Front.* Syndey, NSW, Australia, Allen and Unwin, 2009; E.P.F. Lynch, ed. Will Davies, *Somme Mud: the war experiences of an Australian infantryman in France, 1916–1919*, Australia: Random House, 2006.
17 P. Maze, *A Frenchman in Khaki.* London, William Heinemann, Ltd. 1934.
18 J.A.M.D. Hayward, FRCS. A Casualty Clearing Station. Firstworldwar.com, Memoirs and Diaries: A Casualty Clearing Station, 1930.
19 S. Bennett, *Pozieres: the Anzac Story.* Brunswick, Victoria: Scribe. 2012; C.E.W. Bean, *The Australian Imperial Force in France, 1916.* Sydney, NSW, Australia, Angus and Robertson. 1938.

20 P. Pedersen, with Chris Roberts, *ANZACS on the Western Front Battlefield Guide*, Australia, John Wiley and Son. 2012.

21 L. van Bergen, *Before My Helpless Sight: Suffering, Dying and Military Medicine on the Western Front, 1914–1918*, Netherlands, UK, Ashgate, 2009.

22 J. Damousi, *The Labour of Loss: Mourning, Memory and Wartime Bereavement in Australia*.,, Cambridge University Press, 1999.

23 J. Myer, *Men of War: Masculinity and the First World War*. UK, Palgrave MacMillan, 2009.

24 Rebecca Earle, (ed.), *Epistolatory Selves: Letters and Letter Writers, 1600–1945*, Aldershot, UK: Ashgate, 1999, 5.

25 Michael Roper, *The Secret Battle: Emotional Survival in the Great War*, 1Cultural History of Modern War, Edited by P. Gattrell. Manchester: Manchester University Press, 2009; Earle, *Epistolatory Selves*, 10, 27.

26 Barry Wellman, *Networks in the Global Village: Life in Contemporary Communities*. Boulder, Colorado: Westview Press, 1999, xiii, 20, 21.

27 Michael Roper, 'Nostalgia as an Emotional Experience in the Great War', *The Historical Journal*, 54. 2, (June, 2011), 421–51, 427.

28 Wellman, *Networks in the Global Village*, 19.

29 Ernest Scott, *Official History of Australia in the War of 1914–1918, Volume XI – Australia During the War*, Sydney: Angus and Robertson Ltd, 1936, 7th edition, 1941.

30 Bill Gammage, *The Broken Years: Australian Soldiers in the Great War*, Canberra: Australian National University, 1974, Reprint, Penguin, 1975; John Monash, letter to his wife, 24 April 1915, quoted in Gammage, *The Broken Years*, 46; Warburton, The service, death and memorialisation of an Australian soldier.

31 Michael McKernan, *The Australian People and the Great War*, Sydney: Collins, 1980, 1984.

32 McKernan, *The Australian People and the Great War*, vi, 182–83.

33 John McQuilton, *Rural Australia and the Great War: From Tarrawingee to Tangambalanga*, Melbourne: Melbourne University Press, 2001, 23, 19, 24, 31–37.

34 Phillip Payton, *Regional Australia and the Great War: 'The Boys from Old Kio'*, UK: University of Exeter Press, 2012. 15, 17, 19.

35 Payton, *Regional Australia and the Great War*, 7.

36 Stephen Anstey, The Impact of the Great War on the Beverley, Toodyay and Murchison Goldfield Communities of Western Australia 1914–1917, Honours dissertation, Murdoch University, 1980; B. Oliver, War and Peace in Western Australia, PhD thesis, Nedlands Western Australia: University of Western Australia, 1990.

37 Oliver, *War and Peace*, 1, 2; M. Lake, *A Divided Society – Tasmania*, Melbourne: Melbourne University Press. 1975; Raymond Evans, *Loyalty and Disloyalty: Social Conflict on the Queensland home front, 1914–18*, Sydney: Allen & Unwin, 1987, 13, 22, 26–7, 30.

38 Evans, *Loyalty and Disloyalty*, 3; Lake, *A Divided Society*.

39 Joy Damousi, *The Labour of Loss: Mourning, Memory and Wartime Bereavement in Australia*, Cambridge: Cambridge University Press, 1999, 4, 21.

40 Alistair Thomson, *Anzac Memories: Living with the Legend*, Melbourne: Monash University Publishing, 2013.

41 Ian Gill, *Fremantle to the Front: 11th Battalion AIF, Perth*: Advance Press, 2003;

Walter C. Belford, *Legs-Eleven: Being the Story of the 11th Battalion (A.I.F.) in the Great War of 1914–1918*, Western Australia: John Burridge Military Antiques, 1940, 1992.

42 Jay Winter and Antoine Prost, *The Great War in History, Debates and Controversies 1914 to the Present*. Cambridge University Press, 2005, 141, 142.

43 Ian Tyrrell, 'Ackermann, Jessie A. (1857–1951)', *ADB*, 2005; 'Temperance Demonstration at Fremantle', *The West Australian*, 4 July 1907: 4; 'Visit of Miss Jessie Ackerman to Bunbury', *Southern Times*, 22 September 1910: 5.

44 Carmel Shute, 'Heroines and heroes: Sexual mythology in Australia 1914–18', in Marilyn Lake and Joy Damousi (eds), *Gender and War*, Cambridge: Cambridge University Press, 1995, 30, 31; McQuilton, *Rural Australia and the Great War*, 119–131; Philip Payton, *Australia in the Great War*, London: Robert Hale Ltd, 2015, 98.

45 Marilyn Lake and Joy Damousi, 'Warfare, History and Gender', in Marilyn Lake, Joy Damousi, *Gender and War*, 1; Beverley Kingston, *My Wife, My Daughter and Poor Mary Ann: Women and work in Australia*, Melbourne, Sydney, London: Thomas Nelson (Australia) Ltd. 1975, 195; Bruce Scates, 'The Unknown Sock Knitter: Voluntary Work, Emotional Labour, Bereavement and the Great War', *Labour History*, No. 81 (Nov., 2001), 29–49, 34; Stephen Garton, 'War and masculinity in twentieth century Australia', *Journal of Australian Studies*, 22:56, 1998, 86–95.

46 Ruth Rae, Jessie Tomlins: an Australian army nurse - World War One, PhD thesis, University of Sydney, 2001, published as Ruth Rae, *From Narromine to the Nile: the impact of the Great War on one Australian family*, Narromine NSW, 2004; John McQuilton, Gender and War, *Journal of the Australian War Memorial*, Issue 33, 2000; S. Williams, 'Not Openly Encouraged' - Nurse Soldier Settlers After World War One', University of New England, 2010; Kirsty Harris, 'Work, work, work: Australian Army nurses after the first World War', in *When the Soldiers Return*, 2007 Conference Proceedings, St Lucia, Queensland, 2009, 1, 11; Janice Mary Bassett, 'Australian Army Nursing from the Boer War to the present', PhD thesis, History Department, University of Melbourne, 1991.

47 Alistair Thomson, *ANZAC Memories*, 283–84.

48 'The Perth-Bunbury Railway', *Bunbury Herald*, 24 May 1893: 3.

49 For example, Mrs George Reading, 'Personal', *Southern Times*, 9. August, 1913: 5.

50 Government of Western Australia, Department of the Attorney General, Births, Death and Marriages, henceforth 'DOTAG'.

51 For example, William Spencer, who fathered twelve children, including one William. *Southern Times*, 3 August 1901: 4.

52 For example, A.C. Staples, *They Made Their Destiny*, Smith families: 350.

53 Jeff Pierce, *ANZAC Heroes, Great War 1914–1918*, www.anzacheroes.com. Pierce summarises the attestation papers and war service records (B2455) of the individuals, making this an invaluable reference for the Wellington district. Of these, I have selected around 2000 men and women on the basis of their identification with the Bunbury-Harvey district.

54 Thomson, *ANZAC Memories*, 280; Peter Stanley, 'War Without End', in Ann Clark and Paul Ashton, *Australian History Now*, 2013, Sydney: New South Publishing, 2013, 104, 105.

55 Staples, *They Made Their Destiny*; Theodora Sanders, *Bunbury: Some Early History*, Roebuck Series, 16 Volumes, Canberra: Roebuck Society, 1975.

56 Jeff Pierce, *ANZAC Heroes, Great War 1914–1918.*
57 When referring to the whole district, I will use the term 'Wellington', to distinguish it from individual settlements such as Bunbury, Harvey etc.
58 Larrikin: A boisterous, often badly-behaved young man with apparent disregard for convention, but also good hearted; tends to be associated with urban dwellers. *Oxford Living Dictionaries.*
59 A term that was widely used at the time, both locally and more broadly. For example: 'The Bunbury Herald Thursday, September 16, 1915', *Bunbury Herald,* 16 September 1915: 2; Scott, *Australia During the War,* 324, 399.

1: Private Charles Snell, Service, Death and Commemoration

1 Now the Glen Innes Agricultural Research and Advisory Station.
2 M.J. Warburton, 'The Troop Train Smash at Liverpool Station, December 1916', *Australian Railway History,* Nov. 2015, Vol. 66 no 937, NLA ISSN 1449–6291.
3 4th Infantry Battalion Diary, 1916. *Australian Imperial Force unit war diaries.* Canberra, AWM, First World War Diaries – AWM 4 Class 23/21.
4 P. Pedersen., with Chris Roberts, *ANZACS on the Western Front Battlefield Guide,* Australia, John Wiley and Son. 2012.1
5 G. Sheffield, *The Somme,* UK: Cassell, 2003, 178ff.
6 "The Battle of the Somme", AWM.
7 L van Bergen, *Before My Helpless Sight: Suffering, Dying and Military Medicine on the Western Front, 1914–1918.* Netherlands, UK: Ashgate, 2009. 20.
8 E.P.F. Lynch, ed. Will Davies. *Somme Mud,* 99.
9 1st Australian DIvision Signals Company Diaries. *First World War Diaries - AWM4, Sub-class 22/11.* Canberra, AWM.
10 W. C. Belford, *Legs-eleven : being the story of the 11th Battalion (A.I.F.) in the Great War of 1914–1918,* Claremont, WA, John Burridge Military Antiques.1940, 1992. 240.
11 *1st Brigade Diary,* AWM.
12 Bean, *The AIF in France, 1916,* 260–83. The goal of these raids was to prevent the Germans moving troops to the Somme front.
13 *1st Brigade Diary,* AWM.
14 Bean, *The AIF on the Western Front,* 281, 303–305.
15 CS diary 5.7.1916.
16 Bennett, *Pozieres,* 10.
17 Belford, *Legs-eleven,* 259.
18 Bean, *The AIF on the Western Front,* 454; Sheffield, *The Somme,* 79–82; Ronald J. Austin, *The Fighting Fourth: A History of Sydney's Fourth Battalion, 1914–1919,* Slouch Hat Publications, 2007, 106.
19 Bean, *The AIF on the Western Front,* 449; It was here that photographs of many Australian troops were taken by Mme and M. Thuillier, but Snell's photograph has not been identified; R. Coulthart, *The Lost Diggers.,* Australia, Harper Collins, 2012.
20 Maze, *A Frenchman in Khaki,* 173; Maze, an English-educated Frenchman served General Gough as observer and interpreter.
21 Bean, *The AIF on the Western Front,* 452, 453–54; CS diary, 14, 15 July 1916.
22 CS, 1 May, 21 May, 16 July 1916.
23 Gilbert, *The First World War,* 315.

24 Bean, *The AIF on the Western Front,* 307.
25 Bennett, *Pozieres,* xiv.
26 Maze, *A Frenchman in Khaki*, 149, 153, 156.
27 Bean, *The AIF on the Western Front,* 311, 455, 470, 473.
28 Maze, *A Frenchman in Khaki*, 131, 149.
29 Bean, *The AIF on the Western Front,* 468–69, 447, 490.
30 Bennett, *Pozieres,* 16-1, 30.
31 van Bergen, *Before my Helpless Sight*, 450, 453.
32 Red Cross, Sydney, to Mrs J.A. Martin, Glen Innes, 25 September 1917, Sgt J. Collins, 194, 4th Battalion, 'D' Co., 14th Platoon, No 4 Aust. General Hospital. Randwick; J. Collins, born London, gold miner, enlisted as private, 48 years old, wounded Gallipoli and Pozières, 22.7–27.7, GSW both knees, right arm amputated France, 13.9.17. RTA. July 1917. NAA, B2455.
33 P.W. Hay to Mrs Snell in Hackney, London, 8 October 1916,
34 15th August, 1917, Red Cross, Sydney, to Mrs J.A. Martin, Glen Innes. Informant: Hamilton, Pte. 4th Battalion, 'D' Co., 14th Platoon, No 4 Aust. General Hospital, Randwick. No further information on this soldier has been located.
35 CS *Red Cross Wounded and Missing file*, AWM.
36 Reported to the writer by Frank Caddy around 2000. Leitch's story appears in a later section.
37 Dugald Leitch War Service Record, NAA B2455; *4th Battalion Diary,* AWM.
38 Belford, *Legs-eleven*, 592.
39 44CS Intelligence summary, WO 95/305/1. Numbers can be difficult to interpret, but on July 23rd, the CCS received 383 wounded.
40 *War Service Records*, CS, NAA B2455. All wounds were described as 'gun shot wounds' regardless of cause.
41 3 November 1916, Vera … Secretary, to Lieut. E.A. Boyce, A.D.C. General Sir Newton Moore. The chaplain mentioned has not been identified.
42 Now in the possession of Mrs J. Pollard.
43 Urgent telegram AIF to AJS, 7 August 1916.
44 "Harvey," *Southern Times,* 8 August 1916.
45 AJS to Red Cross 8 August 1916.
46 Red Cross to AJS, 23 August 1916.
47 AJS to YMCA, 25September 1916.
48 J. Beecham, YMCA to AJS 30 September 1916.
49 AJS to YMCA 7 October 1916.
50 Vera - Secretary, to Lieut. E.A. Boyce, A.D.C. General Sir Newton Moore, 3 November 1916,
51 Nellie Gibbs to CAS, 8 August 1916.
52 Mabel Mayne to CAS, 'Sunday' – 13 August 1916
53 Mabel Mayne to CAS 13 August 1916. It seems likely that Mrs Mayne herself wrote it.
54 Gladys Whatham to CAS, 16 August 1916
55 Meyer, *Men of War*, 75.
56 incomplete letter to Nellie Gibbs from her daughter.
57 H. Beigel to AJS 8 August 1916.

58 Alison Moir to CAS 8 August 1916.
59 H. Beigel to AJS 8 August 1916.
60 Steve Snell, Hackney, London, brother to AJS, 15 September 1916.
61 Lorrie Clark to CAS 9 August 1916.
62 Rosa Myatt to CAS 10 August 1916.
63 Geo. Reading to AJS 8 August 1916.
64 Mollie Hurst to CAS 17 August 1916.
65 Emily Daddow to CAS17 August 1916.
66 Mary Newell to CAS 14 August 1916.
67 Alicia O'Connor to CAS 10. September 1916.
68 Mrs Paisley to CAS 9 August 1916.
69 Rebecca Whatham to CAS 9 August 1916.
70 A.P. Cameron, The Manse, Glen Innes to CAS, 13 August 1916.
71 Pollie Snell, London to CAS 15September 1916.
72 Mrs Jefferson, Exmouth, Devonshire, to CAS 15 October 1916.
73 E. Tuxford, Claremont, 7November 1916
74 Gibbs daughter to CAS 9 August 1916.
75 Marion Johnson to CAS, 9 August 1916.
76 A.P. Cameron to CAS, 13 August 1916.
77 H. Beigel to AJS 8August 1916.
78 Lorrie Clark to CAS 9 August 1916.
79 Bessie Lambert, Hampstead, to CAS 3 October 1916.
80 Cousin Susie to CAS 24 October 1916. Isaiah lxvi 13.
81 Elise Clarke to CAS 14 August 1916.
82 Emily Daddow to CAS 17 August 1916.
83 Cousin Pollie, Sydney, to CAS 8 August 1916.
84 Nora Snell, London, to CAS, 12 October 1916. Alf was three years older than Charlie.
85 Meyer, *Men of War,* 74.
86 H. Beigel to AJS 8 August 1916.
87 Alison Moir to CAS 8 August 1916.
88 M. Hymus to CAS 9 August 1916.
89 Alma Shenton to AJS 7 August 1916.
90 Alfred Goss from Goldfields Club Hotel, Perth, to AJS, 10 August 1916.
91 Mrs Jefferson, Devonshire, to CAS 15 October 1916.
92 Bunbury Town Clerk to AJS 26 August 1916.
93 K. Eastman, lawyer to AJS 8 August 1916; Mollie Hurst to CAS 17 August 1916.
94 Ethel Middleton to CAS 11 August 1916.
95 Thomas Paisley, principal of the Bunbury Central School to CAS, 13 August 1916.
96 Isabel Rhead, Malvern Music College to CAS 9. September 1916.
97 Mr Gennys, manager, Experimental Farm, Glen Innes, to CAS., 13 August 1916.
98 Mrs Gennys, Glen Innes, to CAS, 8 August 1916.
99 W.J. Allen, Department of Agriculture in Sydney, to AJS 4. September 1916.
100 R.M. Wilson to CAS 7 August 1916.

101 R. Whatham to CAS 9 August 1916. Hospital matron in Annandale, Sydney.
102 Meyer *Men of War,* 1.
103 Rosa Myatt to CAS 10 August 1916.
104 Dr W.I. Dermer to AJS 11 August 1916.
105 Thomas Paisley to CAS, 13 August 1916.
106 A.P. Cameron, the manse, Glen Innes, 13 August 1916.
107 Mrs Jefferson, Devonshire, 15 October 1916.
108 Meyer, *Men of War,* 80.
109 Mrs Buchanan to CAS 9 August 1916.
110 Kyle Hymus to CAS 11 August 1916; Mrs Whatham to CAS 9 August 1916.
111 Sister in law, Nora Snell, London, 12 October 1916.
112 Alfred Goss to AJS, 10 August 1916.
113 Roy Hayward, business man, to AJS 7 August 1916.
114 Elise Clarke to CAS 14 August 1916.
115 W. Robinson to AJS 3 June 1917.
116 Rupert -, surname undecipherable, to AJS 10 August 1916. The almost illegible handwriting recalls the old German script which was still in use at that time.
117 Steve Snell CAS 15 September 1916.
118 Blanche Martin to CAS 8 August 1916. Mrs Martin's son enlisted: John James Martin, 4335, acting corporal, left Australia November 1916, served UK, France, KIA, July 1917, Polygon Wood. She too had to deal with uncertainty as to his burial place: '*buried nearby*'. NAA B2455.
119 Mrs Jefferson to CAS 15 October 1916.
120 A.P. Cameron, Glen Innes, to CAS, quote: words of an English hymn. 13 August 1916.
121 Dr W.I. Dermer to AJS 11 August 1916.
122 P. Hay to Mrs Snell, London, 8 October 1916. Hay, P.W, mining student, twice wounded in the neck, MC April 1917, returned to Australia 1919. War Service Record, NAA B2455.
123 M. Bostridge, "Vera Brittain – a Testament to War and Peace." Adam Matthew, Sage publishing, UK, 2013.
124 Bessie Lambert, Hampstead to CAS, 13 October 1916.
125 Cousin Susie to CAS 24 October 1916.
126 Nora Snell, London, to CAS 12 October 1916.
127 Lily Port to CAS 8 August 1916.
128 Mrs Jefferson to CAS 15 October 1916.
129 Bessie Lambert to CAS, 3 October 1916.
130 Lady Isobel Moore, wife of Sir Newton Moore to CAS, October 1916.
131 W.J. George, Public Works Department, Claremont, to AJS 12 August 1916.
132 W. Robinson to AJS 22 August 1916.
133 Dr W.I. Dermer to AJS, 11 August 1916.
134 Thomas Paisley to CAS, 13 August 1916.
135 Mrs Paisley to CAS 13 August 1916. Snell reported meeting a Blythe in France.
136 R. Whatham to CAS 9 August 1916. Whatham, Duncan Leslie, labourer, 10th FAB, driver, gunner, Gallipoli, France, VD, AWL, RTA 24 September 1918. NAA B2455.
137 Snell had commented in a letter that his friend 'Smithy' had died.

138 Nora Snell London to CAS 12 October 1916.

139 W.J. Robinson to AJS 22 August 1916. His son's date of arrival in France suggests that he could have been among those who fought at Fromelles. W. J. Robinson, NAA B2455.

140 AJS to Dr William Dermer 2 September 1916.

141 AJS to Geo. Goss, 11 August 1916.

142 AJS to Robinson, 7 October 1916

143 AJS to Harcourt Ward, 11 August 1916.

144 AJS to Dr Dermer, 7 September 1916.

145 AJS to Dr Dermer, 7 September 1916.

146 AJS to H. Beigel, 26 August 1916.

147 AJS to Geo Goss, 11 August 1916.

148 Bennett, *Pozières,* 311, 312.

149 Monumental Masons, Wilson Gray and Co. to AJS, 7 September 1916.

150 Martha Jane Snell, née Baggs, grandmother of the writer.

151 Tanja Luckins, *The Gates of Memory: Australian People's Experiences and Memories of Loss and the Great War,* Western Australia, Curtin University Books, 2004.212-3. That process began in 1927.

2: The Pre-war Wellington Community: 'Something in Between'

1 Jay Winter and Emmanuel Sivan, *War and Remembrance in the 20th Century,* Cambridge: Cambridge University Press, 1999, 41.

2 C.E.W. Bean, *On the Wool Track,* London: Alston Rivers, Ltd, 1912; L.L. Robson, 'The Origin and Character of the First A.I.F., 1914–1918: Some Statistical Evidence', *Australian Historical Studies* 15, no. 61 (1973): 737–49.

3 W. Devine, *The Story of a Battalion,* 4.

4 'Staples—Logue', *Western Mail,* 25 January 1908: 40; 'Obituary', *Southern Times,* 16 April 1914: 5; 'Advertising', *Bunbury Herald,* 18 May 1916: 2.

5 'Harvey Agricultural Alliance', *Southern Times,* 17 May 1903: 5; 'Irrigation and Water Supply at Harvey and Bridgetown', *The Daily News,* 11th December 1917: 6; 'First Harvey Show Opened by Mr George', *The Bunbury Herald and Blackwood Express,* 22nd October 1920: 5.

6 Undated note stating address of Mrs Ibbotson.

7 F. Dannell to CAS, 20 August 1916, Rupert surname illegible] to AJS, August 1916.

8 Toby Manford, 'George, William James (1853–1931)', *ADB,* 1981; 'Death of Mr. J. Fabricius', *Bunbury Herald,* 27 July 1909: 3; *ANZAC Heroes.*

9 Australian Bureau of Statistics, Census of the Commonwealth of Australia 1911.

10 Staples, *They Made their Destiny,* 26, 57–59; Clarke *Early History,* 15; Barker and Laurie, *Excellent Connections,* 6.

11 Clarke, *Early History,* 35, 63–4; Staples, *They Made their Destiny,* 47; Sanders, *Bunbury,* 15–17; Although Snell did not mention any Cliftons by name, the Snell and Clifton names often appeared in the same news item and Snell acquaintances married Cliftons, eg: Clarke–Clifton (DOTAG), Bellamy–Clifton; 'Personal'. *Southern Times,* 3 March 1910: 5.

12 Staples, *They Made their Destiny,* 78; Sanders, *Bunbury,* 114; Clarke, *Early History,* 63.

13 Barnes, *Bunbury Images,* 91; Clarke, *Early History,* 26; Clarke, *Early History,*

40; J. Jones, D. Lindsay, A. Mountford, R. Repacholi, A. Waters, *Bunbury, 'I Remember When',* Bunbury Western Australia: South West Printing and Publishing Co. Ltd, 1998**,** 94; 'Dr Joel Dead', *The West Australian*, 14 February 1935: 13; Clarke, *Early History,* 69.

14 Clarke, *Early History,* 28, 33, 35, 48; Adams, Biography of Sir Newton James Moore, 366; Passey collection of photographs, 1864–1933, Battye Library, 5323B; Staples, *They Made their Destiny,* 213.

15 Barker and Laurie, *Excellent Connections*, 70, 37; Phyllis Barnes, *Bunbury Images, People and Places.* Bunbury Historical Society, 2004. 63; Sanders, *Bunbury,* 28–9; Barnes, *Bunbury Images,* 29; Ian Molyneux, *Bunbury National Estate Study*, City of Bunbury, 1978, 75.

16 Barnes, *Bunbury Images,* 33; Sanders, *Bunbury,* 56–63; *Bunbury Herald,* 2 March 1903: quoted in Clarke, *Early History,* endnote.

17 'Death of Mr. J. Fabricius', *Bunbury Herald,* 27 July 1909: 3; Hal Colebatch, *A Story of 100 years: Western Australia, 1829–1929,* Perth: Government Printer, Western Australia, 1929, 274.

18 Staples, They Made their Destiny, 213.

19 Devine, *The Story of a Battalion*, 3; Frederick Jackson Turner, 'The Significance of the Frontier in American History', Reprinted from Annual report of the American Historical Association, 1893.

20 Staples, *They Made their Destiny,* 83, 86, 195–96, 236, 241; Alf Snell to CS. 17 October 1915.

21 'South Western Railway', *Southern Times,* 9 September 1893: 3.

22 Colebatch, *A Story of 100 Years,* 274; F. K. Crowley, 'Forrest, Sir John (1847–1918)', *ADB,* 1981.

23 Staples, *They Made their Destiny,* 278–85, 359–60, 371, 391, 293, 385, 417–23.

24 'Rambles Round the Harvey', *Bunbury Herald,* 21 March 1906: 2.

25 Staples, They Made Their Destiny, xi.

26 'Agricultural Hall', *The Daily News,* 7 October 1913:16; Staples, *They Made their Destiny,* 186, 195, 450–1; 'Notes on the Harvey District', *Bunbury Herald,* 27 October 1902: 3.

27 Letter of recommendation: W.H. Smith, 'Riverside', Boyanup, 20 April 1911; John Abernethy, State Farm, Brunswick, 1 August 1910; Geo. Gibbs, 'Wannilla Orchard', Harvey, 1914; Roy O. Hayward, Manager, Harvey Fruit Settlement and Harvey Estate, 9 April 1914.

28 Letter AS to CAS, 8 August 1916.

29 Mrs Buchanan to CAS, 6 September 1916.

30 The Snell archive contains a souvenir postcard in old German script.

31 Staples, *They Made their Destiny*, 25, 28, 45, 90.

32 Sanders, *Bunbury,* 25, 39, 45.

33 Census of the Commonwealth of Australia 1911, Volume II - Part IV Education Table 23, Number of Persons in each Statistical Division, at the census of 3rd April 1911, Classified according to Education and Age. 591–594.

34 Suzanne Welborn, *Bush Heroes*, Fremantle, Western Australia: Fremantle Arts Centre Press, 2002, 16.

35 CS letters referring to the Wenn family. There were only two 'Brendas' born within a suitable time range, a Clifton, who is most likely to have been highly literate, and Brenda Wenn, born in 1903, DOTAG; 'Bunbury State School', *Southern Times,* 17 December 1904: 5.

36 Staples, *They Made their Destiny,* 271–73, 275; Sanders, *Bunbury,* 59–62, 89.

37 'Country Letters', *The Inquirer and Commercial News,* 26 June 1878: 3; 'Torrington Ladies' College, Bunbury', *The West Australian,* 2 January 1880: 2.

38 'Bunbury Government Schools', *Southern Times,* 28 December 1892: 3; 'Death of the Hon, W. Spencer, M.L C', *Southern Times,* 25 July 1901: 3; 'Death of Mrs. W. Spencer', *Bunbury Herald,* 10 December 1898: 3.

39 'Correspondence', *Bunbury Herald,* 22 March 1893: 3; 'The Education of Girls', *Bunbury Herald,* 23 July 1908: 3.

40 'Bunbury', *The Inquirer and Commercial News,* 4 November 1898: 1; CS letters to family, 1916.

41 Museums Victoria, *Education Department of Western Australia.* https://collections.museumvictoria.com.au/articles/1934; 'The Story-Teller', *The Herald,* 29 July 1871: 4; 'Legislative Council', *The Herald,* 5 August 1871: 3.

42 'Elementary Education Act, 1871', *The West Australian,* 7 June 1881: 3.

43 'Advertising', *The Inquirer and Commercial News,* 20 October 1875: 4; 'The Rev. A. Buchanan', *Bunbury Herald,* 29 June 1916: 3; 'After Fifty Years', *Southern Times,* 27 June 1916: 2; 'Obituary', *South Western Times,* 10 February 1923: 4.

44 'Advertising', *The Inquirer and Commercial News,* 20 October 1875: 4.

45 'The State School', *Bunbury Herald,* 4 April 1901: 3; 'Bunbury State School', *Southern Times,* 17 December 1904: 5.

46 'Bunbury Infants' State School', *Southern Times,* 31 December 1898: 3; 'The State School', *Bunbury Herald,* 4 April 1901: 3; 'Bunbury State School', *Southern Times,* 17 December 1904: 5.

47 'News of The Week', *The Inquirer and Commercial News,* 30 November 1887: 6.; 'General News', *The Inquirer and Commercial News,* 13 March 1896, 1.

48 Adams, 'Moore, Sir Newton'; Crowley, 'Forrest, Sir John'; G. C. Bolton, 'Forrest, Alexander (1849–1901)', *ADB*, 1981.

49 'A Popular Farewell', *Bunbury Herald*, 5 April 1913: 5.

50 'Wedding', Lowrie-Moore, *Bunbury Herald*, 7 April 1898:3; 'Death, Mr John Lowrie', *The Bunbury Herald and Blackwood Express*, 24 September 1919:3; 'Obituary. Mr John Lowrie', *The Bunbury Herald and Blackwood Express*, Saturday 20 September 1919:5; Alan W. Black, 'Lowrie, William (1857–1933)', *ADB,* 1986; Staples, *They Made their Destiny,* 349, 437, 400–41. Lowrie's son, William Lowrie, Principal of Roseworthy Agricultural College, was invited to Brunswick in 1894 to advise local farmers and was later appointed Director of Agriculture WA, 1909–11 by his brother-in-law, Premier Newton Moore.

51 'A New Fibre', *Western Mail,* 19 September 1908: 5.

52 'Bunbury', *The Inquirer and Commercial News*, 24 February 1869: 3; 'Mechanics' Institute Bunbury', *The Inquirer and Commercial News,* 19 March 1873: 3.

53 'Bunbury Mechanics' Institute', *Southern Times,* 20 January 1900: 6; 'Bunbury Mechanics' Institute', *The Inquirer and Commercial News,* 31 January 1872: 3.

54 'Bunbury Railway Institute', *Southern Times*, 21 November 1912: 5; 'Bunbury Mechanics' Institute', *Southern Times,* 20 January 1900: 6; 'Bunbury Railway Institute', *The West Australian*, 27 November 1905: 7; 'South-Western Railway Notes', *Bunbury Herald*, 31 October 1912: 7; 'Examination Results', *Bunbury Herald,* 14 October 1911: 8.

55 'Mechanics' Institute Bunbury', *The Inquirer and Commercial News,* 19 March 1873: 3; 'Bunbury Mechanics' Institute', *The Inquirer and Commercial News,* 31 January 1872: 3.

56 'Bunbury Railway Institute', *Western Mail,* 30 September 1905: 50.

57 'Local and General', *Bunbury Herald,* 27 February 1905: 2; 'Advertising', *Bunbury Herald,* 18 May 1916: 2.
58 'Men's Class', *Southern Times,* 10 November 1914: 5. Smith returned to Australia, Duce, killed in action, Hurst, POW, returned to Australia.
59 'The Public Library', *The West Australian,* 11 November 1907: 3; 'Examination Results', *Bunbury Herald,* 14 October 1911: 8.
60 'South Bunbury News', *Bunbury Herald,* 14 December 1907: 1.
61 'Anglican Conference', *Bunbury Herald,* 13 February 1915: 5.
62 'Bunbury', *Southern Times,* 16 March 1916: 3; 'Harvey Agricultural Alliance', *Southern Times,* 17 March 1903: 5; 'Bunbury Catholic News', *Southern Times,* 11 March 1916: 5; 'Bunbury Roman Catholic Notes', *Southern Times,* 9 September 1916: 5; Roman Catholic Church Bunbury', *Southern Times,* 7 August 1915: 5; 'Roman Catholic Church', *Bunbury Herald,* 22 May 1915: 3; 'Catholic Literary Society', *Bunbury Herald,* 19 January 1915: 5.
63 'Catholic Girls' Literary Society', *Bunbury Herald,* 22 May 1915: 3.
64 'The Harvey Fatality', *Bunbury Herald,* 12 July 1913: 1.
65 'Sports Gathering Harvey Agricultural Alliance', *Bunbury Herald,* 24 February 1905: 2.
66 B.L., V. and P. Leg Co., 1888, paper 11, quoted in Staples, *They Made their Destiny,* 276, 300 303.
67 W. Devine, *The Story of a Battalion,* 3; 'Rambles Round the Harvey', *Bunbury Herald,* 21 March 1906: 2.
68 Devine, *The Story of a Battalion*, 3.
69 Maud Dunlop to CS, 9 May 1916.
70 Maud Dunlop to CS, second letter, nd.
71 1905 photograph; Wedd Tuxford, Claremont, to CS, c. 1907.
72 'Country Letters', *The West Australian,* 4 August 1883: 3.
73 Photographs, 1905, 1912; Postcard from Mrs Tuxford, Melbourne, to Wedd in Harvey, n.d.
74 Bean, C.E.W., *On the Wool Track.* 40, x, vi.
75 Australian Government, Department of Infrastructure and Regional Development, Bureau of Infrastructure, Transport and Regional Economics (BITRE): Chapter 4, Australia from 1911–2006. Analysis of 1911 census in Report 136: BITRE, *Australian country towns,* 58–61.
76 Robson, L.L. "The Origin and Character of the First A.I.F., 373; J.N.I. Dawes and L.L. Robson. *Citizen to Soldier: Australia before the Great War, Recollections of Members of the A.I.F,* Melbourne: Melbourne University Press, 1977, 14–20.
77 BITRE, *Australian country towns,* 58–61.
78 1911 Census, Summary tables, 2259.
79 1911 Census; 'Collie', *The W.A. Record,* 28 August 1915: 8.
80 'Collie Coalfield', *Bunbury Herald,* 11 December 1897, 3.
81 Census of the Commonwealth of Australia 1911, Volume III - Part XII Occupations, Table 69, Population of Statistical Districts of the State of Western Australia, at the Census of 3rd April 1911, classified according to occupation and sex, 1797, Census of the Commonwealth of Australia 1911, Notes of the Commonwealth Statistician, 11.
82 Rail Heritage WA, South-West Rail and Heritage Centre, Boyanup Western Australia, 6237. http://www.railheritagewa.org.au/museum/pages/swrhc/
83 For example, 'Social Notes', *The West Australian,* 15 December 1908: 6.

84 'Wanted a Manager', *Bunbury Herald,* 24 May 1913: 1.
85 Staples, *They Made their Destiny,* 268–70.
86 Letter AJS to Dr W. Dermer, August 1916.
87 Letters to family, various dates, 1915–1916 and letter from J. Brereton, (NSW) to AJS, August 1916.
88 'Personal', *The West Australian,* 28 August 1925: 10.
89 'Fall from Windmill', *The West Australian,* 3 December 1931: 13; *ANZAC Heroes.*
90 See Appendix 1.
91 AJS to CAS in hospital, c. 1913.
92 D.W. McMillan, 'Sense of community', *Journal of Community Psychology*, 24, 1976, 315–325.
93 Alexis de Tocqueville, 'Of the use Americans make…', in Elinor Ostrom and T.K. Ahn, *Foundations of Social Capital,* Northampton Massachusetts: 2003, 3–21, 3.
94 'Staples—Logue', *Western Mail,* 25 January 1908: 40; 'Social Notes', *The West Australian,* 15 December 1908: 6; 'Forrest-Forrest', *Western Mail,* 23 January 1909: 41; 'Lovegrove—Clifton', *Southern Times,* 25 April 1914: 5.
95 'Obituary', *Southern Times,* 16 April 1914: 5.
96 CS to family, 28 November 1915; 'Bunbury Chamber of Commerce', *Southern Times,* 20 July, 1920: 3; 'A Popular Farewell', *Bunbury Herald,* 5 April 1913: 5.
97 Wedd Tuxford, Sheffield, to CAS, 22 October 1916.
98 Ostrom and. Ahn, *Foundations of Social Capital,* xi; Bankoff, Greg., 'Dangers to Going It Alone: Social Capital and the Origins of Community Resilience in the Philippines', *Continuity and Change,* 22 (2), 2007, 327–355; James S.Coleman, 'Social Capital in the Creation of Human Capital', *American Journal of Sociology,* 94, 1988. 95–120.
99 Grootaert, Christiaan, 'Social capital: the missing link?' *Social Capital Initiative working paper series*: no. 3. Washington, D.C.: The World Bank, 1998.
100 'Brunswick Roads Board', *Southern Times,* 14 April 1906: 4.
101 Staples, *They Made their Destiny,* 437.
102 'Harvey Pruning Competition', *The South-Western News,* 23 June 1905: 3; 'Bunbury', *The Perth Gazette and Independent Journal of Politics and News,* 16 August 1850, 2; 'Farm and Station', *Western Mail,* 4 November 1898.
103 'Harvey Agricultural Alliance', *Bunbury Herald,* 15 August 1894: 3; 'Picnic at the Harvey', *Southern Times,* 13 April 1895: 3; 'This Harvey Area', *Western Mail,* 24 August 1907: 8; 'General News', *The Daily News* 23 July 1894: 2.
104 'Local and General', *Bunbury Herald,* 27 February 1905: 2.
105 'Harvey', *Southern Times,* 4 February 1902: 4; 'Harvey Agricultural Alliance', *Southern Times,* 17 March 1903: 5; 'Harvey Agricultural Alliance', *The West Australian,* 5 February 1896: 3; 'Harvey Agricultural Alliance', *Bunbury Herald,* 26 September 1894: 3.
106 'Harvey Agricultural Alliance', *Bunbury Herald,* 27 October 1894: 3; 'Picnic at the Harvey', *Southern Times,* 13 April 1895: 3; 'Harvey Agricultural Alliance', *Bunbury Herald,* 26 September 1894: 3; 'Harvey Agricultural Alliance', *Bunbury Herald,* 6 April 1895: 3.
107 'Harvey Agricultural Alliance', *Southern Times,* 17 March 1900: 3; 'Harvey Agricultural Alliance', *Southern Times,* 22 March 1900: 5.
108 'News and Notes', *The West Australian,* 29 October 1924: 8; 'First Harvey Show', *The Bunbury Herald and Blackwood Express,* 24 October 1920: 5;

'Harvey Show Luncheon', *Southern Times*, 4 September 1915: 3; 'Harvey', *Bunbury Herald*, 30 July 1919: 4; CS to family, 16 July 1915, 28 November 1915, Alf Snell to CS, 17 October 1915.

109 'Harvey Citrus Society's Picnic', *Southern Times*, 9 April 1914: 5; 'Harvey Citrus Society', *Bunbury Herald*, Thursday 15 July 1909: 3: 'Harvey Citrus Society', *South Western Advertiser*, 12 August 1911: 4; Roy O. Hayward, 'Fertilizing agencies: their constituents, values and methods', Harvey Citrus Society, 1909.

110 'Clare News in Victor', *Northern Argus*, 6 November 1942: 3; 'Harvey Citrus Society', *Southern Times*, 16 June 1914: 4.

111 'Harvey Citrus Society', *Southern Times*, 22 August 1905: 3; 'Harvey Show Luncheon', *Southern Times*, 4 September 1915: 3.

112 'The Agricultural Conference. Opened by the Governor', *Western Mail*, 15 April 1911: 14.

113 Staples, *They Made their Destiny*, 371–371, 374, 399–415, 420, 427.

114 CS to family, 28 November 1915, 16 July 1916.

115 'Harvey Irrigation', *The West Australian*, 18 June 1941: 4; 'The Harvey Irrigation Scheme', *Southern Times*, 4 September 1915: 5.

116 'Irrigation', *The Daily News*, 11 December 1917: 6.

117 'Harvey Citrus Show', *Southern Times*, 17 August 1911: 4.

118 'Harvey Citrus Show', *The West Australian*, 21 August 1905: 3; 'Second Day', *Southern Times*, 5 November 1908: 5; 'Inaugural Citrus Show at Harvey', *Southern Times*, 22 August 1905: 3; 'The Harvey Citrus Show', *Bunbury Herald*, 30 August 1907: 2.

119 'Second Day', *Southern Times*, 5 November 1908: 5.

120 'Bunbury Ploughing Match', *Southern Times*, 1 September 1890: 5.

121 'A Popular Farewell', *Bunbury Herald*, 5 April 1913: 5.

122 'The Hon. Sir John Forrest and his Constituents', *Southern Times*, 23 April 1896: 3; 'South Western Railway', *Southern Times*, 9 September 1893: 3.

123 J.S. Jefferson to CS, 8 July 1916, Mrs Elise Jefferson, 15 October 1916, Exmouth, Devon; Bessie Lambert to Mrs Snell from Hampstead, 3 October, 1916; 'Harvey Agricultural Alliance', *Southern Times*, 17 March 1900: 3; 'Harvey Agricultural Alliance', *Southern Times*, 22 March 1900: 5; Andrew Hassam, *Through Australian Eyes*.

124 J. S. Jefferson to CS, 8 July 1916, Mrs Elise Jefferson to CAS, from Exmouth, Devon 15 October 1916; Bessie Lambert from Hampstead to CAS, 3 October, 1916.

125 Marshall Waller Clifton, grandson of the original Australind Commissioner; 'Sports Gathering Harvey Agricultural Alliance', *Bunbury Herald*, 24 February 1905: 2.

126 'A Popular Farewell', *Bunbury Herald*, 5 April 1913: 5.

127 'Four Bunbury Boys', *Bunbury Herald*, 1 June 1909: 3.

128 'Supposed Attempted Suicide', *The Daily News*, 30 March 1908: 3; 'Johansen's Benefit Committee', *Bunbury Herald*, 14 September 1912: 5.

129 Alistair McIntyre and Donald Fullarton, *Helensburgh Heritage*, Helensburgh Heriatge Trust: 2018; 'News and Notes', *Southern Times*, 26 November 1901: 5; 'Worker Winnowings', *Westralian Worker*, 28 December 1900: 4.

130 'The Goldfields Children', *Southern Times*, 9 February 1901: 3; 'News and Notes', *Southern Times*, 26 November 1901: 5; 'Fresh Air Society', *The Evening*

Star, 29 November 1901: 3.

131 'Bunbury', *Western Mail,* 14 January 1916: 18.

132 'News and Notes', *Southern Times,* 26 November 1901: 5; 'Do You Know', *Southern Times,* 27 January 1916: 5.

133 'Bunbury', *The West Australian,* 22 November 1901: 7; 'The Opening of Goldfields Fresh Air League Home Bunbury', *Southern Times* 24 December 1910: 5.

134 'Bunbury', *Western Mail,* 14 January 1916: 18; 'Do You Know', *Southern Times,* 27 January 1916: 5.

135 'Grand Concert and Dance: Harvey Happenings', *South Western Advertiser,* 16 January 1914: 5; 'At Wellington Mills', *Bunbury Herald,* 21 March 1906: 2; 'Brunswick Roads Board', *Southern Times,* 14 April 1906: 4; 'Harvey Agricultural Alliance', *Bunbury Herald,* 15 August 1894, 3.

136 'Social Notes', *The West Australian,* 13 August 1908: 7; 'Sailors' Rest', *Bunbury Herald,* 5 June 1913: 3; 'Bunbury Ploughing Match', *Southern Times* 1 September 1890: 5; 'A Popular Farewell', *Bunbury Herald,* 5 April 1913: 5; 'Social Evening', *Bunbury Herald,* 24 August 1899: 3; 'St. Paul's Church', *Southern Times,* 4 September 1897: 3.

137 The Clifton piano is displayed at the Bunbury Museum, King Cottage; 'Advertising', *Bunbury Herald,* 21 March 1906: 2.

138 Graeme Skinner (University of Sydney), *A biographical register of Australian colonial musical personnel,* web archive; 'Latest Shipping News', *Sydney Mail,* 4 February 1865: 9; 'The Christy Minstrels', *Freeman's Journal,* 22 February 1865: 116; 'Advertising', *The Inquirer and Commercial News,* 30 September 1868: 2; 'Bunbury', *The Inquirer and Commercial News,* 10 February 1869: 3.

139 'Bunbury', *The Herald,* 27 February 1869: 3.

140 'Western Australian Theatricals', *The Inquirer and Commercial News,* 14 February 1877: 3; 'Local and General', *The Western Australian Times,* 25 April 1879: 2; 'Perth's Old-Time Plays', *Sunday Times,* 31 October 1920: 1; 'Perth Organ-Builder', *The West Australian,* 26 March 1938: 7.

141 'Orchestral Society', *Bunbury Herald,* 2 September 1903: 3.

142 'Bunbury Musical Association', *Bunbury Herald,* 26 June 1913: 5.

143 'Local and General', *Bunbury Herald,* 2 May 1899: 3; 'News and Notes', *Southern Times,* 6 May 1913: 2.

144 'Trinity College of Music London', *Southern Times,* 23 August, 1913: 5.

145 'Advertising', *Bunbury Herald,* 19 July 1913: 6; 'Advertising', *The Bunbury Herald and Blackwood Express,* 16 April 1920: 4; 'Malvern Music College', *Bunbury Herald* 23 December 1913: 5; 'Entertainments', *The West Australian,* 25 August 1904: 9.

146 'Malvern Music College', *Bunbury Herald,* 23 December 1913: 5.

147 'Musical Recital', *Bunbury Herald,* 13 July 1915: 3.

148 'Bunbury', *The Perth Gazette and West Australian Times,* 19 February 1869: 2; 'Bunbury', *The Herald,* 19 February 1869: 3.

149 CS to family, 28 September 1915.

150 CS to family, 15 August 1915, 12 September 1915, 28 September 1915.

151 CS to family, 16 July 1915, 28 November 1915.

152 'Harvey Agricultural Alliance', *Southern Times,* 17 March 1903: 5.

153 'Bunbury Police Court', *Southern Times,* 19 December 1905: 3; 'Bunbury News', *The West Australian,* 4 January 1893: 3; 'The Salvation Army', *Bunbury*

Herald, 27 May 1902: 3.

154 'Cricket', *Bunbury Herald,* 22 December 1894: 3; 'Harvey', *Southern Times,* 16 February 1911: 5.

155 Verna L. Glossop, *Eliza Cons*, Bunbury Historical Society, 1981; 'W.C.T.U.', *The West Australian,* 23 August 1899, 7.

156 'The Bunbury Programme', *Southern Times,* 10 May 1900: 3.

157 The lives of 'public women' will be examined in a later chapter.

158 E. C. Buley, *Australian Life in Town and Country*, New York and London: G. P. Putnam's Sons, 1905, 105, 178, 179.

159 'Rambles Round the Harvey', *Bunbury Herald,* 21 March 1906: 2.

160 AJS to Dr Joel, August – September 1916; 'Dr Joel Dead', *The West Australian,* 14 February 1935: 13.

161 'Bunbury Chamber of Commerce', *Southern Times,* 20 July, 1899: 3.

162 'Bunbury Chamber of Commerce', *Southern Times,* 20 July, 1899: 3.

163 'Local and General', *Bunbury Herald,* 2 May 1899: 3; 'News and Notes', *Southern Times,* 6 May 1913: 2.

164 'Four Bunbury Boys', *Bunbury Herald,* 1 June 1909: 3.

165 Postcards to CS from Wedd Tuxford, 1906–1907; 'Death of Councillor J. J. Tuxford', *Bunbury Herald,* 16 June 1900: 2.

166 'North Ward Election', *Bunbury Herald,* 6 November 1897: 3.

167 'Death of Councillor J. J. Tuxford', *Bunbury Herald,* 16 June 1900: 2.

168 AJS to W.J. George letters, 10–12 August 1916.

169 Manford, 'George, William James', *ADB*, 1981; 'Mr. W. J. George', *Southern Times,* 24 February 1910: 5; 'Mr. W. J. George', *Sunday Times*, 15 March 1931: 9.

170 'Biographical Sketch', *Bunbury Herald*, 25 April 1912: 5.

171 'The Bunbury Programme', *Southern Times,* 10 May 1900: 3.

172 'The State's Fruit Industry', *The West Australian,* 23 November 1909: 6; 'The New Harvey Hall', *Southern Times,* 14 July 1914: 4.

173 Coleman, *Social Capital*, 104, 108.

174 CS to family, May–June 1916.

3: The Wellington Community at War: Civilian and Military Effort

1 Scott, *Australia During the War*, 700–701, 730.

2 McKernan, *The Australian People and the Great War*, 68–69, 73–74; McQuilton, *Rural Australia and the Great War*, 123; Payton, *The Boys from Old Kio*, 12; Beaumont, *Broken Nation*, xv, 38.

3 Carmel Shute, 'Heroines and Heroes', 23; McQuilton, *Rural Australia and the Great War*, 119.

4 Scott, Au*stralia During the War*, 697.

5 'To the People', *Southern Times,* 3 September 1914: 3.

6 Scott, *Australia During the War*, 738; Field Marshall W. R. Birdwood, commander of the AIF during World War I. A. J. Hill, 'Birdwood, William Riddell (Baron Birdwood) (1865–1951)', *ADB*, 1979.

7 'To the People', *Southern Times,* 3 September 1914: 3; 'The Munitions Question', *Southern Times,* 5 October 1915: 3.

8 'The Munitions Question', *Southern Times* 5 October 1915: 3.

9 'Bunbury Munitions Committee', *Bunbury Herald,* 16 October 1915: 3.

10 Scott, Australia During the War, 242.
11 'The Munitions Question', *Southern Times,* 5 October 1915: 3.
12 Nicoletta Gullace, *The Blood of our Sons: men, women, and the renegotiation of British citizenship during the Great War*, New York: Palgrave Macmillan, 2002, 69; 'Women's Peace Army Leaflet No. 2', *Woman Voter*, 14 September 1916: 3; 'Trades Hall and Peace', *Western Argus,* 31 July 1917: 30.
13 Scott, Australia During the War, 191–196.
14 'Lord Kitchener', *Southern Times,* 27 January 1910: 3; 'Lord Kitchener at Bunbury', *Albany Advertiser,* 2 February 1910: 4; Scott, *Australia During the War*, 49, 195, 193.
15 *Bunbury Herald,* April 24 1900: 2; 'Lord Kitchener', *Southern Times,* 27 January 1910: 3; *'Lord Kitchener at Bunbury', Albany Advertiser,* 2 February 1910: 4.
16 'South Bunbury News', *Bunbury Herald,* 14 December 1907: 1.
17 'The Bunbury Show', *The West Australian,* 18 November 1911: 8.
18 Scott, Australia During the War, 204–5, 207.
19 'News and Notes', *The Blackwood Times,* 26 January 1917: 2.
20 Danny Clarke, quoted in *ANZAC Heroes*, 2013; Scott, Australia During the War, 287, 289–91.
21 Ken Inglis, 'Conscription in Peace and War, in Roy Forward and Bob Rees eds, *Conscription in Australia*, Santa Lucia, Queensland: University of Queensland Press, 1968. 1911–1945'. 22–65, 30–32; Anstey, Impact of the Great War, 110.
22 Jennifer McNeice, 'Military exemption courts in 1916: a public hearing of private lives', *Provenance: The Journal of Public Record Office Victoria*, issue no. 14, 2015.
23 'The Call to Arms', *The Sydney Morning Herald,* 11 January 1916: 9.
24 Bart Ziino. Enlistment and Non-enlistment in Wartime Australia: Responses to the 1916 Call to Arms Appeal', *Australian Historical Studies*, Volume 41, Issue 2, 2010, 217–32, 219.
25 Scott, Australia During the War, 312, 314.
26 'The Munitions Question', *Southern Times,* 5 October 1915: 3. Snell's older brother, Alf, was rejected three times. Lists of men rejected were published regularly.
27 'Do you Know', *Southern Times,* 2 September 1915: 5.
28 'White Feathers', *Southern Times* 7 Dec 1915: 5
29 'Bunbury Municipal Council', *The Bunbury Herald and Blackwood Express,* 22 October 1919: 4, 'The Rustics', *Southern Times,* 21 September 1915: 4.
30 'Red Cross', *Bunbury Herald,* 25 January 1916: 3.
31 'Correspondence. Personal Recruiting Papers', *Southern Times,* 12 February 1916: 3.
32 'Bunbury Notes', *The Daily News,* 1 March 1916: 1.
33 'Harvey Honour Roll', *South Western Advertiser*, 4 August 1916: 4.
34 'Recruiting Methods', *The West Australian,* 29 March 1916: 7.
35 Ziino. 'Enlistment and Non-enlistment in Wartime Australia', 217.
36 'Harvey Road Board Monthly Meeting', *South Western Advertiser,* 21 January 1916: 3.
37 'News and Notes', *The Blackwood Times* 26 January 1917: 2.
38 Bunbury's Interest', *The West Australian* 27 Jan 1917: 7.
39 'In the Country', *The West Australian,* 2 February 1917: 8; 'News and Notes', *The South-Western News,* 2 February 1917: 2; Ziino. 'Enlistment and Non-enlistment in Wartime Australia', 219.

40 'In the Country', *The West Australian,* 2 February 1917: 8.
41 *ANZAC Heroes.*
42 Alison Pilger, quoted in Ziino. 'Enlistment and Non-enlistment in Wartime Australia', 220; *ANZAC Heroes.*
43 Ziino, 'Enlistment and Non-enlistment in Wartime Australia', 217, 219.
44 Scott, *Australia During the War*, 338; Beaumont, *Broken Nation*, 377, 233.
45 Scott, *Australia During the War*, 337, 338, Note 3: strictly speaking, the poll was a plebiscite which could guide the government, however, contemporary use the term 'referendum'.
46 Beaumont, *Broken Nation*, 223; McKernan, *The Australian People and the Great War,* 7; Anstey, Impact of the Great War, 138; Oliver, *War and Peace*, 102.
47 McKernan, The Australian People and the Great War, *195.*
48 *Australian Government*, Federal Register of Legislation, 'War Precautions Act 1914' 2; Scott, *Australia During the War*, 353; 'Disloyal Utterances', *Bunbury Herald,* 2 May 1917: 1.
49 Beaumont, *Broken Nation*, 231.
50 'The Bunbury Herald Saturday November 17', *Bunbury Herald,* 17 November 1917: 2. This and many subsequent newspaper citations refers to editorials.
51 NAA, 'Censorship Referendum campaign 1917', A2939, SC147, 963795, 7, 8, memorandum from Prime Minister to editors of various daily newspapers, 19 November 1917.
52 'Leighton-Siebenhaar Inquiry', *The West Australian,* 30 November 1916: 9.
53 'The Bunbury Herald Thursday, September 16, 1915', *Bunbury Herald,* 16 September 1915: 2; www.parliament.uk. 'Conscription: The First World War'.
54 'The Bunbury Herald Thursday, September 16, 1915', *Bunbury Herald,* 16 September 1915: 2.
55 CS to family 9 July 1915.
56 CS to family, 1 January 1916, 10 July 1916.
57 CS to family, 10 July 1916.
58 CS diary 12 July 1916.
59 CS diary, 14 July 1916, 12 July 1916.
60 'Conscription and Democracy', *Bunbury Herald,* 1 January 1916: 3; 'The Bunbury Herald January 8, 1916; 'The Power of Thought', *Bunbury Heral*d, 8 January 1916: 3; 'The Bunbury Herald Saturday, January 15, 1916. Liberty', *Bunbury Herald,* 15 January 1916: 2.
61 'The Bunbury Herald Thursday, February 3. Recruiting', *Bunbury Herald,* 3 February 1916: 2.
62 NAA, 'Conscription referendums, 1916 and 1917 - Fact sheet 161'; 'National Service Referendum', *Southern Times,* 26 October 1916: 3; 'The Referendum Campaign', *Southern Times,* 21 October 1916: 3.
63 'News and Notes', *Southern Times,* 21 October 1916: 5.
64 'Two Disgraceful Meetings', *Southern Times,* 28 October 1916: 5.
65 Scott, *Australia During the War*, 349 – 350.
66 National Service', *The West Australian,* 10 October 1916: 8. Numbers are a 'best estimate' as newspaper reports can be ambiguous.
67 'National Service', *The West Australian,* 10 October 1916: 8.
68 McNeice, 'Military exemption courts in 1916', np.
69 'National Service', *The West Australian,* 10 October 1916: 8; 'Exemption

Courts', *The West Australian,* 2 November 1916: 4. The official records for these proceedings are held in the State Records Office, Perth, 'Register of Applications for Exemption from Military Services, 1916–1955', Series 121, Consignment 3639.

70 'Exemption Courts', *Southern Times,* Thursday 23 November 1916, 4.

71 Occupations were often stated or implied in court reports, others have been identified through other news reports. Individuals not appearing in local news reports are assumed to be itinerant labourers.

72 John McQuilton. 'Enlistment for the First World War in rural Australia: the case of north-eastern Victoria, 1914–1918.' *Journal of the Australian War Memorial* - Issue 33. Canberra: Australian War Memorial, c.2005, paragraph 14.

73 *ANZAC Heroes.*

74 'Found Dead', *South Western Times,* 19 August 1919: 1; 'Funerals', *South Western Times,* 21 August 1919: 3; 'Bunbury Board of Health', *The Bunbury Herald and Blackwood Express,* 27 August 1919: 3.

75 McNeice, 'Military exemption courts in 1916', np.

76 Scott, *Australia During the War,* 357, 359, 361, 368, 369, 375.

77 'The Political Situation', *Bunbury Herald,* 27 January 1917: 3. Mark Lyons, 'Gardiner, Albert (Jupp)', ADB.

78 McQuilton, *Rural Australia and the Great War,* 59; 'The Political Situation', *Bunbury Herald,* 27 January 1917: 3. Lyons, 'Gardiner, Albert '.

79 Scott, *Australia During the War,* 348; Beaumont, *Broken Nation,* 237; 'The Political Situation', *Bunbury Herald,* 27 January 1917: 3; Lyons, 'Gardiner, Albert' ADB.

80 'Recruits Wanted', *Bunbury Herald,* 27 January 1917: 3.

81 Scott, *Australia During the War,* 402; 'The Late Mr. W. B. Castieau', *Sunday Times,* 8 July 1934: 17. The Bunbury Walter Castieau was very likely the brother of the Victorian, since they shared the middle name 'Buckley'.

82 McQuilton, *Rural Australia and the Great War,* 76, 77; 'Recruiting Campaign', *Bunbury Herald,* 17 March 1917: 3.

83 'A Call to Australia', *The West Australian,* 21 March 1917: 8; 'Settling the Returned Soldier', *The Blackwood Times,* 25 August 1916: 4.

84 'Clearing the Atmosphere', *South Western Times,* 14 March 1918: 3.

85 'Recruiting Campaign', *Bunbury Herald,* 17 March 1917: 3.

86 Oliver, *War and Peace,* 114; 'Miss. Adela Pankhurst', *South Western Times,* 3 April 1917: 3.

87 'Miss. Adela Pankhurst', *South Western Times,* 3 April 1917: 3.

88 'Do You Know', South Western Times, 29 March 1917: 3.

89 'Recruiting Speeches', *South Western Times,* 14 April 1917: 5.

90 Privates F.W. Steere, and Jack Donovan, *ANZAC Heroes.*

91 *ANZAC Heroes.*

92 'Banquet to Pte. R. Driver', *South Western Times,* 15 March 1917: 3. The crowd included Becher, Castieau, two Cliftons, Cook, two Haywards, Johnson, Myatt, two Roses, Shenton and Stewart

93 *ANZAC Heroes.*

94 'Local and General', *Bunbury Herald,* 15 December 1917: 4.

95 Scott, Australia During the War, 389.

96 'The War', *South Western Times,* 28 April 1917: 5.

97 'The Minister of Defence', *Bunbury Herald,* 5 May 1917: 3. Minister for Defence, George Pearce. B. Beddie, 'Pearce, Sir George Foster (1870–1952)', ADB.

98 J.R. Robertson, 'The conscription issue and the national movement, Western Australia: June, 1916 to December, 1917', *University Studies in Western Australian History,* Nedlands, WA, University of Western Australia, 1959, 5–57, 32.

99 'War Declaration Anniversary, Patriotic Resolution Passed', *South Western Times,* 7 August 1917: 3.

100 NAA, 'Conscription referendums, 1916 and 1917'; Scott, *Australia During the War,* 415; McKernan, *The Australian People and the Great War,* 197.

101 Beaumont, *Broken Nation,* 384.

102 'Two Disgraceful Meetings', *Southern Times,* 28 October 1916: 5; 'Colonel Brazier. People Don't Understand 'Germany's Aims and Objects, How She "Cut Up" this State', *South Western Times,* 27. November 1917: 3. Brazier, N. M., NAA B2455, 3115159, b. 1866, served 10LH, wounded in eye, Gallipoli, RTA 1916.

103 '[?] (sic) Campaign', *Bunbury Herald,* 5 December 1917: 3; 'Thomas Twaddle, Esq M.L.A', *Bunbury Herald,* 8 December 1917: 5.

104 'Australia's Duty', *South Western Times,* 13 December 1917: 3.

105 'A Voice from the Trenches', *Bunbury Herald,* 29 December 1917: 6.

106 'Two Deliberate Lies', *South Western Times,* 24 April 1917: 3; 'Reinforcements Referendum', *Bunbury Herald,* 5 December 1917: 3;

107 'Senator Henderson', *Bunbury Herald,* 8 December 1917: 7.

108 'Great Speech', *Bunbury Herald,* 19 December 1917: 3.

109 'Reinforcements' Referendum', *Bunbury Herald,* 29 December 1917: 5.

110 'The Recent Referendum. And the War', *South Western Times,* 27 December 1917: 2.

111 'Federal Politics. An Unsatisfactory Position', *South Western Times,* 12 January 1918: 4.

112 'Recruiting appeals by people you know. Living Message from the Dead', *South Western Times,* 13 April 1918: 4;

113 Beaumont, *Broken Nation,* 247; Robertson, 'The conscription issue and the national movement, WA', 21.

114 'Harvey Happenings', *Bunbury Herald,* 19 January 1918: 6.

115 'Bunbury Recruiting Committee', *Bunbury Herald,* 21 December 1918: 6.

116 The military contribution of the Bunbury-Harvey community is explored in a later section.

117 'Repatriation', *Bunbury Herald,* 19 March 1919: 3.

118 Scott, *Australia During the War,* 697.

119 'Belgian Relief Fund', *Bunbury Herald,* 19 November 1914: 1.

120 'Help for Belgians Bunbury's Fine Effort. Just Under £150 Raised', *Bunbury Herald,* 19 December 1914: 5; 'The Belgian Fete', *Bunbury Herald,* 12 December 1914: 5.

121 'Sunday School Anniversary', *Southern Times,* 26 November 1914: 4.

122 'Belgian Relief Fund', *Bunbury Herald,* 6 March 1915: 5.

123 'Concert at Harvey', *Southern Times,* 11 March 1915: 3.

124 'News and Notes', *Southern Times,* 29 June 1915: 2; 'Belgian Relief Fund', *Bunbury Herald* 1 July 1915: 3; 'Belgian Relief Fund', *Bunbury Herald,* 2 March

1916: 2.

125 *Bunbury Herald,* 16 May 1916: 2; 'Unemployed', *The Daily News,* 24 April 1915: 4.

126 Melanie Oppenheimer, *Australian Women and War,* Canberra: Department of Veterans' Affairs, 2008.

127 Scott, Australia During the War, 706.

128 'News and Notes', *Southern Times,* 1916, 21 November 1916: 2.

129 'Red Cross', *Bunbury Herald,* 7 October 1915: 3.

130 'Red Cross', *The Daily News,* 20 October 1915: 8.

131 'Red Cross', *Bunbury Herald,* 25 January 1916: 3.

132 'Red Cross', *Bunbury Herald,* 16 November 1915: 3.

133 'Bunbury War Finds' (sic), *Southern Times,* 25 November 1915: 5.

134 'The Rustics', *Southern Times,* 21 September 1915: 4.

135 'Civilians and Empire', *The Daily News,* 13 April 1915: 3.

136 'News and Notes', *Southern Times,* 29 June 1915: 2.

137 'Red Cross Societies', *South Western Advertiser,* 19 November 1915: 3.

138 'Red Cross', *Bunbury Herald,* 8 August 1916: 3.

139 'News and Notes', *Southern Times,* 21 November 1916: 2.

140 'Bunbury Red Cross Society', *Bunbury Herald,* 9 February 1918: 5.

141 'Bunbury Red Cross', *Bunbury Herald,* 21 December 1918: 5.

142 'Y.M.C.A.', *The Daily News,* 19 September 1918: 6.; 'Y.M.C.A.', *West Australian,* 24 May 1918: 5.

143 Correspondence between AJS and J. Beecham, September-November 1916.

144 'Y.M.C.A.' *The Daily News,* 19 September 1918: 6; 'Western Australia', *The West Australian,* 1 October 1918: 5.

145 'Bunbury Munitions Committee', *Southern Times,* 13 January 1916: 4.

146 'News and Notes', *Southern Times,* 26 February 1916: 2; 'Harvey Roads Board', *Southern Times,* 11 November 1915: 4.

147 'Sand Bags', *Bunbury Herald,* 20 November 1915: 3; CS to family, date censored, May 1916.

148 McQuilton, R*ural Australia and the Great War,* 149–160; 'Orangeism In Bunbury', *Southern Times.* 13 July 1897: 3; 'Gen. Birdwood', *The Daily News,* 1 October 1920: 5; 'Peace', *Bunbury Herald,* 16 November 1918: 5.

149 'Roman Catholic Church', *Bunbury Herald,* 4 November 1915: 3; 'News and Notes', *The West Australian,* 21 March 1916: 6; 'Red Cross', *Bunbury Herald,* 7 October 1915: 3.

150 'Bunbury', *Southern Times,* 16 March 1916: 3.

151 Handwritten note by CAS, n.d.

152 'Bunbury', *Southern Times,* 16 March 1916: 3.

153 CS to family, May 1916.

154 Margaret Tennant, 'Fun and fundraising: the selling of charity in New Zealand's past' *Social History,* Volume 38, no 1, 2013, 46–65, 2.

155 Tennant, 'Fun and fundraising', 47.

156 'Queen Carnival. Explained by Professor Owen Cardston', *Great Southern Herald,* 29 January 1916.

157 'Queen Carnival', *Western Mail,* 18 February 1916: 22.

158 'Queen Carnival', *The West Australian,* 8 February 1916: 8; 'The Queen

Carnival', *Southern Times*, 14 March 1916: 3.

159 'Harvey', *The Daily News* 13 March 1916: 3.

160 'Harvey Notes', *Southern Times,* 4 April 1916: 3.

161 'Harvey Notes', *Harvey Chronicle,* 5 May 1916: 3.

162 'Queen Carnival Final Results', *Harvey Chronicle,* 5 May 1916: 3.

163 'Queen Carnival Odours', *Southern Times,* 22 August 1916: 3.

164 'Bleeding the District', *The Southern Districts Advocate,* 20 December 1916: 2.

165 'Australians In London', *The Daily News,* 18 August 1914: 2; 'Australians At War', *The Daily News,* 20 August 1914: 1; 'London Notes', *The West Australian,* 29 October 1914: 8.

166 'London Notes', *The West Australian,* 12 November 1914: 8.

167 The performers included famous Australian concert performers Percy Grainger and Peter Dawson.

168 'London Notes', *The West Australian,* 12 November 1914: 8.

169 'Australians on Furlough', *The West Australian,* 3 November 1915: 7; 'Mainly About People', *The Daily News,* 24 February 1916: 3.

170 J. Jefferson to Snell family, October 1916.

171 'Anzacs In London', *The Daily News,* 11 August 1916: 5.

172 'Newspapers for Soldiers', *The West Australian,* 13 November 1916: 5.

173 'An Association Wound Up', *The West Australian,* 20 July 1917: 7.

174 A letter in the Snell Archive from the London Red Cross signed by 'Vera' with the surname torn off may have come from Miss Deakin.

175 'The Mine-Sweepers' Fund', *South Western Advertiser,* 4 February 1916: 3.

176 'Sandbags Fund', *The West Australian,* 28 October 1915: 4; 'News and Notes', *Southern Times,* 29 June 1915: 2; 'Motor Ambulance Fund', *The West Australian,* 5 February 1915: 7.

177 'Mainly About People', *The Daily News,* 24 February 1916: 3; 'Mainly About People', *The Daily News,* 19 September 1917: 3.

178 'Mainly About People', *The Daily News,* 9 November 1932: 9; 'Mainly About People', *The Daily News,* 24 February 1916: 3.

179 *ANZAC Heroes.*

180 'Mainly About People', *The Daily News,* 8 November 1916: 3.

181 McQuilton, Rural Australia and the Great War, 19, 23, 24.

182 'News and Notes', *Southern Times,* 29 June 1915: 2.

183 'Bunbury District Nursing Association', *Southern Times,* 25 July 1916: 4.

184 W.C.T.U. *The West Australian,* 23 August 1899: 7.

185 'Timber Topics', *Westralian Worker,* 18 February 1916: 5; 'News and Notes', *Southern Times,* 26 February 1916: 2; 'News and Notes', *The Blackwood Times,* 25 February 1916: 2.

186 'News and Notes', *Southern Times,* 29 June 1915: 2.

187 Marnie Haig-Muir, 'The economy at war', in Joan Beaumont (ed) *Australia's War 1914–1918*, St. Leonards, N.S.W.: Allen and Unwin, 1995, 97, 104.

188 'Unemployed', *The Daily News,* 24 April 1915: 4.

189 'Settling the Returned Soldier', *The Blackwood Times,* 25 August 1916: 4.

190 Alison Moir to CAS. Mrs Moir received news of Snell's death via her child's school.

191 'The Bunbury Show', *Southern Times,* 1 September 1914: 2.

192 'Red Cross', *Bunbury Herald,* 8 August 1916: 3.

193 'Obituary', *The Bunbury Herald and Blackwood Express,* 15 August 1928: 3.

194 'Unveiling of War Memorial', *South Western Times,* 14 December 1920: 4.

195 Welborn, *Bush Heroes.*

196 W. Devine, *The Story of a Battalion*; Walter C. Belford, *Legs-Eleven*; James Hurst, *Game to the Last: the story of the 11th Australian Infantry Battalion at Gallipoli*, Warriewood, New South Wales: Big Sky Publishing, 2005; Stephen Anstey, The Impact of the Great War on the Beverley, Toodyay and Murchison Goldfield Communities of Western Australia 1914–1917, Honours dissertation. Murdoch University, 1980; For example: Hazell Udell, *History of Gingin, 1830–1960*, Gingin Shire Council, 1979; Glen McLaren and William Cooper, *Beverley: our journey through time: a history of the Shire of Beverley*, Shire of Beverley, 2002.

197 Jeff Pierce, *ANZAC Heroes*, web archive.

198 AWM; *ANZAC Heroes*; Census of the Commonwealth of Australia, 1911.

199 Collie', *The Daily News,* 28 February 1916: 5.

200 *ANZAC Heroes.*

201 NAA war service files, B2455; Snell archive, various dates; Wedd Hay Tuxford, NAA MT1139/1, 5910076.

202 Scott, *Australia During the War*, 266–269.

203 Tuxford Wedd, NAA MT1139/1, 5910076 Munitions worker 1021; *Grace's Guide to British Industrial History: W S Laycock*, 4 August 2015.

204 Wenn, Mervyn Bailey, NAA, B2455 8381168.

205 'Country', *The West Australian,* 25 April 1912: 8.

206 Peter Stanley, *Bad Characters: sex, crime, mutiny, murder and the Australian Imperial Force*, Millers Point, N.S.W.: Pier 9, 2010.

207 Wenn, Mervyn Bailey, NAA, B2455 8381168.

208 Thomson, *Anzac Memories*, 58; Stanley, *Bad Characters,* 10–29.

209 CS to family, August–December, 2015; M. J. Warburton, 'Liverpool Troop Train Smash: the December 1915 accident and troop behaviour', *Australian Railway History*, November 2015, Vol. 66 no 937, 4–11.

210 CS to family, 14 December 1915.

211 'Train Smash at Liverpool Station', *Sydney Morning Herald*, Wednesday 15th December, 1915: 15.

212 'Sensational Accident', *The Maitland Weekly Mercury*, Saturday 18 December 1915: 7.

213 'Troop Train Smash', *Barrier Miner* (Broken Hill, NSW). Tuesday 14 December 1915: 4.

214 *The Cumberland Argus and Fruitgrowers Advocate* (Parramatta, NSW) 21 June, 1913.

215 Private Septimus Herbert O'Leary, NAA B2455, 8001429.

216 Private Alfred Brian Chapple, NAA B2455, 3235299.

217 Article annotated by CS: 19 December 1915, 'Overcrowded Trains', *Evening News,* 20 December 1916: 7.

218 Article annotated by CS: 29 December 1915, probably, 'Trains Held Up', *The Sun,* 29 December 1915: 6.

219 'Riot In Sydney', *The Maitland Weekly Mercury,* 18 December 1915: 10; 'When The Riot Was On', *The Cumberland Argus and Fruitgrowers Advocate,*18 December 1915: 5; Robert McKillop, Donald Ellsmore, John Oakes, *A Century*

of Central, Sydney: Australian Railway Historical Society, 2008, 72–73.

220 Valerie Everett, *Blackboy Hill is Calling*, Greenmount, Western Australia: Katharine Susannah Prichard Foundation Incorporated, 2015, Back Cover; Emma Wynne and Lorraine Horsley, 'Blackboy Hill training camp: The birthplace of Western Australia's Anzac forces', ABC Radio Perth, 26 Aug 2014; 'Blackboy Hill Encampment', *The Swan Express*, 29 January 1915: 5.

221 NSW State Archives and records, *NSW ANZAC Centenary*, 'Liverpool Riots 1916'.

222 'Greek Shopkeepers', *The West Australian,* 2 August 1917: 7.

223 'Riotous Soldiery', *The West Australian,* 4 January 1916: 2; 'Candid Criticism', *Southern Times,* 13 January 1916: 3.

224 'The Discipline of the Camp', *Camp Chronicle,* 13 January 1916: 2.

4: The Wellington Community and the Aftermath: Men on the Land, The Public and The Private

1 'Committed for Trial', *The Bunbury Herald and Blackwood Express*, 2 December 1924: 4.

2 'Soldiers' Relatives', *South Western Times,* 18 October 1917: 3. 'Repatriation', *Bunbury Herald,* 19 March 1919: 3.

3 Edward D. Millen, 1917, quoted in Clem. Lloyd and Jacqui Wright, *The Last Shilling: A history of repatriation in Australia*, Carlton Victoria: Melbourne University Press, 1994, 419.

4 For example, Scott, *Australia During the War*; Marilyn Lake, *The Limits of Hope: Soldier settlement in Victoria 1915–1938.* Melbourne: Oxford University Press. 1987; Bruce Scates and Melanie Oppenheimer, *The Last Battle.*

5 Scott, *Australia During the War,* 824–25.

6 Scott, *Australia During the War,* 826, 832, 835–37., 838.

7 'To the People', *Southern Times,* 3 September 1914: 3.

8 'Repatriation', *Bunbury Herald,* 19 March 1919: 3.

9 'Developing the South-West', *Southern Times,* 20 July 1916: 5.

10 'The South-West', *The West Australian,* 5 August 1918: 8.

11 The South-Western Soldiers', *Southern Times,* 25 November 1916: 7; 'The South-West', *The West Australian,* 5 August 1918: 8; 'Developing the South-West', *Southern Times,* 20 July 1916: 5.

12 'Harvey Show Luncheon', *Southern Times,* 4 September 1915*:* 3; 'Western Australia', *The West Australian,* 6 September 1916: 7.

13 For example, Reg. Hemingway (Melbourne), NAA PP2/8 10155153 R9621; B73 20455595 MB21936; B73 20455596 HB21936, and Leonard Baldock (Adelaide), NAA PP2/8, 32500940 R9410. Hemingway's files followed him to Melbourne, Baldock's repatriation record ends when he moved to Adelaide.

14 'The South-Western Soldiers', *Southern Times,* 25 November 1916: 7.

15 'Our Heroes', *The Daily News,* 8 March 1917: 6.

16 Scates and Oppenheimer, *The Last Battle*; 'Agricultural Bank', *Western Mail,* 6 October 1938: 60.

17 'Soldier Settlers', *The West Australian,* 27 March 1917: 6.

18 'Repatriation', *The West Australian,* 16 January 1918: 5.

19 'Repatriation', *South Western Times,* 13 June 1918: 4.

20 'The State and Repatriation', *Bunbury Herald,* 13 July 1918: 5.
21 'Land Settlement Scheme', *Bunbury Herald,* 24 August 1918: 5.
22 'Repatriation', *South Western Times,* 13 June 1918: 4.
23 'The Neglect of Brunswick State Farm', *Bunbury Herald,* 8 May 1918: 3.
24 'Trading Concerns', *The Blackwood Times,* 23 August 1918: 4; 'The South-West', *The West Australian,* 5 August 1918: 8.
25 'Tambellup District', *The Australian,* 10 February 1922: 6.
26 'Plantagenet Road Board', *Tambellup Times,* 14 July 1917: 4; Scates and Oppenheimer, *The Last Battle,* chapters 3 and 5.
27 Scates and Oppenheimer, *The Last Battle,* chapters 3 and 5.
28 'Land Settlement', *Tambellup Times,* 2 June 1917: 2.
29 'Premier's Tour', *Tambellup Times,* 12 July 1919: 2.
30 Hilda Paisley suffered the loss of several infant children. NAA 10113873 HB4981.
31 'Premier's Tour', *Tambellup Times,* 12 July 1919: 2.
32 'Settling the Soldier', *South Western Times,* 6 January 1920: 1.
33 'For Soldiers and Sailors', *Sunday Times,* 15 August 1920: 11 (First Section).
34 'Country', *The West Australian,* 31 March 1920: 8.
35 'Harvey Road Board', *South Western Times,* 8 May 1920: 3.
36 Personal Communication, N. Sherwood. 7 July 2016.
37 George King, b.1871, enlisted twice, discharged twice, 1916, 1917, medically unfit, 'senility and rheumatism', *ANZAC Heroes*; 'Correspondence', *The Bunbury Herald and Blackwood Express,* 4 June 1920: 6.
38 'The I.A.B. Amendment Act', *Primary Producer,* 27 February 1920: 1.
39 'Soldier Settlements', *Tambellup Times,* 11 February 1920: 3.
40 'Tambellup District', *The Australian,* 10 February 1922: 6.
41 'Repatriation Committee', *Tambellup Times,* 11 December 1918: 4.
42 'The I.A.B. Amendment Act', *Primary Producer,* 27 February 1920: 1.
43 'Boyanup', *South Western Times,* 1 July 1922: 7.
44 'A Land Settlement Disclosure' *Westralian Worker,* 10 August 1923: 7; *Royal Commission on repatriated soldiers of the A.I.F., under 'The Discharged Soldiers' Settlement Act, 1918',* Chair: Arthur A. Wilson.
45 'Soldier Settlements', *Tambellup Times,* 11 February 1920: 3.
46 'Soldier Settler', *The West Australian,* 1 June 1923: 8.
47 'Returned Soldiers', *The Bunbury Herald and Blackwood Express,* 29 January 1924: 3.
48 1397 Henry Parkinson, 54 years, 11 Battalion, had suffered a bayonet wound to eye at Gallipoli, NAA, B2455, 8008346; DOTAG, *ANZAC Heroes*; Leigh Straw, *After the War: returned soldiers and the mental and physical scars of World War 1,* Crawley, Western Australia: University of Western Australia Publishing, 2017, 117.
49 'Strange Stock Disease', *South Western Times,* 10 April 1924: 2. Probably Black Leg, an infectious bacterial disease. http://cattletoday.info/blackleg.htm. 'Committed for Trial', *The Bunbury Herald and Blackwood Express,* 2 December 1924: 4. George Herbert Bloor, who, during his military service, spent much time in hospital, *ANZAC Heroes.*
50 'Committed for Trial', *The Bunbury Herald and Blackwood Express,* 2 December 1924: 4.
51 'A Question of Ownership', *South Western Times,* 3 February 1925: 4.

52 Scates and Oppenheimer, *The Last Battle*, 41–65, 55.
53 'An Explanation Wanted', *South Western Times*, 7 March 1925: 3.
54 'Harvey Irrigation Scheme', *The Bunbury Herald and Blackwood Express*, 30 October 1925: 6.
55 CS to family, 28 November 1915.
56 'Harvey Irrigation Scheme', *The Bunbury Herald and Blackwood Express*, 30 October 1925: 6.
57 'Bunbury Repatriation Industry', *South Western Times,* 4 December 1919: 1.
58 'Overdue Rates', *South Western Times,* 14 February 1925: 1.
59 'Amongst the Sheep Farmers', *Great Southern Herald,* 16 May 1925: 5.
60 Lake, *Limits of Hope*, 4, 29.
61 On the published evidence of annual Royal Agricultural Society Show results.
62 'Dairying at Wokalup', *South Western Times,* 9 October 1928: 3.
63 William Ewart White, 1885–1955, mumps, frost bite, trench feet, 1916–1918. d. married a Clifton. *ANZAC Heroes.*
64 'Reso Tourists Visit Bunbury', *The Bunbury Herald and Blackwood Express.* 21 October 1929: 3.
65 'Soldier Settlements', *South Western Times,* 2 May 1929: 1.
66 'Harvey', *Western Mail,* 12 September 1929: 49.
67 'Perth Wool Sales', *Great Southern Herald,* 29 October 1930: 3; 'Country Towns and Districts, Gnowangerup', *Western Mail,* 16 May 1929: 49.
68 'Returned Soldiers' League', *Great Southern Herald,* 17 December 1930: 3.
69 Died 1934, DOTAG. No military records have been found. 'The Dairying Industry. Dairying Progress', *Western Mail,* 10 December 1931: 42.
70 Staples, *They Made their Destiny*, 411–13; Jenny Gregory and Janice Gothard, (eds), *Historical Encyclopedia of Western Australia*, UWA Press, 2009, 273, 437, 893; 'The Harvey River', *South Western Times,* 8 January 1924: 4.
71 'Our City Letter', *Great Southern Leader,* 2 October 1931: 6.
72 'Myalup Camp', *The West Australian,* 4 July 1932: 12; 'Current Comment', *The West Australian,* 30 March 1932: 8; 'News and Notes', *The West Australian,* 13 August 1932: 14; 'Soldiers' Congress,' *The Daily News,* 1 October 1932: 1 (Late Sporting).
73 'The Harvey Weir', *Sunday Times,* 9 August 1936: 34. Jack Lowe, 1919–1952, CS to family 10 July 1916; gunner, 8th FAB, France, severe ear problems, *ANZAC Heroes*; NAA 30806317, 32495853, 32946124. The project is well-remembered by Nancy Snell, and is today one of the waypoints on the Perth – Bunbury highway.
74 'Soldier Settlement Committee', *South Western Times,* 11 November 1922: 5; 'Thriving Centres of the South-West', *Western Mail,* 10 November 1938: 31.
75 Walter N. White, seaman, 11 Battalion, GSW, gassed, pneumonia, MM. RTA 1919, unfit, *ANZAC Heroes.*
76 'Harvey Commonage', *The West Australian,* 23 April 1938: 8.
77 'Assistance to Settlers', *The West Australian,* 23 September 1938: 19.
78 'Gnowangerup', *Great Southern Herald,* 15 September 1937: 3.
79 'Agricultural Bank', *Western Mail,* 6 October 1938: 60.
80 'State Grants', *The West Australian,* 2 December 1938: 28.
81 'Gnowangerup', *Great Southern Herald,* 15 September 1937: 3.

82 Lake, *Limits of Hope,* 11. The plan has similarity to John Forrest's plans in the

1890s for closer settlement in the South West, quoted in Staples, *They Made their Destiny,* 276, 300, 303; 'The South-West', *The West Australian,* 5 August 1918: 8.

83 'Our Heroes'. *The Daily News,* 8 March 1917: 6; 'Settling the Soldier', *South Western Times,* 6 January 1920: 1.

84 Dr Joan Beaumont, Australian National University, Researchers' Projects.

85 'Repatriation', *Albany Advertiser,* 3 July 1918: 4; 'Repatriation,' *South Western Times,* 13 June 1918: 4.

86 'To the People', *Southern Times,* 3 September 1914: 3; 'An Extraordinary Position', *South Western Times,* 19 December 1918: 2.

87 'Bunbury Council Meeting', *Bunbury Herald,* 26 January 1918; 'An Extraordinary Position', *South Western Times,* 19 December 1918: 2.

88 'Repatriation Bungle', *South Western Times,* 17 December 1918: 1; 'Bunbury's Triple Appeal', *Bunbury Herald,* 17 May 1919: 1.

89 'Farmers and Settlers and Repatriation', *The Southern Argus and Wagin-Arthur Express,* 21 July 1917: 2; 'Bunbury Repatriation Committee', *Bunbury Herald,* 30 October 1918: 3; 'Returned Soldiers' Association', *South Western Times,* 8 March 1919: 3.

90 'Bunbury Repatriation Industry', *South Western Times,* 4 December 1919: 1.

91 'Spying Out the Land', *Western Mail,* 8 Jan 1920: 30; 'Country', *The West Australian* 16 Jul 1920: 9.

92 'Bunbury's Woodworking Industry', *South Western Times,* 10 June 1920: 4.

93 'Boyanup', *South Western Times,* 1 July 1922: 7; 'Advertising', *South Western Times,* 14 February 1925: 1.

94 'Fell from Windmill', *The Daily News,* 1 December 1931: 6.

95 Leonard Gordon Gibbs, NAA PP13/1 30808746 C25861; PP2/8 32647544 R25861.

96 Richard John Moore, NAA PP13/1 30802713 C987; PP2/8 32489238 M987; PP2/8 32489237 R987.

97 Reginald Hemingway, NAA PP2/8 10155153 R9621; Edith Hemingway, NAA B73 20455595 MB21936; B73 20455596 HB21936.

98 Grosvenor Hemingway, NAA PP2/8 32643565 M22539.

99 Pension Application, Elizabeth Hemingway, 4 March 1930, NAA PP2/8 30807256 M22539.

100 L. Baldock NAA PP2/8 32500940 R9410

101 Lake, *The Limits of Hope*; Scates and Oppenheimer, *The Last Battle*; Damousi, *The Labour of Loss*; Marina Larsson, *Shattered Anzacs: Living with the legend.* Sydney: UNSW Press Sydney, 2009.

102 Thomson, ANZAC Memories; Straw, *After the War.*

103 Stephen Garton, *The Cost of War,* Oxford: Oxford University Press, 1996. 28, 269, 271–75.

104 Edgar Jones and Simon Wessely, S*hellshock to PTSD" military psychiatry from 1900 to the Gulf War.* Hove; New York, N.Y.: Psychology Press, 2005, 137, 200.

105 Larsson, *Shattered Anzacs*, 25, 273.

106 Thomson, *Anzac Legends*, 10, 327–28.

107 Lloyd and Wright, *The Last Shilling,* 415.

108 'Mainly About People', *The Daily News,* 6 September 1916: 3. This is the correst spelling of 'Ker', DOTAG.

109 Claude Algernon Clifton, NAA 30805443 C 10831.

110 Summary of war history, 17 June 1917, 6 January 1918, NAA 30805443 C10831.

111 Medical report, 4 December 1918, NAA 30805443 C10831; Appeal notes, 13 June 1930.; 3rd Australian FAB, NAA 10155951 M10831.

112 Summary of appeal, 26 March 1919, NAA 30805443 C10831.

113 Medical summary on discharge, 12 August 1920, NAA 30805443 C10831.

114 Garton *The Cost of War* 87; Appeal notes, 13 June 1930, NAA 10155951 M10831.

115 Summary of appeal, 13 June 1930, NAA 10155951 M10831.

116 Summary of appeal, 10 July 1929, NAA, 30805443 C10831; CC to Deputy Commissioner of Repatriation (henceforth DC) 7 August 1920, NAA 10155951 M10831.

117 Note, 16 August 1920, NAA 10155951 M10831; note DC, 23 September 1920, NAA 30805443 C10831.

118 CC to DC, 1 October 1920, NAA 30805443 C10831.

119 Medical summary on discharge, 15 October 1920, NAA 30805443 C10831.

120 DC note, 4 October 1922, NAA 30805443 C10831.

121 G. Warburton, secretary of Brunswick RSL, to DC, 10 July 1929, NAA 30805443 C10831.

122 A.G. Heppinstone, to DC, n.d. 1929, NAA 30805443 C10831.

123 The location was 'Hellfire corner', First World War.com. 'Hellfire Corner'.

124 G. Warburton, 10 July 1929, NAA 30805443 C10831.

125 Doctor's report, 23 July 1929, NAA 30805443 C10831; 'News in Brief', *The Bunbury Herald and Blackwood Express,* 21 October 1924: 2; Medical report, 28 June 1929, NAA 30805443 C10831.

126 Medical report, 28 June 1929, NAA 30805443 C10831.

127 CC to DC, 25 November 1929, NAA 30805443 C10831.

128 Note from DC, 3 March 1930, NAA 30805443 C10831.

129 Summary of appeal, 13 June 1930 NAA 10155951 M10831.

130 Summary of appeal, 13 June 1930, NAA 10155951 M10831.

131 DOTAG; 'Town and Country News', *The Daily News,* 3 December 1932: 6.

132 Prof. S. Fletcher, pers. comm. 23 November, 2017.

133 'Quarter Sessions', *The Perth Gazette and Independent Journal of Politics and News,* 7 October 1853: 2; 'Vasse', *The Inquirer and Commercial News.* 30 December 1857: 2; 'Personal', *Southern Times,* 3 March 1910: 5. This article mentions that three sons has predeceased Claude's grandmother.

134 DOTAG.

135 'Personal', *Southern Times,* 3 March 1910: 5.

136 DOTAG, Robert Ker, Charles Buchanan Ker and Claudius Buchanan Ker.

137 My thanks to Prof. Sue Fletcher, Principal Research Fellow, Centre for Comparative Genomics Western Australia (CCG), Murdoch University, for her interest and contribution to my understanding of this sad case.

138 Garton, *The Cost of War*, 110.

139 First World War.com. 'Hellfire Corner'.

140 DC note, 3 March 1930, NAA 30805443 C10831.

141 A.G. Butler, *Official History of the Australian Army Medical Services, 1914–1918, Section IV – The Aftermath of War*, 1930–1943, 966–69, 839–41.

142 'Limbless Soldiers', *Kalgoorlie Miner,* 15 Novembker 1923: 5.

143 Caddy, *The Rifleman*, no page numbers; DC notes, 22 September 1922, 28 October 1940, 1 June 1951, 18 October 1961, from rehabilitation department to DC, 30 October 1961, DC to son in law, 2 June 1966, NAA 11545183 M23889.

144 'Survey of amputees', 16 January 1950, NAA 11545183 M23889.

145 'Limbless Soldiers Requests', *The Daily News*: 8; 'Their New Home', *The Daily News,* 22 November 1923: 11; 'News and Notes', *The West Australian,* 4 September 1920: 6; 'Legless Boy to Have Limbs', *Sunday Times,* 16 October 1938: 9.

146 'Notes and Comments', *Sunday Times* 27 November 1927: 6; 'Benefit Night and River Trip', *The Daily News,)* 22 January 1920: 5; 'News and Notes', *The Bunbury Herald and Blackwood Express,* 4 April 1928: 2.

147 Letters to DC from daughter and son in law, 28 February 1962, 17 January 1966, 7 January 1966, 24 January 1966, NAA 11545183 M23889.

148 Butler, *Australian Army Medical Services,* 839–41.

149 'Obituary', *The Bunbury Herald and Blackwood Express,* 12 August 1924: 3.

150 'Personal', *Southern Times,* 7 August 1915: 5; *Anzac Heroes.*

151 'Australian In Action', *Kalgoorlie Miner,* 3 October 1916: 2.

152 Anzac Heroes.

153 DOTAG; 'Government Land', *The West Australian,* 16 February 1929: 8.

154 'Hundreds of Mourners at Sister Jones' Funeral', *Mirror,* 13 June 1936: 16. Ruth Victoria Jones aged 47 years. MCB.

155 'Family Notices', *The West Australian,* 18 July 1940: 3.

156 NAA 31847238, 5131792 M2478.

157 DC comment, 28 October 1918, NAA 5131792 M2478; Lloyd and Wright, *The Last Shilling,* 45.

158 DC to TR, 11 May 1921, TR to DC, 13 May 1921, NAA 5131792 M2478.

159 TR to DC, 13 September 1924, NAA 5131792 M2478.

160 DC note, 7 March 1925, 5131792 M2478.

161 'The South-West', *The West Australian,* 5 August 1918: 8.

162 NAA 10065192 C2281, NAA 10154948 M2281; "Our Big Day", *The Bunbury Herald and Blackwood Express,* 7 January 1920: 3.

163 Medical summary on discharge, 14 June 1918; note, DC, 10 April 1920, NAA 10154948 M2281.

164 DOTAG.

165 Note, 20 December 1919, NAA 10154948 M2281.

166 Medical notes, 10 March 1920, NAA 10154948 M2281.

167 Summary of appeal, 17, NAA 10154948 M2281.

168 For example, R. Clarke to DC, 4 February 1960, NAA 10154948 M2281.

169 Summary of appeal, NAA 10065192 K 60, C2281.

170 Appeal notes, 17, NAA 10154948 M2281.

171 M. Clarke to DC, 1 March 1960, 10154948 M2281.

172 Butler, *Australian Army Medical Services,* 811, 804–07, 978: 1931 Study, Table 72, Causes (other than battle casualties) for which, in 1931, Australian pensions had been received in respect of the war of 1914–1918.

173 Scates, 'Finding the Missing from Fromelles', 220.

174 Summary of war service, NAA 32498837 R19287.

175 War summary, 29 August 1915, 18 January 1917, NAA 32501692 M19287.

176 War summary, 14 June 1918, NAA 32501692 M19287.

177 Medical summary on discharge, 14 June 1918, NAA 32501692 M19287.

178 DC notes, 19 July 1919, 31 December 1920, 28 October 1919, NAA 32501692 M19287.

179 'Family Notices', *The West Australian,* 10 May 1930: 1; 'Bunbury', *Western Mail,* 17 July 1930: 29.

180 'Tambellup', *Tambellup Times,* 2 May 1923: 2.

181 'The Annual Training Camp' *Tambellup Times,* 5 April 1924: 4.

182 'Perth Wool Sales', *Great Southern Herald,* 29 October 1930: 3; 'Obituary', *Gnowangerup Star and Tambellup-Ongerup Gazette,* 3 April 1943: 2.

183 Summary of appeal, 8, 14 June 1927, NAA 32501692 M19287.

184 Witness statement, - May 1927, NAA 32501692 M19287.

185 Lloyd and Wright, *The Last Shilling*, 136.

186 Testimonials, E.V. Parnell, O. Saggers,26 June 1927, NAA 32498837 R19287.

187 Summary of appeal, 6–7, 20 May 1927, 29 July 1927, NAA 32498837 R19287.

188 Various dates, summary of appeal, 7–10, NAA 32498837 R19287.

189 Doctor notes, 30 June 1938, 19 October 1938, DC to doctor, 31 October 1938, NAA 32501692 M19287.

190 Doctor notes, 3 March 1946, NAA 32501692 M19287.

191 Summary of appeal, 10, NAA 32501692 M19287.

192 Doctor note, 24 January 1951, NAA 32498837 R19287.

193 Doctor note, 1 March 1949, NAA 32501692 M19287. Dr Beveridge had treated Cyril in 1929, NAA 20423997.

194 Summary of appeal, 11, 1 March 1950, NAA 32498837 R19287; doctor note, 21 April, 1950, NAA 32501692 M19287.

195 Note, 20 April 1951, NAA 32501692 M19287; 23 April 1951, NAA 32498837 R19287.

196 Hospital note, 30 May 1951, DC note, 29 May 1951, DC note, 4 July 1951, NAA 32501692 M19287.

197 LP appeal statement, 18 September 1951,Appeal notes, 22, 23 August 1951, NAA 32501692 M19287; Didier Fassin and Richard Rechtman, *The Empire of trauma: An enquiry into the condition of victimhood*, translated by Rachel Gomme, Princeton, New Jersey: Princeton University Press, 2009. 44, 46.

198 Summary of particulars of application, 29 November 1951, 32501692 M19287; hospital notes, 10 March 1952, 32501693 H19287.

199 DC note, 4 November 1957, 32501692 M19287; Jones and Wessely, *Shell shock to PTSD',* 202.

200 Medical report, 12 November 1957, 32501692 M19287.

201 DC note, 4 December 1957, 32501692 M19287; DC note, 4 February 1958, 32501693 H19287.

202 Spondylitis is a combination of arthritis and other inflammatory conditions which affect both joints and soft tissue, including parts of the digestive tract. This could explain Les's combination of arthritis and gastro-intestinal problems; Hospital notes, 8 June 1959, 28 July 1959, 14 October 1959, 14 October 1959, NAA 32501692 M19287.

203 LP, application for sustenance, 25 June 1958, NAA 32501693 H19287.

204 E.G. Paisley to DC, 14 October 1959, Medical report, 27 October 1959, NAA

32501692 M19287.

205 NAA 32501693 H19287.

206 Medical notes, 2 October 1969, 22 April 1960, 11 May 1961, 32501692 M19287; 28 April 1962, 17 April 1967 – 12 May 1967, NAA 32501693 H19287; 12 April 1969, NAA 32501692 M19287; 7 March 1967, 32501693 H19287.

207 Medical notes, 7 March 1967, 16 December 1963, 11 May 1964, NAA 32501693 H19287.

208 Doctor note, 22 February 1967, NAA 32501692 M19287.

209 18 October 1971 NAA 32501692 M19287; 32501693 H19287; 12 October 1971, 10 January 1972, NAA 32501692 M19287.

210 Doctor note, 12 October 1971, NAA 32501693 H19287.

211 DC note, 18 January 1972, NAA 32501692 M19287.

212 Doctor note, - November 1971, NAA 32501693 H19287.

213 Ruth Rae, 'An historical account of shell shock during the First World War and reforms in mental health in Australia 1914–1939', *International Journal of Mental Health Nursing*, 16 (2007): 266–273.

214 Service record, NAA 31838463 M4981.

215 Service record, NAA B2455 8000688.

216 Evidence of appeal, 2, 12 May 1918, NAA 31838463 M4981.

217 DC note, 22 March 1919, NAA 838463 M4981.

218 DC to SP, 11 November 1920, NAA 31838463 M4981.

219 Doctor note, 3 December 1921, NAA 31838463 M4981.

220 Evidence of appeal, 5, Les Paisley to DC, 8 September 1924, NAA 31838463 M4981.

221 SP to DC, 6 January 1926, NAA 31838463 M4981.

222 Doctor note, 6 January 1926, NAA 31838463 M4981.

223 Doctor note, 3 February 1926, NAA 31838463 M4981.

224 Doctor note, 23 March 1926, NAA 31838463 M4981.

225 SP to DC, 24 January 1927, NAA 20423414 C4981.

226 Doctor notes, 5 May 1927, 21 March 1928, NAA 20423414 C4981.

227 Doctor note, 14 April 1928, NAA 31838463 M4981.

228 RGH ward report, 24 January 1988, NAA 10113873 HB4981.

229 SP to DC, 26 June 1929, NAA 20423414 C4981.

230 SP to DC, 26 June 1929, NAA 20423414; NAA 31838463 M4981.

231 Doctor note, 13 June 1929, NAA 31838463 M4981.

232 Doctor notes, 13 June 1929, NAA 20423414 C4981; 26 November 1929, NAA 31838463 M4981.

233 Doctor notes, 26 November 1929, NAA 20423414 C4981; 13 June 1929, 25 January 1930, NAA 31838463 M4981.

234 Butler, *Australian Army Medical Service*, 68, 835.

235 Butler *Australian Army Medical Service,* Table: Analysis of cases of insanity in returned soldiers in Victoria (accepted as due to or aggravated by war service) treated in mental hospitals. (1935), 836; 837, 835, 833.

236 'Insanity', *The West Australian,* 6 March 1930: 18; 'Medicine and the Public', *The West Australian,* 29 August 1929: 16; 'Public Opinion', *The Daily News,* 31 August 1927: 9.

237 Fassin and Rechtman, *Empire of Trauma,* 59, 60.
238 Doctor notes, 25 January 1930, NAA 20423414 C4981; 11 February 1930, NAA 31838463 M4981.
239 Doctor notes, 11 February 1930, NAA 31838463 M4981; 9 March 1931, NAA 20423414 C4981.
240 DC note, 17 March 1930, NAA 20423414 C4981; Lloyd and Wright, *The Last Shilling*, 187.
241 DC note, 25 March 1931, NAA 20423414C4981.
242 DC note, 9 April 1931, SP to DC, 10 April 1931, NAA 20423414 C4981.
243 Evidence of appeal, 12, 9 July 1931, NAA 31838463 M4981.
244 SP to DC, 15 November 1931, NAA 31838463 M4981; doctor note, 10 November 1931, NAA 31838463 M4981.
245 DC note, 15 June 1938, NAA 20423414 C4981.
246 Death notice inserted by Hilda Paisley, 31 March 1958, copy in file, NAA 30143204 MB4981.
247 HP to DC, 30 April 1970, NAA 10109085 MB4981.
248 DC note, 22 April 1983, NAA 10113873 HB4981.
249 HP to DC, 30 April 1970, NAA 30143204 MB4981; RGH aged care assessment, 22 September 1987, NAA 10113873 HB4981.
250 RGH ward report, 24 January 1988, NAA 10113873 HB4981.
251 Death notice, 6 July 1994 20423414 C4981.
252 Lake, *The Limits of Hope,* 238.
253 Garton, *The Cost of War*, 86–88.
254 Lake, *Limits of Hope*, chapter 8, 195–228.

5: Repatriation: Medical Outcomes for Urban Veterans

1 Straw, *After the War.*
2 Butler, *Australian Army Medical Services*, 839–844.
3 Butler, *Australian Army Medical Services*, 839; Mervyn Ephraim (Dick) Clarke, repatriation files NAA 32924219 C26047; 32924219 C11173; 32502412 H26047; 32502412 M26047.
4 'Chapter VII', *Western Mail,* 10 February 1938: 9.
5 'Personal', *South Western Times,* 29 October 1918: 3; Medical report, 26 October 1920, NAA 32924219 C26047.
6 Medical report, 29 April 1940, NAA 32924219 C11173; 'Personal Pars', *The Bunbury Herald and Blackwood Express* 20 August 1920: 5.
7 'Personal', *South Western Times,* 5 August 1920: 3; 'Personal'. *South Western Times,* 29 October 1918: 3.
8 'Personal', *South Western Times,* 29 October 1918: 3.
9 'Bunbury War Hero', *The Bunbury Herald and Blackwood Express,* 13 August 1920: 1; 'Personal', *South Western Times,* 10 August 1920: 3.
10 MEC to DC, 12 May 1963, NAA 32924219 C11173.
11 MEC to DC, 15 July 1963, NAA 32924219 C11173.
12 MEC to DC, 26 February, 1958, NAA 32924219 C11173.
13 MEC to DC, October 1919, NAA 32502412 M26047.
14 MEC to DC, 23 November 1972, NAA 32502412 M26047.
15 Perth Hospital report, 13 February 1940, NAA 32924219 C11173.

16 Medical report, 4 July 1949, NAA 32502412 M26047.
17 Larsson, *Shattered Anzacs*, 23.
18 Doctor note, 20 March 1985, NAA 32502412 M26047.
19 MEC to DC, 6 October 1976, NAA 32502412 M26047.
20 DC memo, 27 August 1976, NAA 32502412 M26047.
21 Irene Charlotte Benson, b. Sheffield, 1901–1971, married 1926, DOTAG.
22 DC to MEC, 16 June 1933, NAA 32924219 C11173.
23 MEC to DC, 10 September 1941, DC to MEC, 2 November 1950, 3 April 1951, NAA 32924219 C1117310.
24 DC to MEC, 22 March 1963, NAA 32924219 C11173.
25 Medical report, 24 April 1972, 3 October 1972, NAA 32502412 M26047.
26 MEC to DC, 30 October 1975, NAA 32502412 M26047.
27 DC to MEC, 3 September 1959, NAA 32502412 M26047.
28 Statutory declaration, 24 October 1932, NAA 32924219 C11173; Larsson, *Shattered Anzacs*, 106.
29 MEC to DC, 2 July 1954, NAA 32502412 C11173.
30 DC to MEC, 14 February 1964, NAA 32502412 M26047.
31 Mr Inglis to DC, 2 July 1963, 31 January 1964, NAA 32502412 M26047.
32 DC to MEC, 20 September 1963, NAA 32502412 H26047.
33 MEC to DC, 16 January 1973, 32502412 NAA 32502412 M26047.
34 Doctor to DC, 26 January 1973, DC to doctor, 9 February 1973, NAA 32502412 M26047.
35 'Bunbury War Hero', *The Bunbury Herald and Blackwood Express,* 6 August 1920: 5; DC Perth to DC Melbourne, 15 December 1948, NAA 32502412 M26047.
36 MEC to DC, 11 April 1949, NAA 32502412 M26047.
37 MEC to DC, 12 July 1950, DC to MEC, n.d., NAA 32502412 M26047.
38 Red Cross to DC, 26 July 1956, DC to Red Cross, 24 July 1958, Braille Society to DC, 18 September 1967, NAA 32502412 M26047.
39 DC note, 3 July 1970, NAA 32502412 M26047.
40 MEC to DC, 22 March 1963, NAA 32502412, H26047.
41 MEC to DC, 8 September, 1973, 7 November 1972, NAA 32502412 M26047.
42 MEC to DC, 7 November 1972, NAA 32502412 M26047.
43 MEC to DC, 6 October 1976, NAA 32502412 M26047.
44 'Personal', *South Western Times,* 5 August 1920: 3; 'Personal'. *South Western Times,* 29 October 1918: 3.
45 DC note, 24 July 1958, NAA 32502412 M26047.
46 Butler, *Australian Army Medical Services,* 839–43.
47 Margaret J. Warburton, 'Rebuilding Lives: heroism and gender in the Great War community of an Australian soldier', in *Heroism and Wellbeing in the 21st Century: Applied and Emerging Perspectives.* Editors: Olivia Efthimiou, Scott T. Allison, Zeno E. Franco. New York: Routledge, 2018.
48 Larsson, *Shattered Anzacs*; Oppenheimer, 'Caring for severely disabled patients', in Crotty Martin and Marina Larsson. Eds. *Anzac Legacies,* 25ff.
49 Two almost identical photographs of the Snell Christmas 1912 picnic party exist, in which Charlie and Reg exchanged places as they each took one of the pictures. Snell Collection.
50 Medical summary on discharge, NAA 10065573 H769, 10112538 M769.
51 Medical summary on discharge, 23 January 1919, 28 December 1917, 10112538,

M769.

52 Leslie Montague Ibbotson, NAA 31873175 C28591.

53 15 January 1919, NAA 10112538, M769; Colonel Leslie Edward Tilney, D.S.O., V.D., deputy-chairman of the Repatriation Commission, 1915 to 1923. 16th Battalion 1914 to 1916, Commander of Blackboy Hill training camp,1917–1918; 'Funeral of Col. Tilney Tomorrow', *The Daily News,* 22 January 1937: 5; 'Blackboy Hill Command', *The Swan Express,* 25 May 1917: 5.

54 RI to DC, 15 January 1919, doctor note, 23 January 1919, NAA 10112538, M769.

55 RI to DC, 22 January 1919, Summary of appeal, 6 February 1919, NAA 10112538, M769. Leslie Montague Ibbotson, mentioned in letter from Alf Snell to CS, October 1915.

56 Meekatharra repatriation committee to Department of Lands, 15 November 1919; application for assistance, 26 June 1920; DC note, 21 July 1920, 10112538, M769.

57 'Personal', *The Mullewa Mail,* 20 December 1923: 2.

58 'Family Notices', *Daily Telegraph and North Murchison and Pilbarra Gazette,* 21 December 1923: 2; 'Advertising', *Sunday Times,* 26 July 1925: 16.

59 'Harvey', *The Bunbury Herald and Blackwood Express,* 20 June 1927: 2; 'Family Notices', *The West Australian,* 6 August 1927: 1; 'Harvey Show Supplement', *South Western Times,* 20 October 1928: 3; 'Harvey Agricultural Society', *South Western Times,* 7 February 1929: 5.

60 RI to DC, 5 March 1928, NAA 10112538 M769.

61 Medical report, 17 March 1970, NAA 10112538 M769.

62 'Repatriation', *The West Australian,* 1 December 1925: 6.

63 Robert L. Atenstaedt, 'Trench Foot: The Medical Response in the First World War 1914–18', *National Public Health Service for Wales and Institute of Medical and Social Care Research,* University of Wales, Bangor, UK. December 2006, Volume 17, Issue 4, pp. 282–89.

64 For example: *Text Book of Military Medicine, Medical Aspects of Harsh Environments,* 1, Borden Institute, Washington, DC: 2002: 467–490; Thomson, *ANZAC Memories*, 297, 298, 308.

65 Butler, *Australian Army Medical Services*, 810–814; Table: Classification of Cases (In- and Out- Patients) treated during the year, 823.

66 'Harvey Show', *The West Australian,* 3 November 1934: 14; RI to DC, 1 May 1934, NAA 10112538 M769.

67 RI to DC, 23 May 193, NAA 10112538 M769.

68 DC notes, 18 May 1934, 23 May 1934, NAA 10112538 M769.

69 RI to DC, 27 April 1936, NAA 10112538 M769.

70 DC to RI, 1 December 1936, 4 December 1936, NAA 10112538 M769.

71 'Country News', *The West Australian,* 5 November 1937: 5.

72 'Advertising', *The West Australian,* 6 May 1938: 30.

73 RI to DC, 9 September 1938, NAA 10112538 M769.

74 Notice of incident, 6 July 1939, NAA 10112538 M769.

75 RI to DC, 24 September 1941, NAA 10112538 M769.

76 RI to DC, 30 November 1942, NAA 10112538 M769.

77 DC note, 26 February 1943, DC to RI, 30 July 1943, 9 August 1943, NAA 10112538 M769.

78 RI to DC, 23 December 1947, NAA 10065573 H769; DC note, 28 April 1948, NAA 10112538 M769.

79 'Engagements', *The West Australian* 12 August 1948: 15.

80 RI to DC, 24 September 1952, NAA 10112538 M769.

81 DC notes, 5 December 1952, 12 January 1953, 17 February 1953, RI to DC, 12 March 1953, hospital notes, 13 October 1953, DC note, 24 November 1953, NAA 10112538 M769.

82 RI to DC, 13 April 1956, outpatient clinic notes, 24 April 1956, NAA 10112538 M769.

83 RI to DC, 7 May 1957, NAA 10112538 M769.

84 RI to DC, 13 December 1960, NAA 10112538 M769; Butler, *Australian Army Medical Services,* 819.

85 Hospital notes, 28 September 1962, NAA 10065573 H769.

86 Matron to DC, 10 August 1962, 15 August 1962, NAA 10112538 M769.

87 Medical note, 24 March 1964, RI to DC, 18 May 1966, 25 April 1967, NAA 10112538 M769; doctor note, 31 July 1967, NAA 10065573 H769.

88 DC note, 13 December 1970, medical report, 17 March 1970, NAA 10065573 H769; DC to RI son, 1 April 1970, NAA 10112538 M769.

89 RI to DC, 31 August 1971, doctor note, 6 June 1979. NAA 10065573 H769.

90 Medical notes, 5 June 1979, NAA 10112538 M769; 1 June 1979, NAA 10065573 H769; 28 May 1979, NAA 10112538, M769; 29 June 1978, 8 July 1978, NAA 10065573 H769.

91 Medical notes, 13 December 1970, NAA 10112538 M769; 3 May 1979, 31 May 1979, NAA 10065573 H769; 10 July 1978, NAA 10112538 M769.

92 Nursing home report, 23 August 1979, NAA 10112538 M769.

93 Deceased, 2 July 1980, NAA 10112538 M769.

94 'Country News', *The West Australian,* 15 May 1933: 4.

95 'Wills of the Week', *Sunday Times,* 7 August 1927: 3.

96 Joan Beaumont, *Beyond Surrender: Australian Prisoners of War in the 20th Century.* MUP Academic, 2015; Butler, *Australian Army Medical Services*, 777.

97 *Anzac Heroes*; Medical summary on discharge, NAA 827785 H10243, 10082837 M10243; Aaron Pegram, 'Bold bids for freedom: Escape and Australian prisoners *ANZAC Heroes* 1916–1918', in Beaumont, *et al.*, *Beyond Surrender*, 10. Pierce suggests that around 50 Wellington men were taken prisoner, although this number seems high. *ANZAC Heroes.*

98 POW statement taken 7 October 1918, NAA 10082837 M10243.

99 Pegram, 'Bold bids for freedom', 9.

100 Melanie Oppenheimer, ''Our Number One Priority': The Australian Red Cross and prisoners of war in the world wars', in Beaumont, *et al.*, *Beyond Surrender,* 79.

101 POW statement, NAA 10082837 M10243.

102 For example, letter from Beigel to the DC: 'applicant is of good character, honest and reliable', 15 April 1919, 16 September 1919, NAA 10082837 M10243.

103 Report on trainee, 13 August 1919, 29 February 1920; minute paper, 25 December 1920, NAA 10082837 M10243.

104 WHS to DC, 3 February 1921, 11 February 1921, NAA 10082837 M10243.

105 Hospital report, April-May 1934, NAA 10082837 M10243.

106 Doctor notes, 6 October 1941, 23 February 1942, 11 March 1942, NAA 827785 H10243.

107 X ray report, 8 October 1941, NAA 10082837 M10243.

108 Summary of appeal, 2, 23 February 1942, 11 March 1942, NAA 827785 H10243; Jones and Wessely, *Shellshock to PTSD,* 212.

109 Doctor notes, 23 February 1942, summary of appeal, 19 February 1942, NAA 827785 H10243.

110 Case sheet summary, 3, 19 February 1942, NAA 10082837.

111 Medical notes, 27 March 1942, 14 April 1942, 29 June 1942, NAA 10082837 M10243.

112 Case sheet summary, 15 June 1942, NAA 827785 H10243, 10082837 M10243.

113 DC note, 20 August 1942, NAA 10082837 M10243.

114 Medical report, 31 July 1943, NAA 10082837 M10243.

115 Decision of appeal, 24 November 1943 NAA 10082837 M10243.

116 7 November 1957 NAA 827785 H10243, 10082837; 18 October 1966 NAA 10082837 M10243.

117 6 February 1967, 13 February 1967. 25 February 1967, 31 January 1968, NAA 10082837 M10243.

118 3 February 1968, NAA 10082837 M10243.

119 Butler, *Australian army medical services*, 811, 819, 828, 829.

120 Butler, *Australian army medical services*, 804, 809, 811, 812, 813.

121 Straw, *After the War*, chapter 4.

122 Medical summary on discharge, 15 September 1919, NAA 31844379 R17847.

123 DC advice of acceptance for course, 17 October 1919, NAA 31844379 R17847.

124 Application for pension, 14 February 1923, pension appeal, 19 April 1923, NAA 20423997 C17847.

125 'Personal', *South Western Times,* 28 June 1924: 5.

126 Doctor note, 19 November 1925, 20423997 C17847.

127 Butler, *Australian Army Medical Service*, 828, 829, 830.

128 Mary McGregor Craigie, pers. comm., 1 January 2018.

129 DC note, 21 February 1927, NAA 20423997 C17847.

130 Medical notes, 29 March 1928, NAA 20423997 C17847.

131 Doctor note, 14 December 1928, NAA 20423997 C17847.

132 CP to DC, 12 February 1929, NAA 20423997 C17847.

133 Doctor note, 15 February 1929, NAA 20423997 C17847.

134 Butler, *Australian Army Medical Services*, 830, 831.

135 Butler, *Australian Army Medical Services,* 830. As of 1943, Repatriation Commission did not know how many had died while in receipt of a Schedule 2 pension.

136 Doctor notes, 8 March 1929, 13 March 1929, NAA 20423997 C17847.

137 Doctor notes, 8 March 1929, NAA 20423997 C17847.

138 DC note, 17 April 1929, NAA 32498039, M17847.

139 Clinic notes, 2 August 1930, 20 September1931, NAA 20423997 C17847.

140 CP to DC, 2 January 1934, NAA 20423997 C17847.

141 DC to CP, 5 January 1934, NAA 20423997 C17847.

142 Clinical notes, 5 January 1934, 4 April 1934, 22 and 23 March 1934, NAA 20423997 C17847.

143 Doctor notes, 20 November 1934, 29 December 1934, 11 January 1935, 8 December 1934, NAA 32498039 M17847.

144 Summary of appeal, 8, 4 February 1937, NAA 20423997 C17847.

145 Doctor notes, 15 September 1936, NAA 20423997 C17847.

146 'Perth Last Night and the Social Notebook', *Sunday Times,* 26 June 1938: 12.

147 'Trinity College Examinations', *The Northam Advertiser,* 23 July 1913: 2; 'John Morrell', *The West Australian,* 23 September 1933: 4.

148 Doctor notes, 8 February 1938, CP to DC, 20 June 1938, NAA 20423997 C17847.

149 CP to DC, 2 August 1937, NAA 20423997 C17847.

150 Doctor note, 19 April 1939, hospital notes, 2 September 1939, NAA 32498040.

151 Hospital notes, 11 March 1940, NAA 20423997 C17847; pension review, 11 June 1940, hospital notes, 22 July 1940, NAA 32498040.

152 DC notes, 15 January 1946, NAA 20423997 C17847; Larsson, *Shattered Anzacs,* 91.

153 DC note, 8 February 1943, NAA 20423997 C17847.

154 Case sheet, 30 August 1946, Xray report, 6 August 1946, NAA 32498040.

155 DC notes, 15 January 1947, 10 May 1948, 4 February 1949, NAA 32498040.

156 DC notes, 21 February 1949, 17 February 1950, NAA 32498039. M17847.

157 Doctor note, 5 April 1950, DC to CP, 30 May 1950, 20423997 C17847; Butler, *Australian Army Medical Services,* 829.

158 Hospital notes, 26 April 1950, 9 June 1950, doctor note, 7 June 1950, NAA 32498040.

159 Hospital note, 9 June 1950, NAA 20423997 C17847.

160 Clinic notes, 16 August 1950, 22 September 1950, 8 November 1950, NAA 32498040.

161 DC note, 22 May 1951, sustenance claim, 3 May 1951, NAA 32498040.

162 DC note, 10 July 1951, Repat note, 12 October 1951, NAA 32498039 M17847; Butler, *Australian Army Medical Services,* 830.

163 Edith Paisley to RGH, 11 January 1952, NAA 32498039 M17847.

164 Doctor note, 15 August 1955, DC note, 7 February 1956, outpatient notes, 12 October 1961, 13 June 62, NAA 32502870 MB17847.

165 Medical notes, 23 March 1979, 12 April 1979, NAA 32502871 HB17847 Vol 1; doctor note, 4 September 1981, NAA 32502872 MB17847.

166 Crotty and Larsson, *Anzac Legacies,* 7–9; Thomson, *ANZAC Memories,* 15.

167 Butler, *Australian Army Medical Services,* 811, 804–07, 978: 1931 Study, Table 72, Causes (other than battle casualties) for which, in 1931, Australian pensions had been received in respect of the war of 1914–1918; Scates 'Finding the Missing from Fromelles', Chapter 10, in Crotty and Larsson, *ANZAC Legacies,* 220.

168 Medical report, 5 February 1916, 23 November 1916, NAA MT 1486/1, 9554696, B2455 4663108. A varicocele is an abnormal enlargement of the veins in the scrotum which can be exacerbated by physical exertion. Mayo Clinic, Patient Care & Health Information, Diseases & Conditions, Varicocele.

169 Service record, NAA B2455 4663108.

170 Maj. Gen. E.G. Sinclair-Maclagan, 25 September 1916, NAA MT 1486/1, 9554696, B2455, 4663108.

171 DC note, 12 May 1931, NAA 32485400 M14926.

172 Medical summary on discharge, 18 October 1919, NAA 32485400 M14926.

173 DC notes, 21 June 1919, rector of South Perth to DC, 26 March 1920, NAA 10081612 R14926.
174 DC notes, 8 April 1929, 13 April 1920, NAA 10081612 R14926.
175 DC note, 17 April 1920, NAA 10081612 R14926.
176 DC to Base Records, 30 January 1921, medical notes, 29 November 1921, 27 June 1922, NAA 32485400 M14926.
177 Medical note, 2 March 1925, NAA 32485400 M14926.
178 Record of evidence, 11 May 1931, NAA 32485400 M14926.
179 Hospital case sheets, 2 February 1931, NAA 32485400 M14926; medical report, 3 March 1931, NAA 32485401 H14926.
180 Butler, *Australian Medical Service*, 811.
181 Statement of evidence, 27 January 1931, hospital case sheet, 2 February 1931, NAA 32485400 M14926. The Wasserman test is a test for venereal disease. It was routinely conducted, including for Vera Paisley.
182 Testimonial, 12 May 1931, NAA 32485400 M14926.
183 Mrs K. Darlington, n.d. NAA 32485400 M14926.
184 P. Goatcher, testimonial, 13 May 1931, E.C. O'Connor, 14 May 1931, NAA 32485400 M14926.
185 F. Gray to DC, 12 May 1931, doctor note, 14 May 1931, NAA 32485400 M14926.
186 Decision of appeal, 24 June 1931, NAA 32485401 H14926.
187 Decision of appeal, April 1933, NAA 32485401 H14926.
188 Doctor note, 23 October1939, 32485401 H 14926
189 DC note, 16 February 1944, NAA 32485400 M14926.
190 AG application for grant, 13 April 1944, NAA 32485400 M14926.
191 DC notes, 21 April 1944, 2 May 1944 32485401 H14926, 7 September 1944, NAA 32485400 M14926.
192 Outpatient notes, 1 November 1944, NAA 32485400 M14926.
193 'Family Notices', *The West Australian,* 5 August 1948: 1; DC notes, 26 August 1948, 13 September 1948, NAA 10081612 R14926.
194 Post-mortem report, NAA 32485401 H14926.
195 Larsson, *Shattered Anzacs*, 23.
196 Service report, NAA 30143326 WC8061, 32485931 M8061.
197 Medical summary on discharge, 3 March 1919, NAA 32485931 M8061.
198 Butler, *Australian Army Medical services*, 140, 141.
199 Summary of appeal, 9, 26 March 1931, NAA 32485931 M8061.
200 Summary of appeal, 10, 26 January 1934, 12, 17 October 1934, NAA 32485931 M8061.
201 Summary of appeal, 12,19 October 1934, NAA 32485931 M8061.
202 Summary of appeal, 19, 13 March 1946, NAA 32485931 M8061.
203 Scates and Oppenheimer, *The Last Battle*, 86.
204 Dorothy Bird to DC, 25 March 1946, NAA 32485931 M8061.
205 Raymond Bird, NAA (B883) WX18480 6477321, served in Borneo.
206 Dorothy Bird to DC, August 1947, NAA 32485931 M8061; Scates and Oppenheimer, *The Last Battle*, Chapter 3, The Moral Economy, 86.
207 Summary of appeal, 19, Dr Gordon to D. Bird, 28 August 1947, NAA 32485931 M8061.

208 DC note, NAA 32502769 MB8061.

209 R.N. Proctor, 'The History of the Discovery of the Cigarette–Lung Cancer Link: Evidentiary Traditions, Corporate Denial, Global Toll,' *Tobacco Control* 21 (2012): 87–91.

210 Proctor, 'The Cigarette–Lung Cancer Link'.

211 'Roman Catholic Notes', *South Western Times,* 4 February 1919: 3; 'Bunbury Swimming Club', *Southern Times,* 20 January 1910: 3; 'Football', *The Blackwood Times,* 8 July 1910: 4.

212 Summary of war service, NAA 32489914 R1805.

213 Butler, *Australian Army Medical Services,* 786; Garton, *The Cost of War,* 87; Lloyd and Wright, *The Last Shilling,* 415.

214 JB to DC, 9 November 1918, NAA 31838609 M5410.

215 'R.S.L. Social', *South Western Times,* 6 May 1920: 3; 'Do You Know' *South Western Times,* 8 January 1920: 3; NAA 31838609 M5410; 'Local and General', *The Bunbury Herald and Blackwood Express* 24 September 1919: 2.

216 Summary of appeal, 6, NAA 31838609 M5410.

217 F.W. Roberts, (Ethel Forrest's husband) to DC, 27 April 1928, NAA 31838609 M5410; Larsson, *Shattered Anzacs,* 89.

218 Doctor note, 27 April 1928, NAA 31838609 M5410.

219 Summary of appeal, 1953, NAA 31838609 M5410.

220 Summary of appeal, 69, Queenie Blythe to DC, 4 October 1965, NAA 31838609 M5410. I could not find any record of WW2 service in NAA files except for the two references in Blythe's Repat file.

221 Summary of appeal, 12 March 1953, NAA 31838609 M5410; DC note, 27 October 1953, NAA 31846858 M5410.

222 Blythe and Freeth may have known each other from pre-war years spent in the Great Southern. In most cases where veterans have sought assistance from high places, I have been able to trace a likely connection. John Farquharson, 'Freeth, Sir Gordon (1914–2001)', Obituaries Australia, National Centre of Biography, Australian National University; 6 July 1954, NAA 31838609 M5410.

223 Doctor note, 3 December 1959, NAA 31838609 M5410.

224 Summary of appeal, 39, doctor note, A. H. M. Siddons and A. M. Macarthur. 'Carcinomata Developing at the Site of Foreign Bodies in the Lung'. *British Journal of Surgery*, Volume: 39, Issue: 158, 1952. 542–45, ISSN: 00071323; NAA 31838609 M5410.

225 Doctor notes, 25 March 1960, 31 March 1960, NAA 31838609, M5410.

226 Medical report, 18 August 1961, NAA 31846858 M5410.

227 DC notes, 12 September 1961, 22 October 1962, NAA 31838609 M5410.

228 Siddons *et al.*, 'Carcinomata Developing at the Site of Foreign Bodies in the Lung'.

229 J. Jennings, 'Cordite-Eating and Cordite-Eaters', *Journal of the Royal Army Medical Corps* 1903; 1:277–85.

230 J. S. Weiner and M.L., Thomson. 'Observations on the Toxic Effects of Cordite', Royal Naval Personnel, Research Committee of the Medical Research Council, *Brit. J. Industr. Med.,* 1947, 4, 205, 206, 208, 213.

231 Jones and Wessely, *Shellshock to PTSD,* 198.

232 Carl May, 'Lord Moran's memoir: shell-shock and the pathology of fear', *Journal of the Royal Society of Medicine*, 91(1998), 95.

233 The date of opening is shown on individual records and ranges from 2014 to 2016 on the files examined.
234 Lake, *The Limits of Hope*; Damousi, *The Labour of Loss.*
235 Thomson, *Anzac Memories,* 304, 305.
236 Larssons, *Shattered Anzacs,* 151–52.
237 Thomson, *Anzac Memories,* 265, 267.
238 Garton, *The Cost of War,* 94, 143, 151, 165, 226, 236, 242, 252.
239 Butler, *Australian Army Medical Services,* 146; Scates and Oppenheimer, *The Last Battle,* 181, 188, 190.
240 Butler, *Australian Army Medical Services,* 723–786.
241 Straw, *After the War,* 121, 124, 133, 158–161, 162, 166.
242 Butler, *Australian Army Medical Services,* 221, 72–73, 223, 233, 258, 265, 846–980.
243 Butler, *Australian Army Medical Services,* Table 16. Causes for admissions to camp hospitals in Australia during 1915–16 and 1916–17, and percentage of numbers in camp to the yearly total. Also 887: DAH remains a constant in the repatriation files, even after the name was officially changed to 'effort syndrome'.
244 Butler, *Australian Army Medical Services,* 56, 58, 64, 77, 81, 83, 86, 88, 140, 141, 256.
245 'Observations by Colonel H. C. Maudsley, September, 1919. On Members of the A.I.F. Boarded by him In England during the years 1916–1919', in Butler, *Australian Army Medical Services,* Appendix 4. 1012.
246 Butler, *Australian Army Medical Services,* 728, 761, 763, 934, 1015, 1016.
247 Borderline personality disorder (BPD) was introduced to describe patients who seemed to be on the border between neurosis and psychosis. Research is ongoing, and no definite conclusions have yet been reached. Katrin Schroeder, Helen L. Fisher, Inigo Schäfer, 'Psychotic symptoms in patients with borderline personality disorder: prevalence and clinical management', *Current Opinion in Psychiatry,* January 2013 Vol. 26, 113–19.
248 Butler, *Australian Army Medical Services,* 958, 926–927, 930, 833.
249 Butler, *Australian Army Medical Services,* Table 68. 'Classification of Disabilities for Australian War Pensioners'. 965.
250 Butler, *Australian Army Medical Services,* 968, Table 72. 'Causes (other than battle casualties) for which, in 1931, pensions had been received in respect of the war of 1914–1918'. 969, 971.
251 Jones and Wessely, *Shellshock to PTSD,* 202.
252 Butler, *Australian Army Medical Services,* 978–80.
253 Thomson, *Anzac Memories,* 304.
254 Butler, *Australian Army Medical Services,* Table 70 'Classification of Disabilities suffered by Members of the Forces receiving Service Pensions as at 30th June, 1936–1940', 967.
255 Butler, *Australian Army Medical Services,* 810, 811, 813, 832, 835, 965.
256 Straw, *After the War,* 121, 124, 127.
257 Butler, *Australian Army Medical Services,* 142–43, 833. Butler himself was known for his bravery. He was in one of the first boats ashore at Gallipoli, where he won the DSO. In France, he worked in a Field Ambulance and at an advanced dressing station. He was mentioned in dispatches twice in 1917. C.M. Gurner, 'Butler, Arthur Graham (1872–1949)', *ADB,* 1979.

258 Butler, *Australian Army Medical Services,* 142–44.

259 May, 'Lord Moran's memoir', 95.

260 National Institute of Neurological Disorders and Stroke. Guillain-Barré Syndrome Fact Sheet, 2011, NIH Publication No. 11-2902. https://www.nonds.nih.gov/Disorders/Patient-Caregiver-Education/Fact-Sheets/Guillain-Barré-Syndrome-Fact-Sheet; Hirofumi Tsuboi, Naoto Sugeno, 'Retrospective analysis of Guillain–Barré syndrome and Fisher syndrome after the Great East Japan Earthquake', *Brain and Behavior,* 4, Issue 4, (July2014): 595–97.

261 Tsuboi and Sugeno, 'Retrospective analysis of Guillain–Barré syndrome'.

262 A.L. Roberts, S.S. Malspeis, L.D. Kubzansky, C.H. Feldman, S.C. Chang, K.C. Koenan, K.H. Costenbader. 'Association of Trauma and Posttraumatic Stress Disorder with Incident Systemic Lupus Erythematosus in a Longitudinal Cohort of Women', *Arthritis Rheumatol.* 69 No. 11 (November 2017): 2162–2169.

263 Hans Selye, 'A Syndrome produced by Diverse Nocuous Agents', *Nature,* 138 (04 July 1936): 32.

264 May, 'Lord Moran's memoir', 95, 97.

265 Van Bergen, *Before My Helpless Sight*, 211, 219–27; May, 'Lord Moran's memoir', 98.

266 Butler, *Australian Army Medical Services,* 142–144.

267 Joanna Bourke, 'Effeminacy, Ethnicity and the End of Trauma: The Sufferings of 'Shell-shocked' Men in Great Britain and Ireland, 1914–39', *Journal of Contemporary History* 35 no 1, (2000): 57–69, 67–68.

268 Bourke, 'The Sufferings of 'Shell-shocked' Men', 62, 67.

269 Rae, 'Shell shock during the First World War', 2/13 (page numbers not shown).

270 Edgar Jones and Simon Wessely, 'Battle for the mind: World War I and the birth of military psychiatry', *The Lancet*, 384, Issue 9955, (November 2014): 1708 – 1714. 1713.

271 Jones and Wessely, 'Battle for the Mind', 1711, 1712.

272 Jones and Wessely, *Shellshock to PTSD,* 137, *1*84, 213, 216.

273 Shawn P. Cahill, and Kristin Pontoski. 'Post-Traumatic Stress Disorder and Acute Stress Disorder I: Their Nature and Assessment Considerations', *Psychiatry,* 2(4) 2005: 14–25.

274 Straw, *After the War*, 8, 83.

275 Laura di Grande, Y. Neria, R. M. Brackbill, P. Pullam, S. Galea, 'Long-term posttraumatic stress symptoms among survivors of September 11, 2001 attacks', *Am. J. Epidemiol.,* 173(3) 2011: 271–81, 18.

276 Harvard Health Publications, 'Skipping a beat — the surprise of heart palpitations', October 31, 2017.

277 Jenny Edkins, *Trauma and the Memory of Politics,* Cambridge: Cambridge University Press. 2003, 19, 215, 227; Fassin and Rechtman, *Empire of Trauma,* 4.

278 Sharon E. Perlman, Stephen Friedman, Sandro Galea, Hemanth P Nair, Monika Erős-Sarnyai, Steven D Stellman, Jeffrey Hon, Carolyn M Greene, 'Short-term and medium-term health effects of 9/11', *The Lancet,* 378, (September 3 2011): 925–34, 925, 927.

279 Di Grande *et al.*, 'Posttraumatic stress symptoms among survivors of September 11', 8/31 (page numbers not shown).

280 Di Grande *et al.*, 'Posttraumatic stress symptoms among survivors of September 11', 19/31 (see note above).

281 Perlman *et al.*, 'Short-term and medium-term health effects of 9/11', 931.

282 Cahill and Pontoski, 'Post-Traumatic Stress Disorder'.

283 J. H. Binns, N. Cherry, B. A. Golomb, J.C. Graves, R. W. Haley, M.L. Knox, in Veterans' Affairs (ed.) 'Report of research advisory committee on Gulf War veterans' illnesses', Topeka, KS: 2004, 261–262; Gulf War Syndrome, or 'chronic multi-symptom illness' and 'undiagnosed illnesses', is a condition affecting Gulf War (1991–1992) veterans, characterised by a cluster of medically unexplained chronic symptoms that can include fatigue, headaches, joint pain, indigestion, insomnia, dizziness, respiratory disorders, and memory problems. 'Gulf War Veterans' Medically Unexplained Illnesses', US Department of Veterans Affairs, Washington DC. 2017.

284 Gopinath Kaundinya, Parina Gandhi, Aman Goyal, Lei Jiang, Yan Fang, Luo Ouyang, Sandeepkumar Ganji, Bavid Buhner, Wendy Ringe, Jeffrey Spence, Melanie Briggs, Richard Briggs, Robert Haley, 'FMRI reveals abnormal central processing of sensory and pain stimuli in ill Gulf War veterans', *NeuroToxicology,* Elsevier Inc. 33, Issue 3, June 2012: 261–271; National Academies of Sciences, Engineering, and Medicine, *Gulf War and health: Volume 10: Update of serving in the Gulf War, 2016.* Washington, DC: The National Academies Press.

285 Bianca P. Acevedo, Elaine N. Aron, Arthur Aron, Matthew-Donald Sangster, Nancy Collins, Lucy L. Brown, 'The highly sensitive brain: an fMRI study of sensory processing sensitivity and response to others' emotions', *Brain and Behaviour*, 4, Issue 4, (July 2014): 580–94, 242.

286 Jones and Wessely, *Shellshock to PTSD,* 208.

287 During his childhood and war service, his name was spelt 'Holtzmann', but shortened to 'Holtzman' after the war.

288 Discharge papers, NAA M9457 Vol. 1A 31841207

289 'Letter to the Editor', *The Bunbury Herald and Blackwood Express,* 30 March 1923: 5; 'Master David McVicker', *South Western Times,* 2 September 1919: 3.

290 Summary of appeal, 3, doctor notes, 31 December 1919; 4; 7 November 1926, NAA M9457 Vol. 1A 31841207; Medical certificate, Dr Cullen, 24 June 1927, NAA M9457 Vol. 1A 31841207.

291 Summary of appeal, 4, 24 December 1926, testimonial FW Robert; p5, note, Dr Beveridge, NAA M9457 Vol. 1A 31841207

292 Summary of appeal, 5, doctor's note, 10 May 1927, NAA M9457 Vol. 1A 31841207.

293 Summary of appeal, 10, Form K, Drs White and Smyth Yule, 29 August, 1929, NAA M9457 Vol. 1B 31841208

294 Summary of appeal, 10, Norman Holtzman (NH) to DC, 15.8.29, NAA M9457 Vol. 1B 31841208.

295 Perth hospital case sheet, 1 October 1929, 28 October 1929, NAA H9457, Vol. 1, 31841210.

296 Summary of appeal, 13, Form K, Dr Mackay, 5 February 1934, NAA M9457 Vol. 1B 31841208; 'Fall from Windmill', *The West Australian,* 3 December 1931: 13.

297 Summary of appeal, 12, Form K, Dr Mackay, 5 February 1934, NAA M9457 Vol. 1B 31841208

298 Doctor McKay, Form 71, 10 July 1934, NAA M9457 Vol. 1B 31841208

299 'Dice Players Raided', *The Daily News,* 24 July 1939: 16.

300 Leslie Norman Holtzman, captured by Japanese NAA A14171, WX7618 POW

May 1943 – October 1945; Colin Ernest Holtzman, NAA A6770.

301 DC to NH, 25 March 1943, NAA M9457 Vol. 1A 31841207; Dr WL Robinson, DMO to DC, 16 March 1943, 24 March 1943, NAA M9457 Vol. 1B 31841208.

302 Repatriation outpatient clinic, doctor's report, 26 April 1954, NAA M9457 Vol. 1A 31841207; JB Hogg, DMO, notes, 23 April 1954, NAA M9457 Vol. 1B 31841208.

303 NH to DC, 25 November 1957, Dr McKenna to DC, 6 November 1957, DC to Dr McKenna, 9 October 1957, NAA M9457 Vol. 1A 31841207; Summary of appeal, 14, Dr McKenna, Medical report 4 September 1957, 8 August 1957. NAA M9457 Vol. 1B 31841208.

304 Summary of appeal, 17, NH to DC, 9 December 1957; form TF, 12 June 1958, NAA M9457 Vol. 1B 31841208.

305 NH claim for Acceptance of an incapacity as due to war service, 21 December 1960, NAA M9457 Vol. 1A 31841207.

306 DC to Dr McKenna, 25 July 1960, NAA M9457 Vol. 1A 31841207; Summary of appeal, 18, note, 30 September 1960, NAA M9457 Vol. 1B 31841208.

307 DC to NH, 20 February 1961; DC to Dr, 12 October 1962; DC travel permit to doctor, 17 October 1963; Application for travel authority 28 October 1964; DC to NH, 2 October 1968, NAA M9457 Vol. 1A 31841207.

308 To DC from doctor, Victoria, nd, c 23 December 1968, NAA M9457 Vol. 1A 31841207; Form TE, 10 July 1969; Summary of appeal 31, statement of doctor in Victoria, Form K, 31 April 1969, NAA M9457 Vol. 1B 31841208.

309 Dr FC Bourgault, 17 September 1969, NAA M9457 Vol. 1A 31841207.

310 Transfer to Victoria, OIC pensions, 22 November 1971, NAA M9457 Vol. 1A 31841207; Ward report 23 November 1972, H9457, Vol. 1, 31841210.

311 NH, appeal to Repat Commission; DC to NH, 7 December 1972, M9457 Vol 2, 31841209.

312 Summary of appeal, 65, photocopied ward notes, 26 May 1972, NAA M9457 Vol. 1B 31841208; ward report, 27 October 1972, H9457, Vol. 1, 31841210; summary of appeal, 89, 9 January 1973, NAA M9457 Vol. 1B 31841208; Ross Edge to DC 18 September 1972, M9457 Vol 2, 31841209.

313 Summary of appeal, 130, ward notes, 2 April 1976, NAA M9457 Vol. 1B 31841208; case history 6 April 1976, NAA H9457 Vol 2, 31841211.

314 Ward notes, 19 July 1979; NH to DC, n.d., M9457 Vol. 2, 31841209.

315 Application for transfer of patient … to intensive care, 15 May 1979; letter from matron to DC n.d., NAA M9457 Vol 2, 31841209.

316 Deceased 5 September 1979, NAA H9457, Vol. 1, 31841210; Application for grant towards funeral and burial expenses, 18 October 1979, NAA M9457 Vol 2, 31841209.

6: Women and Repatriation

1 Ivy Paisley, 30 August 1946, NAA 32501494 M14276.

2 Ingrid Sharp and Matthew Stibbe, *Aftermaths of War: Women's Movements and Female Activists, 1918–1923*. Leiden, Netherlands: Brill Publishing, 2014, 9; Stephen Garton, 'War and masculinity in twentieth century Australia', *Journal of Australian Studies*, 22:56, 1998, 86–95.

3 Larsson, 'Family caregivers', 39–60.

4 Larsson, 'Family caregivers', 42.
5 Thomson, *ANZAC Memories*, 260.
6 Doctor note, 14 April 1928, NAA 31838463 M4981.
7 'Perth Last Night and the Social Notebook', *Sunday Times*, 26 June 1938: 12 (Sporting Section).
8 Summary of appeal, NAA 10065192 K60, C2281.; Appeal notes, 17, NAA 10154948 M2281.
9 Larsson, 'Family caregivers', 56.
10 Medical notes, 13 December 1970, 3 May 1979, 31 May 1979, NAA 10065573 H769; 10 July 1978, NAA 10112538 M769.
11 Nursing home report, 23 August 1979, NAA 10112538 M769.
12 Medical report, 24 April 1972, 3 October 1972, NAA 32502412 M26047.
13 Doctor notes, 11 February 1930, NAA 31838463 M4981; 9 March 1931, NAA 20423414 C4981.
14 Thomson, *ANZAC Memories*, 286.
15 Doctor notes, 15 February 1929, 8 March 1929, 13 March 1929, NAA 20423997 C17847.
16 Doctor notes, 6 February 1967, 13 February 1967, 25 February 1967, 31 January 1968, NAA 10082837 M10243.
17 Summary of appeal, 5, doctor's note, 10 May 1927, NAA M9457 Vol. 1A 31841207; Summary of appeal, 12, 13, Form K, Dr Mackay, 5 February 1934, NAA M9457 Vol. 1B 31841208.
18 'Fall from Windmill', *The West Australian*, 3 December 1931: 13; Dr McKenna to DC, 6 November 1957, NAA M9457 Vol. 1A 31841207.
19 Summary of appeal, 17, NAA 10154948 M2281.
20 For example, R. Clarke to DC, 4 February 1960, NAA 10154948 M2281; DOTAG.
21 RGH ward report, 24 January 1988, NAA 10113873 HB4981.
22 Doctor note, 15 August 1955, DC note, 7 February 1956, outpatient notes, 12 October 1961, 13 June 1962, NAA 32502870 MB17847.
23 Reginald Hemingway, NAA PP2/8 10155153 R9621; Edith Hemingway, NAA B73 20455595 MB21936; B73 20455596 HB21936.
24 Thomson, *ANZAC Memories*, 284; LP, application for sustenance, 25 June 1958, NAA 32501693 H19287.
25 'Personal', *South Western Times*, 5 August 1920: 3; 'Personal', *South Western Times*, 29 October 1918: 3.
26 Thomson, *ANZAC Memories*, 263.
27 F. Gray to DC, 12 May 1931, doctor note, 14 May 1931, NAA 32485400 M14926.
28 Scates and Oppenheimer, *The Last Battle*, 86; Dorothy Bird to DC, 25 March 1946, NAA 32485931 M8061.
29 Dorothy Bird to DC, August 1947, NAA 32485931 M8061; Scates and Oppenhemer, *The Last Battle*, Chapter 3, The Moral Economy, 86.
30 Kent, *Making peace*, 54, 72.
31 Rae, *From Narromine to the Nile*; John McQuilton, Gender and War, *Journal of the Australian War Memorial*, Issue 33, 2000.
32 Butler, *Australian Army Medical Service*, 582; Garton, *The Cost of War*, 85.
33 Williams, 'Not Openly Encouraged'.
34 Harris, 'Work, work, work: Australian Army nurses after the first World War', in

When the Soldiers Return, 2007 Conference Proceedings, St Lucia, Queensland, 2009, 1, 11.

35 Summary of service, NAA 32502174 M5355.

36 'Mainly About People', *The Daily News,* 23 November 1916: 3.

37 Medical note, 17 March 1917, NAA 32502174 M5355.

38 Doctor notes, 21 December 1956, 27 December 1956, NAA 32502174 M5355.

39 DC notes, 18 January 1957, NAA 32502174 M5355; Harris, 'Work, work, work', 1.

40 'No Title', *Kalgoorlie Western Argus,* 29 April 1902: 16; 'Mainly About People', *The Daily News,* 7 January 1903: 5.

41 'London Notes', *The West Australian,* 29 October 1914: 8; 'Notes on the War', *Williamstown Chronicle,* 5 September 1914: 3; 'An Australian Nurse in Antwerp', *Riverine Herald,* 18 December 1914: 4.

42 'War Nurse's Fine Record. Passing of Kate Bruton', *Williamstown Chronicle,* 8 January 1943: 3; 'Nurse Bruton and the League', *The Australian,* 16 July 1920: 1.

43 'Matron Bruton Retired', *The Australian,* 30 July 1920: 5.

44 Butler, *Australian Army Medical Service,* 545; Chloe Papas, 'The forgotten women of the Great War', ABC Great Southern, 20 August, 2014.

45 'War Nurse's Fine Record. Passing of Kate Bruton', *Williamstown Chronicle,* 8 January 1943: 3.

46 Anzac Heroes.

47 Nancy Sherwood, personal communication, August 2017.

48 'Bunbury Infants' School', *Bunbury Herald,* 29 December 1898: 3; 'Children's Fancy Dress Ball', *The Collie Miner,* 18 July 1908: 4; 'Grand Christmas Fete', *Southern Times,* 22 December 1910: 5. 'Small Bore Rifle Club', *Southern Times,* 27 August 1908: 5; 'News and Notes', *Southern Times,* 24 January 1914: 5; 'Dresses at the Paces'. (sic) *The Bunbury Herald and Blackwood Express,* 18 February 1921: 1; 'Golf', *The Bunbury Herald and Blackwood Express,* 5 May 1922: 5.

49 'Bunbury Notes', *The Blackwood Times,* 4 April 1913: 5; 'Valedictory', *Southern Times,* 3 April 1913: 5.

50 'Social Chatter', *Southern Times,* 24 October 1914: 5; 'Social Notes', *Southern Times,* 9 December 1916: 5.

51 'No 8 AGH', *Camp Chronicle,* 7 June 1917, 6; 'Personal', *South Western Times,* 16 June 1917: 5.

52 'Mainly About People, Franziska', *The Daily News,* 20 June 1917, 3; 'Mainly About People', *The Daily News,* 27 June 1918, 3; WWI file NAA 8000690, 1914–1920; NAA 32501494 M14276.

53 Ashleigh Wadman, AWM Blog, 'Nursing for the British Raj', 28 October 2014; AWM, Suitcase of Staff Nurse Vera Agnes Paisley, REL36908; Ruth Rae, 'Reading between unwritten lines: Australian army nurses in India, 1916–19', *Journal of the Australian War Memorial* 36 (2002).

54 Rae, 'Australian army nurses in India, 1916–19', 8–9.

55 Medical notes on discharge, NAA 32501494 M14276; Rae, 'Shell shock during the First World War', 6/13 (no page numbers).

56 'Mainly About People, Franziska', *The Daily News,* 4 June 1919: 3; 'Personal', *South Western Times,* 3 June 1919: 3; 'Personal', *South Western Times,* 11 September 1919: 3; 'Personal', *South Western Times,* 13 September 1919: 5.

57 Discharge note, 12 November 1919, NAA 8000690, 32501494, M14276.

58 Rae, 'Australian army nurses in India, 1916–19', 4–5.

59 Katie Holmes, 'Day Mothers and Night sisters: World War I nurses and sexuality'

in Lake and Damousi, *Gender and War*, 43–80.

60 Rae, 'Australian army nurses in India, 1916–19', 7–8.

61 Now known as 'Dongara'; 'Personal Pars', *The Bunbury Herald and Blackwood Express,* 21 April 1922: 5.

62 'Social and Personal', *The Bunbury Herald and Blackwood Express,* 30 March 1920: 3; 'Mainly About People', *The Daily News,* 7 November 1923: 9; 'Personal', *South Western Times,* 19 June 1924: 2; 'Personal', *South Western Times,* 28 June 1924: 5; 'Personal', *South Western Times,* 16 September 1924: 3; 'Personal Pars', *The Bunbury Herald and Blackwood Express,* 9 August 1921: 2.

63 'Personal Pars', *The Bunbury Herald and Blackwood Express,* 4 January 1922: 3; 'Social and Personal', *The Bunbury Herald and Blackwood Express,* 11 May 1920. 3; 'Bunbury', *Western Mail,* 28 February 1929: 30; 'Personal', *South Western Times,* 10 April 1923: 2; 'Personal Pars', *The Bunbury Herald and Blackwood Express,* 8 October 1920: 5; 'News and Notes', *The Bunbury Herald and Blackwood Express,* 18 May 1928: 2.

64 'Tenth Light Horse. Bunbury Troop. Inaugural Dinner', *The Bunbury Herald and Blackwood Express,* 28 August 1925: 5; 'Bunbury Period Ball', *The Bunbury Herald and Blackwood Express,* 21 October 1929: 3.

65 'The Social World', *Western Mail,* 10 November 1932: 29.

66 Edkins, *Trauma and the Memory of Politics*, 40.

67 Edkins, *Trauma and the Memory of Politics*, 39.

68 DC note, 16 March 1920, 19 April 1920, NAA 32501494 M14276.

69 Doctor notes, 5 May 1920, NAA 32501494 M14276.

70 Thomas Paisley to DC, 9 August 1920, doctor note, 20 November 1920, NAA 32501494 M14276.

71 Doctor note, 9 August 1921, NAA 32501494 M14276.

72 Doctor note, 12 August 1921, NAA 32501494 M14276.

73 Doctor note, 18 May 1922, NAA 32501494 M14276.

74 Doctor notes, 25 May 1926, NAA 32501494 M14276.

75 Doctor note, 2 August 1927, NAA 32501494 M14276.

76 Doctor note, 8 August 1927, NAA 32501494 R14276; Doctor note, 2 August 1927, NAA 32501494 M14276.

77 Doctor note, 14 July 1931, 32501494, R14276.

78 Doctor notes, 8 September 1931, 14 July 1931, NAA 32501494 M14276.

79 Matthew J. Friedman, 'A brief history of the PTSD diagnosis', National Center for PTSD, U.S. Department of Veterans Affairs, Washington DC, 2015.

80 Summary of appeal, 9, NAA 32501494, R14276.

81 1932–1934, NAA 32501494 M14276.

82 Medical notes, 23 January 1935, Summary of appeal, 15, 27 June 1936, NAA 32501494, R14276.

83 DC notes, 27 June 1936, 32501494 M14276; 'Country News', *The West Australian,* 9 September 1935: 11; 'Golf Match at Dongarra Woorree Team Defeated By Home Club', *Geraldton Guardian and Express,* 11 July 1935, 1.

84 'Dongarra News C.W.A. Activities Trees For Recreation Ground', (Contributed). *Geraldton Guardian and Express,* 22 June 1935, 1.

85 'Country News', *The West Australian,* 23 November 1935: 11; 'Nursing Scheme Work at Dongarra A Successful Year', *Geraldton Guardian and Express,* 23 November 1935, 1; doctor notes, 27 June 1936, NAA 32501494 M14276.

86 'Man's Tragic Death Fall From Midland Train Shocking Affair At Dongarra', *Geraldton Guardian and Express,* 31 December 1936, 2.

87 'Killed By Train Man's Terrible Injuries The Dongarra Accident', *Geraldton Guardian and Express,* 23 January 1937: 4.

88 'Young Man Killed. Motor Cycle Strikes Truck', *The West Australian,* 12 January 1937: 11; 'Pillion Rider's Death Fatality At Dongarra Coronial Inquiry', *Geraldton Guardian and Express,* 30 January 1937: 3. The author's mother passed through Dongara at this time with her family and remembers Sister Paisley going to an inquest.

89 'Local And General', *Geraldton Guardian and Express,* 6 February 1937: 2; 'District Nursing. Dongarra Scheme Ended. Effects of New Award', *The West Australian* 11 June 1937: 19.

90 'District Nursing. Dongarra Scheme Ended. Effects of New Award', *The West Australian* 11 June 1937: 19.

91 Doctor notes, 23 December 1935, NAA 32501494 M14276.

92 Doctor notes, 15 June 1938, NAA 32501494 M14276.

93 Doctor notes, 15 June 1938, NAA 32501494 M14276. Paraphrenia is similar to paranoid schizophrenia but with less Intellectual and personality deterioration. AV Ravindran, Yatham LN, Munro A, 'Paraphrenia redefined', *Canadian Journal of Psychiatry,* 1999 Mar; 44(2):133–7; Doctor notes, 8 November 1938, NAA 32501494 M14276.

94 Doctor notes, 8 November 1938, 7 November 1938, 15 June 1938, 21 June 1938, NAA 32501494 M14276; Stern, 'The Psychopathology of manic-depressive disorder and Involutional Melancholia', *British Journal of Medical Psychology, 1944,* 32.

95 DC notes, 10 November 1938, 32501494 M14276. This again contradicts Rees' assertion that the RSL did not assist nurses. Chloe Papas, 'The forgotten women of the Great War'.

96 Cover notes, 9 October 1940, NAA 32501494, R14276.

97 DC notes, 9 March 1940, NAA 32501494 R14276.

98 Senator Dorothy Tangney to DC, 30 August 1946 NAA 32501494 M14276. Dorothy Tangney, 1907–85, was Australia's first female senator and was involved in women's political organisations. Carmen Lawrence, 'Tangney, Dame Dorothy Margaret (1907–85)', *ADB*; 'Federal Election', *The West Australian,* 11 May 1946: 10.

99 DC to Dorothy Tangney, 10 September 1946, NAA 32501494 M14276.

100 DC notes, 16 November 1949, 29 November 1949, NAA 32501494 M14276.

101 Vera Paisley, *Guide to Nurses*. Perth Western Australia: Perth Public Hospital, Battye Library, 11994865.

102 Doctor to DC, 16 January 1959, NAA 32501494 M14276.

103 Bunbury town clerk to DC, 29 May 1968, NAA 32501494 M14276.

104 Social worker to DC, 22 April 1968; RSL to DC, 25 September 1968, NAA 32501494 M14276.

105 Inside cover; hospital notes, 22 November 1968, 32501495 H14276; DC notes, 29 November 1968, NAA 32501494 M14276.

106 Hospital notes, 14 January 1969, 10 February 1949, NAA 32501495 H14276. Vera was treated with stelazine and mandrax; Ravindran *et al.*, 'Paraphrenia redefined'.

107 Les Paisley to DC, 13 February 1969, 32501495 H14276.

108 Ward reports, Edward Millen Hospital, NAA 32501494 M14276.

109 Stern, 'Manic-depressive disorder and Involutional Melancholia', 31, 32.

110 Rae 'Shell shock during the First World War', 3/13.
111 Rae 'Shell shock during the First World War', 1–3, 4, 7, 11–13.
112 Friedman, 'History of the PTSD diagnosis', 1 – 3.
113 Jen Hawksley, 'Long time coming home: the "unknown patient" of Callan Park', in Crotty and Larsson, *Anzac Legacies*, 61–83.
114 'Valedictory', *Southern Times,* 3 April 1913: 5.
115 Scates and Oppenheimer, *The Last Battle*, Chapter 3, The Moral Economy, 86.
116 Selena Wenn to DC, 24 January 1924, NAA 30804625 C7525.
117 Selena Wenn to DC, 14 November 1919, NAA 30804625 C7525; DC notes, 16 December 1920, NAA 30804625 C7525.
118 M. Beigel, Bunbury Repatriation Committee to DC, 3 February 1919, NAA 32492646 R2716.
119 M. Beigel to DC, 20 February 1919, NAA 32492646 R2716.
120 DC note, 25 February 1919, NAA 32492646 R2716.
121 B. Beigel to DC, 26 May 1919, NAA 32492646 R2716.
122 Bunbury Repat Committee to DC, 11 August 1919, 28 August 1919, NAA 32492646, R2716.
123 Alma Wenn to DC, 1 September 1919, NAA 32492646, R2716.
124 Bunbury Repat Committee to DC, 26 September 1919, NAA 32492646 R2716.
125 C. R. Wenn to DC, 15 June 1922, NAA 32492646 R2716.
126 DC note, 4 September 1924, NAA 32492646 R2716.
127 DC note, 18 May 1942, Alma Wenn to DC, 25 November 1942, DC note, 17 December 1942, NAA 31123640 C2716.
128 Alma Wenn to DC, 29 June 1973, NAA 31123640 C2716; Bunbury Repat Committee to DC, 6 August 1973, NAA 31123640 C2716.
129 'Country', *The West Australian,* 25 April 1912: 8.
130 DC notes, 24 July 1920, MBW to DC, 24 January 1920, NAA 32644956 R24945.
131 MBW to DC, 15 February 1921, DC note, 28 April 1921, NAA 32644956 R24945.
132 DC note, 18 April 1923, NAA 32644956 R24945.
133 DOTAG; 'Lumper Injured', *The West Australian,* 19 January 1945: 8.
134 DOTAG.
135 'Family Notices', *The West Australian,* 27 August 1915: 1; Drummond James Blythe, 1892–1916, Francis Albert Blythe, 1894–1916, *ANZAC Heroes*.
136 Mary Emma Lucinne Blythe, DOTAG; DC note, NAA 31838609, M5410,
137 E. Blythe to DC, 17 October 1916, 15 November 1916, NAA 32489914 R1805; Scates and Oppenheimer, *The Last Battle*, Chapter 3.
138 E. Blythe to DC, 3 November 1916, NAA 32489914 R1805.
139 E. Blythe to DC, 3 November 1916, NAA 32489914 R1805.
140 Mayor G.E. Clarke to DC, 3 November 1916, NAA 32489914 R1805.
141 Q. Blythe to DC, 22 October 1962, NAA 31838609 M5410.
142 DOTAG; Larsson, *Shattered Anzacs*, 75.
143 Q. Blythe to DC, 4 October 1965, NAA 31838609 M5410.
144 Summary of appeal, 67, NAA 31838609 M5410.
145 Larsson, *Shattered Anzacs*, 99; Scates and Oppenheimer, *The Last Battle*, 86.

146 McLarty was closely related to the Sutton family in Harvey, DOTAG.

7: Gender at War in the Wellington Community: The Public and The Private

1 'Red Cross', *Bunbury Herald,* 25 January 1916: 3.

2 Susan Kingsley Kent, 'The Politics of Sexual Difference: World War I and the Demise of British Feminism', *The Journal of British Studies,* Volume: 27: 3, 232–253, 1988, 237, 247, 248, 250, 251.

3 Kingston, *My Wife, My Daughter and Poor Mary Ann*, 129, 195, 194, 94.

4 Kingston, *My Wife, My Daughter and Poor Mary Ann*, 226; Peter A. Murray, Robin Kramar, Peter McGraw, (eds), *Women at Work: Research, Policy and Practice*, Prahran, Victoria, Australia: Tilde University Press, 2011. 23, 27.

5 Kingston, *My Wife, My Daughter and Poor Mary Ann*, 220, 119, 121.

6 Carmel Shute, 'Heroines and heroes', 30, 31.

7 McQuilton, *Rural Australia and the Great War*, 119–131; Philip Payton, *Australia in the Great War*, 98.

8 Meyer, *Men of War,* 3.

9 Scates, 'The Unknown Sock Knitter', 29–49, 34.

10 Scates, 'The Unknown Sock Knitter', 44.

11 Sharp and Stibbe, *Aftermaths of War*, 9, 13.

12 Lenore Davidoff and Catherine Hall, *Family Fortunes: Men and women of the English middle class, 1780–1850*, London: Hutchinson, 1987; 'The New Harvey Hall', *Southern Times,* 14 July 1914: 4; Marjorie to family n.d., c. 1913; Alf Snell to CS 17 October 1915; CS to family, 4 October 1915, 28 November 1915.

13 John Lack, 'Buley, 'Ernest Charles (1869–1933)', *ADB*, 2005; Buley, *Australian Life in Town and Country,* 167; Mesdames Charman, Lambert, Mayne and Smith.

14 Mrs Hymus to CS, 23 March 1916; CS to family, 28 November 1915; 'The Harvey Orchard Area', *Bunbury Herald,* 13 December 1907: 3; CS to family 16 July 1915.

15 Miss Bessie Lambert of Harvey.

16 'Mr. George At Bunbury', *Western Mail,* 21 July 1900: 24.

17 'Torrington Ladies' College, Bunbury', *The West Australian,* 2 January 1880: 2.

18 'The State School', *Bunbury Herald,* 4 April 1901: 3.

19 'Bunbury Evening Classes', *Bunbury Herald,* 3 May 1905: 2; 'Advertising', *Bunbury Herald,* 18 May 1916: 2.

20 Mrs Eastaugh, 'Advertising', *Southern Times,* 20 July 1916: 2.

21 'Bunbury District Nursing Association', *Southern Times,* 25 July 1916: 4; 'The Drink Question', *The West Australian,* 14 April 1915: 6.

22 Stephen Garton, 'War and masculinity in twentieth century Australia', *Journal of Australian Studies*, 22:56, 1998, 86–95.

23 'Help for Belgians Bunbury's Fine Effort. Just Under £150 Raised', *Bunbury Herald,* 19 December 1914: 5; 'The Belgian Fete', *Bunbury Herald,* 12 December 1914: 5.

24 'Bunbury Red Cross', *South Western Times,* 17 August 1918: 7.

25 'The Rustics', *Bunbury Herald,* 4 September 1915: 3; 'News and Notes', *South Western Times* 9 November 1918: 4.

26 'Bunbury Red Cross', *Bunbury Herald* 21 Dec 1918: 5.

27 'White Feathers', *Southern Times* 7 December 1915: 5.
28 'The Rustics', *Bunbury Herald,* 4 September 1915: 3; 'News and Notes', *South Western Times,* 9 November 1918: 4.
29 Scott, *Australia During the War,* 886; Scates, 'The Unknown Sock Knitter', 29.
30 B*unbury Herald,* 8 July 1916; 'Local and General', *Bunbury Herald,* 6 July 1916, 3.
31 'In the Country', *The West Australian* 2 February 1917, 8.
32 Tennant, 'Fun and Fundraising', 64.
33 Scott, Australia During the War, 738.
34 'News and Notes', *Southern Times,* 29 June 1915: 2.
35 'Red Cross Societies', *South Western Advertiser,* 19 November 1915: 3.
36 'Bunbury Red Cross Society', *Bunbury Herald,* 9 February 1918: 5.
37 Scott, *Australia During the War,* 704, 705.
38 'Soldiers' Relatives', *South Western Times,* 18 October 1917: 3; 'Returned Soldiers' Association', *Bunbury Herald,* 1 May 1918: 3; 'Parliamentary Party', *The Bunbury Herald and Blackwood Express,* 8 November 1921: 1.
39 'Soldiers Memorial Fund', *The Bunbury Herald and Blackwood Express,* 22 July 1921: 3; 'Memorial Hall Management Committee', *The Bunbury Herald and Blackwood Express,* 30 September 1927: 5.
40 'Miss Adela Pankhurst', *South Western Times,* 3 April 1917: 3; 'Miss Adela Pankhurst', *Bunbury Herald,* 31 March 1917: 3.
41 'Miss Adela Pankhurst', *South Western Times,* 7 April 1917: 3.
42 'Two Disgraceful Meetings', *Southern Times,* 28 October 1916: 5.
43 Roper, *The Secret Battle*; Steve Snell, London, to AJS, 15 September 1916; Nora Snell to family, 12 October 1916.
44 Winter and Sivan, *War and Remembrance,* 41.
45 Wedd Tuxford, to Snell family, 22 October 1916; CS to family, 28 November 1915.
46 'Dad' Harrington also visited Marjorie in hospital, CS to family 14 July 1915; Luckins, *The Gates of Memory,* 59; CAS handwritten lists, August 1916.
47 CS to family, 21 November 1915.
48 CS to family, 27 December 1915.
49 Blanche Martin, NSW to family, 8 August 1916; Miss M. Treloggen, to family, 20 August 1916
50 Mrs Paisley to family, 9 August 1916; Thomas Paisley to family 9 August 1916.
51 J. Jefferson to CS, 8 July 1916.
52 Mrs Cameron, Glenn Innes, NSW to Snell family, 13 August 1916.
53 W.J. George to Snell family, 12 August 1916.
54 CS to family, 12 August 1915; 29 August 1915; 15 August 1915; 19 September 1915.
55 Mrs Dunlop to CS, 19 May 1916.
56 CS to family, 19 September 1915.
57 Winter and Sivan, *War and Remembrance,* 43; CS to family, 27 December 1915; CS to family, 7 November 1915.
58 CS to family 16 July 1915; J. Robinson to AJS, 15 August 1916.
59 Meyer, *Men of War,* 2009, 1; Alma Shenton to CAS, 9 August 1916; Mrs Jefferson to family, 15 October 1916; Rosa Myatt to CAS, 10 August 1916.

60 M.A. and J. Snell to CS, 11 April 1916.

61 Alfred Goss to AJS, 10 August 1916; Dr W. I. Dermer to AJS, 11 August 1916; T. Paisley to family, 13 August 1916.

62 A. P. Cameron to family 13 August 1916.

63 Winter and Sivan, *War and Remembrance.*, 43.

64 Clive Moore, 'Introduction: Australian Masculinities', *Journal of Australian Studies*, 22:56, 1–16, 1998, 1–16; Coulson Kernahan, *The Experiences of a Recruiting Officer*, London: Hodder and Stoughton, 1915, eg. 53, 54.

65 NAA, 'Conscription referendums, 1916 and 1917 – Fact sheet 161'; Miss M. Treloggen, Sydney, to Snell family, 29 October 1916; 'Home and Society', *Sunday Times*, 9 July 1916: 25; Martha and Margaret Treloggen, b. Tasmania, neither married, both died in NSW, 1926 and 1932. They supported the Women's Patriotic Club which contributed to Catholic children's institutions. Treloggen family website.

66 Maud Dunlop to CS, 9 May 1916.

67 Bessie Lambert, London, to family, 3 October 1916; Mrs Jefferson, Exmouth, Devonshire, 15 October 1916.

68 Roper, *The Secret Battle*, 3, 9, 27.

69 Roper, *The Secret Battle*, 6; Meyer, *Men of War*, 1.

70 Luckins, *The Gates of Memory*, 59.

71 Pat Jalland, *Death in the Victorian Family*. Oxford: Oxford University Press, 1996; Pat Jalland, *Death in War and Peace*. Oxford: Oxford University Press, 2010; Meyer, *Men of War*, 2009, 1.

72 Anna Livia, 'One Man in Two is a Woman: Linguistic Approaches to Gender in Literary Texts', in Janet Holmes and Miriam Meyerhoff (eds) *The handbook of Language and Gender*. Oxford: Blackwell Publishing, 2003, 2005. 142–158, 144.

73 Thomas Paisley to Snell family, 9 August 1916.

74 CS to family, 20 August 1915; CS to Marjorie, 16 May 1916.

75 CS to family, 29 August 1915.

76 Woollacott, *Gender and Empire*, Basingstoke: Palgrave MacMillan, 2006, 88.

77 Kent, *Making Peace*, 13.

78 AJS to Dr Joel, 7 August 1916; AJS to Joel, 8 August 16.

79 Casualty report, 44 CCS, 1916–1917, Australian Red Cross Wounded and Missing Enquiry Bureau Files, 1914–18 War, 1DRL/0428, 3911 Private Charles Snell, 4th Battalion, 19; Mr Gennys to CS, 9 September 1915.

80 John M Dunlop, Bangkok, to CS, 16 May 1916.

81 Lt P.W. Hay to family per Mrs Pollie Snell, London, 8 October 1916.

82 Town Clerk's Office, Bunbury, A. R. Foreman to family, 26 August 1916.

83 K. Eastman to AJS, 8 August 1916.

84 W. C. Robinson to AJS, 22 August 1916. Robinson lost a 14-year-old son in 1911, DOTAG; 'Valedictory to Mr W. C. Robinson', *Bunbury Herald*, 5 September 1908: 3; 'General News', *Mount Magnet Miner and Lennonville Leader*, 10 June 1916: 2; NAA service records, file B2455/1905602. Robinson, WB, SERN 1258.

85 Wedd Tuxford to CAS, 22 October 1916.

86 H.M. Beigel to AJS, 8 August 1916.

87 AJS to W. C. Robinson, 7 October 1916.

88 AJS to W. I. Dermer 7 September 1916.

89 Mrs Dunlop to CS, 19 May 1916.

90 Lorrie Clark to CAS, 9 August 1916.

91 Nellie Gibbs to CAS, 8 August 1916.

92 Eva N. Withers to CAS, 20 August 1916.

93 'Great War Panorama', *The Bunbury Herald and Blackwood Express* 2 February 1923: 1.

94 'Commercial', *Bathurst Free Press and Mining Journal,* 1 November 1892: 3; 'Parisian Parlance', *The Telegraph,* 25 May 1893: 6.

95 'Foreign Notes', *The Queenslander,* 31 March 1894: 6.

96 'Ultra-Democratic', *Launceston Examiner,* 7 June 1895: 3; 'Chiefly Concerning Women', *Worker,* 4 July 1896: 8; 'A Sensible Women's Congress', *The Australasian,* 31 October 1896: 33.

97 'General News', *The Daily News,* 4 June 1896: 2.

98 'Woman's Latest Right', *Albury Banner and Wodonga Express,* 29 July 1898: 11; 'The Great Event of The Century', *The Daily News,* 25 March 1899: 2.

99 Ian Tyrrell, 'Ackermann, Jessie A. (1857–1951)', *ADB*, 2005.

100 'Temperance Demonstration at Fremantle', *The West Australian*, 4 July 1907: 4; 'Visit of Miss Jessie Ackerman to Bunbury', *Southern Times,* 22 September 1910: 5; 'Successful Liberal Rally Held in Bedford Hall Last Night', *Southern Times,* 1 August 1911: 5; There is a portrait of Jessie Ackerman (incorrectly named) among the *Cons Photographs*, State Library of Western Australia, Rb 2083442 PO, 2.

101 Tyrell, 'Jessie Ackerman'.

102 'Mr. George at Bunbury', *Western Mail,* July 21 1900: 24.

103 Campbell, *Man Cannot Speak for Her*, 11, 10.

104 Janice N. Brownfoot, 'Goldstein, Vida Jane (1869–1949)', *ADB,* 1983; Joy Damousi, 'Socialist Women and Gendered Space, anti-conscription and anti-war campaigns, 1914–1918', *Labour History*, No. 60 (May, 1991), 1–15, 11.

105 'Ladies' Column', *The Daily News,* 13 September 1902: 7.

106 'Summary. State News', *Western Mail,* 12 May 1906: 30; 'Orange Blossoms', *Kalgoorlie Miner,* 8 March 1906: 6; 'Mainly About People by Egeria', *The Daily News,* 1 March 1906: 4; 'News and Notes', *The West Australian,* 10 May 1906: 4; 'News and Notes', *The West Australian,* 9 March 1906: 4.

107 'Social Problems', *The West Australian,* 21 February 1911: 3.

108 'What Is Feminism?', *The Bunbury Herald and Blackwood Express,* 29 January 1926: 11.

109 'A Trap Accident', *Southern Times,* 13 April 1911: 2.

110 'A Goldfields Nurse', *The West Australian,* 2 September 1938: 19; DOTAG.

111 Patricia Morison, 'Carnegie, David Wynford (1871–1900)', ADB, National Centre of Biography, Australian National University, 1979; W. J. Hudson, 'Casey, Richard Gavin Gardiner (1890–1976)', ADB, National Centre of Biography, Australian National University, 1993.

112 'Political Labour League', *Southern Times,* 26 March 1901: 3.

113 'The State Elections', *Southern Times,* 19 March 1901: 5; Western Australian women had the vote from 1899, Department of the Premier and Cabinet, A vote of her own, Constitutional Centre of Western Australia, 2019.

114 'The Hon. E. Mclarty at Bunbury', *Southern Times,* 5 May 1904: 5; 'Womens Labour League Conference', *Southern Times,* 28 January 1909: 5.

115 Ann Summers, *Damned Whores and God's Police*, London and Ringwood Victoria: Allen Lane -Penguin, 1975, 21.

116 'Federal Election', *Southern Times,* 22 May 1913: 3.

117 'Topical Subjects', *Bunbury Herald,* 25 May 1911: 3; 'Our Weekly Letter', *The Bunbury Herald and Blackwood Express,* 31 December 1926: 2.

118 'Do You Know?', *Southern Times,* 10 September 1912: 5; Statistiche Bundesamt, https://www.destatis.de/DE/Startseite.html.

119 Bobbie Oliver, 'A Truly Great Australian Woman: Jean Beadle's Work among Western Australian Women and Children 1901–1942', 87–98, in Jenny Gregory, ed., *Western Australia Between the Wars, Studies in Western Australian History,* XI, Centre for Western Australian History, University of Western Australia, Nedlands, 1990, 93, 94.

120 'Our Perth Letter', *Southern Times,* 2 November 1912: 6; 'Saturday', *Southern Times,* 7 June 1910: 5.

121 'Social Notes', *Bunbury Herald,* 26 January 1918: 5.

122 'News and Notes', *Southern Times,* 20 May 1913: 5.

123 'The Bunbury District Nursing Association', *Southern Times,* 4 July 1914: 5.

124 'The Effects of War and Politics on Bunbury', *Bunbury Herald,* 19 November 1914: 1.

125 'Bunbury Roman Catholic Notes', *Southern Times,* 9 September 1916: 5; 'Roman Catholic Church Bunbury', *Southern Times,* 7 August 1915: 5; 'Catholic Girls' Literary Society', *Bunbury Herald* 22 May 1915: 3; 'Roman Catholic Church', *Bunbury Herald,* 22 May 1915: 3; 'Catholic Literary Society', *Bunbury Herald,* 19 January 1915: 5; 'Bunbury', *Southern Times',* 16 March 1916: 3.

126 'The Elections', *South Western Times,* 6 September 1917: 3.

127 Dianne Davidson, 'A Citizen of Australia and the World: A reappraisal of Bessie Mabel Rischbieth', 99–113, in Jenny Gregory, ed., *Western Australia Between the Wars, Studies in Western Australian History,* XI, Centre for Western Australian History, University of Western Australia, 1990, 101, 105.

128 'Perth Ramblings', The Bunbury Herald and Blackwood Express, 21 April 1922: 6.

129 Ann M. George, Elizabeth Weiser and Janet Zepernick, Janet, (eds), *Studies in Rhetorics and Feminisms: Women and Rhetoric between the Wars.* Carbondale, US: Southern Illinois University Press, 2013., 7.

130 Kingston, *My Wife, My Daughter and Poor Mary Ann,* 217.

131 Alison MacKinnon, *Love and freedom, professional women and the reshaping of personal life.* Cambridge University Press, 1997, 214–5; 'Baby Week. Wastage of Infant Life. Must be Curtailed', *South Western Times,* 11 October 1917: 3.

132 'News and Notes', *South Western Times,* 11 November 1920: 2; 'Dr. Roberta Jull To-Night's Lecture', *South Western Times,* 16 June 1927: 2.

133 'Child Welfare Movement. Lecture by Dr. Roberta Jull', *South Western Times,* 21 June 1927: 2; 'Infant Health Centre Bunbury Branch Formed', *South Western Times,* 26 July 1927: 3.

134 'World War I and the Demise of British Feminism', 240; Kent, *Making Peace,* 109, 117, 126, 127, 130, 140.

135 'Anglican Church Notes', *South Western Times,* 27 November 1926: 6; 'Motherhood Endowment', *The Daily News,* 5 June 1922: 5; 'The Wife of The Future', *The Bunbury Herald and Blackwood Express,* 30 March 1923: 7.

136 'Passing Comment', *The Bunbury Herald and Blackwood Express,* 7 January 1927: 4; 'Short Skirts and Brains', *South Western Times,* 28 July 1928: 4.

137 'Good Figure', *South Western Times,* 2 May 1929: 4.

138 'Miss Maude Royden', *Western Mail,* 12 July 1928: 23; 'Miss Maude Royden', *South Western Times,* 29 May 1928: 4.

139 'Miss Maude Royden', *South Western Times,* 29 May 1928: 4;

140 Maude Royden', *The West Australian,* 29 June 1928: 7; 'Miss Maude Royden', *South Western Times,* 29 May 1928: 4; 'Miss Maude Royden', *Western Mail,* 12 July 1928: 23.

141 'Miss Maude Royden', *South Western Times,* 29 May 1928: 4.

142 George *et al., Women and Rhetoric between the Wars,* 3.

143 'The Woman M.P', *The Bunbury Herald and Blackwood Express,* 24 January 1920: 7; Summers, *Gods Police*; 'Of Interest to Women', *South Western Times,* 12 November 1927: 6.

144 'Of Interest to Women', *South Western Times,* 12 November 1927: 6; 'K.C.'S Daughter as Minister', *The Bunbury Herald and Blackwood Express,* 13 March 1928: 4.

145 'Women and Reform', *The West Australian,* 19 May 1923: 8; 'Of Interest to Women', *South Western Times,* 12 November 1927: 6.

146 'General News', *Daily Telegraph and North Murchison and Pilbarra Gazette,* 7 October 1925: 4; Demographia, US population from 1900, http://www.demographia.com/db-uspop1900.htm.

147 'Bunbury Race Club', *South Western Times,* 3 June 1924: 3.

148 'Ladies Section', *South Western Times,* 3 November 1928: 5.

149 'A Son of Bunbury', *The Bunbury Herald and Blackwood Express,* 7 September 1923: 8.

150 'Our Weekly Letter', *The Bunbury Herald and Blackwood Express,* 31 December 1926: 2.

151 'Of Interest to Women', *South Western Times,* 12 November 1927: 6; 'Diocese of Bunbury', *South Western Times,* 23 September 1919, 3.

152 'Diocese of Bunbury Church Notes', *South Western Times,* 29 June 1920: 3.

153 Anglican Communion, Lambeth Conference, 1920.

154 Anglican Communion, *Lambeth conference 1920*, resolution 48.

155 'The Position of Women', *South Western Times,* 14 October 1920: 3.

156 'Anglican Synod', *The West Australian,* 3 November 1921: 8.

157 Brigadier-General Sir Talbot Hobbs; 'Anglican Synod', *The West Australian,* 3 November 1921: 8.

158 'Anglican Synod', *The West Australian,* 4 November 1921: 6.

159 'Anglican Communion, *Lambeth Conference 1920,* resolution 68.

160 'London Life', *The West Australian,* 23 November 1921: 8.

161 'That Touch of Human Nature', *South Western Times,* 25 February 1919: 2.

162 'Thanksgiving Services', *South Western Times,* 21 November 1918: 3.

163 'The Woman's World', The Bunbury Herald and Blackwood Express, 12 July 1929: 6.

164 'Our Perth Letter', *Southern Times,* 26 October 1912: 3; 'Do You Know?', *Southern Times,* 2 November 1912: 5.

165 'Bunbury Tennis Club', *Southern Times*, 19 June 1913: 2.

166 'Clearing the Atmosphere', *South Western Times,* 14 March 1918: 3.

167 'Another Red Cross Window', *South Western Times,* 25 April 1918: 3.

168 'Local and General', *Bunbury Herald,* 12 March 1919: 2;

169 'The New Pope', *The Bunbury Herald and Blackwood Express,* 19 May 1922: 7.

170 'Society', *Call and WA Sportsman,* 3 October 1919: 1.

171 'The Ladies' Sections', *Sunday Times,* 31 January 1915: 25; 'Woman's World', *Bunbury Herald* 12 June 1915: 4; 'Odds and Ends', *Bunbury Herald,* 12 October 1915: 1.

172 'News and Notes', *The West Australian,* 24 September 1915: 6; 'News and Notes', *The Daily News,* 7 February 1916: 4.

173 'The Theatres', *South Western Times,* 16 August 1924: 2; 'Rules for Flappers', *South Western Times,* 30 July 1925: 1.

174 'Maude Royden', *The West Australian,* 29 June 1928: 7.

175 'Background on Postwar', *South Western Advertiser,* 7 November 1947: 18.

8: War, Women, Work and the Census

1 Lake, 'Women's and Gender History', np; Kingston, *My Wife My Daughter and Poor Mary Anne,* 61.

2 'Editorial', *Bunbury Herald,* 16 May, 1916: 2.

3 G. C. Bolton, quoted in Jenny Gregory, (ed), *Western Australia Between the Wars,* Studies in Western Australian History, XI, Centre for Western Australian History, University of Western Australia, 1990, 7, 8.

4 Butler, 'Statistics of the War', *Australian Army Medical Services,* 946–80.

5 1921 Census, Vol. II – Part XVII, Table 25, Australia, Males Nature of Occupation in Conjunction with Age; and with Grade of Occupation, 289.

6 Census 1933, Vol. 1 pt V, Western Australia, Analysis of population in LGAs. Table 17, State of Western Australia, Industry Males, 494–95.

7 'The Common-Sense Dress', *Bunbury Herald,* 23 December 1911: 2.

8 'Advertising', *The Bunbury Herald and Blackwood Express,* 13 December 1919: 4; 'Advertising', *Group Settlement Chronicle and Margaret-Augusta Mail,* 3 February 1925: 2.

9 C.S to family, 15 August 1915, 28 September 1915, 9 October 1915, 17 November 1915, 20 May 1916, Mrs Hymus to CS, 23 March 1916; CS to family, 28 November 1915.

10 The term 'workforce' will refer to female paid workers, while 'breadwinners' refers to women who are working specifically to support themselves and their families. Some judgments have been necessary because census reports do not always distinguish between the two meanings, sometimes referring to 'workers' and 'independents'.

11 See discussion of Bunbury woman, Ivy Paisley, in the next chapter.

12 *Bunbury Herald,* 23 December 1911: 3.

13 *Bunbury Herald,* 23 December 1911: 5; *Bunbury Herald,* 23 December 1911: 8; *Bunbury Herald,* 23 December 1911: 11.

14 'The Ways and Woes of Women', *Westralian Worker,* 9 November 1900.

15 *Bunbury Herald,* 23 December 1911: 4; *Bunbury Herald,* 23 December 1911: 6; George Goss to AJS, August 1916.

16 'The Common-Sense Dress', *Bunbury Herald,* 23 December 1911: 2.

17 *Bunbury Herald,* 23 December 1911: 4.

18 *ANZAC Heroes.*

19 AJS, Letter to Dr Joel. August, 1916.

20 'Guernsey bull, calved before March 1. 1936', Mrs. C. Corker, 1 and champion', in 'Harvey Show', *The West Australian,* 31 October 1938, 13.

21 1921 Census, Bulletin 16, State of Western Australia, 6.
22 Larsson, *Shattered Anzacs*, 268.
23 Butler, 'Statistics of the War' in *Australian Medical Services*, 963–964.
24 Butler, *Australian Medical Services*, Table 67, War Pensions – Summary, 963–4. Butler does not differentiate pensions paid to nurses.
25 Women made up 20% of the unemployed. They will not be considered here.
26 *ANZAC Heroes.*
27 1921 Census, Volume 2, Statistician's Report, 38–39.
28 'Bunbury Benevolent Society', *The Bunbury Herald and Blackwood Express*, 26 September 1922: 3.
29 Campbell, *Man Cannot Speak for Her*, 3.
30 *ANZAC Heroes.*
31 Suzanne Welborn, *Lords of Death: A People a Place a Legend*, Fremantle Western Australia: Fremantle Arts Centre Press, 1982, 157. Butler also made this observation in relation to the Australian forces as a whole, Butler, 267.
32 Figures for the district in 1901 have not been located.
33 Beaumont, *Australia's War*, 75.
34 University of Western Australia, History. https://www.web.uwa.edu.au/university/history.

9: Four Wellington Women: Changes Wartime and Beyond

1 Ivy Paisley, Greta Baldock birth, Janie Sutton, DOTAG; Greta Baldock death: Metropolitan Cemeteries Board; the dates of Kate Joel's birth and death are estimated on the basis of newspaper reports.
2 'News and Notes', *Southern Times,* 14 May 1892: 2; 'Sale of Gifts', *Bunbury Herald,* 25 April 1901: 3; Local and General', *Bunbury Herald,* 23 January 1902: 2.
3 'Convent School', *Southern Times,* 21 December 1901: 5.
4 'Hockey', *Bunbury Herald,* 5 June 1903: 3; 'Personal', *South Western Times,* 20 August 1929: 2.
5 'Newes (sic) and Notes', *Southern Times* 9 April 1907: 2; 'Advertising', *Southern Times,* 20 February 1908: 2; 'Bunbury Rifle Club', *Southern Times,* 23 May 1907: 5; 'Social Notes', *The West Australian,* 7 April 1908: 2.
6 'In the Country', *The Daily News,* 19 February 1929: 10; 'The Second Tennis Ball', *Southern Times,* 8 July 1911: 3.
7 'Bunbury Rifle Club', *Southern Times,* 23 May 1907: 5.
8 'Family Notices', *Southern Times,* 21 March 1901: 3; 'Wedding Bells', *Bunbury Herald,* 30 December 1903: 3; 'Social Notes', *The West Australian,* 3 February 1905: 3; 'Social Notes', *The West Australian,* 26 February 1908: 4; 'Orange Blossoms Rose—Forrest', *Southern Times,* 25 April 1912: 5; 'Mainly About People', *The Daily News,* 30 September 1907: 3.
9 'Personal', *Southern Times,* 5 August 1909: 3; 'Personal', *Southern Times,* 30 October 1909: 3; 'Our Weekly Letter', *The Bunbury Herald and Blackwood Express,* 16 April 1926: 2.
10 'Newes (sic) and Notes', *Southern Times,* 9 April 1907: 2.
11 'Country', *The West Australian,* 15 October 1906: 5; 'Newes (sic) and Notes', *Southern Times,* 9 April 1907: 2.
12 Social Notes', *The West Australian,* 15 March 1910: 2.

13 "Social Notes', *The West Australian,* 29 July 1910: 6.
14 George *et al., Studies in Rhetorics and Feminisms,* 13.
15 'Labour Notes', *The West Australian,* 6 August 1904: 11.
16 'Women in Politics', *The West Australian,* 20 August 1904: 7; 'Country', *The West Australian,* 6 February 1909: 9; 'Local and General', *Bunbury Herald,* 22 September 1910: 3.
17 Sir John Forrest was then a federal parliamentarian, ADB; 'Mainly About People', *The Daily News,* 27 June 1927: 9.
18 'Personal', *The Collie Miner,* 1 February 1916: 2.
19 'Al Fresco Fete', *Southern Times,* 22 January 1916: 5.
20 'News and Notes', *South Western Times,* 29 May 1917: 2.
21 'Bunbury Evening Classes', *South Western Times,* 10 May 1917: 3.
22 'The Late Mrs Caroline Mitchell', *Bunbury Herald,* 14 August 1918: 3; née Caroline Morgan, born Bunbury 1847, m. William Bedford Mitchell, 1865. DOTAG.
23 'Mainly About People', *The Daily News,* 17 September 1919: 3.
24 'Late Miss Ivy Paisley', *South Western Times,* 20 March 1947: 4; 'Personal', *South Western Times,* 16 April 1929: 2; 'Visitors' Guide', *South Western Times,* 4 March 1922: 6.
25 'Who's Who--And Where', *Call,* 19 November 1926: 4.
26 Kingston, *My Wife, My Daughter and Poor Mary Ann*, 92.
27 'C.W.A.', *The Bunbury Herald and Blackwood Express,* 2 August 1929: 4.
28 'Mainly About People', *The Daily News,* 11 October 1922: 8.
29 'Maternity Bonus', *The West Australian,* 22 March 1923: 6; 'The Woman's World', *The Daily News,* 29 September 1923: 2; 'The Daily News', *The Daily News,* 5 October 1923: 6
30 'C.W.A.', *The Bunbury Herald and Blackwood Express,* 2 August 1929: 4.
31 'Bunbury's Centenary Celebrations', *South Western Times,* 12 November 1929: 3; 'Correspondence', *The Bunbury Herald and Blackwood Express,* 15 July 1929: 3; 'Archbishop Riley Presentation Fund', *The South-Western News,* 14 June 1929: 2; 'The Archbishop Riley Presentation Home', *The West Australian,* 21 August 1929: 22.
32 'Reception to Lieut.—Governor', *The West Australian,* 19 March 1934: 7; 'Woman's Realm', *The West Australian,* 16 April 1934: 14; Dry or Wet?', *The Bunbury Herald and Blackwood Express,* 5 August 1924: 3. SS *Clan Matheson,* cargo ship, built 1919; 'At Home on H.M.A.S. Canberra', *Western Mail,* 10 October 1929: 34; 'Warships in Port', *The West Australian,* 31 August 1934: 10. HMAS *Australia 11,* 1927–1954.
33 'In the Country', *The Daily News,* 19 February 1929: 10; Personal', *South Western Times,* 20 August 1929: 2.
34 'The World of Women', *Sunday Times,* 1 August 1937: 1; 'Late Miss Ivy Paisley', *South Western Times,* 20 March 1947: 4. The uncle was D.W. McGregor, Ivy's mother's brother. 'Personal', *The South-Western News,* 13 May 1943: 2; 'Social Gossip', *Sunday Times,* 23 May 1943: 10; McGregor, Martha Rabiney, daughter of Daniel McGregor in 1866. With thanks to Bunbury Historical Society for this information. Quindalup began as a small timber port. *Harwood's Cottage circa 1860*; 'Bunbury', *Western Mail,* 15 January 1931: 26.
35 The Misses Layman of Wonnerup.
36 'The Second Tennis Ball', *Southern Times,* 8 July 1911: 3; 'Obituary.' *The South-Western News,* 10 December 1937: 4. Until this time, Busselton, so close

to Bunbury was geographically isolated from it due to its separate historical development and each having its own port. Land connections by road and rail eventually facilitated closer connections between the two towns. Rail was still used into the 1950s.

37 'Personal', *The South-Western News,* 13 May 1943: 2; 'Social Gossip', *Sunday Times,* 23 May 1943: 10; 'Personal', *The South-Western News,* 12 April 1945: 2.

38 Kingston, *My Wife, My Daughter and Poor Mary Ann*, 130.

39 'Al Fresco Fete', *Southern Times,* 22 January 1916: 5.

40 'Bunbury Notes', *The West Australian,* 3 June 1936: 5; 'C.W.A.', *The Bunbury Herald and Blackwood Express,* 2 August 1929: 4.

41 Doctor notes, 15 June 1938, 8 November 1938, NAA 32501494 M14276.

42 Doctor notes, 8 November 1938, 7 November 1938, 15 June 1938, 21 June 1938, DC notes, 10 November 1938, 32501494 M14276; Cover notes, 9 October 1940, NAA 32501494, R14276.

43 DC notes, 9 March 1940, NAA 32501494 R14276.

44 Case sheet, 30 August 1946, X ray report, 6 August 1946, NAA 32498040.

45 'Perth Wool Sales', *Great Southern Herald,* 29 October 1930: 3; 'Obituary', *Gnowangerup Star and Tambellup-Ongerup Gazette,* 3 April 1943: 2; Doctor notes, 3 March 1946, NAA 32501692 M19287.

46 'Family Notices', *The West Australian,* 7 March 1947: 1.

47 'Late Miss Ivy Paisley', *South Western Times,* 20 March 1947: 4.

48 George *et al.*, *Women and Rhetoric between the Wars*, 4, 10–12.

49 ANZAC Heroes.

50 CS to family, 18 January 1916.

51 'The Red Cross', *South Western Times,* 18 April 1918: 3.

52 'W.C.T.U.', *Southern Times,* 2 April 1901: 6; 'Bunbury Technical School', *Southern Times,* 19 December 1911: 5.

53 'Personal', *Southern Times,* 6 February 1912: 2; 'The Bunbury District Nursing Association', *Southern Times,* 4 July 1914: 5; 'Personal', *South Western Times,* 13 June 1918: 3; 'Bunbury District & Nursing Association', *South Western Times,* 28 July 1917: 6.

54 'The Red Cross', *South Western Times,* 18 April 1918: 3; 'Signaller Skeyhill's Lecture', *Bunbury Herald,* 22 November 1916: 3.

55 'North Perth School', *Call,* 28 November 1924: 1; 'Personal', *South Western Times,* 5 July 1924: 4.

56 'A Little Bird Says', *Call,* 19 February 1926: 2.

57 SRO AU WA S132 cons 3152, Symes, G.F.

58 'Family Notices', *Western Mail,* 14 December 1933: 4; 'Family Notices', *Western Mail,* 7 May 1931: 43.

59 George *et al.*, *Women and Rhetoric between the Wars*, 5, 10, 11.

60 'The Bunbury Herald, Saturday January 15, 1916', *Bunbury Herald,* 15 January 1916: 2.

61 Alison MacKinnon, *Love and freedom*, 194.

62 'Dr. Joel Dead', *The West Australian,* 14 February 1935: 13.

63 'Masquerade Ball', *The Bunbury Herald and Blackwood Express,* 8 October 1928: 2.

64 Scates, 'The Unknown Sock Knitter', 45.

65 '[?]', (sic) The Bunbury Herald and Blackwood Express, 3 December 1920: 6; 'Bunbury Ambulance', The Bunbury Herald and Blackwood Express, 5 May

1922: 3.

66 'Bunbury Benevolent Society', *The Bunbury Herald and Blackwood Express,* 12 September 1922: 3; 'Bunbury Benevolent Society', *The Bunbury Herald and Blackwood Express,* 14 March 1924: 1.

67 'Benevolent Society', *The Bunbury Herald and Blackwood Express,* 11 September 1923: 3.

68 'Bunbury Senior School', *The Bunbury Herald and Blackwood Express,* 28 December 1923: 5; 'Seamen's Mission', *The Bunbury Herald and Blackwood Express,* 29 July 1924: 1; 'Spring Fete', *The Bunbury Herald and Blackwood Express,* 11 September 1925: 6; 'News and Notes', *The Bunbury Herald and Blackwood Express,* 7 September 1926: 2; 'News and Notes', *The Bunbury Herald and Blackwood Express,* 10 September 1928: 2; [?] (sic), *The Bunbury Herald and Blackwood Express,* 3 December 1920: 6; 'Bunbury Ambulance', *The Bunbury Herald and Blackwood Express,* 5 May 1922: 3; 'Bunbury Senior School', *The Bunbury Herald and Blackwood Express,* 28 December 1923: 5; 'Bunbury Benevolent. Society', *The Bunbury Herald and Blackwood Express,* 14 March 1924: 1; 'The South West Club', *The Bunbury Herald and Blackwood Express,* 14 January 1920: 3; 'Masquerade Ball', *The Bunbury Herald and Blackwood Express,* 8 October 1928: 2; 'Seamen's Mission', *The Bunbury Herald and Blackwood Express,* 29 July 1924: 1; 'Spring Fete', *The Bunbury Herald and Blackwood Express,* 11 September 1925: 6.

69 'Advertising', *The Bunbury Herald and Blackwood Express* 13 December 1919: 4.

70 'Dr. Joel Dead', *The West Australian,* 14 February 1935: 13.

71 'The Life of Melbourne', *The Argus,* 30 January 1945: 9; 'W.I.Z.O. War Activities', *The Herald,* (Melbourne), 20 May 1941: 11; 'People and Parties', *The Age,* 23 June 1947: 5; 'Appeal for Children', *The West Australian,* 21 August 1948: 10.

72 'New Hotel for Bunbury', *The West Australian,* 10 September 1949: 9; 'Local Chit Chat', *The Blackwood Times,* 4 June 1948: 12.

73 'Social Notes', *The Age,* 5 June 1941: 3; 'People and Parties', *The West Australian,* 23 March 1950: 23.

74 'Masquerade Ball', *The Bunbury Herald and Blackwood Express,* 8 October 1928: 2; 'Women Who Did Nothing', *The Bunbury Herald and Blackwood Express,* 18 October 1919: 2.

75 'Seamen's Mission', *The Bunbury Herald and Blackwood Express,* 19 September 1924: 5.

76 'Woman's Interests', *The West Australian,* 11 July 1924: 7.

77 'Personal', *Western Mail,* 24 March 1932: 39.

78 'Wesley Church', *Bunbury Herald,* 13 September 1893: 2; 'Ministering Children's League', *Bunbury Herald:* 2 December 1897: 3 'News and Notes', *Southern Times* 7 August 1902: 4; 'Mainly About People', *The Daily News,* 8 July 1920: 3.

79 Mainly About People', *The Daily News,* 20 April 1928: 11; Dr. Elsie Port in China Lectures to Women's Clubs', *The Daily News,* 15 March 1935: 7; 'General News', *The West Australian,* 1 June 1935: 23; 'Bridge Afternoon', *The West Australian,* 6 August 1936: 4.

80 'World of Women. Q'land. Women's Club', *Daily Standard* (Brisbane), 10 September 1934: 10. Elsie Port died in Denver, Colorado in 1948.

81 George *et al.*, *Women and Rhetoric between the Wars,* 7, 14.

82 'Aviation', *The West Australian,* 7 June 1921: 4.

83 'Women's Air Derby', *Kalgoorlie Miner,* 28 August 1929: 5; 'All Went Black', *The Daily News,* 11 March 1930: 1; 'Labor Women of Western Australia', *Westralian Worker,* 11 July 1930: 13; 'Noted Aviatrix on Atom', *The Northam Advertiser,* 18 June 1954: 12.

84 'Women's Interest in Aviation', *Sunday Times,* 15 January 1911: 19; 'The Art of Flying', *The Express and Telegraph,* 7 June 1913: 6.

85 Irene F Lebow, *Before Amelia: women pilots in the early days of aviation*, Washington D.C.: Brassey's Inc., 2002., 4, 5, 273, 274.

86 Lebow, *Before Amelia,* 1, 3, 7, 35, 274; Mrs Eastman and family in car 1911, Battye Library, 007202D.

87 Dierdre Beddoe, *Back to Home and Duty: women between the wars 1918–1939.* London: Pandora, 1989, 8.

88 For example, Summers, *God's Police*; Germaine Greer, *The Female Eunuch*, London: Paladin, 1970.

89 Sara Hillin, *Sweethearts of the Skies*, in Ann George, Weiser, M. Elizabeth, and Zepernick, Janet, (eds), *Studies in Rhetorics and Feminisms: Women and Rhetoric between the Wars,* Carbondale, US: Southern Illinois University Press, 2013, 175–92, 177, 185.

90 'Another Woman Flier', *The Daily News,* 18 June 1928: 5; 'Ten thousand flying women have joined The Ninety-Nines', *Western Mail,* 17 August 1950: 25; Ware, Ware, S. *Still missing: Amelia Earhart and the search for modern feminism*, New York: W.W. Norton & Company. 1994, 29.

91 Ware, *Still Missing*, 33, 37, 80–81, 61, 76.

92 Ware, *Still Missing*, 18, 21, 34, 43, 46, 73, 108, 31, 63, 211.

93 Dance program, 15 August 1913; CS to family, 15 October 1915, 29 May 1916.

94 Sutton's mother was known as 'Granny Sutton' to Nancy Snell, who named her eldest daughter (the writer) after Janie Sutton.

95 4th Squadron 1st Remount Unit, AIF; William John Sutton, NAA, Sern 1012, enlisted 16.10.1915.

96 'In the Country', *The West Australian,* 2 February 1917: 8.

97 Robert Holden and Jane Brummitt, *May Gibbs: More Than a Fairytale*, Melbourne: Hardie Grant Books, 2011., 14, 16.

98 Nancy (Snell) Sherwood, personal communication, August 15, 2016; Jane Ross, *The myth of the digger: the Australian soldier in two World Wars,* Sydney: Hale & Ironmonger, 1985, 142.

99 NAA, Sutton Lilian Jane Davis. 1939–1948, Series Number A9301, SERN 94702, Barcode 4961714; Ware, *Still Missing*, 39.

100 Lebow, *Before Amelia,* jacket; Battye Library, image 007202D, Mrs K. Eastman and family in car, 1911; 'A New Silver Link Sends her Subscription', *Western Mail,* 18 April 1919: 36.

101 'Weddings', *Sunday Times,* 12 September 1920: 7.

102 Australian Stockman's Hall of Fame, Janie Sutton.

103 'No title', *The Daily News,* 16 November 1934: 9

104 'Gossip', *The Daily News,* 11 August 1937: 8; 'She's the only woman pilot', *The Daily News,* 1 August 1938: 8 Australian Stockman's Hall of Fame and Outback Heritage Centre, Object number USH00669.

105 'Gadabout Girl', *The Daily News,* 5 April 1941, 24; 'Gifts For Navy', *The West Australian,* 29 July 1941, 3.

106 Voluntary Aid Detachments (VAD) (1914 –), Australian Women's Archives Project, The Australian Women's Register, National Foundation for Australian Women (NFAW) in conjunction with The University of Melbourne; NAA Sutton Lilian Jane Davis. 1939–1948, A9301, SERN 94702, 4961714.

107 'He's Bought the Ring', *Mirror,* 20 April 1935: 15; 'Family Notices', *The West Australian,* 10 January 1928: 1.

108 'Encouraging Women', *Sunday Times,* 6 July 1930: 14.

109 'Flying Scholarship', *The West Australian,* 8 October 1932: 18.

110 'Aero Club Races', *The West Australian,* 14 November 1932: 10.

111 'Gossip', *The Daily News,* 11 August 1937: 8.

112 'Hepzibah's Gossip', *The Daily News,* 17 June 1937: 8.

113 Ware, *Still Missing*, 49, 51, 52.

114 'Encouraging Women', *Sunday Times,* 6 July 1930: 14; 'Hepzibah's Gossip', *The Daily News,* 17 June 1937: 8.

115 'Hepzibah', *The Daily News,* 21 March 1938: 7.

116 'She's the only woman pilot', *The Daily News,* 1 August 1938: 8.

117 Ware, *Still Missing*, 36, 37; Summers, *Damned Whores and God's Police*, 385.

118 Hillin, *Sweethearts of the Skies*, 179; Battye library image, http://hdl.handle.net/10070/14951.

119 'Gossip', *The Daily News,* 11 August 1937: 8.

120 'Gadabout Girl Roves Round with Rowers', *The Daily News,* 3 August 1938: 10.

121 'Gadabout Girl Finds the Spirit of Shell', *The Daily News,* 15 July 1939.

122 Voluntary Aid Detachments (VAD) (1914–), Australian Women's Archives Project; NAA, Sutton Lilian Jane Davis. 1939–1948, A9301, SERN 94702, 4961714.

123 'The Influence of Women', *Kalgoorlie Miner,* 8 June 1927: 4.

124 Italics mine.

125 'A Smiling Goddess', *Kalgoorlie Miner,* 26 May 1930: 4.

126 'Women Welcome Amy', *Sunday Times* 6 July 1930: 1; The first female opera conductor in Australia, active from 1924 to around 1944.

127 John Curtin Prime Ministerial Library; 'Labor Women of Western Australia', *Westralian Worker,* 11 July 1930: 13. The Labour movement was a pioneer in recognizing gender equality.

128 'Women Welcome Amy', *Sunday Times,* 6 July 1930: 1.

129 'Why I Wouldn't Marry Amy Johnson!', *Mirror,* 21 June 1930: 6.

130 'Aviatrix Resents 'Fatherly' Mr. Thorby', *The Daily News,* 28 October 1938: 2.

131 Elizabeth Gaskell, (1851), has her heroine, Margaret Hale intervening between master and men in her novel of industrial England, *North and South*; Dale Spender, *Writing a New World: Two Centuries of Australian Women Writers*, Spinifex press 1988 Melbourne, 1988, 281; Summers, *God's Police*, 16.

132 Summers, *God's Police.* 380.

133 This was in an illuminated address prepared by the Chinese Kuo Min Tang Society at the request of the Chinese Consul-General of Sydney on behalf of the Chinese in Australia. 'A Smiling Goddess', *Kalgoorlie Miner,* 26 May 1930: 4.

134 Lebow, *Before Amelia*, 275.

135 George *et al.*, *Women and Rhetoric between the Wars*, 12.

10: Conclusion

1 Bolton, quoted in Gregory, (ed), *Western Australia Between the Wars*, Studies in Western Australian History, XI, 7, 8.

INDEX

www.ingramcontent.com/pod-product-compliance
Ingram Content Group UK Ltd.
Pitfield, Milton Keynes, MK11 3LW, UK
UKHW041633190726
13854UKWH00006B/2470